The
Supreme Court
Yearbook
1993-1994

The members of the Supreme Court posed for photographs September 30, 1994, following the investiture ceremony for the newest justice, Stephen G. Breyer. From left, Associate Justices Clarence Thomas, Antonin Scalia, Sandra Day O'Connor, Anthony M. Kennedy, David H. Souter, Breyer, John Paul Stevens, Chief Justice William H. Rehnquist, and Associate Justice Ruth Bader Ginsburg.

The
Supreme Court
Yearbook
1993-1994

Kenneth Jost

Congressional Quarterly Inc.
Washington, D.C.

Congressional Quarterly Inc.

Congressional Quarterly Inc., an editorial research service and publishing company, serves clients in the fields of news, education, business, and government. It combines the specific coverage of Congress, government, and politics contained in the *Congressional Quarterly Weekly Report* with the more general subject range of an affiliated service, the *CQ Researcher*.

Congressional Quarterly also publishes a variety of books, including college political science textbooks under the CQ Press imprint and public affairs paperbacks on developing issues and events. CQ Books researches, writes, and publishes information directories and reference books on the federal government, national elections, and politics, including the *Guide to the Presidency,* the *Guide to Congress,* the *Guide to the U.S. Supreme Court,* the *Guide to U.S. Elections,* and *Politics in America. CQ's Encyclopedia of American Government* is a three-volume reference work providing essential information about the U.S. government. The *CQ Almanac,* a compendium of legislation for one session of Congress, is published each year. *Congress and the Nation,* a record of government for a presidential term, is published every four years.

CQ publishes the *Congressional Monitor,* a daily report on current and future activities of congressional committees, and several newsletters including *Congressional Insight,* a weekly analysis of congressional action. The CQ FaxReport is a daily update available every afternoon when Congress is in session. An electronic online information system, Washington Alert, provides immediate access to CQ's databases of legislative action, votes, schedules, profiles, and analyses.

Cover design: Julie Booth

Photo credits: cover, 2, 14, 305, R. Michael Jenkins; frontispiece, 338, Ken Heinen for the Supreme Court; 5, the White House; 28, Joe Burbank, *Orlando Sentinel*; 45, Jay Koelzer, *Rocky Mountain News;* 47, Texas Department of Criminal Justice; 51, JoAnn Baker; 294, John Sykes, *Arkansas Democrat-Gazette;* 296, U.S. Justice Department; 316, 319, Franz Jantzen, Collection of the Supreme Court of the United States; 323, 325, 327, 329, 331, 332, 334, 336, 340, National Geographic Society, courtesy of the Supreme Court Historical Society.

Published in the United States of America

ISBN 0-87187-815-1
ISBN 0-87187-813-5 (pbk)
ISSN 1054-2701

Contents

Preface   vii

1 *A New Justice*   1
2 *The 1993-1994 Term*   19
3 *Case Summaries*   56

   Business Law   61
   Courts and Procedure   68
   Criminal Law and Procedure   71
   Election Law   86
   Environmental Law   88
   Federal Government   91
   First Amendment   95
   Individual Rights   98
   Labor Law   105
   Property Law   108
   States   109
   Torts   112

4 *Opinion Excerpts*   113
5 *Preview of the 1994-1995 Term*   292

Appendix   309
   How the Court Works   311
   Brief Biographies   323
   Glossary of Legal Terms   342
   United States Constitution   348

Index   367

Preface

As the Supreme Court of the United States prepared to begin its 1994-1995 term, one longtime Court watcher was reminded of Winston Churchill's caustic assessment of a dessert offering: "This pudding has no theme." With a declining caseload and increasingly narrow rulings, the Court too seemed to have no theme other than an apparent desire to lower its profile and defy ideological labels.

Still, even a low-profile Court wields great power. In its 1993-1994 term, the Court upheld limits on abortion protests, approved racial line-drawing in legislative redistricting, and prohibited lawyers from selecting jurors on the basis of sex. While those rulings heartened liberal groups, conservatives were cheered by other decisions. In the most noteworthy of those rulings, the Court gave property owners more power to resist demands from local governments for public use of their land in exchange for permitting development or construction.

As the new term opened, the Court's calendar was thin, but hardly inconsequential. At the top of the justices' agenda was the intense debate over congressional term limits—a reform that was politically popular but constitutionally suspect. The justices also agreed to look again at the rules for legal challenges by death row inmates. The week before the new term was to begin, the Court agreed to review two important cases involving school desegregation and affirmative action in government contracts.

Now in its fifth year, the *Supreme Court Yearbook* provides an overview of the Court's past term along with summaries of each of the Court's signed opinions. Chapter 1 describes the nomination and confirmation of the Court's newest member, Justice Stephen G. Breyer, and examines the voting alignments of the other justices during the term. Chapter 2 gives an overview of the term's decisions and detailed accounts of the most important cases. Chapter 3 contains the comprehensive listing of the Court's decisions from the past term, arranged by subject categories. Chapter 4 consists of excerpts from the Court's major rulings. Chapter 5 previews the 1994-1995 term. The Appendix contains a description of the Court's operations, brief biographies of the justices, a glossary of legal terms, and the U.S. Constitution.

The work in preparing this book is made easier, and more enjoyable, by the capable and friendly assistance provided by the Court's public information office, headed by Toni House. Many of the full-time reporters at the Court have also been helpful during the year. Space does not permit me to personally thank everyone who has shared information or insights, but I do want to express my gratitude again to Joan Biskupic of the *Washington Post,* who wrote the first three volumes of this book while at Congressional Quarterly and who has been generous to me with her time and expertise throughout the year.

At Congressional Quarterly, my thanks go again to Dave Tarr of CQ Books for inviting me to take over the book and to my editors at the *CQ Researcher,* Sandra Stencel and Thomas J. Colin, for giving me the time to work on it. I should also thank Shana Wagger for guiding the book in its formative stages, Barbara de Boinville for polishing the manuscript, and Kerry Kern for overseeing production of the final book.

Finally, by way of a personal dedication, I want to express my appreciation to John Seigenthaler, editor and publisher emeritus of the (Nashville) *Tennessean,* where I began my journalistic career almost twenty-five years ago. In forty years of newspapering, John trained and inspired uncounted numbers of young reporters such as myself to use our energy and talents in a search for truth and justice. Now, in active retirement as head of the Freedom Forum's First Amendment Center at Vanderbilt University, John continues to be a strong voice for courageous and responsible journalism. I hope this book contributes in some way to the goals he has worked for and instilled in others.

1 | A New Justice

Stephen Breyer had a bad year—at least a few bad days—in 1993. First came the bicycle accident. The longtime federal appellate judge, who regularly biked between his work at the U.S. courthouse in Boston and his home in adjacent Cambridge, was hit by a car as he was crossing Harvard Square. Breyer was hospitalized with a punctured lung and broken ribs.

A week later, still in pain, Breyer left his hospital bed to go to Washington for a job interview—not just any job interview but a face-to-face meeting with the president of the United States about a vacancy on the Supreme Court. Breyer went into the session with President Bill Clinton on June 11 as the favored choice to succeed retiring justice Byron R. White. But somehow Breyer left Clinton cold. Aides later said the president found the former Harvard Law School professor detached and didactic.

After the Friday afternoon meeting Breyer lay down on a couch in the White House counsel's office to rest. He was told to begin preparing an acceptance speech. But three days later, after a weekend of leaked stories that Breyer had failed to pay Social Security taxes on a household worker, Clinton settled on someone else for the Court: Ruth Bader Ginsburg, a judge on the federal appeals court in Washington, D.C.

Ginsburg had won the president over with her life story of fighting and overcoming legal discrimination against women. Breyer's more conventional career paled by comparison. Passed over, Breyer returned to his judicial duties in Boston. In August he gamely came to Ginsburg's swearing-in ceremony.

The episode was a rare setback for Breyer, and by all accounts he handled it well. When another Supreme Court seat opened up in April 1994, Breyer was naturally circumspect. When reporters asked him about his chances of succeeding the retiring justice Harry A. Blackmun, Breyer responded blandly. It was an honor to be considered, he said, and he had been considered before.

Indeed, Breyer's chances started as slim. Clinton began with other candidates in mind: Senate Majority Leader George Mitchell, who had already announced his plans to leave the Senate at the end of the year; Interior Secretary Bruce Babbitt, who had been at the top of the short list a year earlier; and federal appeals court judge Richard Arnold, a respected jurist and a personal friend of Clinton's from his home state of Arkansas.

One by one, however, the leading contenders fell by the wayside. Mitchell took himself out of consideration, saying he needed to devote full

Justice Harry A. Blackmun announced his plans to retire after twenty-four years on the Supreme Court at an April 6 news conference at the White House with President Clinton.

attention to his Senate duties, including shepherding the president's health care plan. Babbitt fell victim to sniping from some Republican senators—and to the likelihood of a more difficult confirmation battle over his successor at Interior. Arnold was crossed off the list because he suffered from lymphoma, a form of cancer, which Clinton feared might cut short his tenure on the Court.

Finally, on May 13, after thirty-seven days of embarrassing public vacillation, Clinton turned to Breyer. "He was the one with the fewest problems," White House counsel Lloyd Cutler told reporters in a background session afterward. Clinton announced his selection late Friday afternoon on the White House lawn to a press corps impatient after five days of rampant speculation. The announcement, just in time for the evening newscasts, averted another news cycle of criticism about the delay. Breyer was still in Boston. His formal presentation to the White House press corps had to wait until Monday.

However inelegant the process, Clinton's nominee quickly won nearly unanimous praise. "He's a consensus builder," said Sen. Edward Kennedy, the liberal Massachusetts Democrat who had twice hired Breyer for staff posts on the Senate Judiciary Committee. Kennedy had quietly lobbied Clinton on Breyer's behalf three days earlier.

Republicans also had warm words for Breyer. "He's basically a moderate to liberal jurist, and a good one," said Utah's Orrin Hatch, the Judiciary Committee's ranking Republican. Hatch acknowledged he had warned Clinton that Babbitt's nomination would have faced opposition. But Breyer would sail right through, Hatch assured the president.

A few negative voices were heard, almost exclusively from liberal quarters. Sen. Howard Metzenbaum, an Ohio Democrat and a strong liberal voice on the Judiciary Committee, complained that Breyer was "very strongly on the conservative side" on business issues. Ralph Nader, the consumer activist, called Breyer "a corporate judge." Both men said Breyer's rulings in antitrust cases and his extensive writings on regulation showed a narrow cost-benefit approach that helped business and hurt workers and consumers.

No one expected those criticisms to derail, or even delay, Breyer's confirmation to be the 108th justice of the Supreme Court. In announcing his selection, Clinton himself praised Breyer's "political savvy." "Look at the people supporting his nomination," Clinton told reporters. "He's gotten Senator Kennedy and Senator Hatch together. I wish I had that kind of political skill."

A Charmed Career

Stephen Gerald Breyer reached the threshold of the Supreme Court after a charmed legal and academic career. His résumé boasted enough credentials for two lifetimes: Phi Beta Kappa at Stanford, Marshall Scholar at Oxford, law review at Harvard, a Supreme Court clerkship, a stint at the Justice Department, tenure at Harvard Law School, two leaves of absence to work for the Senate Judiciary Committee in the 1970s, and in 1980 an appointment to the First U.S. Circuit Court of Appeals in Boston.

Breyer's intellect had been recognized from childhood. He was born in San Francisco in 1938 into a middle-class family, the first of two sons. His father was a lawyer for the school board; his mother was active in local Democratic politics. In his confirmation hearings Breyer credited his father with teaching him that "people can work through government to improve their lives." His mother imparted a strong will and a determination to succeed. And, as Breyer recalled, she urged him not to spend too much time with his books but to learn how to "work with other people" as well.

His combination of academic and interpersonal skills stood Breyer in good stead in his work for the Senate Judiciary Committee and later as a federal judge. As special counsel to the Judiciary Subcommittee on Administrative Law from 1974 to 1975, Breyer proposed and then won bipartisan support for a bold plan to deregulate the airline industry that was finally enacted in 1978. As a judge in the 1980s, he played a major part in writing sentencing guidelines for federal judges to follow in criminal cases. In both tasks Breyer was credited with bringing different sides together to produce a consensus.

Breyer's work on deregulation stemmed from a fascination with economics that dated from his two years at Oxford and continued at Harvard Law School. After clerking for Supreme Court Justice Arthur Goldberg, Breyer went on to work in the Justice Department's antitrust division. In 1967 he returned to Harvard to teach administrative law, antitrust, and regulation. As the civil rights revolution moved into the courtroom and the antiwar movement raged in the streets, Breyer directed his passion toward economic issues. He developed a philosophy that looked with favor on the free market and viewed regulation with a skeptical eye.

In a second post with the Judiciary Committee—as staff director in 1979 and 1980—Breyer helped push through legislation deregulating another overregulated industry: trucking. He also participated in a major effort to overhaul the federal criminal code. This work laid the groundwork for passage of legislation creating the federal Sentencing Commission in 1984. Once again Breyer carefully cultivated ties with senators in both parties—bipartisan ties that helped put him on the federal bench.

A seat on the federal appeals court in Boston opened in 1979. Senator Kennedy, Breyer's mentor, favored Archibald Cox, the Harvard professor and former Watergate prosecutor, for the post. But the Carter administration rejected the sixty-seven-year-old Cox, ostensibly because of his age but mainly because of politics: Kennedy was challenging President Carter in the Democratic primaries. After Carter was renominated in 1980, Kennedy decided to push Breyer, and Carter eventually agreed.

The nomination was still pending, however, on election day. After Carter's defeat Republican senators put a hold on judicial nominations to save the posts for Ronald Reagan to fill after he took office. But with support from key Republicans, Kennedy engineered Breyer's approval by the Judiciary Committee and the full Senate. Breyer became the only one of Carter's judicial nominees confirmed after the election. He was sworn in on December 18, 1980.

In fourteen years on the appeals court, Breyer added to his reputation as a pragmatist, a centrist, and a consensus-builder. His record defied ideological labels. He took somewhat liberal positions in civil rights and civil liberties cases and more conservative stands on criminal law and economic questions. But Breyer took cases one at a time, carefully working through the facts and the law to reach practical results. His opinions were judicious to a fault: heavy on analysis and light on rhetoric. And he dissented in only twenty-six cases, fewer than two times a year on a court that came to be dominated by Republican appointees.

In 1985 Breyer was appointed to the newly created U.S. Sentencing Commission. He set about writing sentencing guidelines in the

President Clinton presented Judge Stephen G. Breyer as his choice for the Supreme Court at a May 16 ceremony in the White House Rose Garden. Clinton announced his selection three days earlier, but made his decision too late for Breyer to come to Washington that day.

most practical of ways—by looking at the range of sentences judges were actually handing down and trying to fix the guidelines for each offense around the midpoint. But Breyer's efforts to produce consensus only partly succeeded. Many judges complained that the guidelines were too complicated and too rigid. Congress added mandatory minimum sentences for some offenses, making the guidelines, in the eyes of many, too harsh as well. Breyer drew some of the blame, even though he joined in criticizing mandatory minimums. In one speech he called them "rotten bananas" that were "tending to infect the criminal justice system."

Breyer also drew criticism for his views on regulation. His book *Breaking the Vicious Circle,* published in the fall of 1993, strongly attacked what he depicted as badly skewed priorities in some environmental and health-related regulations. While he faulted some examples of deregulation, Breyer more pointedly criticized certain environmental clean-up regulations that imposed millions of dollars in extra costs for only marginal improvements in health or safety. He blamed regulators and lawmakers for paying too much attention to misguided public opinion. And he ended by calling for a super-elite bureaucracy that could transfer regulatory dollars from one agency to another to maximize the health and safety benefits.

Despite an effort at balance, Breyer's book generated criticism from people more sympathetic to regulation. But the controversy was largely confined to academic and legal circles since Breyer had moved out of the national spotlight by the time the book appeared. The critics returned to the book quickly, however, when Breyer emerged as the Supreme Court nominee on his second go-around. Consumer advocate Nader harshly accused Breyer of "bad scholarship, bad analysis, and an extremely corporatist outlook."

Those criticisms were expected to produce questions but little, if any, opposition to Breyer's confirmation from the eighteen members of the Senate Judiciary Committee. Indeed, Breyer's confirmation hearings would be a homecoming of sorts: nine of the senators were on the committee when Breyer served as staff director.

A Clinton Court?

As Breyer got ready for confirmation hearings, his future colleagues were ending a term with no blockbuster decisions and the fewest signed opinions (only eighty-four) in forty years *(see Figure 3-1, p. 58)*. With the retirement of Blackmun, the most liberal of the current justices, the Court's ideological spectrum was also narrowing. Justices Antonin Scalia and Clarence Thomas remained a determined bloc on the Court's ideological right, but Blackmun's departure left the Court with no similarly consistent voice on the left.

The Court's direction was now controlled by shifting majorities in what one observer called the Court's "mushy middle." That group included conservative justices Sandra Day O'Connor and Anthony M. Kennedy and the more liberal justices John Paul Stevens, David H. Souter, and Ginsburg. Chief Justice William H. Rehnquist sometimes moved away from his conservative past toward more moderate positions. The talk of a conservative Rehnquist Court that might undo liberal precedents of the Warren and Burger Courts had all but disappeared. The question now was whether the newest arrivals would form the nucleus of a Clinton Court and, if so, what direction that Court would follow.

Ginsburg's first year on the Court gave some clues. She supported women's rights in four important rulings in that area, and she sided with civil rights groups in most cases, including two voting rights disputes. Ginsburg generally backed First Amendment claims. For example, she voted to strike down the new law requiring cable operators to carry local broadcast stations on their systems. She also took a strong stand for separation of church and state in the Court's one case in that area.

Table 1-1   Justices' Dissents, 1993-1994 Term

Justice	8-1, 7-1	7-2	6-3, 5-3	5-4	Total	Percentage
		Division on Court				
Rehnquist	—	6	4	4	14	16.7
Blackmun	3	9	7	11	30	36.1
Stevens	2	6	5	11	24	28.6
O'Connor	—	3	1	6	10	12.2
Scalia	—	3	4	4	11	13.1
Kennedy	—	1	3	2	6	7.1
Souter	—	2	4	10	16	19.0
Thomas	1	8	6	6	21	25.0
Ginsburg	—	2	2	10	14	16.7

Note: There were eighty-four signed opinions during the 1993-1994 term. Because of recusals, Justice Blackmun participated in eighty-three cases, Justice O'Connor in eighty-two. The count of dissents includes one 6-3 decision and three 5-4 decisions where justices were unanimous on the result but divided on the legal holding.

On criminal law cases Ginsburg's voting was more mixed. Out of ten cases decided by 5-4 or 6-3 votes, she typically sided with the Court's liberal wing—three times in dissent and four times in the majority. But she voted with the conservative bloc in the three other closely divided cases and parted company with the more liberal justices in five pro-law enforcement rulings decided by 7-2 votes.

Nonetheless, Ginsburg appeared to take a more favorable view of defendants' rights than had her predecessor, Byron R. White. She backed death penalty appeals in five out of seven cases. And she may have changed the outcome in four cases where she provided a needed vote in 5-4 decisions backing criminal appeals. The rulings included decisions making it easier for death row inmates to challenge their convictions in federal appeals courts, limiting the government's power to seize property from criminals, and striking down a state tax on illegal drugs. White's views in the specific cases are impossible to know, but his general support for law enforcement suggests that some of the cases would have come out differently had he still been on the Court.

Overall, Ginsburg voted most often with Souter and next most often with Stevens. She dissented in about one-sixth of the cases—less often than the other liberal-leaning justices, more frequently than Kennedy, O'Connor, or Scalia *(see Table 1-1)*. Typically for a junior justice, the nine decisions she wrote included no major rulings, but she was an energetic presence on the Court.

From her first day Ginsburg was an unusually active questioner on the bench. She was counted as having asked seventeen questions in one hour-long argument on her first day. After receiving some critical comments she eased up, but she remained one of the most active questioners throughout the term. She also made a point of introducing gender-free terminology into arguments and opinions. During one argument, when one of the justices posed a hypothetical involving a "postman," Ginsburg changed the term in her questions to "letter carrier."

Among the other liberal-leaning justices, Souter drew attention as an emerging leader. "Souter has really found his voice as the moderate leader of the current Court," said Harvard law professor Laurence Tribe. Souter wrote two of the Court's major decisions in its final days.

Both decisions represented liberal victories in areas where conservative justices had seemed on the verge of shifting the Court's position. In one the Court upheld racially drawn lines in a redistricting plan for Florida's legislature. Just one year earlier the Court had cast doubt on the constitutionality of racial redistricting. In the other decision, the Court struck down a New York law creating a special school district for a Jewish community, saying the state had gone too far in trying to accommodate the community's religion. The ruling provoked an angry dissent from Scalia, which Souter answered in his own opinion by accusing Scalia of being "as blind to history as to precedent."

The result in both of those cases depended in part on Justice O'Connor, who voted with the Court's liberal wing while carefully distancing herself a bit from its views. She joined only part of Souter's opinion in the church-state case and wrote a concurrence to underline the narrowness of the Court's holding in the redistricting case.

In most other cases O'Connor continued to take conservative stands. She lined up more than 80 percent of the time with each of the conservatives: Rehnquist, Scalia, Kennedy, and Thomas *(see Table 1-2)*. She voted for the government in all of the most closely divided criminal law rulings and wrote the Court's significant decision refusing to expand the *Miranda* ruling on police interrogation. In civil cases she joined the Court's three most important conservative victories of the term; these decisions helped landowners challenge land-use policies, gave businesses more leverage to fight punitive damage awards, and cut back some federal securities fraud suits against lawyers, accountants, and other professionals.

O'Connor shared the Court's middle position with another moderate conservative, Kennedy. For the third year in a row, Kennedy had the lowest percentage of dissents of any of the justices. He formally dissented in just four cases. In two others he concurred in the outcome but effectively dissented from the legal holding. Based on a total of six dissents, that gave Kennedy a 93 percent voting record for the 1993-1994 term—half a percentage point lower than his record in the previous term, when he dissented in 7 out of 107 cases.

Table 1-2   Justices' Alignment, 1993-1994 Term

This table shows the percentage of decisions in which each justice agreed with each of the other members of the Court. Of the eighty-four signed decisions for the 1993-1994 term, thirty (or 36 percent) were unanimous.

The voting pattern suggested increased polarization between the most liberal and the most conservative justices and somewhat reduced cohesiveness among the other members of the Court. Conservative justices Scalia and Thomas both voted less frequently with liberal justices Blackmun and Stevens than they did in the 1992-1993 term. Thomas agreed with Blackmun and Stevens each less than half the time.

Chief Justice Rehnquist and Justice Kennedy also voted somewhat less often with Scalia and Thomas than they did in the previous term. But, along with Justice O'Connor, the conservative majority still showed a high degree of alignment. The five justices all voted with each of the others in at least three-fourths of the cases.

Justice Souter voted with Blackmun and Stevens more than 80 percent of the time—a marked increase over his alignment with the two liberals in the previous term. In her first term Justice Ginsburg had a moderate-to-liberal voting record. She voted most often with Souter and Stevens but agreed with O'Connor and Kennedy more than she did with Blackmun.

	Rehnquist	Blackmun	Stevens	O'Connor	Scalia	Kennedy	Souter	Thomas	Ginsburg
Rehnquist		32.1	29.6	73.6	72.2	66.7	48.1	68.5	51.9
		56.1	54.8	83.1	82.1	78.6	66.7	79.8	69.0
Blackmun	32.1		73.6	28.8	26.4	39.6	73.6	13.2	54.7
	56.1		82.9	54.3	52.4	61.0	82.9	43.9	70.7
Stevens	29.6	73.6		45.3	35.2	51.9	74.1	20.4	70.4
	54.8	82.9		65.1	58.3	69.0	83.3	48.8	81.0
O'Connor	73.6	28.8	45.3		75.5	73.6	52.8	71.7	62.3
	83.1	54.3	65.1		84.3	83.1	69.9	81.9	75.9
Scalia	72.2	26.4	35.2	75.5		72.2	50.0	81.5	57.4
	82.1	52.4	58.3	84.3		82.1	67.9	88.1	72.6
Kennedy	66.7	39.6	51.9	73.6	72.2		66.7	64.8	63.0
	78.6	96.2	69.0	83.1	82.1		78.6	77.4	76.2
Souter	48.1	73.6	74.1	52.8	50.0	66.7		31.5	74.1
	66.7	82.9	83.3	69.9	67.9	78.6		56.0	83.3
Thomas	68.5	13.2	20.4	71.7	81.5	64.8	31.5		46.3
	79.8	43.9	48.8	81.9	88.1	77.4	56.0		65.5
Ginsburg	51.9	54.7	70.4	62.3	57.4	63.0	74.1	46.3	
	69.0	70.7	81.0	75.9	72.6	76.2	83.3	65.5	

Note: The first number in each cell represents the percentage of agreement in divided cases. The second number represents the percentage of agreement in all signed opinions.

For the most part Kennedy, like O'Connor, took conservative stands. In the Court's 5-4 decisions he provided needed votes for nine rulings that could be classified as conservative, and he wrote the ruling limiting federal securities suits. In four other 5-4 decisions, however, Kennedy lined up with liberals in rulings that favored criminal defendants. He wrote the Court's decision requiring the government to give property owners notice and opportunity for a hearing before seizing land in criminal forfeiture proceedings. And he joined in two rulings that set back antidrug enforcement. One overturned a state tax on illegal drugs as a violation of the Double Jeopardy Clause, and the other raised the prosecution's burden of proof under a new federal money-laundering statute.

Kennedy voted with the liberals as well in the legislative redistricting and church-state cases, but he wrote separate concurrences, distancing himself more than O'Connor from the Court's holding in both cases. Kennedy based his vote on precedent but repeated his criticisms of race-based redistricting and overly strict views of separation of church and state.

For Rehnquist the term provided one major personal victory: the Court's property rights ruling, which capped several years of effort by Rehnquist to strengthen legal protections for private property. Conservative groups were especially heartened by Rehnquist's declaration that property rights should not be "relegated" below other constitutionally protected rights.

Rehnquist also continued to take conservative stands on other issues. Out of nineteen nonunanimous criminal law decisions, Rehnquist voted against the government's position only once. He wrote three closely divided rulings that broadened the government's ability to use prior convictions against defendants in sentencing decisions. But the Court shifted somewhat on criminal law issues, leaving Rehnquist in dissent more often than the year before. Overall, he dissented in one-sixth of the cases for the term; in the 1992-1993 term he had dissented only one-tenth of the time.

Rehnquist ended the term with a notable break from his conservative colleagues. He wrote the Court's final opinion strengthening the power of judges to protect abortion clinics from violent antiabortion demonstrations. And he even included in his opinion a citation to the *Roe v. Wade* abortion rights ruling—a decision that he had voted to overturn just two years earlier. Earlier in the year Rehnquist also wrote the Court's opinion allowing abortion clinics to use the federal antiracketeering law to sue violent protesters. That decision, however, was unanimous.

The strengthening of the Court's center left the justices at the ideological edges more isolated than a year earlier. Court watchers noted, in particular, that Scalia and Thomas were often alone in taking sharply conservative positions. "The term showed the increasing marginalization of Scalia and Thomas," observed Stephen Shapiro, legal director of the American Civil Liberties Union. "That was a further indication that the balance of power is shifting from the far right to the moderates."

Scalia and Thomas continued to be the most closely aligned of the justices. They voted together 88 percent of the time, compared with 90 percent of the time in the previous year. Even more significantly, they often paired off alone in opinions that bluntly called for scrapping prior liberal rulings by the Court.

When the Court overturned Montana's tax on illegal drugs as a violation of the Double Jeopardy Clause, for example, Rehnquist and O'Connor based their dissents on existing case law, while Scalia and Thomas advocated overturning the five-year-old ruling that the majority relied on. Similarly, in the Court's end-of-term voting rights cases, Thomas and Scalia called for dismantling cases dating back to 1969 that used the federal Voting Rights Act to help minorities get elected to office.

Despite their ideological ties, Scalia and Thomas had different styles. Scalia continued as the Court's most active inquisitor, vigorously interrogating lawyers with questions aimed at taking arguments in his direction. Thomas, on the other hand, was a sullen and silent presence on the bench. Close Court watchers said he went through the entire term without asking a single question from the bench. Thomas also dissented more often than Scalia—twenty-one times compared with Scalia's eleven dissents. The difference stemmed in part from four criminal law rulings in which Scalia joined the majority in decisions favoring criminal defendants while Thomas backed the government's position.

Blackmun and Stevens continued as the Court's most liberal members, voting together 83 percent of the time. They were also the justices most often in dissent. Blackmun dissented in more than one-third of the cases, Stevens in more than one-fourth. They dissented together in twenty cases, usually taking liberal positions in criminal law or individual rights cases. Blackmun dissented in an additional ten cases that showed an even stronger liberal orientation. He voted alone, for example, to overturn part of California's death penalty statute and to apply a new law favoring plaintiffs in job discrimination suits retroactively. He also differed with Stevens in voting to uphold three protectionist state laws that the Court struck down as interfering with interstate commerce.

In a more dramatic departure from the rest of the Court, Blackmun announced in February 1994 that he would no longer vote to uphold death sentences in any cases. The impassioned 7,000-word announcement was attached to the Court's decision denying review in an otherwise unexceptional death penalty case (*Callins v. Collins, Director, Texas Department of Criminal Justice, Institutional Division* (Feb. 22, 1994)). Blackmun said he had become convinced that it was impossible to administer capital punishment fairly. "From this day forward," Blackmun declared, "I no longer shall tinker with the machinery of dissent." No one joined Blackmun's statement; Scalia responded by accusing Blackmun of trying to "thrust a minority's view on the people."

Blackmun had some notable successes, however, in the last of his twenty-four years on the Court. He wrote the Court's main opinions in two rulings backing death penalty appeals. In one the Court gave federal judges the power to delay state executions while inmates challenged their convictions. The other ruling gave defendants the right to counter some prosecution arguments for the death penalty by telling the jury about the alternative sentence of life imprisonment without parole. Blackmun also wrote an important opinion broadening the right to jury trial in contempt cases. And he wrote the Court's opinion barring the use of gender in jury selection.

With Blackmun's retirement Stevens was to become the senior member of the Court's liberal wing. Under Court procedures that meant he would have the power to assign the writing of opinions more often—that is, whenever he was in the majority and Rehnquist in dissent. But Stevens was not seen as a leader in the Court's internal deliberations. "He's no groupie," one reporter remarked in a postmortem on the term. Stevens had a penchant for taking distinctive positions, often alone. Court observers doubted that he would step into the role of trying to forge moderate-to-liberal coalitions to counter the Court's still predominantly conservative orientation.

That perception led liberals to pin their hopes for moderating the Court's conservative tendencies on Breyer. Some viewed Breyer hopefully as an intellectual heavyweight who could fortify the Court's liberal wing while using a mixture of persuasion and charm to reach out to the more moderate conservatives. But conservatives voiced few fears about Breyer's ascension to the Court. On many issues Breyer appeared less liberal than Blackmun. And business groups had special praise for Breyer's views on regulatory issues. "He's someone who understands the cost of regulation and will look at it with a jaundiced eye," said Stephen Bokat, director of the National Chamber Litigation Center.

A One-Snag Confirmation

From the time of Breyer's selection, the White House wanted to soften his image as a judicial technocrat. Clinton introduced Breyer at a Rose Garden ceremony May 16, 1994, as a judge who had shown an "impressive ability to build bridges in the pursuit of fairness and justice." Breyer followed suit, promising that he would "try to make law work for people because that is its defining purpose in a government of the people."

The "Robin Hood" spin on Breyer's nomination—as one reporter dubbed it—produced snickers among some Senate staffers. Breyer's opinions, in fact, displayed no special passion for social justice. And thanks to a fortunate marriage, Breyer was a millionaire several times over. His wife, the former Joanna Hare, was the daughter of a wealthy British press lord and Conservative Party politician. Financial disclosure statements put Breyer's net worth somewhere between $3 million and $6 million or perhaps higher.

Still, a bit of disingenuousness was hardly unknown in Washington and, surely, was no obstacle to Breyer's confirmation. A more substantive problem arose, however, on the eve of Breyer's initial appearance before the Judiciary Committee. Senator Metzenbaum said he planned to question Breyer about a possible conflict of interest stemming from his investment in the famous British insurance syndicate, Lloyd's of London. The investment, first disclosed by the Long Island newspaper *Newsday* on June 24, raised questions whether Breyer should have recused himself from some cases involving liability for cleaning up toxic waste sites, one of the areas of Lloyd's coverage.

Breyer had first invested in Lloyd's in the 1970s and continued investing in the syndicate through most of the 1980s. He resigned from Lloyd's in 1988, but he still faced potential losses for a 1985 investment in a syndicate called Merrett 418 that insured companies involved with asbestos and other environmental pollution risks. Breyer had been concerned enough to step out of asbestos-related cases, but Metzenbaum said the judge had sat in at least eight cases involving cleanup costs under the federal Superfund law. Metzenbaum said Breyer's rulings in the cases might have had an impact on his investment. And he noted that in two of the rulings, Breyer had voted to limit enforcement activities by the Environmental Protection Agency (EPA).

White House aides minimized the issue. Counsel Lloyd Cutler called it "a nitpick." The administration released letters from legal ethics experts saying Breyer need not have recused himself from the pollution cases because they could not have affected his investment. And Breyer himself sought to preempt the issue as the Judiciary Committee began hearings July 12.

Breyer opened with a prepared statement that traced a life devoted to law and public service and ended with the most general of promises, if confirmed, to "work hard," "listen," and "try to interpret the law carefully in accord with its basic purpose." Then he turned to defending himself against the ethics charge. "There is nothing more important to me than my integrity and my reputation for impartiality," Breyer said firmly. "So I have reviewed those cases, and the judicial recusal statute. And I am personally confident that my sitting in those cases did not present any conflict of interest."

Judge Stephen G. Breyer talked with Senate Judiciary Committee members July 12 as he prepared to testify in his confirmation hearings before the committee. Senators, from left, were Strom Thurmond, Republican of South Carolina; Orrin Hatch of Utah, the committee's ranking Republican; and committee chair Joseph R. Biden, Jr., Democrat of Delaware.

Lloyd's had not been a party in any of the cases, Breyer emphasized. He had resigned from Lloyd's and was trying to get out of any remaining liability as soon as possible. To try to allay any remaining concerns, Breyer said he would divest himself of all holdings in insurance companies.

Breyer's pronouncement provided a moment of drama, but the moment passed. None of the senators followed up with questions on the issue in Breyer's first day on the witness stand, although Metzenbaum said he planned to ask about it later. Instead, the senators began the delicate game of probing Breyer's views on legal issues, while he tried to avoid committing himself to specific positions on questions that he might have to decide later.

Senators had felt frustrated in their efforts to get answers during the last three Supreme Court confirmation hearings. President Bush's two nominees, Souter and Thomas, had deflected liberal senators' questioning about abortion, among other issues, while Republicans chafed at Ginsburg's limited answers on capital punishment. Abortion and capital punishment remained hot-button issues, and Breyer's record gave limited clues about his stands. He had never sat on a capital punishment case, and his record on abortion was limited to two rulings. In one case he had voted to strike down a rule prohibiting abortion counseling by federally financed family planning centers. In the other he had voted to prevent abortion rights supporters from challenging a law requiring parental notification before abortion on minors.

To deal with those issues, Breyer fell back on the Court's own rulings, saying that the Court had settled the broad questions and he accepted the decisions. The issues were raised by Strom Thurmond, the ninety-one-year-old conservative Republican from South Carolina. Thurmond asked first about the death penalty, prefacing the question by noting Blackmun's decision earlier in the year to oppose capital punishment. Breyer's answer appeared to fault Blackmun's stance.

A judge should consider taking himself out of a case if he has "strong personal views on a matter as important as the death penalty," Breyer said. "I have no such personal view on the death penalty," he continued. And he noted that the Court had ruled that the death penalty could be imposed under some circumstances. That issue, he said, "is, in my opinion, settled law. At this point, it is settled."

So too with abortion. "The case of *Roe v. Wade* has been the law for twenty-one years," he told Senator Thurmond, adding that the Court had reaffirmed it in 1992 in another case, *Casey v. Planned Parenthood of Pennsylvania*. "That is the law."

Breyer's responses gave an appearance of candor, but he avoided detailed questions about death penalty procedures or legislative restrictions on abortion. On other issues, too, Breyer managed to satisfy senators' inquiries while steering clear of specifics. He distanced himself from the Court's new property rights ruling by saying that he did not favor using the Constitution's takings clause to impose "significant practical obstacles" on government regulation. He assured senators that he thought judges should look to legislative intent in interpreting statutes—a sharp contrast to Justice Scalia's criticism of legislative history. In addition, he voiced support for privacy rights and separation of church and state and indicated an open mind on televising Supreme Court proceedings.

In a revealing passage Breyer also discussed his approach to judicial decision making. He portrayed himself as a determined pragmatist, always conscious of the practical effects of ruling one way or another. And he linked his emphasis on building consensus to the same pragmatic goal. "Consensus is important," Breyer explained, "because law is not theoretical. And consensus helps produce the simplicity that will enable the law to be effective."

As a witness, Breyer was just like his opinions: judicious and analytical. He explained Court precedents and his own opinions with an impressive memory for factual details and a solid command of the law. Yet he also appeared relaxed, delivering answers in a conversational tone. At times he thumbed through a pocket-sized copy of the Constitution before giving an answer.

His emotions surfaced only occasionally during his twenty-two hours on the witness stand. Asked about affirmative action, Breyer spoke strongly of the need to fulfill what he called the "basic promise of fairness" in the Fourteenth Amendment, ratified after the Civil War. "It's not surprising to me that, given the years of neglect, that it will be decades, decades before that promise is met," Breyer said. "But we're trying. And trying is absolutely correct."

Breyer also signaled a strict approach on women's rights, using his two daughters, seated behind him, to make his point. "Think of Chloe or Nell or their equivalents all over the country going into the workplace and think of some kind of rule that makes their life worse because they're women," Breyer said. "Wouldn't you say, but what kind of justification for that could there be?"

Breyer's strongest displays of emotion, however, came under critical questions from Metzenbaum, first about his views on antitrust and then about the Lloyd's issue. On antitrust, Metzenbaum charged that Breyer had voted in sixteen out of sixteen cases "against the people the antitrust laws are designed to protect." Breyer responded tartly: "I don't count up how many victories are for plaintiffs and for defendants." He went on to say that in some of the cases, his rulings for antitrust defendants helped promote competition and lower prices for consumers.

Metzenbaum provoked Breyer again when he turned to the subject of Lloyd's on the third day of the hearing. Focusing on a 1982 decision that had limited EPA cleanup of a toxic dump site in New Hampshire, Metzenbaum repeatedly insisted Breyer had a clear conflict in sitting on the case. "I think the question is whether there is a real direct impact on the investment, and I think the answer was no," Breyer replied. Then, with anger in his voice, he insisted that the appeals court had sided with the EPA on one issue in the case while merely upholding the rest of the lower court's ruling.

The questioning ended inconclusively, but no one joined in Metzenbaum's criticisms. Later Senator Biden closed by tying up one loose end: the issue of Breyer's failure to pay Social Security taxes on a household worker several years earlier. Breyer explained that the problem involved an elderly woman who had cleaned their house for several years while also working for other families. In that capacity the woman was classified as an "independent contractor" and the Breyers did not need to pay Social Security taxes for her. But eventually she dropped her other work and became their "employee" for Social Security purposes. When they discovered the mistake, Breyer said, he and his wife paid the taxes and a penalty. Biden said the explanation satisifed him, and no other senator voiced concern about the matter.

The committee allotted one day for public witnesses. A string of bar leaders and law professors came in with high praise for Breyer. Nader repeated his criticisms of Breyer's views on economic issues. Two other groups registered opposition—an antiabortion organization and a home schooling group, which faulted Breyer's opinion upholding a state law setting standards for church-run schools. For much of the day, only one of the senators was present to keep the hearing going.

Four days later the committee voted to recommend Breyer's confirmation. Metzenbaum said he was voting for him "with some reservations but also a great deal of hope." Some Republicans complained that Breyer was soft on property rights and too liberal on social issues. But the final vote was unanimous, 18-0. The committee met Tuesday morning. The word was that Breyer would be confirmed by Friday.

But then came a hitch. The Senate's calendar was busy, and the nomination had to wait. Then came another snag. Sen. Richard Lugar, a respected moderate Republican from Indiana, decided to oppose Breyer, saying he had shown "bad judgment" in investing in Lloyd's. Then another problem: the *New York Times* called for reopening the hearings, saying Breyer had not been completely candid on the Lloyd's issue. Despite the delays, Senate staffers insisted the nomination was still on track and the only problem was finding time to bring it to the Senate floor.

The time finally arrived on July 29—two weeks after the conclusion of the hearings. The Senate chamber was largely empty for most of the five hours of desultory debate. Kennedy and Hatch opened with bipartisan praise for Breyer. Biden endorsed him, too, but criticized his views on regulation. After a few more speakers Lugar took the floor. Breyer had shown "extraordinarily bad judgment" in signing documents that exposed him to "unlimited liability," Lugar said in his hour-long speech. Moreover, Breyer was "trapped" in the syndicate, raising the possibility that he would have to recuse himself from some cases "for a long time."

Lugar's views were echoed only by two Republicans and by Metzenbaum, who nonetheless repeated his plan to vote for confirmation. Others defended him. "He's a man of integrity," Hatch said as the debate ended. When the roll call began shortly after 2:30 p.m., no one doubted the outcome. But the final vote, 87-9, fell short of what many had expected two months earlier. The nine senators voting no were all Republicans: Lugar (Ind.), Conrad Burns (Mont.), Dan Coats (Ind.), Paul Coverdell (Ga.), Jesse Helms (N.C.), Trent Lott (Miss.), Frank H. Murkowski (Alaska), Don Nickles (Okla.), and Robert C. Smith (N.H.). Three of the senators—Helms, Nickles, and Smith—also voted against Ginsburg's confirmation in 1993. Most of the senators who voted against

Breyer's confirmation were conservatives more concerned with his legal views than his ethics. Four senators were absent when the vote was taken on the Senate floor.

Breyer's confirmation margin was lower than that of Clinton's first nominee, Ginsburg, who had been approved one year earlier by a vote of 96-3. But at a White House celebration Breyer evinced no disappointment. "The responsibility of that position is awesome, rather humbling," he said. "I'll do my best."

2 | *The 1993-1994 Term*

As the justices of the Supreme Court mounted the bench for the final day of the 1993-1994 term, they had some of the year's most difficult cases yet to decide. The six cases awaiting rulings on June 30 covered explosive subjects: abortion protests, capital punishment, and racial redistricting. The issues were contentious for the public and, as the various opinions showed, contentious for the justices, too.

In one case Clarence Thomas, the Court's only black justice, argued in a massive concurring opinion that courts should stop drawing redistricting plans to help blacks or other minorities get elected to legislative bodies. Retiring Justice Harry Blackmun underlined his opposition to capital punishment with a plaintive protest against the inadequate legal representation for defendants in death penalty cases. And Justice Antonin Scalia bitterly accused his colleagues of curtailing freedom of speech by allowing judges to set up "buffer zones" around abortion clinics to protect them from antiabortion demonstrations.

The rulings produced sharp reactions outside the courtroom. Abortion rights leaders said the abortion clinic ruling would protect patients and clinic staff from violence or even death. Antiabortion forces said the real victim in the case was the First Amendment. Civil rights organizations rued the Court's decisions cutting back legal remedies in two voting rights cases. Conservative groups saw encouraging signs of a turning away from what they called "racial balkanization." Texas's attorney general said a decision helping death row inmates challenge their sentences in federal court would add to the delay in carrying out executions. But the lawyer who won the case maintained the ruling would help ensure that death penalty cases received "meaningful review" in federal courts.

By the time reporters had finished their stories on June 30, however, emotions had already started to subside. And as court-watchers conducted more deliberative postmortems, the justices received good marks from a surprisingly broad range of interest groups and experts.

The American Civil Liberties Union (ACLU), a strong critic of the Court's conservative trend in recent years, said the term had been "relatively successful for civil liberties." From the other end of the political spectrum, conservative activist Clint Bolick of the Institute for Justice in Washington called the term "quiet but overall excellent." And Stephen Bokat, head of the National Chamber Litigation Center, an arm of the U.S. Chamber of Commerce, said business fared "reasonably well" during the term.

Many academic experts who follow the Court had similarly positive assessments. Law professors from across the ideological spectrum gave the Court credit for steering a middle course—and steering it reasonably well.

"The Court decided fewer cases and, by and large, decided cases on their own terms rather than setting forth a larger philosophy or comprehensive view," observed Douglas Kmiec, a conservative constitutional law professor at Notre Dame Law School. "I thought they confronted some difficult cases and acquitted themselves reasonably well."

"We've seen that instead of this being a radical right court, it's now a centrist court," said Erwin Chemerinsky, a liberal constitutional law expert at the University of Southern California Law Center. "The middle is taking control.'

The chorus of carefully modulated approval was, of course, not unanimous. Harvard's liberal law professor Laurence Tribe complained that the Court was "in a state of disarray and confusion" and was failing to give clear guidance for lower courts to follow. Overall, however, few disparaging remarks followed the justices as they dispersed for a three-month recess.

The Court itself could take the credit for the muted reaction to its work from politicians, interest groups, experts, and the public at large. The Court appeared to be working hard to lower its profile. It issued only eighty-four signed opinions, the lowest number in four decades. The cases the justices did agree to decide presented narrower issues than the memorable decisions of the past three decades. And the Court generally decided the cases on narrow grounds and with a minimum of legal rhetoric.

Just over half of the Court's decisions—forty-four in all—involved interpretations of statutes or regulations. Only thirty cases, about one-third of the total, were decided on constitutional grounds. Constitutional rulings are most likely to force broad legal changes and provoke strong reactions, pro and con. But the Court rejected new claims of individual rights in fifteen—exactly half—of the constitutional rulings. When the justices did recognize constitutional claims, they usually were only following established legal doctrines.

In criminal law cases the Court refused to broaden the *Miranda* rule on police interrogation, strike down a widely used jury instruction defining "reasonable doubt," or tighten the standards for capital punishment statutes. In one decision the Court even cut back on constitutional rights by permitting federal judges to lengthen a defendant's sentence on the basis of a prior misdemeanor conviction if the defendant had not been represented by a lawyer. The decision overturned a ruling the Court had handed down in 1980. It was the only time during this term that the Court explicitly reversed one of its prior rulings *(see Table 2-1)*.

Table 2-1   Reversals of Earlier Rulings

The Supreme Court issued one decision during the 1993-1994 term that reversed a previous ruling by the Court, either explicitly or in effect. The ruling brought the total number of such reversals in the Court's history to 208.

New Decision	Overruled Decision	New Holding
Nichols v. United States (1994) [p. 84]	*Baldasar v. Illinois* (1980)	Uncounseled prior misdemeanor conviction can be used to increase prison term in new case

Source: Johnny Killian, American Law Division, Congressional Research Service, Library of Congress.

The justices sustained new constitutional claims in only three of the term's criminal law decisions. Two of those rulings were setbacks for drug enforcement. The Court struck down a Montana tax on illegal drugs as a violation of the Double Jeopardy Clause. The justices also said the government ordinarily could not seize land in a criminal forfeiture proceeding without first giving the owner notice and an opportunity for hearing. In a capital punishment case the Court said juries in some cases had to be told about the option of sentencing a defendant to life without possibility of parole as an alternative to the death penalty.

The Court recognized constitutional rights more often in other areas. The justices prohibited lawyers from excluding potential jurors on the basis of sex by extending precedents that already barred racially motivated peremptory challenges in jury selection. Property rights groups and tort reform organizations won constitutional victories, but the rulings arguably did little more than fill in blanks left in earlier Court decisions. Similarly, the Court's ruling in a prisoner rights case simply settled the question of what burden of proof inmates must meet in suits under the Eighth Amendment.

In the First Amendment area two rulings striking down a local ban on yard signs and protecting advertising by accountants plowed no new ground. The Court also upheld First Amendment interests in an important copyright law case by strengthening legal protections for parody and satire.

Two other First Amendment cases produced mixed results in terms of freedom of expression. The Court said public employees could not be fired for comments on public issues without some form of prior investigation short of a legal trial. And the cable industry won greater First Amendment protection, but the Court left it to a lower court to decide the actual issue in the case—the validity of the so-called must-carry rules requiring cable operators to carry local broadcast stations on their systems.

Business interests won four constitutional law victories as the Court struck down protectionist state or local measures on grounds they discriminated against interstate commerce. Four additional rulings invalidated state or local laws on constitutional grounds *(see Table 2-2)*. Business groups failed, however, in five cases challenging state or federal tax measures, including a controversial state tax scheme that multinational corporations said amounted to double taxation.

In two other constitutional law rulings the Court favored the federal government. It refused to allow individuals to sue federal agencies for violations of constitutional rights. And it rejected a due process attack on the method of appointing judges in the military justice system. Both decisions were unanimous.

Finally, two of the Court's most significant constitutional rulings involved conflicting claims under the First Amendment. In the abortion clinic case the Court rejected the free speech claims of protesters in order to help protect the abortion rights of the clinic's patients. And in a church-state case the Court struck down a state law creating a special school district for an orthodox Jewish community as an unconstitutional establishment of religion.

In many statutory cases the Court continued to follow the "plain language" of laws enacted by Congress or state legislatures rather than attempt a broad reading of legislative intent. This formalistic approach, most strongly advocated by Justice Scalia, sometimes hurt and sometimes helped individuals claiming legal protection under federal laws. But the Court departed from its plain-language approach in several cases. Typically, those decisions curtailed the coverage of federal laws and found conservative justices in the majority and the more liberal justices in dissent.

In one of its most significant statutory decisions, the Court refused to allow suits under the federal securities laws for aiding and abetting securities fraud. The 5-4 ruling narrowly interpreted the Securities Exchange Act of 1934 to bar suits that virtually all federal appeals courts had previously allowed. In another important case the Court refused to give retroactive effect to a 1991 law broadening legal remedies in federal employment discrimination cases. The law contained no retroactivity provision, and the Court said it would not read one into the statute.

In some other cases the Court's formalistic approach to reading statutes favored groups claiming protection under federal laws. Most notably, the Court allowed abortion clinics to use the broadly written federal antiracketeering law to sue antiabortion demonstrators, who had argued that the statute was intended to be used against organized crime,

Table 2-2   State and Local Laws Held Unconstitutional

The Supreme Court invalidated eight state constitutional provisions or statutes or local ordinances during the 1993-1994 term.

Decision (in chronological order)	State or Local Law Ruled Invalid
Oregon Waste Systems, Inc. v. Department of Environmental Quality (p. 90)	Surcharge for disposal of out-of-state solid waste
C & A Carbone, Inc. v. Town of Clarkstown (p. 89)	"Flow-control" ordinance requiring garbage to be processed at designated facility
Associated Industries of Missouri v. Lohman (p. 110)	Higher sales tax on out-of-state goods than in-state purchases
Montana Department of Revenue v. Kurth Ranch (p. 77)	State tax on illegal drugs
City of Ladue v. Gilleo (p. 97)	Ordinance banning most yard signs
West Lynn Creamery, Inc. v. Healy (p. 109)	Assessment on out-of-state milk producers used to subsidize dairy farmers inside state
Honda Motor Co., Ltd. v. Oberg (pp. 112, 143)	State constitutional provision limiting judicial review of punitive damage awards
Board of Education of Kiryas Joel Village School District v. Grumet (pp. 96, 168)	State law creating school district for religious community

not political protesters. In an important environmental ruling the Court literally enforced the federal law governing disposal of hazardous wastes. This decision imposed costly regulatory controls on municipal trash incinerators. The opinion was written by Scalia, who usually voted against environmentalists.

In several cases, however, the Court scaled back legal remedies by creating judicial exceptions in the face of broad statutory language and legislative intent. The Court barred minority groups from using the Voting Rights Act to enlarge governing bodies to gain better representation. In a labor law case the Court adopted a legal doctrine, rejected by most states, that limited the ability of railroad workers to sue under an expansive turn-of-the-century statute. In a bankruptcy case the Court made it harder for debtors to use a statutory provision to nullify home foreclosure sales. All three decisions were closely divided, with the liberal-leaning justices in the minority.

The Court's movement toward the center was reflected in the shifting fortunes of various interest groups during the term. In criminal law, individual rights, and business-related cases, the best description for the term seemed to be "mixed results." Prosecutors and business interests continued to fare better than did criminal defendants or organized labor. Most claims to broaden individual rights failed.

For all sides, however, most of the victories or defeats were at the legal margins. "What this Court is doing is what the Court historically has done," said Dennis Hutchinson, a law professor at the University of Chicago and former Supreme Court law clerk. "It's carving out a middle course."

In criminal law cases the Court backed prosecutors in fifteen out of twenty-five rulings, or 60 percent of the time. In the previous term prosecutors had a better success rate, winning twenty out of thirty rulings. Prosecutors' success rate in capital punishment cases also declined. The Court upheld death sentences in four out of seven decisions, compared with six out of seven cases in the 1992-1993 term.

"It was hardly a pro-defendant or pro-government term," said Barry Friedman, a professor at Vanderbilt Law School who follows the Court's criminal law decisions. "Everybody was batting .500, and the result depended very much on the issues."

Business groups won in seventeen out of thirty cases where business interests lined up against government, labor, or consumers. The property rights and punitive damages rulings topped the list of business victories; both opinions included commentary that business groups thought would be helpful in future cases.

In the punitive damages case Justice John Paul Stevens warned that arbitrary awards and potentially biased juries pose a danger for the rights of big corporations. Stephen Bokat of the National Chamber Litigation Center called the 7-2 decision "a recognition by a significant number of members of the Court that punitive damages are a substantial problem for businesses and that the process has to be watched carefully."

Similarly, Chief Justice William Rehnquist cheered property rights forces by declaring that the Fifth Amendment's Takings Clause, which prevents the government from taking property without just compensation, should not be "relegated" to a lower status than other provisions in the Bill of Rights. "This is an idea that's been a long time coming, and it's high time it came," said Michael Berger, a Los Angeles lawyer who represents landowners and developers in property rights cases.

In labor-related rulings the Court sided with unions or workers about half the time, but most of the issues were narrow. In one important ruling the Court said the National Labor Relations Board could award reinstatement and back pay to workers in an unfair labor practice case even if the workers lied in administrative hearings. In other cases the Court made it somewhat harder for unions to organize nurses or federal workers. It also raised the burden of proof for coal miners and longshore workers seeking benefits under federal laws for work-related injuries.

Labor unions had one major victory in a decision that also had implications in other areas. The Court unanimously threw out a $52 million contempt-of-court fine against the United Mine Workers for allegedly violating an antiviolence injunction during a coal strike in 1989. The ruling, which broadened the requirement for jury trials in criminal contempt cases, could benefit not only labor unions but any individuals or groups accused of violating court injunctions.

The Court's rulings in individual rights cases were also mixed and generally narrow. The justices looked most favorably on claims under the First Amendment or under explicit federal statutes. In one ruling, for example, the Court reinforced the right of parents of youngsters with disabilities to use a federal law to force school districts to pay for special education services not being offered by the public schools. But the Court was reluctant to create new legal protections under vaguely written constitutional or statutory provisions. For example, the justices barred the use of the Due Process Clause to bring a federal civil rights suit for malicious prosecution even though most lower federal courts had allowed such actions.

Women's rights groups, however, had an exceptionally good year at the Court. They prevailed in two cases giving abortion clinics stronger legal protections against disruptive demonstrations. They won a closely watched sexual harassment case in which the justices reaffirmed a broad test favoring plaintiffs. And women's groups also supported the Court's decision to bar gender-based challenges in jury selection even though the ruling favored a man who had been ordered to pay child support in a paternity suit.

The Court's shift toward the center could be seen clearly by comparing the most important decisions of the term with those from the previous session. In the 1992-1993 term conservative groups could claim substantial victories in eight of the ten major rulings. In the 1993-1994 term, however, conservatives were clear victors in only four of the eleven highest-profile rulings. Liberal groups, on the other hand, prevailed in five major decisions. One voting rights case was best counted as a draw, while the cable industry's challenge to the must-carry rules awaited a ruling by a lower court.

Abortion and Free Speech

Clinics Gain Tools to Curb Antiabortion Protests

Madsen v. Women's Health Center, Inc., decided by a 6-3 vote, June 30, 1994; Rehnquist wrote the opinion; Scalia, Kennedy, and Thomas dissented. *(See excerpts, p. 266.)*

National Organization for Women, Inc. v. Scheidler, decided by a 9-0 vote, January 24, 1994; Rehnquist wrote the opinion. *(See excerpts, p. 113.)*

Frustrated in their efforts to overturn abortion rights rulings in the Supreme Court or Congress, opponents of abortion in the 1990s took their fight to the streets. Militant groups such as Operation Rescue openly proclaimed their intent to close clinics where abortions were performed. Protesters engaged in clamorous, occasionally violent demonstrations, chanting antiabortion slogans over bullhorns and taunting patients and staff on their way into clinic buildings.

Abortion rights groups turned to the courts and to Congress for relief. Local trespass laws provided only minimal help. In 1993 the Supreme Court rebuffed an effort to invoke a Reconstruction-era civil rights law to limit demonstrations *(Supreme Court Yearbook, 1992-1993, pp. 23-25)*. But in its 1993-1994 term the Court cleared the way for abortion clinics to use two other legal strategies.

In one case, *National Organization for Women, Inc. v. Scheidler,* the Court upheld use of the federal antiracketeering law to bring civil damage suits against antiabortion organizations that engage in unlawful demonstrations. In the other ruling, *Madsen v. Women's Health Center, Inc.,* the Court held that judges can set up "buffer zones" requiring protesters to keep a minimum distance—36 feet in this case—away from clinics.

The racketeering suit was part of a broad action brought by the National Organization for Women (NOW) and two abortion clinics— Delaware Women's Health Organization and Summit Women's Health Organization in Milwaukee. Defendants included an umbrella group called the Pro-Life Action Network and one of its leaders, Joseph Scheidler; Operation Rescue and its founder, Randall Terry; and several other antiabortion activists and groups.

NOW and the clinics hoped to hit the antiabortion groups with heavy financial penalties. The original suit charged that the pro-life groups were violating the Sherman Antitrust Act by trying to drive abortion clinics out of business for the benefit of their own pregnancy counseling centers. Later the complaint was amended to include a count under the federal Racketeering Influenced and Corrupt Organizations Act, popularly known as RICO.

RICO allows plaintiffs to recover triple damages for economic harms inflicted by an "enterprise" engaged in a "pattern of racketeering activity." The clinics charged that the antiabortion groups were committing extortion—one of the offenses covered by RICO—by using force or violence to deny women their right to medical services and clinic staff their right to employment.

The antiabortion groups, however, contended RICO was intended to be used against organized crime, not political protest groups engaged in civil disobedience. A federal district court judge in Chicago and the Seventh U.S. Circuit Court of Appeals agreed. Both courts said RICO could be used only if the defendants were motivated by "economic gain." The lower courts also dismissed the antitrust allegations.

Before the Supreme Court the antiabortion groups secured the services of the nation's preeminent expert on RICO. Notre Dame law professor G. Robert Blakey helped write the law when he was a Senate Judiciary Committee staffer in 1970. Blakey told the justices the law "can be summed up in two words: illicit gain." But Fay Clayton, a Chicago lawyer representing the clinics, contended that the law contained no such limitation. "We are asking this Court to apply the statute as Congress wrote it," she said.

Less than two months later the Court unanimously sided with the clinics. "Nowhere [in the statute] is there any indication that an economic motive is required," Chief Justice Rehnquist wrote in a short, low-key opinion on January 24. All eight justices joined the opinion.

In a brief concurrence Justice Souter, joined by Justice Kennedy, stressed that political groups could raise free speech arguments in defending against RICO suits. Rehnquist dealt with the issue only in a footnote, saying the issue had not been adequately raised for the Court to consider.

After the ruling antiabortion groups vehemently denounced the decision as violating First Amendment rights and trampling on the American tradition of civil disobedience. "Under this decision, Martin Luther King, Jr., would have been a racketeer," Randall Terry told reporters. For their part, NOW leaders said the ruling would help abortion clinics put a stop to "antiabortion terrorism." The decision had no immediate impact, however. It merely returned the case to lower courts, where the clinics still had to prove their accusations and show evidence of economic injury before they could recover any damages.

One week before the RICO ruling, the Court had agreed to decide another case pitting abortion rights against freedom of speech—this one a protracted legal dispute stemming from antiabortion demonstrations at a women's clinic in Melbourne, Florida. Lawyers for the Aware Woman Center for Choice went to state court; they claimed the demonstrators

Staff members at the Aware Woman Center for Choice in Melbourne, Florida, celebrated the Supreme Court's decision June 30 upholding parts of an injunction limiting antiabortion protests near the clinic.

were trying to close the facility, and they asked for an injunction to limit the protests.

In response the judge, Robert McGregor, in September 1992 prohibited demonstrators from trespassing on clinic property, blocking the center, or physically abusing anyone associated with it. When demonstrations continued, the clinic returned to court with evidence that the protesters had violated the restrictions. In April 1993 the judge substantially expanded the injunction.

The new injunction prohibited demonstrations within a 36-foot buffer zone around the clinic. McGregor also set up a 300-foot buffer zone where protesters were forbidden from physically approaching any person "unless such person indicates a desire to communicate." The order prohibited, during surgical and recovery periods, any "singing, chanting, whistling, shouting, yelling, use of bullhorns, auto horns, sound amplification equipment or other sounds or images observable to or within the earshot of the patients inside" the clinic. Finally, the judge prohibited demonstrations within 300 feet of the residences of clinic staff.

Operation Rescue challenged the injunction before the Florida Supreme Court and in federal courts, calling it vague, overbroad, and discriminatory against antiabortion views. The Florida Supreme Court upheld the order in October. But one week later the Eleventh U.S. Circuit Court of Appeals in Atlanta agreed with the protesters, saying the injunction was a viewpoint-based restriction that could be justified only if a compelling state interest was shown. The appeals panel ordered a lower court to determine whether the injunction met that test. Before that could happen, however, the Supreme Court took up the issue by agreeing to review the protesters' appeal of the Florida high court's ruling.

The Court heard arguments in the case on April 28, while abortion rights and antiabortion forces rallied with signs and slogans outside. Inside the chamber the justices appeared sympathetic to the protesters' First Amendment arguments. Justices Scalia and Kennedy both said they had viewed a videotape of the demonstrations entered into evidence by the clinic and found the protests fairly orderly. Other justices doubted the position taken by the clinic's lawyer and the Clinton administration that the injunction could be upheld under the lax test applied to "time, place, and manner" regulations affecting speech.

The Court's decision, however, went against the protesters. Surprisingly, the ruling was announced by Chief Justice Rehnquist, a consistent opponent of abortion rights since the original *Roe v. Wade* ruling in 1973.

Rehnquist began by rejecting the protesters' argument that the injunction should be subjected to the highest level of judicial review—the "strict scrutiny" test—because it singled out antiabortion speech on the basis of content or viewpoint. An injunction necessarily "applies only to a particular group," he said. The judge had restrained the protesters not because they were opposed to abortion, Rehnquist explained, but because they had "violated the court's order."

Even as a content-neutral injunction, however, Rehnquist said the judge's order warranted a measure of heightened judicial review. ". . . [O]ur standard time, place, and manner analysis is not sufficiently rigorous," he wrote. "We must ask instead whether the challenged provisions of the injunction burden no more speech than necessary to serve a significant government interest."

To determine the interests protected by the injunction, Rehnquist turned to the Florida Supreme Court's opinion. First on the list was "the strong interest in protecting a woman's freedom to seek lawful medical or counseling services in connection with her pregnancy." And here Rehnquist added, with no further comment, a legal citation to *Roe v. Wade*, a decision that he had voted to overrule as recently as 1992.

Rehnquist also noted that the Florida court had said the injunction helped protect public safety and order, promote the free flow of traffic, protect property rights, and safeguard residential privacy. ". . . [T]he combination of these interests is quite sufficient to justify an appropriately tailored injunction to protect them," Rehnquist concluded.

With the legal standards established, Rehnquist evaluated the judge's injunction point by point. The 36-foot buffer zone passed muster, partly in deference to the judge's ruling that the first injunction had failed to "accomplish its purpose." The Court also accepted the "limited noise restrictions" imposed during the hours when abortions were performed.

The judge's other restrictions were struck down, however. The 300-foot "no-approach" zone "burdens more speech than is necessary to prevent intimidation and to ensure access to the clinic," Rehnquist said. The ban on signs visible from within the clinic also went too far, he added, since patients could simply "pull the curtains" to avoid seeing the placards. And the clinic had failed to present enough evidence, Rehnquist concluded, to justify the 300-foot ban on picketing near the homes of clinic staff.

Overall, the opinion was a model of understatement: only twenty-one pages long, carefully tied to the facts of the case, and with no rhetorical flourishes. Four justices—Blackmun, O'Connor, Souter, and Ginsburg—joined all of Rehnquist's opinion. Justice Stevens joined most of it, but said he would have upheld the "no-approach" zone.

Scalia, joined in dissent by Kennedy and Thomas, was bitter at the outcome and contemptuous of the majority's reasoning. In any other context, he complained, the injunction would have been "a candidate for summary reversal." But special rules applied to the abortion issue, he said, nullifying established legal doctrines: "Today, the ad hoc nullification machine claims its latest, greatest, and most surprising victim: the First Amendment."

The injunction, Scalia said, should have been reviewed under the Court's traditional strict scrutiny standard. As for the legal standard Rehnquist did adopt, Scalia mocked it as "intermediate-intermediate scrutiny." Even under that test, he said, the limitations could not be upheld. Except for the noise restriction, all the limits burdened more speech than necessary, in his view.

With a final punch Scalia compared the ruling to the Court's infamous 1944 decision, *Korematsu v. United States*, which upheld the wartime military internment of Japanese-Americans. Borrowing phrasing from Justice Robert Jackson's dissent in that case, he said the Court's decision to uphold a "misguided trial-court injunction . . . left a powerful loaded weapon lying about today." The ruling, he concluded, "ought to give all friends of liberty great concern."

Outside the courtroom abortion foes echoed Scalia's stridency. "The victim of the decision is the First Amendment," said Jay Alan Sekulow, director of the conservative American Center for Law and Justice. He called the ruling "a devastating blow for the pro-life movement."

But Eleanor Smeal, director of the Feminist Majority Foundation, said the ruling "established that a woman doesn't have to walk a gauntlet to exercise her right to an abortion." She voiced regret that the Court had struck down the residential buffer zone, but predicted that the ruling would buttress the new law making it a federal crime to intimidate abortion providers or women seeking abortions. Antiabortion groups had challenged the law in federal court in Washington.

Commentators had more mixed reactions to the ruling. Laurence Tribe, a strong abortion rights advocate, criticized Scalia's dissent— especially his closing reference to the *Korematsu* case. "He really went off the wall," Tribe said. Tribe also said the ruling "will give the Court some difficulty in the future in areas where everybody agrees speech ought to be protected."

Douglas Kmiec, a conservative professor at Notre Dame Law School and an opponent of abortion rights, also warned the ruling could have damaging consequences. Kmiec conceded the ruling may have reached "the right result." He noted that the demonstrators themselves had testified that the protest could be just as effective across the street from the clinic. But he said the ruling invited judges to issue injunctions "in a content-based way" and to be "insensitive to the ways in which they're being misused."

Reapportionment and Redistricting

"Rough Proportionality" Is Test for Minority Districts

Johnson, Speaker of the Florida House of Representatives v. De Grandy, decided by a 7-2 vote, June 30, 1994; Souter wrote the opinion; Thomas and Scalia dissented. *(See excerpts, p. 219.)*

The Supreme Court closed its 1992-1993 term with a controversial decision, *Shaw v. Reno,* that cast doubt on racially drawn legislative districting plans *(Supreme Court Yearbook, 1992-1993, pp. 20-23).* The justices returned to the emotionally charged issue on the first day of their new session. Civil rights groups braced for another ruling limiting the ability of lawmakers or courts to promote the election of more minorities to legislative or other government posts by redrawing district lines. The Court's decision, however, left the power to consider race in redistricting and reapportionment cases largely intact.

The case arose in ethnically diverse Miami-Dade County, Florida. It pitted against each other two historically disadvantaged minority groups— African-Americans and Florida's rapidly growing Hispanic population. The legal issue was how many minority districts were needed to satisfy the federal Voting Rights Act, the major tool for racial and ethnic minorities in redistricting suits.

Florida's legislature redrew district lines for the state House and Senate in 1992. In the Miami area—where 1 million Hispanics comprised about 45 percent of the population—the plan created Hispanic majorities in nine out of twenty House districts and three out of seven Senate districts. Blacks formed majorities in four House districts and two Senate districts.

A group of Hispanics, led by a Republican state representative, Miguel De Grandy, challenged the plan in federal court under the Voting Rights Act. They argued that the Demo-cratic-controlled legislature could have created two additional House districts and one more Senate district with Hispanic majorities. The plan that was adopted, they argued, "diluted" Hispanic voting strength in violation of the federal act. One subtext in the case: Miami's Cuban-American population voted predominantly Republican; blacks mostly voted Democratic.

Miguel De Grandy

A three-judge federal court heard evidence in a five-day trial and issued a ruling from the bench in July 1992 that gave the Hispanics half of what they wanted. The panel agreed that the districting plan violated the Voting Rights Act and ordered use of a new plan for House seats. The new plan created two additional Hispanic-majority districts. But the panel refused to order a new Senate map, saying an extra Hispanic district could only come at the expense of one of the black-majority seats.

The ruling left no one satisfied: the legislature, the Hispanics, or the Bush administration, which had sided with the Hispanic group. Three separate appeals reached the Supreme Court, which decided to leave the legislature's plan in place for the 1992 election and then put the case on the calendar for the first day of the 1993-1994 term.

The justices had difficulty with their introduction to Florida's tripartite ethnic politics. At one point during arguments, Chief Justice Rehnquist struggled to follow the colors on a multihued map De Grandy's lawyer used to illustrate the ethnic composition of the various districts. The justices' questions were similarly hard to read, yielding few strong clues about the outcome. The Court compounded the suspense by holding the case—along with a second Voting Rights Act dispute argued the same day—until the final day of the term.

When the decision finally came, it was almost anticlimactic. In a low-key opinion Justice Souter acknowledged the history of racial voting in Florida but said the three-judge court was wrong to think the Voting Rights Act required lawmakers to create as many black- or Hispanic-majority districts as possible. "One may suspect vote dilution from political famine," Souter wrote, "but one is not entitled to suspect . . . dilution from mere failure to guarantee a political feast."

Instead, Souter said, courts should look to see whether the number of minority districts is "roughly proportional" to the minority's share of the population. That would not be "dispositive," Souter said, but it would be "a relevant fact" in evaluating "the totality of the circumstances." Since the legislature's plan met that test, Souter concluded there was no Voting Rights Act violation and the remap scheme should be left in place.

Souter's opinion was supported by Justices Blackmun, Stevens, and Ginsburg on the left and Rehnquist and O'Connor on the right. Conspicuously absent from the opinion was any reference to the *Shaw v. Reno* decision. Souter was one of four dissenters in that case.

Shaw did appear, however, in a separate opinion by Justice Kennedy. While joining much of Souter's opinion, Kennedy cited *Shaw* in warning against racial line-drawing. ". . . [E]xplicit race-based redistricting embarks us on a most dangerous course," Kennedy said. Any redistricting scheme had to pass constitutional muster under the Equal Protection Clause, he added. Since the plaintiffs had not raised any constitutional issues, however, Kennedy said he concurred in the decision.

Justices Thomas and Scalia, while technically dissenting, agreed that the plaintiffs' challenge should be rejected. Thomas explained his vote by pointing to his opinion in another case decided the same day, *Holder v. Hall (see next section)*. In *Holder* he argued the Voting Rights Act only prohibited practices that prevented minorities from voting at all. On that basis Thomas said he would decide the Florida case by holding "that an apportionment plan is not a 'standard, practice, or procedure' that may be challenged under section 2 [of the act]."

In Florida De Grandy made the best of the setback by telling reporters the Court's emphasis on proportional representation might aid Hispanics in gaining seats on local governing bodies. For his part, state representative Peter Wallace, the St. Petersburg Democrat who chaired the legislature's reapportionment committee, was bitter about the long legal fight. "It never made sense to me," Wallace told the *Miami Herald*, "that states would have to maximize minority districts in a manner that was unfair to other segments of the community."

Nationally, conservatives took more heart from the ruling than did civil rights groups. Clint Bolick, litigation director for the conservative Institute for Justice in Washington, said the ruling showed that the Court "was not going to engage in wholesale social engineering through the Voting Rights Act." But Theodore Shaw, associate director of the NAACP Legal Defense and Educational Fund, told the *New York Times* that the ruling could be used as a "road map" to draw districting plans reducing minority voting strength that would be "beyond the reach of the Court."

Voting Rights

Court Bars Challenges to Size of Governing Bodies

Holder v. Hall, decided by a 5-4 vote, June 30, 1994; Kennedy wrote a plurality opinion; Blackmun, Stevens, Souter, and Ginsburg dissented. *(See excerpts, p. 232.)*

Black voters in a tiny county in central Georgia mounted a legal challenge to an unusual form of local government. The Court had to decide whether the Voting Rights Act could be used to change the size of an existing government body. The justices said no in a ruling that might have gone largely unnoticed but for an impassioned argument against racial redistricting written by the Court's only black justice, Clarence Thomas.

The 1990 census showed 10,430 people in Bleckley County in central Georgia: three-fourths of them white, slightly under one-fourth black. Like a dwindling number of other small counties in the state, about a dozen by 1994, Bleckley County had a distinctive form of government. A single "commissioner" exercised all executive and legislative power for the county—from controlling property and maintaining roads to levying taxes and appropriating funds. Other counties in the state had multimember governing bodies—typically, with five commissioners elected from single-member districts.

In 1985 black voters challenged the single-commissioner government as a violation of their rights under the federal Voting Rights Act and the post-Civil War Fourteenth and Fifteenth Amendments. In a four-day trial the plaintiffs showed that no black person had ever been elected to a countywide office or even run for office before 1984. Nonetheless, U.S. District Court Judge Wilbur C. Owens, Jr., rejected the suit. He ruled the plaintiffs had failed to show intentional discrimination as required to sustain their constitutional claims. They also failed to show two conditions needed to prove minority vote "dilution" under the Voting Rights Act— bloc voting by whites and political cohesiveness among black voters.

The federal appeals court in Atlanta reversed that ruling and ordered the judge to fashion a remedy—presumably, judicially mandated creation of a multimember board for the county. But County Commissioner Jackie Holder, who had held the post since 1977, asked the Supreme Court to review the case. He argued the Voting Rights Act gave federal courts no power to order a change in the size of a local or state governing body. A ruling in favor of the plaintiffs, he warned the justices, would invite challenges to a host of single-person offices, such as mayors, sheriffs, or even state governors.

The justices heard arguments in the case on the first day of the term in October, but they did not decide it until the last day of the session nine months later. The justices produced six opinions in the case: three from the five justices in the majority who rejected the suit and three from the four dissenters. Longest of all was a fifty-nine-page concurrence written by Thomas. He boldly argued for throwing out twenty-five years of case law that allowed the Voting Rights Act to be used to require racial line-drawing in redistricting and reapportionment plans.

The Court's main opinion was narrower. Justice Kennedy, joined by Chief Justice Rehnquist and in part by Justice O'Connor, said the black plaintiffs could not prove vote "dilution" because there was no "princi-pled" way to decide the best size of the county's governing body. ". . . [W]here there is no objective and workable standard for choosing a reasonable benchmark by which to evaluate a challenged voting practice, it follows that the voting practice cannot be challenged under section 2 [of the Act]," Kennedy wrote.

In her separate opinion O'Connor made the same point. "The wide range of possibilities makes the choice inherently standardless," she wrote.

Writing for the four dissenters, Justice Blackmun agreed with the plaintiffs that the single-commissioner system denied black voters "the ability . . . to have their votes count." Georgia's prevailing pattern of five-member county commissions provided "an appropriate benchmark" to use in fixing the size of a new commission, he said. "Traditional" single-person offices such as mayor or governor would be safe from challenge, however. Justices Stevens, Souter, and Ginsburg joined his dissent. Ginsburg added a brief separate dissent.

In his opinion Thomas, joined by Scalia, argued the Court had been on the wrong track since 1969, when it first allowed lower courts to use the Voting Rights Act to challenge a change from a system of electoral districts to an at-large system. The result, he said, was to encourage courts "to segregate voters into racially designated districts to ensure minority success." Thomas continued, "In doing so we have collaborated in what may aptly be termed the racial balkanization of the Nation."

To correct this "disastrous adventure in judicial policymaking," Thomas said he would interpret the Voting Rights Act to apply only to practices that prevent minorities from going to the polls at all. To support his view, Thomas had to challenge not only Supreme Court case law but also Congress's reenactment of the law three times after the Court had adopted the broader interpretation. But Thomas was unflinching.

"In my view," he concluded, "our current practice should not continue. Not for another Term, not until the next case, not for another day."

Stevens answered Thomas in a separate opinion joined by the other three dissenters. He called Thomas's view a "radical reinterpretation" of the Voting Rights Act effectively calling for it to be "repealed or amended in important respects." Those arguments, Stevens said, were properly addressed to Congress. But given the reenactment of the statute, he concluded, "judges have an especially clear obligation to obey settled law."

Thomas's opinion provoked sharp reactions, pro and con. Clint Bolick, director of the conservative Institute for Justice in Washington, said Thomas "called into question the underlying logic of those who would use the Voting Rights Act to balkanize American society." But Laughlin McDonald, southern regional director of the American Civil Liberties Union and one of the lawyers for the plaintiffs, called Thomas's opinion "the most extraordinary example of judicial activism."

McDonald said the plaintiffs would continue with their constitutional attack on the single-commissioner system, but he acknowledged they faced a difficult burden of proof. For his part, Holder said he was pleased with the outcome. And he insisted that race had nothing to do with keeping the single-commissioner system.

"The people like this form of government," Holder said. "It's cheaper, and they like a full-time commissioner they can always come in and see."

Jury Selection

Lawyers Cannot Bar Potential Jurors on Basis of Sex

J. E. B. v. Alabama ex rel. T. B., decided by a 6-3 vote, April 19, 1994; Blackmun wrote the opinion; Scalia, Rehnquist, and Thomas dissented. *(See excerpts, p. 131.)*

In picking a jury, trial lawyers use a combination of research, questions, and intuition. Every lawyer has his or her own pet theory about the best kind of juror in particular kinds of cases. But one widely used assumption is that women tend to side with defendants in criminal cases and to sympathize with injured plaintiffs in civil cases.

Judges can disqualify potential jurors if there is a specific reason to question their ability to be openminded in a case. For centuries English and American courts have also allowed lawyers to exclude a given number of potential jurors for any reason at all—or no reason. Trial lawyers cherish these "peremptory challenges" as a way to try to prevent one bad apple from spoiling the jury for their client.

In a series of cases beginning in 1986, the Supreme Court said lawyers could not use peremptory challenges to exclude someone from jury service on the basis of race *(see box, p. 37)*. The justices ruled that the practice violated the right to a fair trial and equal rights to jury service. Trial lawyers warned the rulings meant the beginning of the end of peremptory challenges.

Court's Rulings on Peremptory Challenges

1986

Batson v. Kentucky
Bars prosecutors from
   excluding jurors on the
   basis of race

1991

*Edmonson v. Leesville
   Concrete Co.*
Prohibits race-based
   peremptory challenges
   in civil trials

1992

Georgia v. McCollum
Bars criminal defendants
   from excluding jurors
   on the basis of race

1994

*J. E. B. v. Alabama
   ex rel. T. B.*
Prohibits use of peremp-
   tory challenges on the
   basis of sex

The Court added to those fears in 1994 by extending the ruling to gender. In a 6-3 decision the Court held that excluding a potential juror on the basis of his or her sex amounted to unconstitutional discrimination. The decision provoked a sharp dissent as well as a troubled concurrence from one of the Court's female justices, Sandra Day O'Connor, about the potential costs of the ruling.

The issue reached the Court in a paternity suit from the small town of Scottsboro in rural northern Alabama. James Bowman, a married salesman from across the border in Tennessee, had a liaison in February 1988 with Teresia Bible. Bible later testified that Bowman promised to marry her but left her when she became pregnant. After the child was born, Bible got the district attorney's office to file a paternity suit on her behalf seeking child support. Bowman admitted the affair but said someone else must have been the father. Bible said it had to be Bowman.

The pool of jurors selected at random for the trial included twice as many women as men. The local prosecutor used nine of his ten peremptory challenges to strike men from the panel. Bowman's lawyer, John Porter, objected, although he countered by using ten of his eleven challenges to remove women.

The jury finally chosen included twelve women and no men. After hearing the evidence—including a DNA test that indicated a 99.92 percent probability Bowman was the father—the jury ruled for Bible. In appealing the verdict Porter argued the state's use of peremptory challenges to exclude men from the jury violated his client's constitutional rights. When the Alabama Supreme Court rejected his plea, Porter took the case to the U.S. Supreme Court. The Clinton administration and a variety of civil rights and women's rights groups sided with him.

The Court's ruling came as no surprise. In a broadly written opinion Justice Harry A. Blackmun said that the use of gender-based peremptory challenges "serves to ratify and perpetuate invidious, archaic, and overbroad stereotypes about the relative abilities of men and women." Blackmun dismissed the state's argument that men might be unduly sympathetic to a man accused in a paternity suit as an unsupported generalization—"the very stereotype the law condemns." Justices Stevens, O'Connor, Souter, and Ginsburg concurred in the opinion. Kennedy agreed with the result but did not join Blackmun's opinion.

Even though she joined Blackmun's opinion, O'Connor wrote separately to voice some doubts. Lawyers often were able to "correctly intuit" a juror's sympathies, she said, even if they could not explain the intuition. And studies indicated that women were in fact more likely than men to vote to convict in rape cases, she noted. ". . . [T]o say that gender makes no difference as a matter of law is not to say that gender makes no difference as a matter of fact," O'Connor concluded. She said the new ruling should not be applied to criminal defendants or to civil cases, but she acknowledged it probably would be.

In a dissent Justice Scalia echoed some of O'Connor's concerns but added more biting commentary. He mocked the opinion as "an inspiring demonstration of how thoroughly up-to-date and right-thinking we Justices are in matters pertaining to the sexes." Scalia dismissed Blackmun's account of the discrimination against women in jury service as "irrelevant, since the case involves state action that allegedly discriminates against men." And the logic of the ruling, he concluded, cast doubt on all peremptory challenges, which he said had been "considered an essential part of a fair jury trial since the dawn of the common law." Chief Justice Rehnquist and Justice Thomas joined the dissent.

Women's rights groups praised the ruling and denied any contradiction in establishing a new limit on sex discrimination in a case brought by a man trying to avoid child support for an out-of-wedlock child. "We believe sexual equality is advanced whenever it is illegal to take sex into account—whether for women or against women," said Deborah Ellis, legal director of the National Organization for Women's Legal Defense Fund.

Many trial lawyers predicted the ruling would make it harder to pick a fair jury, but John Porter discounted the problem. "I think they're making much more of it than it will be in practice," Porter said.

As for the new trial, Porter acknowledged the verdict might be the same unless he could exclude the DNA test as evidence. But the lawyer who represented Alabama in the appeal said she worried about the second trial.

"This was a good case," said Lois Brafield, an assistant state attorney general. "Now, it's going back to a small town where John Porter is a hero. You don't have that many lawyers from Scottsboro, Alabama, who win a case before the Supreme Court."

Property Rights

Permit Conditions Must Be "Proportional" to Impacts

Dolan v. City of Tigard, decided by a 5-4 vote, June 24, 1994; Rehnquist wrote the opinion; Stevens, Blackmun, Souter, and Ginsburg dissented. *(See excerpts, p. 154.)*

John Dolan opened a modest plumbing supply store in Portland, Oregon, in 1960. Over the next thirty-three years he built it into a bustling, family-operated business with eleven outlets in the Portland area. In 1989 he applied for a construction permit from the suburban city of Tigard (population 32,000) so he could replace the existing store with a new building about twice as big.

Tigard's zoning board approved the plan, but with two conditions. Dolan had to turn over approximately 7,000 square feet—10 percent of the 1.7-acre parcel—for a "public greenway," supposedly to help storm water drain into an adjacent creek. He was also told to put in part of a pedestrian and bicycle pathway to ease the impact of the additional traffic his expanded store would create.

Dolan decided to fight city hall. With the help of a statewide property rights organization, Oregonians in Action, he argued that the permit conditions amounted to a taking of his property without compensation in violation of the Fifth Amendment. Oregon courts rejected his argument, finding the conditions "reasonably related" to the impact of the development on the community.

Dolan died in March 1993, but his wife Florence and son Dan kept the fight going. The Supreme Court sustained the Dolans' claim. The decision gave landowners and developers a new legal tool to resist demands by local governments to set aside part of their property for public purposes.

The Court's conservative bloc—especially Chief Justice Rehnquist and Justice Scalia—had been looking for a good case to use to broaden property rights. The Dolans' suit built on a ruling in Rehnquist's first term as chief justice, *Nollan v. California Coastal Commission* (1987). In that case, the Court ruled, 5-4, that local governments must show a connection—in legal terms, a "nexus"—between the impact of a proposed development and any permit conditions ("exactions") they wanted to impose.

Florence Dolan and her son Dan won an important property rights ruling from the Supreme Court when the justices blocked zoning authorities in Tigard, Oregon, from requiring them to set aside part of their land for a flood control plain and a bicycle and pedestrian pathway.

The Dolans' lawyer, David Smith, told the justices in March that the city had to go further and show "some sort of proportional relationship" between the exactions and the impact of the development. Three months later the Court agreed.

Writing for the five-justice majority, Rehnquist acknowledged that Oregon had followed most state courts in using a "reasonable relaship" test to evaluate permit conditions. Calling that standard too lax, Rehnquist said that "a term such as 'rough proportionality' best encapsulates what we hold to be the requirement of the Fifth Amendment."

Smith had urged the justices to require cities to make some "specific quantification" of the impact of a proposed development before imposing permit conditions. Rehnquist said that went too far. "No precise mathematical calculation" was needed, Rehnquist wrote. Cities must make an "individualized determination" that the conditions were "related both in nature and extent to the impact of the proposed development."

Applying that test, Rehnquist found Tigard's justifications for the conditions on the Dolans' property wanting. He said the city had failed to show an adequate relationship between the expansion of the store and the need for the floodplain easement or the bike path. Justices O'Connor, Scalia, Kennedy, and Thomas concurred in the ruling.

Rehnquist heartened conservatives with an added comment that answered one of the points made by Justice Stevens in his dissenting opinion. In the past, Stevens said, land-use policies had been given a presumption of validity, just like other business regulations. That attitude, in Rehnquist's view, downgraded the importance of property rights. "We see no reason," Rehnquist wrote, "why the Takings Clause of the Fifth Amendment, as much a part of the Bill of Rights as the First Amendment or Fourth Amendment, should be relegated to the status of a poor relation."

Stevens, who emphasized his dissent by reading portions of it from the bench, argued that local governments needed the benefit of the doubt in devising land-use policies because of the uncertainty in predicting the impact of new developments on the environment. "When there is doubt concerning the magnitude of these impacts," Stevens wrote, "the public interest in averting them must outweigh the private interest of the commercial entrepreneur."

Stevens also picked up a point made by the Clinton administration in supporting Tigard's position. He said the Dolans would actually benefit from the added flood control and new bike path the city wanted. Justices Blackmun and Ginsburg joined Stevens's opinion; Justice Souter dissented separately.

Property rights groups were elated with the ruling. "It's a great victory for property rights, a great victory for the country, a great victory for the Dolans," rejoiced Bill Moshofsky, president of Oregonians in Action, which represented the Dolans for free in the case. Clint Bolick, litigation director of the Washington-based Institute for Justice, which filed a brief siding with the Dolans, said the decision would reduce "the garden-variety extortion that many local governments are involved with around the country."

For cities and counties the ruling seemed likely to mean more work, and higher costs, in crafting land-use policies. One expert wryly commented that the ruling amounted to "a planners' full employment act." But some lawyers for municipalities and environmental organizations played down the ruling's likely effects. They said most cities and counties already did careful impact studies before setting conditions for developers and property owners.

In Tigard city officials blandly commented that they hoped the dispute with the Dolans could be resolved "now that the law has been clarified." But Dan Dolan sounded a triumphant note as he talked with a television reporter on the day of the ruling. "Now if the city wants this land," Dolan said, "they're going to have to get it the old-fashioned way. They're going to have to pay for it."

Punitive Damages

States Must Provide Review of Punitive Damage Awards

Honda Motor Co., Ltd. v. Oberg, decided by a 7-2 vote, June 24, 1994; Stevens wrote the opinion; Ginsburg and Rehnquist dissented. *(See excerpts, p. 143.)*

Five times since 1980, business and insurance groups had gotten the Supreme Court's attention with pleas to rein in what they regarded as out-of-control punitive damage awards in personal injury cases. And five times, critics of the civil justice system were left, for the most part, holding the bag. This term they finally won one and hailed the ruling as a major victory even though it affected just one state: Oregon.

Tort reform advocates had been surprised when the Court decided to review the Oregon punitive damages case. Honda Motor Co. had been ordered to pay $735,000 in compensatory damages and $5 million in punitive damages in a suit brought by Karl Oberg, who suffered a crushed skull when his 1985 Honda all-terrain vehicle overturned on him. Honda's lawyers argued the punitive damages award was excessive, but Oregon courts upheld it. They based their ruling in part on a provision of the Oregon constitution that prohibited judicial review of damage awards "unless the court can affirmatively say there is no evidence to support the verdict."

Honda's lawyers argued that this limitation—added in 1911— violated the company's due process rights under the U.S. Constitution. But the Oregon Supreme Court held that the detailed jury instructions in state law gave adequate protection against arbitrary awards. Differing with some other state courts, the Oregon justices said that the Supreme Court's 1991 decision upholding jury discretion in punitive damages cases, *Pacific Mutual Life Insurance Co. v. Haslip*, did not require states to provide post-verdict review of the amounts of awards.

Although Oregon's limit on judicial review was unique among the states, the case attracted a number of briefs from business groups on the one hand and plaintiffs lawyers on the other. The argument before the Court seemed to go badly for Honda. Harvard law professor Laurence Tribe, the winning lawyer in the Court's 1993 punitive damages case, crafted an ingenious argument that Oregon law actually gave judges a variety of ways to prevent arbitrary punitive damage awards, including the power—before the verdict—to set a maximum amount the jury could consider in a case.

In his time before the Court, Honda's lawyer, Washington attorney Andrew Frey, drew mostly skeptical questions from the justices. Embarrassingly, he had no ready answer when Justice Antonin Scalia asked him for the "best case" to show that judicial review of punitive damages was an established historical practice at the time of the adoption of the Constitution.

Two months later, however, the Court ruled for Honda in a 7-2 decision written by Justice Stevens. After reviewing tort cases from eighteenth-century England on through American history, Stevens concluded that judicial review of damage awards was a well-established practice in Anglo-American law. "Oregon's abrogation of a well-established common law protection against arbitrary deprivations of property," he wrote, "raises a presumption that its procedures violate the Due Process Clause."

Echoing the tort reformers' arguments, Stevens said the risk of "arbitrary awards and potentially biased juries" had, if anything, increased in recent years because of "the rise of large, interstate and multinational corporations." Jurors typically have wide discretion in setting punitive damages, Stevens continued, and could use verdicts "to express their biases against big businesses, particularly those without strong local presences." Despite that danger, Stevens said, Oregon had eliminated judicial review of punitive damage awards "without providing any substitute procedure."

As for Tribe's arguments, Stevens dismissed them one by one. He noted in particular that no Oregon judge had ever done what Tribe suggested to cap the damages before jury deliberations.

Six justices joined with Stevens. Scalia, who takes a narrow view of the Due Process Clause, explained in a brief opinion that he concurred because Oregon had removed a historically recognized procedural protection.

In a dissent Justice Ginsburg, joined by Chief Justice Rehnquist, challenged Stevens's reading of history and of Oregon law. She argued that American law had always recognized a broad discretion for juries in civil cases and that Oregon's procedures "adequately" guided juries on the criteria for awarding punitive damages. Ginsburg also questioned the need for extra safeguards. She said the verdict against Honda was only the second punitive damage award in a product liability suit in Oregon in nearly thirty years.

The Court's ruling had a direct effect only on Oregon, but tort reform groups saw a larger message in the decision. "The Court has recognized the need to place some reasonable limits on punitive damage awards," said Martin Connor, president of the American Tort Reform Association. "Judicial scrutiny of punitive damage awards is imperative if the civil justice system is to function fairly."

Professor Tribe, however, did not consider the ruling a major setback for plaintiffs. He said the ruling did not encourage judges to reexamine damage awards "as if they were playing the role of the thirteenth juror." And he predicted that, given Oberg's serious injuries, Oregon courts would uphold his award anyway.

Securities Law

Court Curbs Investors' Suits for Aiding Fraud

Central Bank of Denver, N.A. v. First Interstate Bank of Denver, N.A., decided by a 5-4 vote, April 19, 1994; Kennedy wrote the opinion; Stevens, Blackmun, Souter, and Ginsburg dissented. *(See excerpts, p. 119.)*

The financial fallout of a soured community development project in Colorado resulted in an unexpected Supreme Court decision that took away an important legal weapon for investors suing lawyers, accountants, and other professionals in cases of securities fraud.

Federal courts have interpreted federal securities laws since 1946 to allow private investors to bring civil damage suits in cases involving deceptive or misleading financial information. The number of those suits—brought under the broadly worded antifraud section 10(b) of the Securities Exchange Act of 1934 and its companion regulation, Rule 10b-5—grew after the Supreme Court in 1971 began to accept the legal theory. Over the next two decades the Court sometimes expanded and sometimes narrowed the scope of securities litigation while leaving many questions unanswered.

Among the unsettled issues was whether an investor could sue someone for "aiding and abetting" a securities fraud. Lower federal courts allowed plaintiffs to sue lawyers, accountants, or other professionals for aiding fraudulent schemes by keeping silent about misleading financial information. These "secondary liability" suits sometimes gave investors their only chance to recover any money, since the main promoters were often bankrupt, in jail, or both. But the Supreme Court had twice—in 1976 and 1983—specifically reserved its own decision on the question.

A Colorado branch of First Interstate Bank included an aiding-and-abetting count in a securities fraud suit in 1989 after a municipal authority defaulted on bonds issued for construction of a new residential community in Colorado Springs. The bank, which bought $2.1 million of the bonds, sued the municipal authority, the private developer, and the bank—Central Bank—that served as trustee for the bonds.

As the trustee, Central Bank, which was later merged into Colorado National Bank, had the responsibility of making sure that the value of land put up as collateral was worth at least 160 percent of the total bond issue. In 1988 Central Bank became concerned that property values were declining in the area and called for a new appraisal. After meetings with the developers and the authority, the bank agreed to delay the reappraisal until after the bonds were sold.

First Interstate claimed the bank's delay aided the securities fraud by concealing misleading information. In ruling on the suit, two lower federal

The Supreme Court blocked investors in a financially troubled development in Colorado Springs, Colorado, from using federal securities law to try to recover losses from the bank that issued bonds for the project.

courts differed on whether First Interstate needed to prove Central Bank guilty of recklessness in order to recover. When it agreed to review the case, however, the Supreme Court asked the two banks to address the broader question of whether aiding-and-abetting suits were allowed at all. By a 5-4 vote the justices ruled that they were not.

Writing for the majority, Justice Kennedy said that section 10(b) simply did not provide liability for aiding a securities fraud. "Congress knew how to impose aiding and abetting liability when it chose to do so," Kennedy wrote, but it did not do so in the antifraud provision. Chief Justice Rehnquist and Justices O'Connor, Scalia, and Thomas concurred in the opinion.

While Kennedy said the statutory language settled the issue, he also considered and rejected one by one other arguments made by First Interstate and by the Clinton administration in urging a broader interpretation of the law. He then closed by appearing to side with critics of what he called "excessive" securities litigation against professionals. Kennedy said professionals had to spend "large sums" to defend or settle such cases, and the risks of such litigation could deter professionals from advising new companies or businesses at all.

Stevens, joined in dissent by Justices Blackmun, Souter, and Ginsburg, began by noting that the courts and the Securities and Exchange Commission (SEC) had permitted aiding-and-abetting suits in "hundreds" of proceedings. The broadened liability, Stevens said, had "become a part of the established system of private enforcement. We should leave it to Congress to alter that scheme."

Stevens also warned that the ruling appeared to take away the power of the SEC itself to bring civil enforcement actions under an aiding-and-abetting theory. Kennedy did not address the issue, but within a month the SEC urged Congress to pass legislation to neutralize the effects of the ruling on the agency's powers. SEC Chairman Arthur Levitt, Jr., said the ruling "fundamentally curtailed well-established and vital investor rights."

The ruling was hailed, however, by bankers, accountants, and securities lawyers. "This is a signal that looking for deep pockets won't be countenanced," Harvey Pitt, a Washington securities lawyer, commented to the *Washington Post.*

As the dust settled, some plaintiffs lawyers and other experts commented that the ruling's effects might have been exaggerated. John Coffee, a Columbia law school professor, said Kennedy's opinion still allowed investors to sue lawyers or accountants who help prepare misleading financial statements. "The line's going to be between those who were involved in the actual transmission of the information and those who were merely silent when they had a duty to speak," Coffee said.

Capital Punishment

Death Row Inmates Get Help and Time to Block Executions

McFarland v. Scott, Director, Texas Department of Criminal Justice, Institutional Division, decided by 6-3 and 5-4 votes, June 30, 1994; Blackmun wrote the opinion; O'Connor dissented in part; Thomas, Rehnquist, and Scalia dissented. *(See excerpts, p. 256.)*

Frank McFarland came within less than an hour of being executed in a Texas prison on the evening of October 26, 1993. The convicted murderer was spared only because the Supreme Court granted a last-minute stay to consider whether McFarland was entitled under federal law to a lawyer to challenge his death sentence—and the time to find the lawyer and file the challenge in federal court. Eight months later the Court backed McFarland's plea in a ruling that also safeguarded the rights of dozens of other inmates without lawyers on Texas's death row.

With 376 prisoners on death row as of June 1994, Texas was the buckle on the nation's death penalty belt—the dozen or so states stretching

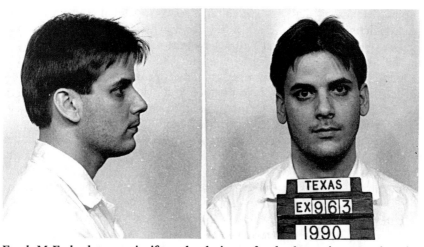

Frank McFarland won a significant legal victory for death row inmates when the Supreme Court upheld a lower court ruling blocking his execution in Texas until a court-appointed lawyer could file a new challenge to his murder conviction.

across the southern United States that held the vast majority of condemned prisoners in the country. Frustration with delays in imposing the death penalty ran high in Texas among police, prosecutors, lawmakers, and the public. To speed the process, Texas courts adopted guidelines calling for an execution to be scheduled forty-five days after the end of the inmate's normal round of appeals.

The lawyers who handled death penalty cases protested, saying extra legal proceedings were needed to make sure defendants' rights were protected at trial. But Texas was the only state to rely primarily on volunteer lawyers to represent death row inmates in state postconviction or federal habeas corpus proceedings. The Texas Resource Center, a federally funded nonprofit law office, worked to recruit lawyers for death row challenges. But when McFarland's case reached the Supreme Court, he was one of more than sixty death row inmates in Texas with no lawyer to represent them in filing habeas corpus petitions.

McFarland had been convicted and sentenced to death in 1989 for the rape-murder of a woman he met in a bar. State courts upheld the conviction, and the U.S. Supreme Court refused to review the case in June 1993. The trial judge set McFarland's execution for September 23 and then postponed it one month to the early morning of October 27.

As the execution date neared, McFarland filed motions on his own in state and federal courts seeking a stay of execution to allow him time to find a lawyer to challenge his conviction and sentence. In federal court he relied on a little-noticed provision of the 1988 federal antidrug act that a capital defendant "shall be entitled" to a court-appointed attorney in "any postconviction proceeding" under the federal habeas corpus statute.

A federal district court judge, however, refused to appoint a lawyer or stay the execution because McFarland had no habeas corpus petition pending. The Fifth U.S. Circuit Court of Appeals upheld that ruling on the evening of October 26, hours before McFarland was scheduled to be put to death. The Supreme Court stayed the execution later that night and then set the case for argument in late March.

McFarland's case drew support from the American Bar Association and the American Civil Liberties Union, which echoed the complaints from the Texas Resource Center of a "crisis" in death penalty representation. But the Texas attorney general's office blamed the problem on "brinksmanship" by death penalty lawyers in waiting until the last minute to file habeas corpus petitions.

During arguments before the Court, Justice Antonin Scalia appeared to adopt that criticism. "I am not happy with the performance of the Texas Resource Center in the cases that come before me," Scalia told the center's executive director, Mandy Welch, who argued McFarland's case.

Other justices appeared openly disturbed at the state's argument that an inmate could be put to death while looking for a lawyer to challenge the sentence. Three months later—on the final day of the term—the justices rejected the position by the narrowest of margins, 5-4.

"We conclude," Justice Blackmun wrote for the majority, "that a capital defendant may invoke [his] right to a counseled federal habeas corpus proceeding by filing a motion requesting the appointment of habeas counsel, and that a district court has jurisdiction to enter a stay of execution where necessary to give effect to that statutory right."

Blackmun strained to reach the result—first by enlarging the definition of "postconviction proceeding" and then by broadly construing federal courts' power to impose stays under the habeas corpus statute. But he argued any other interpretation would defeat Congress's purpose in mandating appointed counsel and would render the death row inmate's right "meaningless." Justices Stevens, Kennedy, Souter, and Ginsburg joined the opinion.

In his dissent Justice Thomas offered an alternative interpretation of the appointed counsel provision. Congress could have intended, he said, that a lawyer be appointed only after a death row inmate had first filed a habeas corpus petition presenting adequate grounds for challenging his or her sentence. As for the stay of execution, Thomas said the Court's ruling went against the normal rule that federal courts have only limited power "to interfere with state proceedings through granting stays." Chief Justice Rehnquist and Justice Scalia joined Thomas's opinion.

In a partial dissent Justice O'Connor said McFarland was entitled to a court-appointed lawyer but not to a stay of execution. A stay would be unnecessary, she added, if prisoners asked for a lawyer "well in advance of a scheduled execution."

The ruling was criticized by Texas Attorney General Dan Morales, who called it "another mechanism for delaying the punishment handed down by juries." But Welch said the decision was "an important victory in seeing that death penalty cases get an informed, meaningful review by the courts."

Church and State

Special School District for Religious Community Barred

Board of Education of Kiryas Joel Village School District v. Grumet, decided by a 6-3 vote, June 27, 1994; Souter wrote the opinion; Scalia, Rehnquist, and Thomas dissented. *(See excerpts, p. 168.)*

The village of Kiryas Joel, lying about forty miles northwest of New York City, is a tiny enclave inhabited exclusively by members of a small, rigidly orthodox Jewish sect—the Satmar Hasidim. In Kiryas Joel ("community of Joel"), religious rituals are scrupulously observed, the outside world is shunned, and almost all the children are taught in private religious schools.

In 1990, however, a small number of the villagers' children—all of them handicapped or learning-disabled—began attending a public school in a newly created school district. New York's legislature carved out the new district to try to accommodate the religious views of the Satmars with the Supreme Court's mandate to keep church and state separate in public education.

The Kiryas Joel school district's lone public school had secular teachers, a secular curriculum, and no religious trappings. But its pupils were all Hasidic children with disabilities who lived in Kiryas Joel or other nearby communities. To church-state separationists the school represented a clear violation of the Constitution's ban on establishment of religion. In a splintered ruling the Supreme Court agreed, holding that the special school district violated the principle of government neutrality on religion.

The New York legislature created the Kiryas Joel district in 1989 after the villagers reached an impasse with the Monroe-Woodbury School District on providing special education services—as required by state and federal law—for youngsters with physical or mental disabilities.

Before 1985 the disabled youngsters received special services in an annex, operated by the school district, adjacent to the private religious schools. But in 1985 the Supreme Court ruled in a pair of cases that providing compensatory educational services at private religious schools violated the separation of church and state.

The school district told the Hasidim that the youngsters had to attend a public school outside the village. Some did, but they reported feeling traumatized by attending school in what the village leaders called a "foreign setting." The legislature responded in 1989 with a measure to make the village into its own school district so that it could establish a "public" school strictly for its special-needs students.

Leaders of the New York State School Boards Association quickly challenged the law as unconstitutional. In July 1993 the New York Court of Appeals, the state's highest court, agreed. In a 4-2 ruling the court said the law setting up the school district created a "symbolic union" between church and state in violation of the Establishment Clause.

When the Supreme Court agreed to review the case in November, religious accommodationists hoped the justices would relax the test adopted for church-state issues in a 1971 case, *Lemon v. Kurtzman.* That ruling barred any law benefiting religion unless it had a secular purpose and effect and did not entangle the government in religious issues. Church-state separationists warned that upholding the special school district would invite the "religious balkanization" of public schools in America.

When the case was argued in March, the justices appeared sharply divided. Chief Justice Rehnquist and Justice Scalia repeatedly asked why the villagers should not be allowed to have their own school district. Significantly, however, Justices O'Connor and Kennedy, who voted sometimes to permit government accommodation of religion, appeared troubled that the state had carved out a special district for a specific religious community. Three months later O'Connor and Kennedy provided the critical votes in the 6-3 decision to strike down the law.

In the Court's main opinion Justice Souter said that the New York law gave the power over public education "to an electorate defined by common religious belief and practice, in a manner that fails to foreclose religious favoritism." For that reason, he said, it violated "the general principle that civil power must be exercised in a manner neutral to religion." He added that there was "no assurance" that the legislature would create a similar school district for a different religious group. Justices Blackmun, Stevens, and Ginsburg joined Souter's opinion in full, and O'Connor joined the section doubting the likelihood of equal treatment for other religious groups.

In a separate opinion, however, O'Connor said the case would be different if New York had a general law permitting municipalities to set up separate school districts. Kennedy also wrote a separate opinion that concluded the law was impermissible "religious gerrymandering" under the Court's precedents. Both he and O'Connor called for reconsidering the 1985 decisions that prevented public school systems from providing special education services at religious schools.

New York Gov. Mario Cuomo met in August with residents of the village of Kiryas Joel after signing legislation aimed at preserving the village's separate school district. The Supreme Court ruled that an earlier state law carving out the school district was an unconstitutional establishment of religion.

Justice Scalia ridiculed the ruling in a caustic dissent joined by Chief Justice Rehnquist and Justice Thomas. Scalia began by mocking the idea that a small Jewish sect that fled religious persecution in Europe had become "so powerful, so closely allied with Mammon, as to have become an 'establishment' of the Empire State." He went on to depict the challenged law as a neutral statute aimed at accommodating the villagers' cultural rather than religious views.

In any event, Scalia continued, a law accommodating a group's religious beliefs promoted rather than violated religious freedom. And he criticized the majority for assuming that New York lawmakers might not create a special school district for a different religious community—"presumably those less powerful than the Satmar Hasidim."

The Court's ruling left the status of the *Lemon* test unchanged. Souter mentioned the case just once. He relied mostly on a different precedent that overturned a law giving churches the power to block liquor stores from being operated nearby. Scalia said Souter had skirted the controversial ruling, but Justice Blackmun wrote a separate concurrence to insist that *Lemon* remained good law.

With that much confusion some experts minimized the likely impact of the ruling. "The case had the look of special treatment, and it ended up being resolved largely on those grounds," said Douglas Kmiec, a professor of constitutional law at Notre Dame Law School. "I don't think the case stands for much."

In Kiryas Joel, however, leaders and most of the villagers were crestfallen. Abraham Weider, president of the school board, was in tears at a news conference. But he promised to "continue our search for a suitable way to provide a quality education for the most vulnerable of our children."

New York lawmakers had a more concrete reaction. Taking up the suggestion in O'Connor's opinion, legislative leaders rushed through a law allowing any municipality that fit specified criteria to establish a new school district. Gov. Mario Cuomo supported the bill and signed it into law.

Louis Grumet, executive director of the state school boards association, promptly said the group would challenge the new law. "The [Court's] ruling is crystal-clear," Grumet told the *New York Times*. "It says you cannot politically gerrymander for religious purposes."

Cable Television

"Must-Carry" Rule for Cable TV Left Up in the Air

Turner Broadcasting System, Inc. v. Federal Communications Commission, decided by a 5-4 vote, June 27, 1994; Kennedy wrote the opinion; O'Connor, Scalia, Thomas, and Ginsburg dissented in part. *(See excerpts, p. 193.)*

Cable television and broadcasting came before the Court this term in a high-stakes legal fight. Both industries claimed to have the interests of viewers at heart and the First Amendment on their side. Cable television emerged with a heightened status under the First Amendment, but the justices left it to another court to decide the real issue: whether Congress could require cable operators to carry all local broadcast stations on their systems.

Cable television began, in the 1950s, as nothing more than a giant antenna for bringing TV stations to communities where broadcast signals could not be received clearly. By the 1980s, however, cable grew into a communications medium in its own right. Cable systems still depended on over-the-air TV stations for a major part of their service, but they added movies, sports, news, public affairs, and a host of other specialized entertainment and information channels.

Cable's growth made its chilly relationship with broadcasters even colder. Broadcasters and cable systems were now competing for viewers and advertisers. Since most people kept their sets tuned to cable, broadcasters depended on their competitor to be seen by viewers.

Broadcasters came to fear that some day cable operators might decide they did not need TV stations at all and drop some or all of them from their channel lineup to make room for other programming.

To safeguard their place on cable, broadcasters twice during the 1980s persuaded the Federal Communications Commission (FCC) to enact rules requiring all but the smallest cable systems to carry all local broadcast stations. Twice the federal appeals court in Washington threw the must-carry rules out, saying the agency had not presented adequate justification for the regulation. In 1992, however, Congress decided to include must-carry provisions in a cable regulation bill enacted over President George Bush's veto. The lawmakers accepted broadcasters' argument that cable now had a "bottleneck" power over the fate of existing TV stations.

The cable industry promptly challenged the law. Turner Broadcasting System—the broadcasting-cable conglomerate founded by Ted Turner—filed the first suit within an hour of the law's enactment. Four more separate suits followed. Some were filed by owners of other cable systems. Others were filed by cable programmers, who said they were being squeezed out of cable systems because of the decision to reserve so much space for local broadcasters.

In their suits the cable interests argued that cable was entitled to the same First Amendment protections as print media. Any interference with their right to choose their programming, they argued, had to be subject to "strict scrutiny" and struck down unless it furthered a "compelling government interest."

Even if the law were examined only under a lower "intermediate scrutiny" test, cable operators said it could not be upheld. They maintained that broadcasters had exaggerated the dangers to their competitive position. Cable operators had dropped very few broadcast stations, they insisted, and had every reason to continue to carry popular TV stations to maintain their subscribers.

In response, the FCC contended the must-carry law was economic regulation that did not warrant any special First Amendment scrutiny. Even under an intermediate scrutiny test, the commission said the law passed constitutional muster because it was only a minimal intrusion on cable operators' editorial discretion.

The three-judge court upheld the rules in a 2-1 decision in April 1993. The appeal went directly to the Supreme Court, where broadcasters and cable systems filed voluminous briefs to back their opposing positions. When the case was argued in January, the justices appeared uncertain. Solicitor General Drew Days, arguing the case for the FCC, was sharply challenged on the justification for the law. But attorney H. Barstow Farr, a Washington lawyer representing the cable industry, was also questioned about the dangers to broadcasters from cable's "bottleneck" power.

The Court's ambivalence was reflected in its ruling five months later. By a 5-4 vote the justices sent the case back to the three-judge court for a full trial, saying the government had to offer more evidence to justify the law. The dissenting justices said they would have thrown out the must-carry rules without further ado.

In the Court's main opinion Justice Kennedy began by saying that cable operators "engage in and transmit speech" and are entitled to First Amendment protection. In addition, he said, the rationale used to justify regulation of broadcasters—the scarcity of broadcast frequencies—does not apply to cable. Any laws regulating cable television, Kennedy concluded, can be evaluated under "settled principles of our First Amendment jurisprudence."

In effect, the Court decided that for purposes of government regulation, cable was more like newspapers or other print media than broadcasting. The ruling represented a major legal victory for an industry that the Court had previously described as "ancillary to broadcasting." And the Court was nearly unanimous on the point. Seven justices—all but Stevens—joined that part of Kennedy's opinion.

The justices divided, however, in evaluating the must-carry rules themselves. Kennedy led five justices in concluding that the rules were content-neutral and could be judged under the intermediate level of scrutiny. "... [T]he must-carry provisions are not designed to favor or disadvantage speech of any particular content," Kennedy wrote. "Rather, they are meant to protect broadcast television from what Congress determined to be unfair competition by cable systems."

Kennedy followed this blow to the cable industry's position by agreeing that the government had failed to show broadcasters were really "in jeopardy." The government had no evidence, he said, of local broadcasters going bankrupt, turning in their licenses, curtailing operations, or suffering serious losses in revenue. To explore those issues, Kennedy concluded, the case needed to go back to the three-judge court for a full trial.

The justices' voting on the divided issues crossed normal ideological lines. Chief Justice Rehnquist and Justices Blackmun, Stevens, and Souter joined Kennedy in taking a favorable view of the law. Stevens split from the group on the need for a trial. He said the law should be upheld, and he questioned the need to second-guess Congress's fear of future harm to broadcasters. But Stevens said he voted with the other four justices to form a majority for one position in the case.

Justice O'Connor led four dissenters in urging that the law be struck down. She called the must-carry provisions an "impermissible restraint on the cable operators' editorial discretion as well as on the cable program-mers' speech." She noted that by reserving up to one-third of cable channels for broadcast stations, the law reduced access for cable services such as CNN, C-SPAN, and the Discovery Channel "with as much claim as PBS to being educational or related to public affairs." Justices Scalia and Ginsburg joined all of O'Connor's opinion; Justice Thomas joined most of it.

After the ruling the rival industry lobbying groups both claimed partial victory. The National Cable Television Association voiced disappointment that the must-carry rules remained in effect. But the cable group said the Court had "overwhelmingly" found that the rules had not been adequately justified and had ordered them to be subject to "a much higher level of scrutiny."

The National Association of Broadcasters, on the other hand, said the Court had rejected "most of the cable industry's constitutional arguments" and accepted Congress's reasons for enacting the law as "legitimate government interests." The broadcasters said they were "confident" the three-judge court would uphold the rules again.

Whatever the three-judge court did, the case was certain to come back to the Supreme Court, probably in two years or so. By then a new justice would be on the case: Stephen Breyer, who succeeded Harry Blackmun in summer 1994. Blackmun voted to leave the must-carry rules in place. Breyer's stance on the issue was difficult to predict. In confirmation hearings he stressed his willingness to defer to Congress on statutory issues. But Breyer was also a strong First Amendment supporter and an administrative law expert who believed in closely scrutinizing the practical effect of regulations.

3 | *Case Summaries*

For four years as the Bush administration's solicitor general, Kenneth Starr had a ringside seat to watch the Supreme Court in action. The solicitor general's office is involved in about two-thirds of the cases before the Court, either representing the federal government as a direct party or filing "friend-of-the-court" briefs to give the justices guidance. The solicitor general even has an office in the Court building itself.

From that vantage point the solicitor general is in a better position than anyone outside the Court to evaluate the justices' most mysterious function: the selection of the hundred or so cases the justices will hear and decide each year among the thousands filed. Nine months after leaving government to practice law in Washington, Starr wrote an article for the *Wall Street Journal* evaluating the case selection process. The article, published just after the Court opened its 1993-1994 term, was not complimentary.

Under the headline "Trivial Pursuits at the Supreme Court," Starr complained that the justices picked bizarre or obscure cases to hear while passing up more important disputes. Starr cited examples. For one, he scoffed at the case from the Court's 1992-1993 term that decided whether Antarctica is a foreign country for purposes of the law allowing individuals to sue the federal government for torts. "That issue," Starr said wryly, "arises every twenty years or so in litigation somewhere in the U.S."

By contrast, Starr noted that the justices had declined to hear several major business cases, including the AT&T antitrust suit of the early 1980s, a restructuring of the natural gas industry later in the decade, and a recent trademark dispute that his law firm had unsuccessfully asked the Court to review. And Starr noted the Court had room on its calendar for more cases. He criticized what he called its "embarrassingly skimpy docket"—around 100 cases in recent terms compared with "the traditional level" of 150 cases per term.

Nine months later the Court's docket had gotten even skimpier. For the 1993-1994 term the Court issued only eighty-four signed opinions. That was one-fifth lower than the output from the two previous terms (107) and the lowest number since the Court issued eighty-two opinions in the 1955-1956 term. Moreover, the number of opinions was falling even though the number of petitions for review filed with the Court again reached a new high. A total of 7,786 cases were filed during the term—a 7 percent increase from the previous year *(see Figure 3-1)*.

With the lower number of decisions, the Court was somewhat more divided than in the previous term. The justices were unanimous in thirty of the cases, or 36 percent; they had been unanimous in 43 percent of the decisions the previous term. The percentage of cases with only one dissenting vote also dropped to 7 percent from 11 percent. While the proportions for 6-3 and 5-4 decisions remained unchanged, the percentage of 7-2 decisions jumped to 24 percent from 13 percent.

After the justices ended the term, business groups renewed the criticism of the Court's reduced output. "One of the great disappointments was the small number of cases," complained Stephen Bokat of the National Chamber Litigation Center. Business interests could point to any number of cases where the justices had spurned their calls for a second look, among them a high-stakes patent dispute between two computer chip makers, a closely watched sexual harassment case from Columbia University, and a defense contractor's constitutional challenge to a century-old law allowing private individuals to bring fraud suits on behalf of the government and keep part of any winnings.

The Court showed no greater interest in individual rights cases than in business cases, but civil liberties groups were less concerned. "By and large, the civil rights and civil liberties community is still wary of the Supreme Court," said Stephen Shapiro of the American Civil Liberties Union. "We have seen increasing reliance on state courts and state constitutions. I don't think that's going to change even though the Supreme Court is moderating." Still, Shapiro did note one disappointment: the Court's refusal to hear an appeal by civil rights groups and the Clinton administration to reinstate an Equal Employment Opportunity Commission regulation banning English-only rules in the workplace.

The justices have shed little light on the trend toward fewer decisions. Court observers have posited several explanations, among them the elimination of laws requiring the justices to take certain kinds of cases, ideological compatibility with Republican-appointed federal judges, and a deliberate decision to lower the Court's profile. An examination of some of the cases passed over during the past year also shows that the justices engage in ideological sparring among themselves in trying to get cases onto the Court's calendar.

For example, five weeks after the Court's ruling barring sex-based peremptory challenges in jury selection, two of the dissenters—Justices Scalia and Thomas—complained about the Court's refusal to hear a similar case. The case involved a member of the Jehovah's Witnesses who said that he had been barred from jury service because of his religion. In a four-page dissent Thomas said the action demonstrated the Court's "unwillingness to confront forthrightly the ramifications of its decision" in the earlier case.

Figure 3-1 Supreme Court Caseload, 1960 Term -1993 Term

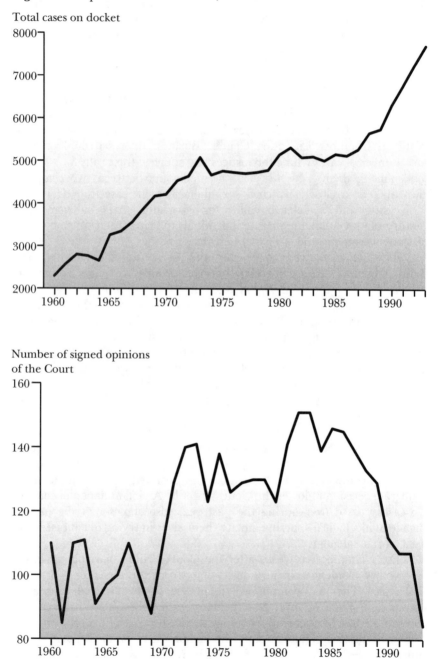

Total cases on docket

Number of signed opinions
of the Court

Thomas and Scalia also dissented from the Court's refusal to hear a plea from a Kentucky man to reinstate a federal civil rights suit against two state social workers; the social workers had charged him with molesting his daughter. The lower court had ruled the social workers had the same absolute immunity from lawsuits granted by prosecutors. Scalia wrote a four-page dissent questioning the reasoning.

In other cases Justices Scalia and O'Connor dissented from the Court's refusal to hear a procedurally complex case from Oregon that they said cast doubt on private property rights on beaches for the entire length of Oregon's seacoast. O'Connor and Chief Justice Rehnquist dissented when the Court rejected a case seeking to bar punitive damage awards in arbitration cases. And Justice Blackmun—in line with his newly declared opposition to capital punishment in February—dissented in every subsequent death penalty case that the Court declined to hear.

Under Court procedures four justices are needed to vote to hear a case, so Blackmun's solitary votes or the votes by the two-justice blocs were not enough to put the cases on the calendar. But the dissents—exceptions to the Court's usual custom of giving no indication of the reasons for rejecting a case—gave a few clues about the tactical maneuvering that goes on behind the scenes in the case selection process.

Court watchers also noted evidence that cast doubt on the justices' skill in picking cases. The Court's meager output for the term would have been higher but for four cases that the justices decided not to decide, even after reading all the briefs and listening to the opposing lawyer's arguments. Technically, the Court declared that the writ of certiorari it had granted in order to review each of the cases was "dismissed as improvidently granted." In Court parlance the cases were said to have been "digged"—an apt acronym.

Usually, the Court digs no more than one or two cases a term. Sometimes the Court gives a reason for refusing to decide a case—and sometimes not. The unusually high number of cases digged in the 1993-1994 term raised eyebrows among Court watchers. And the justices themselves disagreed in three of the four cases about whether they should have decided the disputes instead of dropping them.

In one of the cases, the justices had no choice but dismissal. The Court had agreed to review a South Carolina law that retroactively limited parole consideration for violent offenders. During oral argument, however, the justices were told the South Carolina legislature had changed the law four and a half months earlier. Neither of the lawyers had noticed until just before the argument.

In three other cases, however, one or more justices dissented from the decision to dig. In one the Court was reviewing a ruling by the Tennessee Supreme Court that had limited the state's death penalty law. Belatedly, the justices learned that the state court had based its ruling on state constitutional grounds—protecting it from review by federal courts. Justice Blackmun wanted to rule on the case anyway.

In another case, the Court had agreed to review a little-known but highly controversial procedure that allowed the parties in a civil suit to wipe out (technically, "vacate") a court ruling after settling their dispute. Insurance companies and other businesses often used the procedure to erase unfavorable decisions. Plaintiffs' lawyers and consumer groups said the practice essentially allowed "deep-pocket" defendants to pay off individual litigants and nullify legal precedents that could prove more costly in the long run.

The Court heard arguments on the issue in October in a case arising from a three-way patent dispute between a Japanese company and two U.S. corporations. The two U.S. companies settled their dispute and joined in asking the judge to vacate his ruling, which would have benefited the Japanese concern. After listening to arguments, the Court ruled on November 30 that the Japanese company had not properly raised the question of its right to intervene in the case. For this reason the case was digged.

Justices Blackmun and Stevens complained that the Court was using a "technicality" to refuse to decide the issue. Four months later the Court found another case presenting the question—a bankruptcy case that the parties had settled just before the Court had decided to review it. One side favored and the other side opposed vacating the lower court ruling. The Court ordered up a new round of arguments on the procedure and set it on the calendar for the new term (see p. 299).

In the fourth of the digged cases, the Court had agreed to rule on a technical but important civil procedure issue, this one involving "class action" suits. A class action allows an individual consumer with a small claim against a business to file a suit on behalf of a "class" of people that might have similar claims. The procedure is a potent consumer remedy, but business groups say it gives plaintiffs' attorneys the power to effectively blackmail companies into cash settlements that often include large fees for the lawyer and little money for the consumer.

The issue the Court agreed to decide was whether individual consumers had a constitutional right to "opt out" of class action suits and pursue any monetary claims on their own. But in April the Court voted 6-3 to dig the case. The majority said the constitutional issue was premature because the Federal Rules of Civil Procedure might allow consumers to pull out of the case anyway. In a dissent Justice O'Connor, joined by Chief Justice Rehnquist and Justice Kennedy, called for ruling on the case. "The issue has been thoroughly briefed and argued by the parties," O'Connor wrote. "We should decide it."

Following are case summaries for the eighty-four signed opinions issued during the 1993-1994 term. They are organized by subject matter:

business law, courts and procedure, criminal law and procedure, election law, environmental law, federal government, First Amendment, individual rights, labor law, property law, states, and torts. The summaries include two *per curiam* (unsigned) opinions—*Morgan Stanley & Co., Inc. v. Pacific Mutual Life Insurance Co.,* summarily affirmed on a 4-4 vote; and *Stansbury v. California,* decided by a 9-0 vote.

Business Law

Aviation

Northwest Airlines, Inc. v. Kent County, decided by a 7-1 vote, January 24, 1994; Ginsburg wrote the opinion; Thomas dissented; Blackmun did not participate.

The Court rejected an airline industry challenge to fees imposed by local airports but fortified the power of the federal Department of Transportation to regulate the charges.

The ruling shifted the focus of a growing, high-stakes controversy between airlines and local airports from federal courts to the Transportation Department. The department promised after the decision to take a more active role in airport fee disputes.

The case stemmed from a challenge by seven commercial airlines to fees imposed by the Kent County International Airport in Grand Rapids, Michigan. The airlines claimed the charges violated the 1973 Anti-Head Tax Act, which limits airport user fees to "reasonable rental charges, landing fees, and other service charges . . . for use of airport facilities."

Lower federal courts had upheld the bulk of the fees even though they had generated a large surplus for the Grand Rapids airport. But the rulings took a narrower approach to enforcing the law than had another federal appeals court in 1984, which struck down somewhat lower fees imposed by the Indianapolis airport.

In her opinion for the Court, Ginsburg said the airlines had failed to show that the fees of the Grand Rapids airport were unreasonable or that they discriminated against interstate commerce. But she said the ruling did not foreclose the airlines from challenging the fees before the Transportation Department, which she said was better equipped than the courts "to regulate . . . based on a full view of the relevant facts and circumstances."

In a lone dissent Thomas argued the Anti-Head Tax Act gave the Transportation Department no broad power to regulate airport user fees. He said the case should have been remanded for a ruling on the interstate commerce issue.

Bankruptcy

BFP v. Resolution Trust Corporation, as receiver of Imperial Federal Savings and Loan Association, decided by a 5-4 vote, May 23, 1994; Scalia wrote the opinion; Souter, Blackmun, Stevens, and Ginsburg dissented.

The Court limited the ability of debtors in bankruptcy to nullify a foreclosure sale of real property they owned before seeking court protection from creditors.

In a closely divided ruling the Court held that debtors cannot use a bankruptcy code provision to undo a properly conducted foreclosure sale even if the price paid is less than the property's market value.

The bankruptcy code allows debtors to get out of transactions that occurred up to one year before filing for bankruptcy if they received "less than a reasonably equivalent value" for the property. A partnership in California invoked the law to try to rescind the $433,000 foreclosure sale of a beachfront house that it said was worth at least $725,000. Lower federal courts said they had no power to undo the sale.

Writing for the Court, Scalia agreed that a proper foreclosure sale "conclusively satisfies" the bankruptcy code's requirement. "A fair and proper price, or a 'reasonably equivalent value,' for foreclosed property, is the price in fact received at the foreclosure sale, so long as all the requirements of the State's foreclosure sale have been complied with," he wrote.

Dissenting justices argued that the ruling went against the "straightforward language" of the bankruptcy code. ". . . [T]he bankruptcy avoidance power will apparently be a dead letter in reviewing real estate foreclosures," Souter wrote.

Copyright

Campbell, a/k/a Skyywalker v. Acuff-Rose Music, Inc., decided by a 9-0 vote, March 7, 1994; Souter wrote the opinion.

A parody of a copyrighted work may be legally protected even if it copies a substantial part of the original and is produced for commercial purposes.

The unanimous ruling ordered a new trial in a copyright infringement suit brought against the rap group 2 Live Crew for doing its own version of the rock classic "Pretty Woman," cowritten and performed by the late Roy Orbison. The closely watched case pitted songwriters and composers wanting to protect the market for copyrighted works against satirists and civil liberties groups defending what they called the "rich tradition" of musical parody in the United States.

The Court ruled that 2 Live Crew was entitled to raise the copyright doctrine of "fair use" as a defense to the infringement suit. The Sixth U.S. Circuit Court of Appeals had ruled that the group could not rely on the fair use doctrine, which allows limited use of copyrighted material without permission for some purposes, because the recording was for a commercial purpose.

Souter rejected arguments that parody should be given automatic protection under the fair use doctrine. Instead, Souter said courts must decide copyright suits against parodies on a case-by-case basis after weighing the four factors recognized under the doctrine: the purpose and nature of the new work, the nature of the original work, the amount of copying, and the effect on the market for the original work. The commercial character of the work, Souter said, "is only one element to be weighed in a fair use enquiry."

In returning the case to lower courts, the Court said 2 Live Crew still had to show that it had not copied more of Orbison's song than necessary and that it had not hurt the market for the original song or the potential market for a new version.

In a separate opinion Kennedy expressed doubt that 2 Live Crew's song was "a legitimate parody." He said the court's ruling "leaves room for the District Court to determine on remand that the song is not a fair use."

Fogerty v. Fantasy, Inc., decided by a 9-0 vote, March 1, 1994; Rehnquist wrote the opinion.

The Court made it easier for a successful defendant in a copyright infringement suit to be awarded attorney's fees.

In a unanimous ruling the Court said plaintiffs and defendants are to be treated alike under the Copyright Act provision permitting judges to award attorney's fees to the prevailing party in an infringement suit. Some federal appeals courts had held that a defendant could be awarded attorney's fees only if the defendant showed that the plaintiff's suit was frivolous or in bad faith.

Writing for the Court, Rehnquist said nothing in the text or legislative history of the Copyright Act called for a different test for defendants than plaintiffs. He added that defendants "should be encouraged" to advance meritorious copyright defenses "to the same extent that plaintiffs are encouraged to litigate meritorious infringement claims."

The ruling gave John Fogerty, one-time lead singer for the rock group Creedence Clearwater Revival, a second chance to collect attorney's fees after winning a copyright infringement suit brought by the music publishing house that owned the copyright to his 1972 song "Run Through the Jungle." The company had claimed that a later Fogerty composition was the same melody with different words.

Insurance

John Hancock Mutual Life Insurance Co. v. Harris Trust &
Savings Bank, as Trustee of Sperry Master Retirement Trust No. 2,
decided by a 6-3 vote, December 13, 1993; Ginsburg wrote the opinion;
Thomas, O'Connor, and Kennedy dissented.

The Court required insurance companies to comply with the federal
Employee Retirement Income Security Act (ERISA) in managing a
common type of retirement account bought by employee pension plans.

The dispute involved group annuity contracts sold by insurance
companies that provide for fixed annual benefits to retirees plus
supplemental benefits that vary depending on investment results. Insurance companies typically had included these funds as part of their
general assets instead of setting up separate accounts. ERISA requires
separate accounting and imposes other fiduciary standards on pension
plan assets, but the 1974 law contains an exemption for "guaranteed
benefit" policies.

The Court rejected insurance industry arguments that the exemption
applies to accounts that include variable benefits. In a densely written
opinion Ginsburg said that Congress intended to impose "fiduciary
standards on persons whose actions affect the amount of benefits retirement plan participants will receive." She said Congress had "specifically
instructed" that the exemption be "closely contained."

The ruling allowed the bank that served as trustee of a Unisys Corp.
employee pension plan to proceed with a ten-year-old suit against the
John Hancock insurance company's management of the plan. More
broadly, it appeared to require insurers either to set up separate accounts
or rewrite annuity contracts for pension plans unless Congress changed
the law.

In a dissent Thomas, joined by O'Connor and Kennedy, complained
that the ruling "abruptly overturns the settled expectations of the
insurance industry."

Maritime Law

American Dredging Co. v. Miller, decided by a 7-2 vote, February
23, 1994; Scalia wrote the opinion; Kennedy and Thomas dissented.

A state may block ship owners and operators from using a standard
legal doctrine to try to move seaman injury suits to another jurisdiction
if the state is not the most "convenient" place for the case to be
tried.

The ruling allowed a Mississippi seaman who had been injured
while working on a tug operating on the Delaware River to proceed with
a suit against the tug owner in Louisiana state court. The company, a

corporation chartered in New Jersey with its principal place of business in Pennsylvania, sought to dismiss the suit under a doctrine called *"forum non conveniens."* But the Louisiana Supreme Court refused, citing a state law that barred use of the doctrine in maritime law cases.

In a 7-2 ruling the Court ruled federal law does not preempt the state statute. Scalia said the state's refusal to recognize *forum non conveniens* did not prejudice a "characteristic feature" of maritime law or hamper uniformity in maritime cases.

Kennedy, in a dissent joined by Thomas, argued that the ruling "condones the forum shopping and disuniformity that admirality jurisdiction is supposed to prevent."

Boca Grande Club, Inc. v. Florida Power & Light Co., Inc., decided by a 9-0 vote, April 20, 1994; Stevens wrote the opinion.

Losing defendants in maritime lawsuits are not entitled to seek a contribution from defendants that settle claims before trial.

The one-paragraph decision followed the Court's ruling in a related case announced the same day, *McDermott, Inc. v. AmClyde (see below)*.

Howlett v. Birkdale Shipping Co., S.A., decided by a 9-0 vote, June 13, 1994; Kennedy wrote the opinion.

Shipowners can be held liable for injuries to longshoremen only if the vessel's crew knew of a latent safety hazard or were negligent in failing to learn of the danger.

The unanimous ruling narrowly defined a shipowner's "turnover duty" under the federal Longshore and Harbor Workers' Compensation Act as amended in 1972. The law gives an injured dock worker fixed benefits from a stevedore—the independent contractor that supervises cargo loading and unloading—but also permits an open-ended damage suit against the shipowner for failing to warn the stevedore of hazardous conditions.

Writing for the Court, Kennedy said the 1972 amendments put primary responsibility for avoiding injuries to longshoremen on stevedores, not shipowners. ". . . [T]he vessel's turnover duty to warn of latent defects in the cargo stow and cargo area is a narrow one," Kennedy wrote. Shipowners have no duty to supervise loading or unloading or to inspect cargo areas for hazards, he said.

The ruling came in a suit by a Philadelphia dock worker permanently disabled after slipping on a sheet of plastic in the cargo stow of a ship. Lower courts dismissed the suit, but the Court sent the case back for reconsideration under its holding.

McDermott, Inc. v. AmClyde, decided by a 9-0 vote, April 20, 1994; Stevens wrote the opinion.

Losing defendants in a maritime lawsuit must pay their proportionate share of damages instead of getting a reduction for any settlements paid by other defendants.

The decision backed a company that had sued five other companies for a construction accident on an offshore oil rig in the Gulf of Mexico. Three defendants settled before trial for $1 million. A jury found two other defendants liable for 70 percent of the $2.1 million in damages. Those two companies then sought to reduce their payments by the amount the plaintiff had already received.

In a unanimous ruling the Court adopted the pro-plaintiff "proportionate share" rule for federal courts to follow in maritime suits. It also ruled that defendants that go to trial may not try to recover any amounts paid from the settling defendants. Stevens said that allowing an offset would be unfair to defendants that settle their claims and could discourage settlements and increase burdens on courts.

Securities Law

Central Bank of Denver, N.A. v. First Interstate Bank of Denver, N.A., decided by a 5-4 vote, April 19, 1994; Kennedy wrote the opinion; Stevens, Blackmun, Souter, and Ginsburg dissented.

The Court sharply limited the ability of defrauded investors to recover losses from accountants, lawyers, or other professionals for indirectly aiding a securities fraud.

In a 5-4 ruling the Court held that private plaintiffs may not maintain an action for aiding-and-abetting a violation of the broad antifraud section 10(b) of the federal Securities Exchange Act of 1934 or its companion regulation, Rule 10b-5.

Writing for the majority, Kennedy said the text of the federal securities law did not authorize aiding and abetting suits and that policy considerations argued against recognizing such a cause of action.

Dissenting justices complained that the ruling wiped out federal court precedents dating to 1966 and also cast doubt on the power of the Securities and Exchange Commission to file civil suits against outside professionals.

The ruling threw out part of a suit filed by First Interstate Bank of Denver to recover its losses after a municipal building authority defaulted on $26 million in bonds. First Interstate blamed Central Bank of Denver, the trustee on the bonds, for failing to tell investors that property values in the area being developed were falling.

In his opinion Kennedy said that "excessive litigation" could make accountants or lawyers reluctant to give advice to new companies. But Stevens, writing for the dissenters, said there was no evidence that the aiding-and-abetting theory had caused "such deleterious consequences that we should dispense with it on those grounds." *(See entry, p. 44; excerpts, p. 119.)*

Morgan Stanley & Co., Inc. v. Pacific Mutual Life Insurance Co., judgment affirmed by an equally divided Court, May 23, 1994; *per curiam* (unsigned) opinion; O'Connor did not participate.

The Court failed on a tie vote to decide the constitutionality of a law reinstating some federal securities suits dismissed after the Court changed the time limit for bringing such cases.

The issue arose from the Court's 1991 ruling *Lampf, Pleva, Lipkind, Prupis & Petigrow v. Gilbertson,* which established a three-year statute of limitations for federal securities fraud suits. Congress responded by passing a law to block application of the new deadline to pending suits and to permit reinstatement of suits already dismissed because of the ruling.

One federal appeals court ruled that the provision permitting suits to be revived was an unconstitutional violation of the doctrine of separation of powers. But the Fifth U.S. Circuit Court of Appeals upheld the law, allowing an insurance company to revive a securities fraud suit against three investment banking firms and an accounting firm.

The Court's 4-4 vote had the effect of upholding the appeals court ruling. As is customary, the Court did not indicate how individual justices voted. O'Connor did not participate because the ruling could have affected the value of what was described as "a small amount of stock" she owned. Two weeks later the Court agreed to review in the coming term another case posing the same issue (*Plaut v. Spendthrift Farm, Inc.*).

Taxation

United States v. Carlton, decided by a 9-0 vote, June 13, 1994; Blackmun wrote the opinion.

Congress has broad discretion to enact retroactive tax changes if the revisions are rationally related to a legitimate purpose and extend to a "modest" period before enactment.

The unanimous ruling upheld a law passed by Congress in 1987 to close an estate tax loophole adopted one year earlier. The loophole threatened to cost the Treasury $7 billion. The executor of an estate who was blocked from taking a $2.5 million deduction under the new law challenged the retroactive provision as a due process violation. A federal appeals court agreed, but the Court rejected the argument.

Writing for a six-justice majority, Blackmun said retroactive tax legislation is valid if it is "supported by a legitimate legislative purpose furthered by rational means." The challenged law was valid because Congress had "acted to correct . . . a mistake . . . that would have created a significant and unanticipated revenue loss," and it had "acted promptly and established only a modest period of retroactivity"—a little more than one year.

Blackmun rejected the executor's argument that his rights had been violated because he had relied on the superseded tax provision. "Tax legislation is not a promise," Blackmun wrote, "and a taxpayer has no vested right in the Internal Revenue Code."

Three justices concurred separately. O'Connor agreed with the decision but warned that a longer retroactivity period would raise "serious constitutional questions." Scalia, joined by Thomas, concurred on grounds that the Due Process Clause has no application to retroactive taxes. "[T]he Due Process Clause guarantees *no* substantive rights, but only (as it says) process."

United States v. Irvine, decided by an 8-0 vote, April 20, 1994; Souter wrote the opinion; Blackmun did not participate.

The government can collect gift tax on a taxpayer's delayed decision to give up interest in a trust even if the trust was created before the gift tax was passed.

The ruling allowed the Internal Revenue Service (IRS) to collect $10 million in taxes, interest, and penalties from the children of a Minnesota woman who, in 1979, disclaimed her right to a trust established by her grandfather in 1917. Under terms of the trust, the money was divided among her five children.

An IRS regulation, which the Court upheld in 1982, allows a taxpayer to avoid the gift tax in such a situation only if he or she disclaims the interest "within a reasonable time." The woman's children contended, however, that the 1932 gift tax did not apply to a trust created earlier.

In a unanimous opinion Souter rejected the argument. He said the gift tax applied to the decision to give up the money, not to the creation of the trust.

Courts and Procedure

Contempt of Court

United Mine Workers v. Bagwell, decided by a 9-0 vote, June 30, 1994; Blackmun wrote the opinion.

The Court threw out a $52 million contempt of court fine imposed on the United Mine Workers (UMW), ruling the penalty was too serious to be imposed without a jury trial.

A state judge in Virginia imposed the fine after finding the union in contempt of court for violating an injunction aimed at preventing violence in a 1989 coal strike. The Virginia Supreme Court ruled the fine was a proper sanction for civil contempt because it was designed to force compliance with the injunction, not to punish the union.

In a unanimous ruling the Court disagreed. Blackmun said the fine could not be regarded as a civil penalty because it was not designed to compensate a private party, the alleged contempt did not take place in the judge's presence, and the conduct involved a broad range of activities instead of a single, discrete act. He said the $52 million fine was "unquestionably ... a serious contempt sanction" and "constitutionally could not be imposed absent a jury trial."

Six justices joined Blackmun's opinion. Ginsburg, joined by Rehnquist, concurred separately in a briefer opinion that stressed the state was "pursu[ing] the fines on its own account ... without tying the exactions exclusively to a claim for compensation."

Scalia, who did join Blackmun's opinion, wrote in a separate concurrence that the ruling would apply to contempt proceedings in broad institutional litigation such as school desegregation suits.

Federal Courts

O'Melveny & Myers v. Federal Deposit Insurance Corporation, as receiver for American Diversified Savings Bank, decided by a 9-0 vote, June 13, 1994; Scalia wrote the opinion.

State law, not federal law, governs professional negligence suits brought by the Federal Deposit Insurance Corporation (FDIC) as receiver for a failed savings and loan association.

The unanimous ruling came in a suit filed by the FDIC as receiver for an insolvent state-chartered thrift in California. The agency sought to recover losses from a real estate deal from a Los Angeles law firm. It charged the firm with negligence and breach of fiduciary duty. The firm argued state court decisions barred the suit, but a federal appeals court said the issue should be decided on the basis of "a federal common-law rule."

Writing for the Court, Scalia emphatically disagreed. "There is no federal general common law," Scalia objected, quoting a famous 1938 decision (*Erie Railroad Co. v. Tompkins*). "... [T]he remote possibility that corporations may go into federal receivership," he added, "is no conceivable basis for adopting a special federal common-law rule divesting States of authority" over the legal issue in the case.

The ruling returned the case to lower federal courts. In a concurring opinion Stevens, joined by three other justices, stressed that the decision "avoids any suggestion about how the merits of the [legal] issue should be resolved."

Judicial Disqualification

Liteky v. United States, decided by 9-0 and 5-4 votes, March 7, 1994; Scalia wrote the opinion; Kennedy, Blackmun, Stevens, and Souter concurred in the judgment but disagreed with the ruling on the legal issue.

Federal judges generally cannot be disqualified from a case for bias on the basis of their comments or conduct in the courtroom.

The ruling unanimously upheld the refusal by a federal judge in Georgia to step aside from the 1991 trial of three peace activists for a protest at a military base. The defendants claimed the judge made prejudicial remarks during the proceedings and during an earlier trial of one of the defendants for similar charges in 1983.

Although all nine justices agreed the judge's remarks did not require disqualification, they split 5-4 on the legal issue in the case. Writing for the majority, Scalia said that a judge cannot be removed for "critical, disapproving . . . or even hostile" remarks during a trial unless they indicate "such a high degree of favoritism or antagonism as to make fair judgment impossible."

In an opinion concurring in the result, Kennedy said a judge should be removed from a case whenever there are "reasonable questions about the judge's impartiality." He also said the majority opinion placed "undue emphasis" on whether the allegations of bias arose from the judge's conduct on the bench or from an "extrajudicial source."

Jury Selection

J. E. B. v. Alabama ex rel. T. B., decided by a 6-3 vote, April 19, 1994; Blackmun wrote the opinion; Scalia, Rehnquist, and Thomas dissented.

Lawyers may not exclude people from serving on juries solely because of their sex.

The Court held, 6-3, that the Equal Protection Clause prohibits discrimination in jury selection based on gender. The ruling extended the reasoning of a line of cases beginning in 1986 that had barred lawyers from excluding potential jurors on account of race.

"Discrimination in jury selection, whether based on race or on gender, causes harm to the litigants, the community, and the individual jurors who are wrongfully excluded from participation in the judicial process," Blackmun wrote.

The decision ordered a new trial for a Tennessee man in a paternity case tried by an all-female jury in Alabama. The state's attorney had used so-called peremptory challenges to remove nine men as potential jurors without giving reasons for excluding them. The jury found that the man was the father of the child in question.

Blackmun insisted the ruling would not eliminate all use of peremptory challenges. But in an acerbic dissent, Scalia, joined by Rehnquist and Thomas, said that the Court was weakening lawyers' ability to select a fair jury "simply to pay conspicuous obeisance to the equality of the sexes." *(See entry, p. 36; excerpts, p. 131.)*

Settlements

Digital Equipment Corp. v. Desktop Direct, Inc., decided by a 9-0 vote, June 6, 1994; Souter wrote the opinion.

A party to a civil suit is not entitled to an immediate appeal of a judge's refusal to enforce a settlement agreement that would preclude trial of the case.

The unanimous ruling came in a trademark infringement suit filed by a small computer company, Desktop Direct, against the giant Digital Equipment Corp. A judge set aside a settlement in the case after Desktop alleged misrepresentation and fraud. Digital then tried to appeal the ruling, claiming that it had a contractual right to avoid trial of the case.

The justices declined to enlarge the exception to the general statutory rule barring appeals of most pretrial rulings. Souter said that a litigant's right to avoid trial "does not rise to the level of importance needed for recognition" under the limited provision for immediate appeals.

Kokkonen v. Guardian Life Insurance Co. of America, decided by a 9-0 vote, May 16, 1994; Scalia wrote the opinion.

A federal court cannot enforce the terms of an agreement settling a suit unless the agreement specifically provides for court enforcement.

The brief, unanimous ruling came in a wrongful termination case between an insurance company and one of its agents in California. The insurer and the agent settled the case and agreed to a dismissal of the suit. But the company went back to court, contending the man had failed to turn over files as the agreement provided.

Scalia said the dispute over the settlement amounted to a breach of contract suit that was for state courts, not federal courts, to handle. But he noted parties to a suit can provide in a settlement that a federal court retains jurisdiction to enforce the agreement.

Criminal Law and Procedure

Arrest

Powell v. Nevada, decided by a 7-2 vote, March 30, 1994; Ginsburg wrote the opinion; Thomas and Rehnquist dissented.

A Nevada man won a second appeal of his conviction in a child abuse-murder case because the state's supreme court failed to apply a decision requiring suspects to be brought before a magistrate within forty-eight hours of their arrest. The Court left open the possibility, however, that the state justices could affirm the defendant's conviction and death sentence after a second appeal.

The defendant, Kitrich Powell, was convicted and sentenced to death in the November 1989 beating death of his girlfriend's four-year-old daughter. Powell was arrested on November 3 and was in custody four days before a magistrate determined there was probable cause for his arrest.

The Nevada Supreme Court upheld his conviction in 1992 after deciding that the U.S. Supreme Court's 1991 decision setting a forty-eight-hour rule for a suspect's initial court hearing did not apply retroactively.

In a 7-2 decision the Court ruled that the state justices were wrong. Under a 1987 decision, Ginsburg said, new Supreme Court rulings on the conduct of criminal prosecutions generally apply to any case pending at the time. But Ginsburg said the Nevada justices still had to consider whether Powell's statement to police should have been suppressed because of the delayed hearing.

In a dissent Thomas, joined by Rehnquist, argued that Powell's statement could be used despite the delay and that the Court should have upheld the conviction.

Capital Punishment

McFarland v. Scott, Director, Texas Department of Criminal Justice, Institutional Division, decided by 6-3 and 5-4 votes, June 30, 1994; Blackmun wrote the opinion; O'Connor dissented in part; Thomas, Rehnquist, and Scalia dissented.

Federal judges must appoint a lawyer for a death row inmate who requests assistance in drawing up a habeas corpus petition and can stay the inmate's execution until the petition is filed.

The closely divided ruling interpreted a provision of the Anti-Drug Abuse Act of 1988 that created a right to counsel for capital defendants in federal habeas corpus proceedings. Federal judges in Texas, however, ruled the law did not require appointment of counsel until after a habeas corpus petition had been filed and did not permit judges to stay executions in the meantime.

Writing for the Court: Blackmun said the right to counsel began earlier: "this interpretation is the only one that gives meaning to the statute as a practical matter." Inmates cannot be expected to prepare habeas corpus petitions on their own, Blackmun said, because the petitions "must meet heightened pleading requirements" and are subject to summary dismissal if they fail to present grounds for challenging the conviction or sentence.

Similarly, the appointment of counsel "would have been meaningless," Blackmun said, unless judges could stay an execution until the habeas corpus petition was filed. But he added that a federal judge could deny a stay if "a dilatory capital defendant inexcusably ignores" the opportunity to get legal help.

O'Connor agreed with the ruling on appointment of counsel, but she said the law did not authorize federal judges to delay executions. Death row inmates "can avoid the need for a stay by filing a prompt request for appointment of counsel well in advance of the scheduled execution," she added.

In a dissent Thomas, joined by Rehnquist and Scalia, criticized the majority's "expansive interpretation" of the new law. *(See entry, p. 46; excerpts, p. 256.)*

Romano v. Oklahoma, decided by a 5-4 vote, June 13, 1994; Rehnquist wrote the opinion; Ginsburg, Blackmun, Stevens, and Souter dissented.

A defendant sentenced to death is not entitled to a new penalty hearing if the jury was told the defendant had already been sentenced to death in a prior case.

The narrowly divided ruling rejected a plea by an Oklahoma death row inmate for a new sentencing for a 1986 robbery-murder. Over his objections the jury in the case was informed of his prior conviction and death sentence for a 1985 robbery-murder. An Oklahoma appeals court said evidence of the earlier death sentence was irrelevant and concluded the information did not affect the jury's decision.

In his opinion for the Court, Rehnquist said that prosecutors' use of the evidence "did not amount to constitutional error." He added, "We do not believe that the admission of evidence regarding petitioner's prior death sentence affirmatively misled the jury regarding its role in the sentencing process so as to diminish its sense of responsibility."

Writing for the four dissenters, Ginsburg said introduction of the evidence created a "grave" risk that jurors "might well believe that [the defendant's] fate had been sealed by the previous jury, and thus was not fully their responsibility."

Schiro v. Farley, Superintendent, Indiana State Prison, decided by a 7-2 vote, January 19, 1994; O'Connor wrote the opinion; Stevens and Blackmun dissented.

A judge may impose a death sentence for intentional murder even if a jury fails to return a verdict for that offense.

The Court's ruling upheld a death sentence imposed on Thomas Schiro after he was convicted of raping and killing an Indiana woman in her home in 1981. The jury convicted Schiro of one capital count—murder while committing a rape—but did not specify a verdict on two other capital counts, including intentional murder.

Although the jury unanimously recommended against imposition of capital punishment, the judge imposed the death penalty after finding that Schiro had "committed the murder by intentionally killing the victim." In a habeas corpus challenging the sentence, Schiro contended the jury had acquitted him of intentional murder, and the judge's sentence therefore violated the Double Jeopardy Clause prohibiting two trials for the same offense.

In a 7-2 decision the Court disagreed. O'Connor said the Double Jeopardy Clause does not apply to the sentencing phase of a single prosecution. She also said the legal doctrine of "collateral estoppel," which bars a party to a case from trying an issue a second time, did not apply. The verdict the jury returned on the intentional murder count, she wrote, was not unambiguously guilty.

Stevens, joined by Blackmun, argued in a dissenting opinion that it was "constitutionally impermissible" for the trial judge to "re-examine" the issue of intent after the jury verdict.

Simmons v. South Carolina, decided by a 7-2 vote, June 17, 1994; Blackmun wrote a plurality opinion for four justices; O'Connor wrote a concurring opinion for three justices; Scalia and Thomas dissented.

Jurors in a capital case must be told about the possibility of sentencing a defendant to life in prison without parole if the prosecution uses the defendant's dangerousness as an argument for the death penalty.

The ruling ordered a new sentencing hearing for a South Carolina death row inmate convicted of the beating death of an elderly woman. After the prosecution urged the jury to consider his future dangerousness in weighing his sentence, the defendant's lawyer asked that the jury be told the defendant would be ineligible for parole under state law if sentenced to life imprisonment. The judge refused.

In a splintered decision the Court ruled that the failure to tell the jury of the defendant's ineligibility for parole violated his rights to due process.

Writing for four justices, Blackmun said the judge's refusal to give the jury information about parole created a "grievous misperception" about its sentencing decision. ". . . [I]t had the effect of creating a false choice between sentencing petitioner to death and sentencing him to a limited period of incarceration," Blackmun wrote. Stevens, Souter, and Ginsburg joined in his opinion.

O'Connor, joined by Rehnquist and Kennedy, concurred in the decision in a briefer opinion that said information about parole ineligibility could be given to the jury either by the judge or by the defense lawyer in argument. She noted that the prosecution could still argue that a defendant would be dangerous in prison.

In a dissent Scalia, joined by Thomas, complained that the ruling meant that opponents of capital punishment had "successfully opened another front in their guerrilla war to make this unquestionably constitutional sentence a practical impossibility."

Tuilaepa v. California, decided by an 8-1 vote, June 30, 1994; Kennedy wrote the opinion; Blackmun dissented.

The Court rejected pleas by two California death row inmates to strike down three factors listed in state law for juries to consider in deciding whether to impose the death penalty.

Among nineteen factors in all, the state's capital murder law instructed jurors to consider "the circumstances of the crime," "the presence or absence of criminal activity [involving] the use or attempted use of force or violence . . .," and the age of the defendant. Two death row inmates challenged the factors as unconstitutionally vague.

In a near unanimous ruling the Court upheld use of the factors in the two cases. Kennedy said the criteria "provide common and understandable terms to the sentencer," and the law did not need to instruct jurors how to weigh each of the factors. Five justices concurred in Kennedy's opinion.

Stevens, joined by Ginsburg, concurred separately, saying that "references to such potentially ambiguous, but clearly relevant factors actually reduce the risk of arbitrary capital sentencing."

In a lone dissent Blackmun complained that the law did not give sufficient guidance to jurors. ". . . [O]pen-ended factors and a lack of guidance," he wrote, "create a system in which . . . improper arguments can be made in the courtroom and credited in the jury room."

Criminal Offenses

Posters 'N' Things, Ltd. v. United States, decided by a 9-0 vote, May 23, 1994; Blackmun wrote the opinion.

The Court somewhat eased the government's burden of proof under a federal law prohibiting the sale of "drug paraphernalia."

The Court held that a defendant may be convicted under the law for selling merchandise generally used with illegal drugs. The justices unanimously rejected arguments by the owner of a "head shop" that the government had to prove she specifically knew that a particular customer intended to use the items with drugs. "It is sufficient that the defendant be aware that customers in general are likely to use the merchandise with drugs," Blackmun wrote.

In a separate opinion Scalia, joined by Kennedy and Thomas, also said the law could apply to the sale of an otherwise innocent item, such as a razor blade or paper clip, if the defendant knew it was to be used with drugs.

Ratzlaf v. United States, decided by a 5-4 vote, January 11, 1994; Ginsburg wrote the opinion; Blackmun, Rehnquist, O'Connor, and Thomas dissented.

The Court made it harder for the government to prosecute individuals who keep their cash transactions with banks under $10,000 in order to avoid federal currency reporting requirements. The ruling weakened the 1986 Money Laundering Act, which Congress passed to help the government detect proceeds from drug trafficking, gambling, or other lucrative criminal activities.

In a closely divided decision the Court said the government must prove that the defendant knew he was violating the law in structuring the transactions to stay under the threshold for the cash reporting requirement. Ginsburg said the law provided criminal penalties for any person "willfully violating" the section. She said the willfulness requirement could not be met without proof of "the defendant's knowledge of the illegality of the structuring."

The ruling ordered a new trial for an Oregon couple who obtained a number of cashier's checks, all just under $10,000, to get cash to pay off a $160,000 gambling debt to a Nevada casino. The couple were facing a tax audit and apparently wanted to keep their gambling from coming to the Internal Revenue Service's attention.

Dissenting justices argued that the decision conflicted with the "fundamental principle" that ignorance of the law does not excuse a crime. Ginsburg responded: "In particular contexts, however, Congress may decree otherwise."

Staples v. United States, decided by a 7-2 vote, May 23, 1994; Thomas wrote the opinion; Stevens and Blackmun dissented.

The Court somewhat tightened the government's burden of proof under the federal law prohibiting possession of unregistered machine guns.

The 7-2 ruling overturned the conviction of a man for owning an unregistered semiautomatic rifle that had been modified to fire automatically. The government argued the weapon fell under the National Firearms Act's definition of a machine gun. The defendant said he had not known that the rifle had been modified.

Writing for a five-justice majority, Thomas agreed that the law required the government to prove that the defendant "knew the weapon he possessed had the characteristics that brought it within the statutory definition of a machinegun."

Thomas noted that the country has a "long tradition of private ownership of guns." He concluded, ". . . [I]f Congress had intended to make outlaws of gun owners who were wholly ignorant of the offending characteristics of their weapons, and to subject them to lengthy prison terms, it would have spoken more clearly to that effect." Ginsburg, joined by O'Connor, concurred on narrower grounds.

The dissenting justices said the majority had misread the law. ". . . Congress did not intend to require knowledge of all the facts that constitute the offense of possession of an unregistered weapon," Stevens wrote.

Double Jeopardy

Montana Department of Revenue v. Kurth Ranch, decided by a 5-4 vote, June 6, 1994; Stevens wrote the opinion; Rehnquist, O'Connor, Scalia, and Thomas dissented.

The Court struck down a stiff state tax on illegal drugs, saying the measure was punitive and violated the constitutional prohibition against multiple punishments.

The ruling invalidated a 1987 Montana law that set a tax of $100 per ounce on marijuana and similarly high levies on other illegal drugs. Montana authorities used the law to try to collect $181,000 from six members of an extended family after they had been prosecuted for growing marijuana on a ranch in central Montana. Lower federal courts ruled the tax violated the Constitution's Double Jeopardy Clause.

In a narrowly divided decision, the Court agreed. The ruling marked the first time the Court had used the Double Jeopardy Clause—which prohibits successive criminal prosecutions—to strike down a tax.

Writing for the Court, Stevens said Montana's tax had "an unmistakable punitive character" because it was so high, was imposed only after a criminal proceeding, and was based on the value of property that the government presumably had already confiscated and destroyed. "Taken as a whole, this drug tax is a concoction of anomalies, too far-removed in crucial respects from a standard tax assessment to escape characterization as punishment for the purpose of Double Jeopardy analysis," he wrote.

The four dissenting justices took different approaches. Rehnquist disagreed that the tax amounted to a punishment and criticized the majority opinion as "a hodgepodge of criteria." O'Connor said she would have returned the case to lower courts to give Montana a chance to justify the size of the tax. She also warned the ruling could jeopardize similar drug tax laws in twenty-two other states.

Separately, Scalia, joined by Thomas, called for reconsidering the 1989 ruling that first used the Double Jeopardy Clause to limit punitive civil fines imposed after criminal prosecutions.

Evidence

Williamson v. United States, decided by 9-0 and 6-3 votes, June 27, 1994; O'Connor wrote the opinion; Kennedy, Rehnquist, and Thomas concurred in the judgment but disagreed with the ruling on the legal issue.

The Court limited prosecutors' ability to introduce out-of-court statements made by an accomplice who does not testify in person at the defendant's trial.

The ruling reopened the federal cocaine trafficking conviction of a Florida man, Fredel Williamson. The conviction was based in part on a statement by a purported accomplice, Reginald Harris. When Harris refused to testify at Williamson's trial, prosecutors were allowed to introduce Harris's statement despite the general rule against using hearsay evidence. The Federal Rules of Evidence contain an exception to the hearsay rule for self-incriminating statements.

Writing for a six-justice majority, O'Connor said that provision allows prosecutors to introduce statements in which an accomplice directly implicates himself or herself. But she said the government normally cannot introduce "collateral statements" that are either neutral in effect or shift the blame to someone else.

Three of the justices—Kennedy, Rehnquist, and Thomas—called for a narrower restriction on the use of accomplices' statements. Kennedy said the Court's ruling contradicted past interpretations of the hearsay exception in state and federal courts.

The decision returned the case to the federal appeals court in Atlanta to rule on what parts of Harris's statement could be introduced. Four of the justices in the majority—Ginsburg, Blackmun, Stevens, and Souter— said they believed Harris's confession should be excluded in its entirety. O'Connor and Scalia said the appeals court should decide first.

Forfeiture

United States v. James Daniel Good Real Property, decided by a 5-4 vote, December 13, 1993; Kennedy wrote the opinion; Rehnquist, O'Connor, Scalia, and Thomas dissented.

The Court made it harder for law enforcement officers to use strengthened forfeiture laws to seize property from drug traffickers or other suspected criminals.

In a closely divided decision the Court ruled that a property owner is ordinarily entitled to notice and a hearing before the government can seize real estate through civil forfeiture.

The ruling favored James Daniel Good, a Hawaii man whose house and four-acre parcel of land were seized by the government in 1989—four years after he had pleaded guilty in state court to growing marijuana on the site. The Ninth U.S. Circuit Court of Appeals agreed with his argument that due process required notice and hearing before the seizure.

The Court agreed with the appellate ruling on the due process issue after applying a three-part analysis from an earlier case that examines the property owner's interests, the risk of an erroneous property seizure, and the government's interest.

Kennedy said that Good's "right to maintain control over his home" was "a private interest of historic and continuing importance." He also said seizure of property without a prior hearing "creates an unacceptable risk of error," especially in forfeiture cases where the government "has a direct pecuniary interest in the outcome of the proceeding."

As to the government's interest, Kennedy said there was "no pressing need" for an expedited seizure of property since real estate "cannot abscond," and the government could take other steps to make sure the property was not sold or destroyed.

The government could seize property without a hearing, Kennedy added, if it showed that "less restrictive measures" would not prevent "the sale, destruction, or continued unlawful use of the property." The government had made no showing of such "exigent circumstances" in Good's case.

The ruling came less than six months after the Court's decision from the 1992-1993 term holding that the Eighth Amendment's Cruel and Unusual Punishment Clause limits the government's power to seize property in forfeiture proceedings.

In a broadly written dissenting opinion Rehnquist called the new decision "ill-considered and disruptive" and said it conflicted with prior cases that upheld summary proceedings in civil forfeitures. Scalia joined Rehnquist's dissent in full; O'Connor agreed with most of it. In a separate dissent Thomas rejected Good's claim but said he "sympathize[d] with the impulses motivating the Court's decision."

The Court backed the government in a secondary issue in the case, however. It ruled unanimously that lower courts cannot dismiss a forfeiture action because of delays in initiating the proceeding as long as it was filed within the five-year statute of limitations.

Habeas Corpus

Caspari, Superintendent, Missouri Eastern Correctional Center v. Bohlen, decided by an 8-1 vote, February 23, 1994; O'Connor wrote the opinion; Stevens dissented.

The Court denied habeas corpus relief to a Missouri inmate who claimed the Double Jeopardy Clause prevented prosecutors from having a second chance to enhance his sentence under the state's persistent offender statute.

Without deciding the merits of the inmate's claim, the Court held he was not entitled to rely on a "new rule" of law to win habeas corpus relief. O'Connor said that at the time of the inmate's conviction, courts had not applied the Double Jeopardy Clause to sentence proceedings in noncapital cases. On that basis, she applied a ruling by the Court in 1989 that generally bars retroactive use of new constitutional rulings in habeas corpus cases.

Insanity

Shannon v. United States, decided by a 7-2 vote, June 24, 1994; Thomas wrote the opinion; Stevens and Blackmun dissented.

Federal judges are not required to tell jurors that a defendant found not guilty by reason of insanity may be committed to a mental hospital after a further hearing.

By a 7-2 vote the Court refused to impose the requirement under the Insanity Defense Reform Act. The 1984 law recognized a "not guilty by reason of insanity" verdict in federal court and required a civil commitment hearing for defendants acquitted under an insanity plea. A Mississippi man sought to overturn his firearms conviction because the jury that rejected his insanity plea was not told about the involuntary commitment procedure.

In his opinion for the Court Thomas cited the "well established" principle that juries "are not to consider the consequences of their verdicts."

In a dissent Stevens, joined by Blackmun, noted that Congress modeled the 1984 law on procedures in the federal courts in the District of Columbia, which since 1957 had given juries instructions about the consequences of an insanity verdict. But Thomas said that an isolated passage in legislative history endorsing the D.C. procedures was "not entitled to authoritative weight."

Interrogation

Davis v. United States, decided by 9-0 and 5-4 votes, June 24, 1994; O'Connor wrote the opinion; Souter, Blackmun, Stevens, and Ginsburg concurred in the judgment but disagreed with the legal ruling.

Police do not need to stop questioning a suspect who makes an ambiguous statement about wanting an attorney or try to clarify the suspect's wishes about having legal help.

The ruling rejected an effort by a sailor convicted of murder in a pool hall shooting to widen the *Miranda* rule on police interrogation. The sailor told navy investigators at one point, "Maybe I should talk to a lawyer." When the agents asked if he was asking for a lawyer, however, the sailor said he was not. The sailor's statement was used in his court martial trial.

Writing for a five-justice majority, O'Connor said police need not stop questioning unless a suspect makes "an unambiguous or unequivocal request for counsel." She also refused to require police to ask clarifying questions if a suspect makes an ambiguous statement, but she said that procedure "may often be good police practice."

Souter, joined by Blackmun, Stevens, and Ginsburg, argued that police should be required to clarify any statement by a suspect "that could reasonably be understood to express a desire to consult a lawyer." Since the navy investigators did so, they voted to uphold the conviction.

Stansbury v. California, decided by a 9-0 vote, April 26, 1994; *per curiam* (unsigned) opinion.

A California man convicted of the rape-murder of a young girl was given a second chance to win a new trial because police failed to give him *Miranda* warnings at the start of interrogation.

The Court said the California Supreme Court applied the wrong standard in upholding use of a statement the defendant gave to police while being questioned about the 1982 slaying.

The California court ruled that no *Miranda* warnings were required because police initially considered the defendant to be a witness, not a suspect. But the Court said that objective circumstances, not a police officer's subjective belief, determine whether an individual is in custody and must be given *Miranda* warnings. The ruling returned the case to the California court for a decision under that standard.

United States v. Alvarez-Sanchez, decided by a 9-0 vote, May 2, 1994; Thomas wrote the opinion.

A suspect who confesses to a federal crime while in state custody cannot use a federal law governing the time of the initial hearing before a magistrate to block the use of the confession.

The decision reinstated the federal counterfeiting conviction of a California man who admitted possession of bogus currency while in jail three days after his arrest by Los Angeles police on drug charges. The Ninth U.S. Circuit Court of Appeals ruled the confession inadmissible.

A federal law provides that a confession is not inadmissible because of delay in bringing a suspect before a magistrate if the hearing takes place within six hours of the arrest. The appeals court interpreted that provision to permit suppression of a statement if a six-hour deadline is not met. Some courts, however, ruled the law did not set a deadline but merely safeguarded the use of voluntary confessions obtained within the six-hour period.

In its ruling the Court did not resolve the issue. Instead, Thomas said the federal law does not apply to a person who is being held solely on state charges. "Plainly, a duty to present a person to a federal magistrate does not arise until the person has been arrested for a *federal* offense," Thomas wrote.

Juries

Victor v. Nebraska, decided by 9-0 and 7-2 votes, March 22, 1994; O'Connor wrote the opinion; Blackmun and Souter dissented in part.

The Court criticized but refused to prohibit jury instructions used in many states to define the prosecution's burden to prove a criminal defendant guilty beyond a reasonable doubt.

The ruling rejected separate challenges to jury instructions in California and Nebraska brought by defendants who had each been convicted of first-degree murder and sentenced to death. The California instruction told jurors they must be convinced of a defendant's guilt "to a moral certainty"—a phrase used in fifteen other states. The Nebraska instruction also at one point equated "reasonable doubt" with "actual or substantial doubt."

Writing for the Court, O'Connor said that "taken as a whole" both instructions "correctly conveyed the concept of reasonable doubt" and that there was "no reasonable likelihood" the jurors misunderstood the prosecution's burden of proof. Nonetheless, O'Connor said the Court "does not condone" the instructions and criticized the language as confusing—as did Kennedy and Ginsburg in separate opinions.

The vote in the California case *(Sandoval v. California)* was unanimous, but Blackmun, joined by Souter, voted to find the Nebraska instruction unconstitutional.

Prisons and Jails

Farmer v. Brennan, Warden, decided by a 9-0 vote, June 6, 1994; Souter wrote the opinion.

Prison officials may be held liable for injuries to an inmate only if they know the prisoner faces a substantial risk of harm and fail to take reasonable measures to prevent it.

The ruling set a strict standard for prisoners to meet in civil rights suits brought under the Court's 1991 decision *Wilson v. Seiter.* That ruling allowed prison authorities to be held liable for "deliberate indifference" to an inmate's health or safety. The Court had to define that standard in a suit brought by a male transsexual who was raped after being placed in the general population of a high-security penitentiary. Lower federal courts dismissed the suit because the inmate had not complained about the transfer.

Writing for the Court, Souter adopted what he termed a "subjective recklessness" standard. "A person must consciously disregard a substantial risk of serious harm," Souter explained. He rejected the inmate's argument that officials be held liable for failing to notice an obvious risk. But Souter said circumstantial evidence could be used to prove prison officials knew of safety risks.

The ruling reinstated the suit to allow lower courts to consider whether they used too strict a standard in their earlier rulings. Blackmun and Stevens concurred in the opinion but repeated criticisms of the "deliberate indifference" standard. At the same time Blackmun said the ruling "sends a clear message to prison officials that their affirmative duty under the Constitution to provide for the safety of inmates is not to be taken lightly."

In a separate concurrence Thomas approved what he called the Court's "restrictive definition of deliberate indifference." But he refused to join Souter's opinion, citing his previous view that the Eighth Amendment does not provide a basis for inmate suits over prison conditions.

Sentencing

Beecham v. United States, decided by a 9-0 vote, May 16, 1994; O'Connor wrote the opinion.

A state's decision to restore the civil rights of a convicted felon does not wipe out a prior federal conviction for purposes of the federal law prohibiting possession of firearms by felons.

The brief, unanimous ruling rejected pleas by two felons convicted of federal offenses under the federal firearms law even though their home states had restored their citizenship. Federal appeals courts had disagreed on the issue.

Writing for the Court, O'Connor said the statute provides that the status of a conviction is to be determined "in accordance with the law of the jurisdiction in which the proceedings were held." On that basis, she said, a state's decision to restore citizenship has no effect on the status of a prior federal conviction.

O'Connor acknowledged that Congress has not established a procedure for restoring civil rights to a federal felon. But she said the Court was not ruling on the "complicated question" of whether a federal felon has any means of regaining his civil rights.

Custis v. United States, decided by a 6-3 vote, May 23, 1994; Rehnquist wrote the opinion; Souter, Blackmun, and Stevens dissented.

The Court sharply limited defendants' ability to challenge the constitutionality of prior conviction used to impose stiffer prison sentences under a federal law on armed "career criminals."

The Court ruled that a defendant being sentenced under provisions of the Armed Career Criminal Act of 1984 cannot, with one exception, contest the validity of earlier state court convictions used to lengthen the defendant's new prison term. The only exception, the Court said, is in cases where the defendant had been denied the right to counsel.

The issue was raised by a Maryland man convicted of cocaine possession and possession of a firearm by a felon. Under the career criminal law he was sentenced to twenty years instead of thirteen years because of three prior convictions. Before sentencing, he argued that two of the convictions were constitutionally defective, but lower federal courts refused to consider the claim.

Writing for the Court, Rehnquist said the career criminal law does not provide for defendants to challenge prior convictions, and the Constitution does not require federal courts to hear such claims before sentencing. Allowing defendants to attack earlier convictions, Rehnquist warned, would pose administrative problems and undermine the "interest in promoting finality of judgments."

In explaining the limited exception, Rehnquist said that the Court had historically treated failure to provide counsel as "a unique constitutional defect."

Souter, in a dissent joined by Blackmun and Stevens, argued that the 1984 law did not bar courts from considering the constitutionality of prior convictions. Earlier Court rulings had indicated a broad prohibition against use of defective convictions to enhance sentences, he said. He also contended that the decision actually would add to courts' workloads because defendants could still contest prior convictions in separate habeas corpus proceedings.

Nichols v. United States, decided by a 6-3 vote, June 6, 1994; Rehnquist wrote the opinion; Blackmun, Stevens, and Ginsburg dissented.

Judges can use a defendant's prior misdemeanor conviction to lengthen a new prison sentence even if the defendant had no lawyer in the earlier case.

The ruling overturned a splintered decision in a 1980 case, *Baldasar v. Illinois.* In that case the Court held that the Sixth Amendment's right to counsel prevented the use of an uncounseled misdemeanor conviction to convert a later misdemeanor into a felony. Citing *Baldasar,* a Tennessee man tried to prevent the use of a 1983 drunken driving conviction from raising his new sentence on felony drug charges to 235 months from 210 months.

Writing for a five-justice majority, Rehnquist said the *Baldasar* ruling had caused great confusion in lower courts and should be overturned. He said that judges traditionally have considered "a wide variety of factors" in sentencing, including "a defendant's prior convictions."

Concurring separately, Souter skirted the constitutional issue. Instead, he called for interpreting the federal sentencing guidelines to permit but not require judges to consider a prior uncounseled misdemeanor conviction in setting a defendant's new sentence.

Writing for the three dissenters, Blackmun said that misdemeanor convictions without legal representation "lack the reliability this Court has always considered a prerequisite for the imposition of any term of incarceration."

United States v. Granderson, decided by a 7-2 vote, March 22, 1994; Ginsburg wrote the opinion; Scalia and Kennedy concurred in the judgment; Rehnquist and Thomas dissented.

The Court eased the impact of a law requiring a prison term for any defendant found in possession of drugs while on probation.

The drug possession provision—part of the 1988 Anti-Drug Act—requires a judge to revoke a defendant's probation and "sentence the defendant to not less than one-third of the original sentence." Some federal appeals courts interpreted the law to mean a prison term equal to one-third of the length of the probation. Others read it to require imprisonment for one-third of the possible sentence for the defendant's crime.

Writing for a five-justice majority, Ginsburg said that tying the new sentence to a typically longer probation term would be too severe. The provision, she explained, calls for a minimum sentence of one-third of the maximum term that the defendant could have received originally.

All nine justices criticized the provision—which was added to the drug law in the early morning hours of the last day of the 1988 congressional session—as poorly written. Scalia called the provision "wretchedly drafted." Ginsburg acknowledged difficulty in interpreting the amendment but called her interpretation "securely plausible."

Rehnquist, in a dissent joined by Thomas, argued for basing the new sentence on the length of the probation—as the government had urged in the case. In a third interpretation of the law, Kennedy and Scalia said the defendant should not be imprisoned but should be given a new probation equal to one-third of the original term. They concurred in the judgment only because the defendant had already served eleven months in prison, longer than he would have been given under the majority's approach or under theirs.

Speedy Trial

Reed v. Farley, Superintendent, Indiana State Prison, decided by a 5-4 vote, June 20, 1994; Ginsburg wrote a plurality opinion; Blackmun, Stevens, Kennedy, and Souter dissented.

The Court barred federal habeas corpus relief to an Indiana prison inmate who was brought to trial after the deadline set by an interstate agreement for handling prisoners from other states.

The splintered ruling involved a provision in the Interstate Agreement on Detainers (IAD) that required an inmate transferred from one state for prosecution in another state to be brought to trial within 120 days. The compact provides for dismissal of the charge if the deadline is not met.

An Indiana inmate serving a long prison term asked a federal court to set aside his 1983 conviction and sentence because the trial did not start within 120 days of his transfer from a federal penitentiary. But a federal appeals court said habeas corpus could not be used to enforce the provisions of the detainer agreement.

The five-justice majority split into two camps in rejecting the inmate's plea. In a plurality opinion Ginsburg stressed the inmate's failure to object to the delay at the time. Habeas corpus was not available, Ginsburg wrote, "when the defendant registered no objection to the trial date at the time it was set, and suffered no prejudice attributable to the delayed commencement." Rehnquist and O'Connor joined in the opinion.

In a broader concurring opinion Scalia, joined by Thomas, said he would bar habeas corpus relief for violation of the agreement's deadline under any circumstances. "If there was ever a technical rule," Scalia wrote, "the IAD's 120-day rule is one."

Writing for the dissenters, Blackmun said the interstate compact— approved by Congress—should be enforced through federal habeas corpus. ". . . [T]he congressional imposition of the drastic sanction of dismissal forecloses any argument that a violation of the IAD time limits is somehow a mere 'technical' violation too trivial to warrant habeas review," Blackmun wrote.

Election Law

Reapportionment and Redistricting

Johnson, Speaker of the Florida House of Representatives v. De Grandy, decided by a 7-2 vote, June 30, 1994; Souter wrote the opinion; Thomas and Scalia dissented.

The federal Voting Rights Act does not require legislative districting plans to maximize the number of districts in which minority groups are in the majority.

Instead, the Court ruled, state legislatures usually can satisfy the Voting Rights Act if minority voters form "effective voting majorities in a number of districts roughly proportional to the minority voters' respective shares in the voting-age population."

The decision left in place a redistricting plan for the Florida legislature. Hispanics challenged the plan, which gave Hispanics majorities in nine out of twenty House districts in the Miami-Dade County area and three out of seven Senate districts. A three-judge federal court found the plan violated the Voting Rights Act and ordered the House plan drawn to create eleven majority-Hispanic districts. But the court left the Senate plan standing, saying that another majority-Hispanic district could not be created without reducing the number of majority-black seats.

In an opinion for the Court, Souter criticized the lower court for using a "maximization principle" to require lawmakers to draw the largest possible number of majority-minority districts. Lower courts must consider the "totality of the circumstances" in deciding whether a redistricting plan complies with the Voting Rights Act, Souter said. Proportional representation, he explained, was "an indication" but "no guarantee" that minority voters have equal political opportunities as required by the law.

Five justices joined all of Souter's opinion, and Kennedy joined most of it. Writing separately, Kennedy said that race-based districting could violate the Equal Protection Clause but acknowledged that the plaintiffs had not raised any constitutional issues.

Thomas, joined by Scalia, filed what was technically a dissenting opinion even though he and Scalia agreed that the redistricting plan should not be disturbed. Citing his opinion in another case released the same day, *Holder v. Hall*, Thomas said redistricting plans should not be subject to challenge under the Voting Rights Act. The lower court should have been ordered to dismiss the original suit on that basis, he added. *(See entry, p. 31; excerpts, p. 219.)*

Voting Rights Act

Holder v. Hall, decided by a 5-4 vote, June 30, 1994; Kennedy wrote a plurality opinion; Blackmun, Stevens, Souter, and Ginsburg dissented.

The size of a governing body—in this case a single county commissioner with executive and legislative authority—is not subject to challenge under the federal Voting Rights Act.

The splintered decision barred a statutory challenge to the unusual governmental structure used in rural Bleckley County, Georgia. Blacks, who made up about 20 percent of the county's population, claimed the single-member commission violated the Voting Rights Act by "diluting" their opportunity to elect blacks to office.

Writing for three justices, Kennedy rejected the claim by saying there was "no objective and workable standard" to use in deciding how many members the county commission should have. Rehnquist joined Kennedy's opinion in full; O'Connor joined that part of the opinion.

Thomas wrote a massive, fifty-nine-page concurring opinion that more broadly attacked the use of the Voting Rights Act in any legislative districting case. He said use of the law to encourage "racially designated districts" had been a "disastrous adventure in judicial policymaking." Scalia joined Thomas's opinion.

Writing for the four dissenters, Blackmun said courts could use the prevailing pattern of five-member county commissions in Georgia as "an objectively reasonable alternative practice" to judge the county's single-member commission. Separately, Stevens, joined by the other dissenters, answered Thomas by saying his views "should be addressed to Congress, which has ample power to amend the statute." *(See entry, p. 34; excerpts, p. 232.)*

Environmental Law

Hazardous Waste

City of Chicago v. Environmental Defense Fund, decided by a 7-2 vote, May 2, 1994; Scalia wrote the opinion; Stevens and O'Connor dissented.

Federal law does not exempt the ash produced by municipal incinerators from the costly regulations that govern disposal of hazardous waste.

The decision literally interpreted a 1984 amendment to the federal Resource Conservation and Recovery Act, which gives the Environmental Protection Agency (EPA) broad powers to regulate generation, transportation, storage, and disposal of hazardous waste. Municipalities contended that incinerators, which burn trash and produce energy in the process, were exempt from the regulations under the 1984 amendment and an earlier EPA regulation.

A federal appeals court in New York agreed with the municipalities. But the Seventh U.S. Circuit Court of Appeals, ruling in an environmentalist organization's suit against a waste-to-energy plant operated by the city of Chicago, held that the so-called municipal waste combustion ash was not exempt from hazardous waste regulation.

Ruling in the Chicago case, the Court agreed. Scalia said that the 1984 amendment exempts incinerators from hazardous waste regulations but not the incinerator residue. "The provision quite clearly does *not* contain any exclusion for the *ash itself,*" Scalia wrote.

The EPA had sided with the municipalities. The dissenting justices argued that the EPA's reading of the law was "a correct and permissible interpretation of the Agency's broad congressional mandate."

Key Tronic Corp. v. United States, decided by a 6-3 vote, June 6, 1994; Stevens wrote the opinion; Scalia, Blackmun, and Thomas dissented.

Private parties cannot recover attorneys' fees for legal proceedings under the federal Superfund law to force others to share the costs of cleaning up toxic waste sites.

The ruling settled a conflict between lower federal courts over how to interpret provisions of the Comprehensive Environmental Response, Compensation, and Liability Act, first passed in 1980 and amended in 1986. The law seeks to spread the cost of toxic waste cleanups by permitting one party—typically, the property owner—to sue polluters for "any . . . necessary costs of response" incurred in cleaning up the site.

In a 6-3 decision the Court ruled the law does not authorize recovery of legal fees related to litigation or negotiation over cleanup liability. Stevens noted that attorneys' fees generally are not awarded without explicit statutory authorization. The cost-recovery provisions of the Superfund law, he said, did not specifically cover legal fees. But the Court did allow recovery for fees paid to lawyers or other experts for identifying other parties responsible for cleanup costs.

In a dissent Scalia, joined by Blackmun and Thomas, argued that the law's "plain language" permits private parties to recover the costs of "enforcement activities." "Obviously, attorney's fees will constitute the major portion of those enforcement costs," Scalia wrote.

Solid Waste

C & A Carbone, Inc. v. Town of Clarkstown, decided by a 6-3 vote, May 16, 1994; Kennedy wrote the opinion; Souter, Rehnquist, and Blackmun dissented.

The Court barred local governments from passing laws requiring all trash generated within their borders to be processed at a designated waste-treatment facility.

The ruling, which came in a case involving a small town north of New York City, was important to the growing private waste-treatment industry on one side and municipalities and municipal bond markets on the other. The town passed the so-called flow control law to ensure an adequate supply of waste for a new waste-treatment plant that was to be privately operated for five years and then turned over to the town.

Writing for a five-justice majority, Kennedy said that the flow control law violated the Constitution because it "allows only the favored operator to process waste that is within the limits of the town." He argued the ruling was in line with "well-settled principles of our Commerce Clause jurisprudence" and cited decisions dating as far back as 1890 striking down local or state laws giving local industries advantages over out-of-state businesses.

O'Connor, concurring separately, called the law unconstitutional because the burden it imposed on interstate commerce outweighed the benefits to the municipality. But she said Congress could use its power over interstate commerce to authorize local flow control laws if it wanted.

Souter, in a dissent joined by Rehnquist and Blackmun, argued the law should have been upheld because it "directly aids the government in satisfying a traditional governmental responsibility."

Oregon Waste Systems, Inc. v. Department of Environmental Quality, decided by a 7-2 vote, April 4, 1994; Thomas wrote the opinion; Rehnquist and Blackmun dissented.

A surcharge imposed by the state of Oregon for disposing of out-of-state solid waste was struck down as an unconstitutional discrimination against interstate commerce.

Oregon imposed the $2.25 per ton surcharge on out-of-state waste in 1991, while setting the fee for handling in-state waste at $.85 per ton. Two waste-treatment companies that shipped garbage into Oregon from other states challenged the surcharge.

The Supreme Court in 1992 struck down an Alabama surcharge on out-of-state hazardous waste. Oregon officials tried to get around that decision by saying the state's levy was designed to make shippers of out-of-state garbage pay their "fair share" of the costs of disposing of waste in Oregon landfills. But the Court rejected the argument.

The Oregon levy "patently discriminates against interstate commerce," Thomas wrote for the Court. He said the state had not shown that out-of-state garbage costs more to dispose of than in-state waste.

In a dissent Rehnquist, joined by Blackmun, said the ruling "ties the hands of the States in addressing the vexing national problem of solid waste disposal."

Water

PUD No. 1 of Jefferson County v. Washington Department of Ecology, decided by a 7-2 vote, May 31, 1994; O'Connor wrote the opinion; Thomas and Scalia dissented.

States can set stricter environmental standards, including minimum water flow requirements, for hydroelectric projects than those imposed by federal law.

The 7-2 decision upheld efforts by Washington State to limit the diversion of water by a planned dam on a river in the Olympic National Forest in order to protect fish habitats. A local public utility district and the city of Tacoma argued that the federal Clean Water Act did not give states authority to regulate the quantity of water in rivers and streams.

Writing for the Court, O'Connor said the 1972 law authorizes states to set standards for water quality and water quantity, which in many cases are closely related. "... [A] sufficient lowering of the water quantity in a body of water could destroy all of its designated uses, be it for drinking water, recreation, navigation, or, as here, as a fishery."

In a dissent Thomas, joined by Scalia, agreed with the utility district's argument that the law only allowed states to regulate "discharges." He said the ruling would give states an effective veto over hydroelectric projects.

Federal Government

Federal Regulation

MCI Telecommunications Corp. v. American Telephone & Telegraph Co., decided by a 5-3 vote, June 17, 1994; Scalia wrote the opinion; Stevens, Blackmun, and Souter dissented; O'Connor did not participate.

The Federal Communications Commission (FCC) exceeded its statutory authority in exempting AT&T's long-distance competitors from filing tariffs of rates and services.

The ruling overturned the "permissive detariffing" policies that the FCC began adopting in the early 1980s to enhance competition in long-distance telephone service. The FCC said rate-filing requirements hindered the ability of MCI Telecommunications Corp. and other new long-distance carriers to compete with AT&T. But the agency kept the requirements in place for AT&T.

In a 5-3 decision the Court agreed with AT&T that the detariffing policies went beyond the FCC's authority under the Communications Act of 1934 to "modify" rate-filing requirements. Scalia said the policies— "much too extensive to be considered a 'modification' "—amounted to "a fundamental revision of the statute."

Writing for the three dissenters, Blackmun accused the majority of adopting "a rigid literalism that deprives the FCC of the flexibility Congress meant it to have in order to implement the core policies of the Act in rapidly changing conditions."

Security Services, Inc. v. Kmart Corp., decided by a 7-2 vote, May 16, 1994; Souter wrote the opinion; Thomas and Ginsburg dissented.

The Court limited the ability of bankrupt motor carriers to use defective rate filings with the Interstate Commerce Commission (ICC) to collect higher-than-agreed charges from shippers.

The 7-2 decision narrowed an earlier ruling—*Maislin Industries, U.S., Inc. v. Primary Steel* (1990)—that allowed a bankrupt motor carrier to collect its "filed rate" from shippers even if they negotiated a lower rate. As a result of trucking deregulation, many carriers did offer lower rates during the 1980s. Some went bankrupt, however, and then tried to collect "undercharges" from the shippers by insisting on the rates filed with the ICC.

In the dispute before the Court, the ICC ruled that rates filed by one shipper were void because the company had failed to pay a required fee to an industry bureau that establishes standard mileage between cities. On that basis the agency refused to allow the company to collect undercharges from the shipper. The Court agreed.

Writing for the Court, Souter said the company's failure to pay the fee was not a "technical defect." Bankrupt truckers "may rely on the filed rate doctrine to collect for undercharges," Souter wrote, "but they may not collect for undercharges based on filed, but void, rates."

In separate dissents Thomas and Ginsburg argued the decision would allow the ICC to evade the Court's previous ruling.

Thomas Jefferson University dba Thomas Jefferson Hospital v. Shalala, Secretary of Health and Human Services, decided by a 5-4 vote, June 24, 1994; Kennedy wrote the opinion; Thomas, Stevens, O'Connor, and Ginsburg dissented.

Teaching hospitals are not entitled to reimbursement from Medicare for the administrative costs of training medical interns and residents.

The 5-4 ruling upheld the interpretation by the Department of Health and Human Services (HHS) of a regulation regarding reimbursement of university-affiliated hospitals for treating elderly patients under the federal Medicare program.

The regulation—known as the "anti-redistribution principle"—says "it is not intended" that Medicare pay "increased costs resulting from redistribution of costs from educational institutions ... to patient care institutions."

HHS invoked the regulation in 1985 to deny a request by Thomas Jefferson Hospital in Philadelphia for a $2.8 million reimbursement for administrative costs of so-called graduate medical education services. In an opinion by Kennedy, the Court upheld HHS's position, saying it was "faithful to the regulation's plain language."

Dissenting justices argued the regulation had no substantive effect because it was "cast in vague aspirational terms."

Freedom of Information

United States Department of Defense v. Federal Labor Relations Authority, decided by a 9-0 vote, February 23, 1994; Thomas wrote the opinion.

Federal agencies may not disclose workers' home addresses to public employee unions.

In a unanimous ruling the Court said that the federal Privacy Act prohibits agencies from providing the workers' addresses unless required to do so by other federal law. The Court said that disclosure was not required by the federal employee labor-management relations law or by the Freedom of Information Act (FOIA), which itself contains privacy exemptions.

The decision overturned the policy of the Federal Labor Relations Authority, which had been upheld by most courts to rule on the issue. The case before the Supreme Court involved two unions that represented civilian employees of military base exchanges in Mississippi and Texas. The unions wanted to obtain the addresses of workers who did not belong to the unions.

Writing for the Court, Thomas said the workers' privacy interest in preventing communications from the union at their homes was "far from insubstantial." He said the FOIA did not override that interest because disclosure would not further the act's "core purpose . . . of contributing significantly to public understanding of the operations or activities of government."

In separate opinions Souter, who joined Thomas's opinion, and Ginsburg, who did not, both stressed that Congress could revise the federal labor statute to guarantee unions access to federal workers' home addresses. Although Ginsburg voiced doubts about the majority's view of the "core purpose" of the Freedom of Information Act, she deferred to "the position solidly approved by my colleagues."

Military

Dalton, Secretary of the Navy v. Specter, decided by a 9-0 vote, May 23, 1994; Rehnquist wrote the opinion.

Courts cannot review decisions to close defense bases under a 1990 law aimed at making it easier to close unneeded military and naval facilities.

The Court unanimously held that the Defense Base Closure and Realignment Act of 1990 bars judicial review. Under the law a special commission recommended bases for closure and submitted its recommendations to the president, who had to accept or reject the package as a whole. If the president agreed, Congress could disapprove, but again only by rejecting the whole package.

The law was designed to reduce political maneuvering over the issue, but several members of Congress from Pennsylvania filed suit seeking to prevent the recommended closure of the Philadelphia Naval Shipyard. They alleged that the Pentagon and the commission had violated several substantive and administrative requirements. Republican senator Arlen Specter personally argued the case before the Court—the first time a member of Congress had done so since 1972.

Writing for the Court, Rehnquist said the suit had to be dismissed because the law gave the president power to make the decision but did not provide for judicial review of his action. "Where a statute . . . commits decisionmaking to the discretion of the President judicial review of the President's decision is not available," Rehnquist wrote in part of the opinion joined by all nine justices.

Rehnquist also said the base closure decisions could not be reviewed under the Administrative Procedure Act, which permits court review of "final decisions" by federal agencies. He said the commission's recommendations could not be reviewed because they were not final, and the president's action could not be contested because he was not an "agency." Four justices—O'Connor, Scalia, Kennedy, and Thomas—joined that part of the opinion.

Souter, joined by Blackmun, Stevens, and Ginsburg, concurred separately in an opinion that rejected judicial review under the base closure law but did not address the administrative law issue. Blackmun also wrote a separate opinion, saying that courts could entertain suits on some issues, such as requiring the commission to comply with open meeting laws.

Weiss v. United States, decided by a 9-0 vote, January 19, 1994; Rehnquist wrote the opinion.

The Court unanimously rejected a constitutional challenge to the method of appointing military judges. It refused to require that officers be given a separate presidential appointment before serving as military judges or that military judges be given a fixed term of office.

Under existing procedures, any commissioned military officer who was also a lawyer could be appointed to serve as a military judge by the military Judge Advocate General of his or her branch of service. Two Marines who had been forced out of the service after court-martial convictions argued that the method of appointment for military judges violated the constitutional requirement that "Officers of the United States" be nominated by the president and confirmed by the Senate. The former servicemen also contended that military judges' lack of tenure protection violated their rights to due process.

Writing for the Court, Rehnquist said that all commissioned officers are already subject to presidential appointment and Senate confirmation and that they need no additional appointment to exercise judicial duties. As to due process, Rehnquist said military judges do not need a fixed term of office to ensure independence or impartiality.

Ginsburg wrote a brief concurring opinion. The Court's careful handling of the case, she said, "demonstrates once again that men and women in the Armed Forces do not leave constitutional safeguards and judicial protection behind when they enter the military service."

Native Americans

Hagen v. Utah, decided by a 7-2 vote, February 23, 1994; O'Connor wrote the opinion; Blackmun and Souter dissented.

The Court upheld Utah state court jurisdiction over an area that had been located in the Uintah Indian Reservation but was opened to non-Indians in 1902. The ruling permitted Utah courts to try an Indian man arrested on drug charges in the area.

O'Connor said a 1902 act of Congress restoring parts of the reservation to the "public domain" had been intended to terminate reservation status. She noted that the population in the disputed area—located in northeastern Utah—was now 85 percent non-Indian.

Dissenting justices argued that the decision conflicted with previous rulings requiring more explicit evidence of congressional intent before finding that an Indian reservation had been diminished.

First Amendment

Cable Television

Turner Broadcasting System, Inc. v. Federal Communications Commission, decided by a 5-4 vote, June 27, 1994; Kennedy wrote the opinion; O'Connor, Scalia, Thomas, and Ginsburg dissented in part.

The Court extended to cable television First Amendment protections comparable to those enjoyed by print media. But it left unresolved a constitutional challenge to the 1992 law requiring cable systems to carry local broadcast stations.

A three-judge court had upheld the "must-carry" provision of the Cable Television Consumer Protection and Competition Act. By a 5-4 vote the Supreme Court ordered it to hear more evidence in the case. Broadcasters, who supported the law, and cable operators and programmers, who opposed it, both claimed victory.

Writing for the Court, Kennedy said cable television is not subject to the kind of regulations imposed on broadcasters because of the scarcity of radio and television channels. Seven justices, all except Stevens, joined that part of his opinion.

On the must-carry provision itself, however, Kennedy rejected the bulk of the cable industry's arguments. He said the law did not infringe the free speech rights of cable operators or cable programmers. He also said the government had a substantial interest in preventing cable systems from using their "bottleneck" power to disadvantage television broadcasters. Four justices—Rehnquist, Blackmun, Stevens, and Souter—joined that part of the ruling.

Kennedy concluded that the government had failed to show that local broadcasters were in economic jeopardy or that the must-carry provisions were narrowly tailored to address the problem. Rehnquist, Blackmun, and Souter concurred. Stevens said he voted with the group to provide a majority even though he favored upholding the law.

In a partial dissent O'Connor, joined by Scalia, Thomas, and Ginsburg, said that the law violated the First Amendment by infringing on cable operators' editorial discretion. *(See entry, p. 52; excerpts, p. 193.)*

Church and State

Board of Education of Kiryas Joel Village School District v. Grumet, decided by a 6-3 vote, June 27, 1994; Souter wrote the opinion; Scalia, Rehnquist, and Thomas dissented.

A New York law creating a special school district to serve disabled children of a Hasidic sect was struck down as an unconstitutional establishment of religion.

The law designated the village of Kiryas Joel, inhabited exclusively by members of the Satmar Hasidic sect, as a state school district. Villagers sent almost all of their children to religious schools, but those schools did not provide services for students with disabilities.

In the Court's main opinion Souter said that the law improperly created a "fusion of governmental and religious functions." Three justices—Blackmun, Stevens, and Ginsburg—joined that part of the opinion.

O'Connor provided a fifth vote for a narrower part of Souter's opinion that said there was no assurance New York would provide the same benefit "equally to other religious (and nonreligious) groups." In a separate opinion Kennedy also voted to strike down the law, calling it "religious gerrymandering."

In a lengthy and biting dissent Scalia, joined by Rehnquist and Thomas, called the law a proper accommodation of religion. He said the decision turned the Establishment Clause into "a repealer of our Nation's tradition of religious toleration." *(See entry, p. 49; excerpts, p. 168.)*

Commercial Speech

Ibanez v. Florida Department of Business and Professional Regulation, Board of Accountancy, decided by 9-0 and 7-2 votes, June 13, 1994; Ginsburg wrote the opinion; O'Connor and Rehnquist dissented in part.

States may not prohibit lawyers from truthfully advertising themselves as certified public accountants (CPAs) or certified financial planners.

Florida's Board of Accountancy reprimanded lawyer Silva Safille Ibanez for including the identifications on her business cards and stationery and in a telephone directory. The board claimed the advertising was deceptive because Ibanez was not practicing as an accountant and because her certification as financial planner came from a private group, not a state agency.

Writing for the Court, Ginsburg said the board "has not demonstrated with sufficient specificity that any member of the public could have been misled by Ibanez' constitutionally protected speech or that any harm could have resulted from allowing that speech to reach the public's eyes."

In a partial dissent O'Connor, joined by Rehnquist, said she would have upheld the reprimand because Ibanez's listing as financial planner was "inherently misleading." She agreed Ibanez could advertise herself as a CPA, but also said the board could discipline Ibanez if she violated regulatory rules for accountants.

Freedom of Speech

For two cases involving free speech rights of antiabortion protesters, see the Individual Rights section of this chapter.

City of Ladue v. Gilleo, decided by a 9-0 vote, June 13, 1994; Stevens wrote the opinion.

Cities may not completely prohibit residents from displaying signs on their property.

The unanimous ruling struck down a St. Louis suburb's ordinance aimed at minimizing "visual clutter" by prohibiting most signs on residential property. A community activist who had sought to post signs opposing the Persian Gulf War in 1990 in her yard and window challenged the ordinance as a violation of her free speech rights.

In a broadly worded decision Stevens said the ordinance "almost completely foreclosed a venerable means of communication that is both unique and important."

Waters v. Churchill, decided by a vote of 7-2, May 31, 1994; O'Connor wrote a plurality opinion; Stevens and Blackmun dissented.

A splintered Court gave public employees limited procedural rights against being fired for things they say.

The ruling prohibits a government employer from discharging a worker for something the worker said unless it has a "reasonable belief" that the comments were either disruptive or unrelated to matters of "public concern." The decision did not spell out procedures for employers to use, but three of the justices complained of what they called the "proposed right to an investigation before dismissal for speech."

A nurse fired by a public hospital in Macomb, Illinois, for criticizing management filed a federal civil rights suit. She claimed her comments qualified as "protected speech" because they involved hospital policies, but administrators said the remarks were disruptive. A federal trial judge ruled for the hospital, but the Seventh U.S. Circuit Court of Appeals said the nurse was entitled to a trial to determine exactly what was said.

In the Court's main opinion O'Connor faulted the appeals court's decision to require a full trial. She said it gave "insufficient weight to the government's interest in efficient employment decision making." Employers can use "personnel procedures that differ from the evidentiary rules used by courts," she wrote, and courts reviewing a firing need only "look to the facts as the employer *reasonably* found them to be." Rehnquist, Souter, and Ginsburg joined in O'Connor's opinion.

In a separate opinion Scalia, joined by Kennedy and Thomas, agreed the appeals court decision should be set aside. But Scalia criticized the plurality opinion for creating "a broad new First Amendment right" that was "unprecedented and unpredictable in its application and consequences."

In a dissent Stevens, joined by Blackmun, said the ruling gave inadequate protection to public employees' freedom of speech. "A proper regard for that principle," Stevens wrote, "requires that, before firing a public employee for her speech, management get its facts straight."

Individual Rights

Abortion

Madsen v. Women's Health Center, Inc., decided by a 6-3 vote, June 30, 1994; Rehnquist wrote the opinion; Scalia, Kennedy, and Thomas dissented.

Judges can establish "buffer zones" preventing antiabortion protesters from getting too close to clinics where abortions are performed, but they cannot restrict "more speech than necessary" to protect access to clinics or other government interests.

The ruling upheld some parts of an injunction a state judge issued to limit demonstrations around a women's clinic in Melbourne, Florida. Other parts of the judge's order were struck down. Abortion rights groups called the ruling a victory, while antiabortion forces strongly denounced it.

Writing for the Court, Rehnquist rejected protesters' arguments that the injunction was subject to the highest level of judicial review—"strict scrutiny"—because it singled out antiabortion views. Instead, the injunction was "content-neutral," Rehnquist said, and could be upheld if it "burdens no more speech than necessary to serve a significant government interest."

Rehnquist listed "a woman's freedom to seek lawful medical counseling or counseling services in connection with her pregnancy" as one of the interests that would justify "an appropriately tailored injunction." On that basis he upheld a thirty-six-foot buffer zone around most of the clinic and a broad noise ban during hours when abortions were performed.

The Court struck down three other restrictions: a ban on use of signs visible from within the clinic; a 300-foot "no approach" zone limiting demonstrators from trying to speak with staff or patients or offering them literature; and a 300-foot buffer zone around homes of clinic doctors and staff. Rehnquist said that a smaller residential buffer zone might be permissible, however.

Stevens concurred with most of the ruling, but he dissented from the decision to strike down the restriction on physically approaching clinic patients and staffs. He said the restriction limited conduct, not speech.

In a dissent Scalia, joined by Thomas, said the ruling violated the First Amendment rights of the protesters. The evidence did not show a need for the injunction, he argued, and the Court was too lax in scrutinizing the order. *(See entry, p. 26; excerpts, p. 266.)*

National Organization for Women, Inc. v. Scheidler, decided by a 9-0 vote, January 24, 1994; Rehnquist wrote the opinion.

Abortion clinics can bring a civil damage suit under the federal antiracketeering law for violent protests or demonstrations even if the protesters have no economic motive for their actions.

The decision reinstated a closely watched suit by two abortion clinics against a coalition of antiabortion groups called the Pro-Life Action Network. The clinics claimed the protesters were using force and violence to try to close them down and asked for damages under the Racketeer Influenced and Corrupt Organizations Act, commonly called RICO. But two lower federal courts said RICO could not be used because the antiabortion groups had no economic motive for their actions.

The Court unanimously rejected the argument. "RICO contains no economic motive requirement," Rehnquist wrote. He said the plaintiffs could maintain the suit as long as they showed that the defendants constituted an "enterprise" that was engaged in "a pattern of racketeering activity" as defined by the act.

In a concurring opinion Souter, joined by Kennedy, stressed that a RICO defendant can raise free-speech claims as a defense. In some cases, he said, the First Amendment might require dismissal of a suit or limit the remedies available to the plaintiff. *(See entry, p. 26; excerpts, p. 113.)*

Damage Suits

Albright v. Oliver, decided by a 7-2 vote, January 24, 1994; Rehnquist wrote a plurality opinion; Blackmun and Stevens dissented.

Someone who has been falsely accused of a crime and arrested cannot use the Fourteenth Amendment's guarantee of due process of law to bring a federal civil rights suit against the officials responsible for the baseless prosecution.

In a splintered decision the Court upheld the dismissal of a federal civil rights suit filed against a police officer and the city of Macomb, Illinois, by a man who had been wrongfully accused of selling drugs.

Writing for four justices, Rehnquist said a suit for false arrest can be based on a violation of the Fourth Amendment's prohibition against unreasonable search and seizure but not on the "generalized" protections of the Due Process Clause. The plaintiff did not base his claim on the Fourth Amendment, apparently because he thought the deadline for filing a false arrest suit had passed.

Kennedy, joined by Thomas, rejected the suit on a different ground, saying the plaintiff had an adequate remedy for malicious prosecution under state law. Souter, in a separate concurrence, left open the possibility that a due process claim could be brought in some false arrest cases.

Most federal courts of appeals that had ruled on the issue had permitted such suits. In a lengthy dissent Stevens, joined by Blackmun, said the plurality opinion took a "cramped view" of due process.

Elder v. Holloway, decided by a 9-0 vote, February 23, 1994; Ginsburg wrote the opinion.

Appellate courts should consider all relevant case law, not just cases cited by opposing lawyers, in reviewing a lower court decision on the defense of qualified immunity in federal civil rights suits.

The decision reinstated a suit by a man who was injured in April 1987 in a warrantless arrest by federal officers surrounding his home. A lower court found that no warrant was required because the officers had not entered the house. The Ninth U.S. Circuit Court of Appeals discovered an earlier case requiring warrants for arrests outside a suspect's home but disregarded it because the plaintiff's lawyer had not cited the precedent.

In a unanimous opinion Ginsburg said the appeals court made a mistake. ". . . [A]ppellate review of qualified immunity dispositions is to be conducted in light of all relevant precedents," she wrote.

Federal Deposit Insurance Corporation v. Meyer, decided by a 9-0 vote, February 23, 1994; Thomas wrote the opinion.

Federal agencies cannot be sued for money damages for violating an individual's constitutional rights.

The Court's unanimous decision barred a suit by a former California savings and loan executive who was fired when the Federal Savings and Loan Insurance Corporation took over the failed thrift. The executive claimed the action by the agency—later renamed the Federal Deposit Insurance Corporation—unconstitutionally deprived him of a property right without due process of law.

In rejecting the suit the Court refused to extend a 1971 decision *(Bivens v. Six Unknown Fed. Narcotics Agents)* that had allowed suits against individual federal agents or officers for so-called constitutional torts. Thomas explained that allowing similar suits against federal agencies would weaken the deterrent effect of permitting damage awards against federal officers and could create "a potentially enormous burden for the Federal Government."

Heck v. Humphrey, decided by 9-0 and 5-4 votes, June 24, 1994; Scalia wrote the opinion; Souter, Blackmun, Stevens, and Ginsburg concurred in the judgment but disagreed with the legal ruling.

A defendant in a state criminal prosecution ordinarily cannot bring a federal civil rights suit for damages if the suit challenges the legality of the conviction or sentence.

The complex ruling barred an Indiana man's suit under a federal civil rights law—42 U.S.C. § 1983—against two prosecutors and a state police investigator involved in his conviction for involuntary manslaughter. Lower federal courts dismissed the suit, filed while the man was appealing his conviction in state court, on the grounds that he had not exhausted state remedies for challenging the prosecution.

The Court unanimously upheld the dismissal but split into two groups that adopted different reasoning for barring the suit. Writing for a five-justice majority, Scalia said the correct rule for deciding the case was "the hoary principle" that civil suits cannot be used to challenge criminal convictions. On that basis Scalia said a section 1983 suit effectively challenging the legality of a conviction was not "cognizable" unless the conviction was first "reversed on direct appeal, expunged by executive order, declared invalid by a state tribunal . . ., or called into question by a federal court's issuance of a writ of habeas corpus."

In a separate opinion Souter, joined by Blackmun, Stevens, and Ginsburg, criticized the decision as too restrictive. He said the ruling would bar any legal remedy for a state defendant who was never imprisoned or had already been released. Scalia dismissed the problem, saying "no real life examples come to mind."

Disability Rights

Florence County School District Four v. Carter, decided by a 9-0 vote, November 9, 1993; O'Connor wrote the opinion.

The Court made it easier for parents of students with disabilities to obtain reimbursement for private school tuition costs if public school districts do not provide an appropriate education as required by federal law.

The decision upheld rulings by two lower federal courts in favor of a South Carolina family who pulled their teenage daughter out of public school and enrolled her in a private school serving students with learning disabilities. The family claimed they were entitled to reimbursement for the tuition under a 1985 Supreme Court decision interpreting the federal Individuals with Disabilities Education Act. But school authorities refused, saying the school had not been certified by the state for serving special-needs students.

In a unanimous opinion O'Connor said the parents' failure to select a state-approved school did not bar reimbursement. Quoting the federal appeals court ruling in the case, O'Connor said that "it hardly seems consistent with the [Disabilities] Act to forbid parents from educating their child at a school that provides an appropriate education simply because that school lacks the stamp of approval of the same public school system that failed to meet the child's needs in the first place."

O'Connor noted the school district's argument that allowing reimbursement for private tuition would burden financially strapped school systems. But she said schools could avoid the costs by providing an appropriate education in public schools. And she added that federal courts can limit reimbursements if "the cost of the private education was unreasonable."

Job Discrimination

Landgraf v. USI Film Products, decided by an 8-1 vote, April 26, 1994; Stevens wrote the opinion; Blackmun dissented.

Provisions of a 1991 civil rights act giving plaintiffs the right to jury trials and compensatory and punitive damages in job discrimination suits do not apply to cases pending when the law was passed.

The ruling—and a companion decision announced the same day, *Rivers v. Roadway Express, Inc. (see below)*—rejected civil rights plaintiffs' efforts to win retroactive application of liberal provisions contained in the 1991 law. Congress passed the law in part to overturn a series of Supreme Court rulings in 1989 that had narrowed plaintiffs' remedies in employment discrimination cases.

The 1991 law did not explicitly say whether Congress intended it to have retroactive effect. President George Bush had vetoed an earlier version that included a retroactivity provision. A Texas woman who filed a sexual harassment complaint against her former employer in 1989 argued on appeal that the law entitled her to a new trial with a right to a jury and damages.

In a near unanimous decision the Court said laws that impair rights, increase liability, or impose new duties typically do not apply to pending cases unless there is "clear evidence" Congress intended the law to have retroactive effect. "The presumption against statutory retroactivity is founded upon sound considerations of general policy and practice, and accords with long held and widely shared expectations about the usual operations of legislation," Stevens wrote.

Stevens said the compensatory and punitive damages provisions were both subject to the presumption against retroactivity because they increased employers' liability for employment discrimination. He said the right to a jury trial would ordinarily be a procedural provision that could be applied retroactively but could not be given extended effect because it was tied to the damages provision.

Stevens reached his conclusion after conducting a lengthy analysis of the legislative history of the 1991 act. In a separate opinion Scalia, joined by Kennedy and Thomas, argued the Court should have looked solely at the text of the law and not the legislative history.

In a lone dissent, Blackmun argued that retroactive application of the law would not be unfair. "There is nothing unjust about holding an employer responsible for injuries caused by conduct that has been illegal for almost 30 years," Blackmun wrote.

Rivers v. Roadway Express, Inc., decided by an 8-1 vote, April 26, 1994; Stevens wrote the opinion; Blackmun dissented.

Provisions of a 1991 civil rights act allowing employees to sue in federal court for racial harassment in the workplace do not apply to cases pending when the law took effect.

The justices rejected arguments that the provisions should be applied retroactively because Congress intended to overturn the Court's 1989 decision rejecting racial harassment suits. "We cannot find in the 1991 Act any clear expression of congressional intent to reach cases that arose before its enactment," Stevens wrote.

Stevens acknowledged that Congress may have intended the law to overturn the Court's earlier ruling. But he said that the 1991 law—in contrast to a 1990 version vetoed by President Bush—did not have language describing the measure as "restoring" the right to sue for racial harassment.

The ruling rejected an effort by two black mechanics on Ohio to use the new provision in a racial harassment suit against their former employer. In a companion decision released the same day—*Landgraf v. USI Film Products*—the Court also rejected retroactive application of provisions of the law giving job discrimination plaintiffs the right to a jury trial and compensatory and punitive damages.

Blackmun dissented alone, as he did in *Landgraf.*

Sexual Harassment

Harris v. Forklift Systems, Inc., decided by a 9-0 vote, November 9, 1993; O'Connor wrote the opinion.

An employee claiming job discrimination on the basis of sexual harassment must prove the existence of a "hostile" or "abusive" work environment but does not need to show that he or she suffered serious psychological injury as a result.

The decision, in a case closely watched by employers and by civil rights groups, reinstated a sexual harassment suit by Teresa Harris, who had worked for two and a half years as a manager for an equipment rental company. She said she quit her job in October 1987 because the firm's president, Charles Hardy, had made sexually suggestive comments to her throughout her employment.

A federal magistrate dismissed the suit, saying the comments were not "so severe as to seriously affect [Harris's] psychological well-being" or cause her to suffer injury. The Sixth U.S. Circuit Court of Appeals affirmed that ruling, but the Supreme Court reversed it in a brief decision handed down four weeks after oral argument.

Writing for the Court, O'Connor said the prohibition on sex discrimination contained in Title VII of the Civil Rights Act of 1964 "comes into play before the harassing conduct leads to a nervous breakdown." She added, "So long as the environment would reasonably be perceived, and is perceived, as hostile or abusive, there is no need for it also to be psychologically injurious."

O'Connor acknowledged that the standard was not "mathematically precise." She said "no single factor" was required but listed several circumstances that could show a hostile work environment, including "the frequency of the discriminatory conduct; whether it is physically threatening or humiliating or a mere offensive utterance; and whether it unreasonably interferes with an employee's work performance."

All of the justices joined in O'Connor's opinion, but two commented briefly in separate concurrences. Scalia said the terms "abusive" and "hostile" were not clear, but he said he knew of "no test more faithful to the inherently vague statutory language." Ginsburg, in her first opinion as a justice, said the ruling did not require an employee to show that sexual harassment interfered with her work performance in order to recover damages.

Labor Law

Labor Relations

National Labor Relations Board v. Health Care & Retirement Corporation of America, decided by a 5-4 vote, May 23, 1994; Kennedy wrote the opinion; Ginsburg, Blackmun, Stevens, and Souter dissented.

The Court made it more difficult for nurses with supervisory responsibilities to organize collectively or enjoy other protections of federal labor law.

The closely divided ruling struck down a National Labor Relations Board (NLRB) decision that had protected four licensed practical nurses at a private nursing home from being fired for protesting job conditions. Federal labor law denies collective bargaining and other rights to employees who exercise supervisory roles "in the interest of the employer." But the board said nurses were not supervisors because they carry out their functions in the interest of patients, not the employer.

Writing for the Court, Kennedy rejected the NLRB's interpretation as "a false dichotomy" because "[p]atient care is the business of a nursing home." He continued, "We thus see no basis for the Board's blanket assertion that supervisory authority exercised in connection with patient care is somehow not in the interest of the employer."

In a lengthy dissent Ginsburg argued that the majority misinterpreted the law. She also said the ruling would deny protections to professional employees in many other industries if they supervise other workers. But Kennedy insisted the ruling applied only to nursing cases.

Mine Safety

Thunder Basin Coal Co. v. Reich, decided by a 9-0 vote, January 19, 1994; Blackmun wrote the opinion.

Mining companies cannot go to federal court to challenge implementation of mine safety regulations in advance of an agency action to enforce the rules.

The unanimous decision prevented operators of a nonunionized coal mine in Wyoming from blocking a requirement that union representatives be allowed to participate in mine safety inspections. Even though the federal Mine Safety and Health Administration had not started any enforcement action, the company went to federal court, claiming that it would suffer irreparable harm if the union representatives were given access to the mine site.

In affirming an appeals court's dismissal of the suit, Blackmun said that Congress precluded "pre-enforcement challenges" when it tightened the federal mine safety law in 1977. He said the act's "detailed structure" permits mine operators to challenge enforcement of the act only after receiving a citation or penalty for an alleged violation.

Remedies

ABF Freight System, Inc. v. National Labor Relations Board, decided by a 9-0 vote, January 24, 1994; Stevens wrote the opinion.

The Court upheld a decision by the National Labor Relations Board (NLRB) to order back pay and reinstatement to an employee fired for union activities even though the worker lied under oath about the events prior to his dismissal.

Ruling unanimously, the Court said the board was not "obligated to adopt a rigid rule" denying relief to employees who lied during administrative proceedings. The decision upheld an NLRB order in favor of a dockworker fired by a New Mexico truck terminal ostensibly because of tardiness. The employee lied about why he was late, but the board concluded the company fired him because of previous grievances he had filed against the company.

Stevens said the board did not abuse its "broad discretion" in the case and was justified in deciding that the employee's false testimony was "ultimately irrelevant" to the real reasons for his discharge. He said a different ruling might require the NLRB to "devote unnecessary time and energy to resolving collateral disputes about credibility."

Scalia, joined by O'Connor, complained in a separate opinion that the board was "really not very much concerned about false testimony." He said the board could have referred the case for prosecution for perjury or refused to reinstate the employee, but he agreed that the Court could not order the board to do so.

Consolidated Rail Corporation v. Gottshall, decided by a 6-3 vote, June 24, 1994; Thomas wrote the opinion; Ginsburg, Blackmun, and Stevens dissented.

Railroads are liable to employees for negligent infliction of emotional distress only if the employee sustains a physical impact or is placed in immediate risk of physical impact as a result of the negligence.

The ruling adopted a restrictive "zone of danger" test for suits under the Federal Employers' Liability Act (FELA), a 1908 law protecting railroad workers injured on the job. The issue reached the Court in separate suits brought by two Conrail employees. In one case a member of a work crew claimed he suffered emotional distress after watching a colleague die of a heat-induced heart attack. In the other a dispatcher claimed emotional distress from overwork.

In a 6-3 decision the Court reversed rulings by the federal appeals court in Philadelphia that favored the plaintiffs. Thomas agreed that a railroad "has a duty under FELA to avoid subjecting its workers to negligently inflicted emotional injury." The appeals court, however, should have used a more restrictive test to prevent "the specter of unlimited and unpredictable liability." The decision threw out the jury award won by the dispatcher and ordered the appeals court to reconsider whether the work crewman should be allowed to take his suit to trial.

Writing for the dissenters, Ginsburg said the ruling "leaves severely harmed workers remediless, however negligent their employers."

Hawaiian Airlines, Inc. v. Norris, decided by a 9-0 vote, June 20, 1994; Blackmun wrote the opinion.

The federal labor law covering railway and airline industry workers does not prevent employees from filing wrongful discharge suits in state courts.

The unanimous ruling allowed an airline mechanic to proceed with two suits in state court against Hawaiian Airlines. The mechanic claimed he was fired illegally for refusing to sign a safety certification for a plane he considered unsafe. The airline argued the suit was barred by a mandatory arbitration provision in the Railway Labor Act (RLA), which also covers airline workers.

Writing for the Court, Blackmun said the provision applies only to disputes under a labor contract and not to rights protected by state law. ". . . [S]ubstantive protections provided by state law, independent of whatever labor agreement might govern, are not pre-empted under the RLA," he wrote.

Livadas v. Bradshaw, California Labor Commissioner, decided by a 9-0 vote, June 13, 1994; Souter wrote the opinion.

The Court struck down a state policy of refusing to enforce a state wage law in complaints brought by union workers covered by collective bargaining agreements.

Unanimously, the Court held that federal labor law preempted a policy of the California labor commissioner. The commissioner had refused to enforce a state law requiring employers to immediately pay all wages due to a fired worker. The state argued union workers' claims under the law should be subject to arbitration as provided in collective bargaining pacts.

Writing for the Court, Souter said the policy left workers with the "unappetizing choice" of "having state-law rights ... enforced" or "exercising the right to enter into a collective-bargaining agreement with an arbitration clause." The ruling allowed a fired grocery clerk to proceed with a civil rights suit claiming the state labor commissioner violated her rights under federal labor law.

Workers' Compensation

Director, Office of Workers' Compensation Programs, Department of Labor v. Greenwich Collieries, decided by a 6-3 vote, June 20, 1994; O'Connor wrote the opinion; Souter, Blackmun, and Stevens dissented.

The Court struck down a Labor Department rule that made it easier for injured workers to recover benefits under federal laws protecting longshore workers and coal miners.

The ruling involved separate claims filed by workers under the Black Lung Benefits Act and the Longshore and Harbor Workers' Compensation Act. In sustaining the claims, the administrative law judges applied the Labor Department's so-called "true doubt" rule, which called for awarding benefits in cases where evidence offered by the worker and employer was evenly balanced.

In a 6-3 decision the Court held the rule was inconsistent with a general burden of proof requirement in the federal Administrative Procedure Act (APA). O'Connor said the APA meant that claimants had a "burden of persuasion"—not only to offer evidence but also to convince the hearing officer or judge they were entitled to the benefit.

Writing for the dissenters, Souter argued a worker could satisfy the burden of proof by producing evidence to support a claim. He said the Labor Department had discretion to decide that the employer, rather than the employee, should lose in cases where the evidence was uncertain.

Property Law

Dolan v. City of Tigard, decided by a 5-4 vote, June 24, 1994; Rehnquist wrote the opinion; Stevens, Blackmun, Souter, and Ginsburg dissented.

The Court limited the power of local governments to force landowners to permit public use of their property in return for approval of development or construction on the site.

In a closely divided ruling the Court held that municipalities have the burden of showing a connection and a "rough proportionality" between conditions imposed on a development permit and any claimed harm to the public from the development. The decision cleared the way for the family owners of an Oregon hardware store to challenge a requirement that they provide land for flood control and a bike path before expanding the store.

Writing for the Court, Rehnquist said the city action amounted to "an uncompensated taking of property" in violation of the Due Process Clause because it failed to justify the conditions for the building permit. ". . . [T]he city must make some sort of individualized determination that the required dedication is related in nature and extent to the proposed development," he wrote.

In a dissenting opinion Stevens, joined by Blackmun and Ginsburg, said the Court "has stumbled badly" by shifting to cities the burden of justifying land-use permit conditions. Souter filed a briefer dissent, saying the city had adequately justified the conditions anyway. *(See entry, p. 39; excerpts, p. 154.)*

States

Commerce Clause

West Lynn Creamery, Inc. v. Healy, decided by a 7-2 vote, June 17, 1994; Stevens wrote the opinion; Rehnquist and Blackmun dissented.

The Court struck down a Massachusetts dairy farmer subsidy scheme on grounds that it discriminated against out-of-state milk producers.

Massachusetts imposed an assessment on all milk sold in the state—about two-thirds of it produced out of state—and distributed the funds to dairy farmers inside the state. In a challenge brought by an in-state milk dealer, the state's supreme court upheld the system, saying that the scheme was "evenhanded" and did not unduly burden interstate commerce.

Writing for a five-justice majority, Stevens said the system was "clearly unconstitutional." He said the scheme "allows Massachusetts dairy farmers who produce at higher cost to sell at or below the price charged by lower cost out-of-state producers."

Scalia, joined by Thomas, concurred separately in an opinion that sought to limit the majority's holding. Scalia said a state should be allowed to subsidize domestic industry "so long as it does so from nondiscriminatory taxes that go into the State's general revenue fund."

The dissenting justices also complained about the ruling's potential effect on other state subsidy schemes. Rehnquist said the ruling reflected "a messianic insistence on a grim sink-or-swim policy of laissez-faire economics" that "bodes ill for the values of federalism."

Taxation

Associated Industries of Missouri v. Lohman, Director of Revenue of Missouri, decided by a 9-0 vote, May 23, 1994; Thomas wrote the opinion.

States may not impose higher taxes on goods bought from outside the state than on in-state purchases even if the difference is small and due to local-option sales taxes.

The unanimous ruling struck down a tax system that Missouri adopted in 1991. Under the system, goods bought from outside the state were subject to a uniform, statewide tax of 5.725 percent, while in-state purchases were subject to a statewide levy of 4.225 percent plus any city or county sales tax.

A business trade group challenged the taxing scheme as discriminating against interstate commerce because the combined tax on out-of-state purchases was higher in many places than the levy on in-state sales. But the Missouri Supreme Court upheld the system, saying the difference was insignificant. Because of local taxes added in the state's most populous areas, overall interstate sales were taxed less than in-state purchases, the state court added.

The Supreme Court, however, ruled that the system was "impermissibly discriminatory" in any locality where the use tax exceeded the sales tax. Thomas said the "resulting disparity" could not be justified as a "compensatory tax" on interstate sales that escaped local levies. "Missouri's use tax scheme . . . runs afoul of the basic requirement that, for a tax system to be 'compensatory,' the burdens imposed on interstate and intrastate commerce must be equal," he wrote.

Thomas said the ruling would not affect local option sales tax schemes used in twenty-eight states. These states ensured that interstate purchases were not subject to higher rates than in-state sales. State tax experts said only one other state, Tennessee, had a system similar to Missouri's.

Blackmun concurred in the decision but did not join Thomas's opinion or write one himself.

Barclays Bank PLC v. Franchise Tax Board of California, decided by 9-0 and 7-2 votes, June 20, 1994; Ginsburg wrote the opinion; O'Connor and Thomas dissented in part.

States can tax multinational corporations on the basis of their worldwide income instead of on their earnings within a state unless Congress acts to prevent the practice.

The ruling rejected pleas by international business groups, Britain, and other U.S. trading partners to bar the so-called "worldwide combined reporting" accounting method for taxing multinational firms. They claimed the system—used in California until 1988 and in some form in six other states—subjected multinationals to double taxation.

In her opinion for the Court, Ginsburg rejected many of the firms' claims on the basis of a 1983 ruling that upheld California's tax system as applied to domestic corporations. She then said Congress, not the Court, had to decide whether the states should be required to adopt a uniform method for taxing multinational enterprises.

". . . [W]e leave it to Congress—whose voice, in this area, is the Nation's—to evaluate whether the national interest is best served by tax uniformity, or state autonomy," Ginsburg wrote.

The decision came in separate challenges brought by the British-based Barclays Bank and the U.S.-based Colgate-Palmolive Co. The Court was unanimous in the Colgate case, but O'Connor and Thomas dissented on Barclays' plea.

O'Connor, who dissented in the Court's 1983 ruling, said that decision governed Colgate's suit. But she said she would sustain the challenge by Barclays on the ground that states need express authority from Congress to adopt a taxing system that subjects foreign corporations to multiple taxation.

Although California changed its taxing system under lobbying by the business community, the state faced up to $4 billion in refunds if the Court had ruled the method illegal. The Clinton administration urged the Court not to declare the taxing scheme invalid even though the Carter, Bush, and Reagan administrations had opposed the system. As a candidate in 1992, Clinton had promised to side with California in the case.

Department of Revenue of Oregon v. ACF Industries, Inc., decided by an 8-1 vote, January 24, 1994; Kennedy wrote the opinion; Stevens dissented.

The Court rejected a railroad industry challenge to state property tax systems that do not give railroads the same tax exemptions accorded to other businesses.

The Ninth U.S. Circuit Court of Appeals had ruled that a 1976 federal law aimed at prohibiting discriminatory tax treatment of railroads required states to give railroad companies the same tax exemption for commercial property as other businesses received. Evidence in the case showed that Oregon exempted about 25 percent of commercial property from taxation but all railroad equipment was subject to taxation.

In his opinion for the Court, Kennedy said that the federal act did not affect states' discretion to grant traditional property tax exemptions as long as they do not single out railroads for discriminatory treatment. State tax officials had warned that a ruling in favor of the railroads could have cost states about $100 million annually.

Department of Taxation and Finance of New York v. Milhelm Attea & Bros., Inc., decided by a 9-0 vote, June 13, 1994; Stevens wrote the opinion.

The Court upheld New York State regulations aimed at preventing evasion of millions of dollars in taxes in the sale of untaxed cigarettes to non-Indians at stores on Indian reservations.

States cannot tax the sale of cigarettes to tribal members on Indian reservations, but purchases by non-Indians are subject to tax. To control widespread evasion of the tax at Indian stores, New York limited the number of cigarettes that wholesalers could distribute to retail outlets on reservations. A Buffalo-based wholesaler challenged the regulations, arguing they were preempted by federal Indian Trader Statutes.

The Court rejected the argument. "Indian traders are not wholly immune from state regulation that is reasonably necessary to the assessment or collection of lawful state taxes," Souter wrote.

Torts

Punitive Damages

Honda Motor Co., Ltd. v. Oberg, decided by a 7-2 vote, June 24, 1994; Stevens wrote the opinion; Ginsburg and Rehnquist dissented.

States must permit judicial review of the amount of punitive damage awards by juries in civil suits.

The ruling struck down a provision of Oregon's constitution that prohibited courts from reviewing the amount of punitive damages awarded by juries unless there was "no evidence" to support the verdict. No other state had a similar restriction. Honda Motor Co. challenged the provision after a jury awarded $735,000 in compensatory damages and $5 million in punitive damages to a man injured in an accident involving an all-terrain vehicle manufactured by the company.

Writing for the Court, Stevens said judicial review of the amount of punitive damage awards had been established in England and the United States as a protection against the "acute danger" of biased verdicts. He said Oregon violated the Due Process Clause when it "removed that safeguard without providing any substitute procedure and without any indication that the danger of arbitrary awards has in any way subsided over time."

In a dissent Ginsburg, joined by Rehnquist, said Oregon's procedures were "adequate to pass the Constitution's due process threshold." *(See* *entry, p. 42; excerpts, p. 143.)*

4 Opinion Excerpts

Following are excerpts from some of the most important rulings of the Supreme Court's 1993-1994 term. They appear in the order in which they were announced. Footnotes and legal citations are omitted.

No. 92-780

National Organization for Women, Inc., etc., et al., Petitioners v. Joseph Scheidler et al.

On writ of certiorari to the United States Court of Appeals for the Seventh Circuit

[January 24, 1994]

CHIEF JUSTICE REHNQUIST delivered the opinion of the Court.

We are required once again to interpret the provisions of the Racketeer Influenced and Corrupt Organizations (RICO) chapter of the Organized Crime Control Act of 1970. Section 1962(c) prohibits any person associated with an enterprise from conducting its affairs through a pattern of racketeering activity. We granted certiorari to determine whether RICO requires proof that either the racketeering enterprise or the predicate acts of racketeering were motivated by an economic purpose. We hold that RICO requires no such economic motive.

I

Petitioner National Organization for Women, Inc. (NOW) is a national nonprofit organization that supports the legal availability of abortion; petitioners Delaware Women's Health Organization, Inc. (DWHO) and Summit Women's Health Organization, Inc. (SWHO) are health care centers that perform abortions and other medical procedures. Respondents are a coalition of antiabortion groups called the Pro-Life Action Network (PLAN), Joseph Scheidler and other individuals and organizations that oppose legal abortion, and a medical laboratory that formerly provided services to the two petitioner health care centers.

Petitioners sued respondents in the United States District Court for the Northern District of Illinois, alleging violations of the Sherman Act and RICO's §§ 1962(a), (c), and (d), as well as several pendent state-law claims stemming from the activities of antiabortion protesters at the clinics. According to respondent Scheidler's congressional testimony, these protesters aim to shut down the clinics and persuade women not to have abortions. Petitioners sought injunctive relief, along with treble damages, costs, and attorneys' fees. They later amended their complaint, and pursuant to local rules, filed a "RICO Case Statement" that further detailed the enterprise, the pattern of racketeering, the victims of the racketeering activity, and the participants involved.

The amended complaint alleged that respondents were members of a nationwide conspiracy to shut down abortion clinics through a pattern of racketeering activity including extortion in violation of the Hobbs Act. Section 1951(b)(2) defines extortion as "the obtaining of property from another, with his consent, induced by wrongful use of actual or threatened force, violence, or fear, or under color of official right." Petitioners alleged that respondents conspired to use threatened or actual force, violence or fear to induce clinic employees, doctors, and patients to give up their jobs, give up their economic right to practice medicine, and give up their right to obtain medical services at the clinics. Petitioners claimed that this conspiracy "has injured the business and/or property interests of the [petitioners]." According to the amended complaint, PLAN constitutes the alleged racketeering "enterprise" for purposes of § 1962(c).

The District Court dismissed the case pursuant to Federal Rule of Civil Procedure 12(b)(6). Citing *Eastern Railroad Presidents Conference v. Noerr Motor Freight, Inc.* (1961), it held that since the activities alleged "involve[d] political opponents, not commercial competitors, and political objectives, not marketplace goals," the Sherman Act did not apply. It dismissed petitioners' RICO claims under § 1962(a) because the "income" alleged by petitioners consisted of voluntary donations from persons opposed to abortion which "in no way were derived from the pattern of racketeering alleged in the complaint." The District Court then concluded that petitioners failed to state a claim under § 1962(c) since "an economic motive requirement exists to the extent that some profit-generating purpose must be alleged in order to state a RICO claim." Finally, it dismissed petitioners' RICO conspiracy claim under § 1962(d) since petitioners' other RICO claims could not stand.

The Court of Appeals affirmed. As to the RICO counts, it agreed with the District Court that the voluntary contributions received by respondents did not constitute income derived from racketeering activities for purposes of § 1962(a). It adopted the analysis of the Court of Appeals for the Second Circuit in *United States* v. *Ivic*, which found an "economic motive" requirement implicit in the "enterprise" element of the offense. The Court of Appeals determined that "non-economic crimes committed in furtherance of non-economic motives are not within the ambit of RICO." Consequently, petitioners failed to state a claim under § 1962(c).

The Court of Appeals also affirmed dismissal of the RICO conspiracy claim under § 1962(d).

We granted certiorari (1993) to resolve a conflict among the courts of appeals on the putative economic motive requirement of 18 U.S.C. § 1962(c) and (d).

II [omitted]

III

... Section 1962(c) makes it unlawful "for any person employed by or associated with any enterprise engaged in, or the activities of which affect, interstate or foreign commerce, to conduct or participate, directly or indirectly, in the conduct of such enterprise's affairs through a pattern of racketeering activity or collection of unlawful debt." Section 1961(1) defines "pattern of racketeering activity" to include conduct that is "chargeable" or "indictable" under a host of state and federal laws. RICO broadly defines "enterprise" in § 1961(4) to "includ[e] any individual, partnership, corporation, association, or other legal entity, and any union or group of individuals associated in fact although not a legal entity." Nowhere in either § 1962(c), or in the RICO definitions in § 1961, is there any indication that an economic motive is required.

The phrase "any enterprise engaged in, or the activities of which affect, interstate or foreign commerce" comes the closest of any language in subsection (c) to suggesting a need for an economic motive. Arguably an enterprise engaged in interstate or foreign commerce would have a profit-seeking motive, but the language in § 1962(c) does not stop there; it includes enterprises whose activities "affect" interstate or foreign commerce. Webster's Third New International Dictionary 35 (1969) defines "affect" as "to have a detrimental influence on—used especially in the phrase *affecting commerce*." An enterprise surely can have a detrimental influence on interstate or foreign commerce without having its own profit-seeking motives.

The Court of Appeals thought that the use of the term "enterprise" in §§ 1962(a) and (b), where it is arguably more tied in with economic motivation, should be applied to restrict the breadth of use of that term in § 1962(c). . . .

We do not believe that the usage of the term "enterprise" in subsections (a) and (b) leads to the inference that an economic motive is required in subsection (c). The term "enterprise" in subsections (a) and (b) plays a different role in the structure of those subsections than it does in subsection (c). Section 1962(a) provides that it "shall be unlawful for any person who has received any income derived, directly or indirectly, from a pattern of racketeering activity . . . to use or invest, directly or indirectly, any part of such income, or the proceeds of such income, in acquisition of any interest in, or the establishment or operation of, any enterprise which is engaged in, or the activities of which affect, interstate or foreign commerce." Correspondingly, § 1962(b) states that it "shall be unlawful for any person through a pattern of racketeering activity or through collection of an unlawful debt to acquire or maintain, directly or indirectly, any interest in or control of any enterprise which is engaged in, or the activities of which affect, interstate or foreign commerce." The "enterprise" referred to in subsections (a) and (b) is thus something acquired through the use of illegal activities or by money obtained from illegal activities. The enterprise in these subsections is the victim of unlawful activity and may very well be a "profit-seeking" entity that represents a property interest and may be acquired. But the statutory language in subsections (a) and (b) does not mandate that the enterprise be a "profit-seeking" entity; it simply requires that the enterprise be an entity that was acquired through illegal activity or the money generated from illegal activity.

By contrast, the "enterprise" in subsection (c) connotes generally the vehicle through which the unlawful pattern of racketeering activity is committed, rather than the victim of that activity. Subsection (c) makes it unlawful for "any person employed by or associated with any enterprise . . . to conduct or participate . . . in the conduct of such enterprise's affairs through a pattern of racketeering activity. . . ." Consequently, since the enterprise in subsection (c) is not being acquired, it need not have a property interest that can be acquired nor an economic motive for engaging in illegal activity; it need only be an association in fact that engages in a pattern of racketeering activity. Nothing in subsections (a) and (b) directs us to a contrary conclusion.

The Court of Appeals also relied on the reasoning of *United States* v. *Bagaric* (1983) to support its conclusion that subsection (c) requires an economic motive. In upholding the dismissal of a RICO claim against a political terrorist group, the *Bagaric* court relied in part on the congressional statement of findings which prefaces RICO and refers to the activities of groups that "drain billions of dollars from America's economy by unlawful conduct and the illegal use of force, fraud, and corruption." The Court of Appeals for the Second Circuit decided that the sort of activity thus condemned required an economic motive.

We do not think this is so. Respondents and the two courts of appeals, we think, overlook the fact that predicate acts, such as the alleged extortion, may not benefit the protestors financially but still may drain money from the economy by harming businesses such as the clinics which are petitioners in this case.

We also think that the quoted statement of congressional findings is a rather thin reed upon which to base a requirement of economic motive neither expressed nor, we think, fairly implied in the operative sections of the Act. . . .

The Court of Appeals also found persuasive guidelines for RICO prosecutions issued by the Department of Justice in 1981. The guidelines provided that a RICO indictment should not charge an association as an enterprise, unless the association exists "for the purpose of maintaining operations directed toward an *economic* goal. . . ." The Second Circuit . . . believed these guidelines were entitled to deference under administrative law principles. Whatever may be the appropriate deference afforded to such internal rules, for our purposes we need note only that the Department of Justice amended its guidelines in 1984. The amended guidelines provide that an association-in-fact enterprise must be "directed toward an economic *or other identifiable goal*" (emphasis added).

Both parties rely on legislative history to support their positions. We believe the statutory language is unambiguous, and find in the parties' submissions respecting legislative history no such "clearly expressed legislative intent to the contrary" that would warrant a different construction.

Respondents finally argue that the result here should be controlled by the rule of lenity in criminal cases. But the rule of lenity applies only when an ambiguity is present. . . . We simply do not think there is an ambiguity here which would suffice to invoke the rule of lenity. . . .

We therefore hold that petitioners may maintain this action if respondents conducted the enterprise through a pattern of racketeering activity. The questions of whether the respondents committed the requisite predicate acts, and whether the commission of these acts fell into a pattern, are not before us. We hold only that RICO contains no economic motive requirement.

The judgment of the Court of Appeals is accordingly

Reversed.

JUSTICE SOUTER, with whom JUSTICE KENNEDY joins, concurring.

I join the Court's opinion and write separately to explain why the First Amendment does not require reading an economic-motive requirement into RICO, and to stress that the Court's opinion does not bar First Amendment challenges to RICO's application in particular cases.

Several respondents and *amici* argue that we should avoid the First Amendment issues that could arise from allowing RICO to be applied to protest organizations by construing the statute to require economic motivation, just as we have previously interpreted other generally applicable statutes so as to avoid First Amendment problems. The argument is meritless in this case, though, for this principle of statutory construction applies only when the meaning of a statute is in doubt and here "the statutory language is unambiguous."

Even if the meaning of RICO were open to debate, however, it would not follow that the statute ought to be read to include an economic-motive requirement, since such a requirement would correspond only poorly to free-speech concerns. Respondents and *amici* complain that, unless so limited, the statute permits an ideological organization's opponents to label its vigorous expression as RICO predicate acts, thereby availing themselves of powerful remedial provisions that could destroy the organization. But an economic-motive requirement would protect too much with respect to First Amendment interests, since it would keep RICO from reaching ideological entities whose members commit acts of violence we need not fear chilling. An economic-motive requirement might also prove to be underprotective, in that entities engaging in vigorous but fully protected expression might fail the proposed economic-motive test (for even protest movements need money) and so be left exposed to harassing RICO suits.

An economic-motive requirement is, finally, unnecessary, because legitimate free-speech claims may be raised and addressed in individual RICO cases as they arise. Accordingly, it is important to stress that nothing in the Court's opinion precludes a RICO defendant from raising the First Amendment in its defense in a particular case. Conduct alleged to amount to Hobbs Act extortion, for example, or one of the other, somewhat elastic RICO predicate acts may turn out to be fully protected First Amendment activity, entitling the defendant to dismissal on that basis. And even in a case where a RICO violation has been validly established, the First Amendment may limit the relief that can be granted against an organization otherwise engaging in protected expression.

This is not the place to catalog the speech issues that could arise in a RICO action against a protest group, and I express no view on the possibility of a First Amendment claim by the respondents in this case. . . . But I think it prudent to notice that RICO actions could deter protected advocacy and to caution courts applying RICO to bear in mind the First Amendment interests that could be at stake.

□□□

No. 92-854

Central Bank of Denver, N. A., Petitioner v. First Interstate Bank of Denver, N. A., and Jack K. Naber

On writ of certiorari to the United States Court of Appeals for the Tenth Circuit

[April 19, 1994]

JUSTICE KENNEDY delivered the opinion of the Court.

As we have interpreted it, § 10(b) of the Securities Exchange Act of 1934 imposes private civil liability on those who commit a manipulative or deceptive act in connection with the purchase or sale of securities. In this case, we must answer a question reserved in two earlier decisions: whether private civil liability under § 10(b) extends as well to those who do not engage in the manipulative or deceptive practice but who aid and abet the violation. See *Herman & MacLean* v. *Huddleston* (1983); *Ernst & Ernst* v. *Hochfelder* (1976).

I

In 1986 and 1988, the Colorado Springs-Stetson Hills Public Building Authority (Authority) issued a total of $26 million in bonds to finance public improvements at Stetson Hills, a planned residential and commercial development in Colorado Springs. Petitioner Central Bank served as indenture trustee for the bond issues.

The bonds were secured by landowner assessment liens, which covered about 250 acres for the 1986 bond issue and about 272 acres for the 1988 bond issue. The bond covenants required that the land subject to the liens be worth at least 160% of the bonds' outstanding principal and interest. The covenants required AmWest Development, the developer of Stetson Hills, to give Central Bank an annual report containing evidence that the 160% test was met.

In January 1988, AmWest provided Central Bank an updated appraisal of the land securing the 1986 bonds and of the land proposed to secure the 1988 bonds. The 1988 appraisal showed land values almost unchanged from the 1986 appraisal. Soon afterwards, Central Bank received a letter from the senior underwriter for the 1986 bonds. Noting that property values were declining in Colorado Springs and that Central Bank was operating on an appraisal over 16 months old, the underwriter expressed concern that the 160% test was not being met.

Central Bank asked its in-house appraiser to review the updated 1988 appraisal. The in-house appraiser decided that the values listed in the appraisal appeared optimistic considering the local real estate market.

He suggested that Central Bank retain an outside appraiser to conduct an independent review of the 1988 appraisal. After an exchange of letters between Central Bank and AmWest in early 1988, Central Bank agreed to delay independent review of the appraisal until the end of the year, six months after the June 1988 closing on the bond issue. Before the independent review was complete, however, the Authority defaulted on the 1988 bonds.

Respondents First Interstate and Jack Naber had purchased $2.1 million of the 1988 bonds. After the default, respondents sued the Authority, the 1988 underwriter, a junior underwriter, an AmWest director, and Central Bank for violations of § 10(b) of the Securities Exchange Act of 1934. The complaint alleged that the Authority, the underwriter defendants, and the AmWest director had violated § 10(b). The complaint also alleged that Central Bank was "secondarily liable under § 10(b) for its conduct in aiding and abetting the fraud."

The United States District Court for the District of Colorado granted summary judgment to Central Bank. The United States Court of Appeals for the Tenth Circuit reversed.

The Court of Appeals first set forth the elements of the § 10(b) aiding and abetting cause of action in the Tenth Circuit: (1) a primary violation of § 10(b); (2) recklessness by the aider and abettor as to the existence of the primary violation; and (3) substantial assistance given to the primary violator by the aider and abettor.

Applying that standard, the Court of Appeals found that Central Bank was aware of concerns about the accuracy of the 1988 appraisal. Central Bank knew both that the sale of the 1988 bonds was imminent and that purchasers were using the 1988 appraisal to evaluate the collateral for the bonds. Under those circumstances, the court said, Central Bank's awareness of the alleged inadequacies of the updated, but almost unchanged, 1988 appraisal could support a finding of extreme departure from standards of ordinary care. The court thus found that respondents had established a genuine issue of material fact regarding the recklessness element of aiding and abetting liability. On the separate question whether Central Bank rendered substantial assistance to the primary violators, the Court of Appeals found that a reasonable trier of fact could conclude that Central Bank had rendered substantial assistance by delaying the independent review of the appraisal.

Like the Court of Appeals in this case, other federal courts have allowed private aiding and abetting actions under § 10(b)....

After our decisions in *Santa Fe Industries, Inc.* v. *Green* (1977) and *Ernst & Ernst* v. *Hochfelder* (1976), where we paid close attention to the statutory text in defining the scope of conduct prohibited by § 10(b), courts and commentators began to question whether aiding and abetting liability under § 10(b) was still available....

We granted certiorari [1993] to resolve the continuing confusion over the existence and scope of the § 10(b) aiding and abetting action.

II

In the wake of the 1929 stock market crash and in response to reports of widespread abuses in the securities industry, the 73d Congress enacted two landmark pieces of securities legislation: the Securities Act of 1933 (1933 Act) and the Securities Exchange Act of 1934 (1934 Act). The 1933 Act regulates initial distributions of securities, and the 1934 Act for the most part regulates post-distribution trading. Together, the Acts "embrace a fundamental purpose . . . to substitute a philosophy of full disclosure for the philosophy of *caveat emptor*."

The 1933 and 1934 Acts create an extensive scheme of civil liability. The Securities and Exchange Commission (SEC) may bring administrative actions and injunctive proceedings to enforce a variety of statutory prohibitions. Private plaintiffs may sue under the express private rights of action contained in the Acts. They may also sue under private rights of action we have found to be implied by the terms of § 10(b) and § 14(a) of the 1934 Act. This case concerns the most familiar private cause of action: the one we have found to be implied by § 10(b), the general antifraud provision of the 1934 Act. Section 10(b) states:

> "It shall be unlawful for any person, directly or indirectly, by the use of any means or instrumentality of interstate commerce or of the mails, or of any facility of any national securities exchange—
>
> "(b) To use or employ, in connection with the purchase or sale of any security registered on a national securities exchange or any security not so registered, any manipulative or deceptive device or contrivance in contravention of such rules and regulations as the [SEC] may prescribe." 15 U.S.C. § 78j.

Rule 10b-5, adopted by the SEC in 1942, casts the proscription in similar terms:

> "It shall be unlawful for any person, directly or indirectly, by the use of any means or instrumentality of interstate commerce, or of the mails or of any facility of any national securities exchange,
>
> "(a) To employ any device, scheme, or artifice to defraud,
>
> "(b) To make any untrue statement of a material fact or to omit to state a material fact necessary in order to make the statements made, in the light of the circumstances under which they were made, not misleading, or
>
> "(c) To engage in any act, practice, or course of business which operates or would operate as a fraud or deceit upon any person,
>
> "in connection with the purchase or sale of any security." 17 CFR 240.10b-5 (1993).

In our cases addressing § 10(b) and Rule 10b-5, we have confronted two main issues. First, we have determined the scope of conduct prohibited by § 10(b). Second, in cases where the defendant has committed a violation of § 10(b), we have decided questions about the elements of the 10b-5 private liability scheme: for example, whether there is a right to contribution, what the statute of limitations is, whether there is a reliance requirement, and whether there is an *in pari delicto* defense.

The latter issue, determining the elements of the 10b-5 private liability scheme, has posed difficulty because Congress did not create a private § 10(b) cause of action and had no occasion to provide guidance about the elements of a private liability scheme. We thus have had "to infer how the 1934 Congress would have addressed the issue[s] had the 10b-5 action been included as an express provision in the 1934 Act."

With respect, however, to the first issue, the scope of conduct prohibited by § 10(b), the text of the statute controls our decision. In § 10(b), Congress prohibited manipulative or deceptive acts in connection with the purchase or sale of securities. It envisioned that the SEC would enforce the statutory prohibition through administrative and injunctive actions. Of course, a private plaintiff now may bring suit against violators of § 10(b). But the private plaintiff may not bring a § 10b-5 suit against a defendant for acts not prohibited by the text of § 10(b). . . . We have refused to allow § 10b-5 challenges to conduct not prohibited by the text of the statute. . . .

Our consideration of statutory duties, especially in cases interpreting § 10(b), establishes that the statutory text controls the definition of conduct covered by § 10(b). That bodes ill for respondents, for "the language of Section 10(b) does not in terms mention aiding and abetting." To overcome this problem, respondents and the SEC suggest (or hint at) the novel argument that the use of the phrase "directly or indirectly" in the text of § 10(b) covers aiding and abetting. . . .

The federal courts have not relied on the "directly or indirectly" language when imposing aiding and abetting liability under § 10(b), and with good reason. There is a basic flaw with this interpretation. . . . The problem, of course, is that aiding and abetting liability extends beyond persons who engage, even indirectly, in a proscribed activity; aiding and abetting liability reaches persons who do not engage in the proscribed activities at all, but who give a degree of aid to those who do. A further problem with respondents' interpretation of the "directly or indirectly" language is posed by the numerous provisions of the 1934 Act that use the term in a way that does not impose aiding and abetting liability. . . . In short, respondents' interpretation of the "directly or indirectly" language fails to support their suggestion that the text of § 10(b) itself prohibits aiding and abetting. . . .

Congress knew how to impose aiding and abetting liability when it chose to do so. . . . If, as respondents seem to say, Congress intended to impose aiding and abetting liability, we presume it would have used the words "aid" and "abet" in the statutory text. But it did not. . . .

We reach the uncontroversial conclusion, accepted even by those courts recognizing a § 10(b) aiding and abetting cause of action, that the text of the 1934 Act does not itself reach those who aid and abet a § 10(b) violation. Unlike those courts, however, we think that conclusion resolves the case. It is inconsistent with settled methodology in § 10(b) cases to extend liability beyond the scope of conduct prohibited by the statutory text. To be sure, aiding and abetting a wrongdoer ought to be actionable in certain instances. The issue, however, is not whether imposing private civil liability on aiders and abettors is good policy but whether aiding and abetting is covered by the statute.

As in earlier cases considering conduct prohibited by § 10(b), we again conclude that the statute prohibits only the making of a material misstatement (or omission) or the commission of a manipulative act. . . . The proscription does not include giving aid to a person who commits a manipulative or deceptive act. We cannot amend the statute to create liability for acts that are not themselves manipulative or deceptive within the meaning of the statute.

III

Because this case concerns the conduct prohibited by § 10(b), the statute itself resolves the case, but even if it did not, we would reach the same result. When the text of § 10(b) does not resolve a particular issue, we attempt to infer "how the 1934 Congress would have addressed the issue had the 10b-5 action been included as an express provision in the 1934 Act." For that inquiry, we use the express causes of action in the securities Acts as the primary model for the § 10(b) action. The reason is evident: Had the 73d Congress enacted a private § 10(b) right of action, it likely would have designed it in a manner similar to the other private rights of action in the securities Acts. . . .

Following that analysis here, we look to the express private causes of action in the 1933 and 1934 Acts. In the 1933 Act, § 11 prohibits false statements or omissions of material fact in registration statements; it identifies the various categories of defendants subject to liability for a violation, but that list does not include aiders and abettors. Section 12 prohibits the sale of unregistered, nonexempt securities as well as the sale of securities by means of a material misstatement or omission; and it limits liability to those who offer or sell the security. In the 1934 Act, § 9 prohibits any person from engaging in manipulative practices such as wash sales, matched orders, and the like. Section 16 prohibits short-swing trading by owners, directors, and officers. Section 18 prohibits any person from making misleading statements in reports filed with the SEC. And § 20A, added in 1988, prohibits any person from engaging in insider trading.

This survey of the express causes of action in the securities Acts reveals that each (like § 10(b)) specifies the conduct for which defendants may be held liable. Some of the express causes of action specify categories of defendants who may be liable; others (like § 10(b)) state only that "any person" who commits one of the prohibited acts may be held liable. The important point for present purposes, however, is that none of the express causes of action in the 1934 Act further imposes liability on one who aids or abets a violation.

From the fact that Congress did not attach private aiding and abetting liability to any of the express causes of action in the securities Acts, we can infer that Congress likely would not have attached aiding and abetting liability to § 10(b) had it provided a private § 10(b) cause of action. . . . There is no reason to think that Congress would have attached aiding and abetting liability only to § 10(b) and not to any of the express private rights of action in the Act. . . .

IV

Respondents make further arguments for imposition of § 10(b) aiding and abetting liability, none of which leads us to a different answer.

A

The text does not support their point, but respondents and some *amici* invoke a broad-based notion of congressional intent. They say that Congress legislated with an understanding of general principles of tort law and that aiding and abetting liability was "well established in both civil and criminal actions by 1934." Thus, "Congress intended to include" aiding and abetting liability in the 1934 Act. A brief history of aiding and abetting liability serves to dispose of this argument.

Aiding and abetting is an ancient criminal law doctrine. Though there is no federal common law of crimes, Congress in 1909 enacted what is now 18 U.S.C. § 2, a general aiding and abetting statute applicable to all federal criminal offenses. The statute decrees that those who provide knowing aid to persons committing federal crimes, with the intent to facilitate the crime, are themselves committing a crime. . . .

. . . Congress has not enacted a general civil aiding and abetting statute—either for suits by the Government (when the Government sues for civil penalties or injunctive relief) or for suits by private parties. Thus, when Congress enacts a statute under which a person may sue and recover damages from a private defendant for the defendant's violation of some statutory norm, there is no general presumption that the plaintiff may also sue aiders and abettors.

Congress instead has taken a statute-by-statute approach to civil aiding and abetting liability. . . . Indeed, various provisions of the securities laws prohibit aiding and abetting, although violations are enforceable only in actions brought by the SEC.

With this background in mind, we think respondents' argument based on implicit congressional intent can be taken in one of three ways. First, respondents might be saying that aiding and abetting should attach to all federal civil statutes, even laws that do not contain an explicit aiding and abetting provision. But neither respondents nor their *amici* cite, and we have not found, any precedent for that vast expansion of federal law. . . .

Second, on a more narrow ground, respondents' congressional intent argument might be interpreted to suggest that the 73d Congress intended to include aiding and abetting only in § 10(b). But nothing in the text or history of § 10(b) even implies that aiding and abetting was covered by the statutory prohibition on manipulative and deceptive conduct.

Third, respondents' congressional intent argument might be construed as a contention that the 73d Congress intended to impose aiding and abetting liability for all of the express causes of action contained in the 1934 Act—and thus would have imposed aiding and abetting liability in § 10(b) actions had it enacted a private § 10(b) right of action. As we have explained, however, none of the express private causes of action in the Act imposes aiding and abetting liability, and there is no evidence that Congress intended that liability for the express causes of action. . . .

B

When Congress reenacts statutory language that has been given a consistent judicial construction, we often adhere to that construction in interpreting the reenacted statutory language. Congress has not reenacted the language of § 10(b) since 1934, however, so we need not determine whether the other conditions for applying the reenactment doctrine are present.

Nonetheless, the parties advance competing arguments based on other post-1934 legislative developments to support their differing interpretations of § 10(b). . . .

Respondents observe that Congress has amended the securities laws on various occasions since 1966, when courts first began to interpret § 10(b) to cover aiding and abetting, but has done so without providing that aiding and abetting liability is not available under § 10(b). From that, respondents infer that these Congresses, by silence, have acquiesced in the judicial interpretation of § 10(b). We disagree. This Court has reserved the issue of 10b-5 aiding and abetting liability on two previous occasions. Furthermore, our observations on the acquiescence doctrine indicate its limitations as an expression of congressional intent. . . .

Central Bank, for its part, points out that in 1957, 1959, and 1960, bills were introduced that would have amended the securities laws to make it "unlawful . . . to aid, abet, counsel, command, induce, or procure the violation of any provision" of the 1934 Act. . . . These bills . . . were not passed. . . . According to Central Bank, these proposals reveal that those Congresses interpreted § 10(b) not to cover aiding and abetting. We have stated, however, that failed legislative proposals are "a particularly dangerous ground on which to rest an interpretation of a prior statute.". . .

C

The SEC points to various policy arguments in support of the 10b-5 aiding and abetting cause of action. It argues, for example, that the aiding and abetting cause of action deters secondary actors from contributing to fraudulent activities and ensures that defrauded plaintiffs are made whole.

Policy considerations cannot override our interpretation of the text and structure of the Act, except to the extent that they may help to show that adherence to the text and structure would lead to a result "so bizarre" that Congress could not have intended it. . . . That is not the case here.

Extending the 10b-5 cause of action to aiders and abettors no doubt makes the civil remedy more far-reaching, but it does not follow that the objectives of the statute are better served. Secondary liability for aiders and abettors exacts costs that may disserve the goals of fair dealing and efficiency in the securities markets.

As an initial matter, the rules for determining aiding and abetting liability are unclear, in "an area that demands certainty and predictability." That leads to the undesirable result of decisions "made on an ad hoc basis, offering little predictive value" to those who provide services to participants in the securities business. . . . Because of the uncertainty of the governing rules, entities subject to secondary liability as aiders and abettors may find it prudent and necessary, as a business judgment, to abandon substantial defenses and to pay settlements in order to avoid the expense and risk of going to trial.

In addition, "litigation under Rule 10b-5 presents a danger of vexatiousness different in degree and in kind from that which accompanies litigation in general." . . . Litigation under 10b-5 thus requires secondary actors to expend large sums even for pretrial defense and the negotiation of settlements. . . .

This uncertainty and excessive litigation can have ripple effects. For example, newer and smaller companies may find it difficult to obtain advice from professionals. A professional may fear that a newer or smaller company may not survive and that business failure would generate securities litigation against the professional, among others. In addition, the increased costs incurred by professionals because of the litigation and settlement costs under 10b-5 may be passed on to their client companies, and in turn incurred by the company's investors, the intended beneficiaries of the statute.

We hasten to add that competing policy arguments in favor of aiding and abetting liability can also be advanced. The point here, however, is that it is far from clear that Congress in 1934 would have decided that the statutory purposes would be furthered by the imposition of private aider and abettor liability.

D

At oral argument, the SEC suggested that 18 U.S.C. § 2 is "significant" and "very important" in this case. . . .

. . . [W]hile it is true that an aider and abettor of a criminal violation of any provision of the 1934 Act, including § 10(b), violates 18 U.S.C. § 2, it does not follow that a private civil aiding and abetting cause of action must also exist. We have been quite reluctant to infer a private right of action from a criminal prohibition alone. . . . If we were to rely on this reasoning now, we would be obliged to hold that a private right of action exists for every provision of the 1934 Act, for it is a criminal violation to violate any of its provisions. And thus, given 18 U.S.C. § 2, we would also have to hold that a civil aiding and abetting cause of action is available for every provision of the Act. There would be no logical stopping point to this line of reasoning: Every criminal statute passed for the benefit of some particular class of persons would carry with it a concomitant civil damages cause of action. . . .

We decline to rely only on 18 U.S.C. § 2 as the basis for recognizing a private aiding and abetting right of action under § 10(b).

V

Because the text of § 10(b) does not prohibit aiding and abetting, we hold that a private plaintiff may not maintain an aiding and abetting suit under § 10(b). The absence of § 10(b) aiding and abetting liability does not mean that secondary actors in the securities markets are always free from liability under the securities Acts. Any person or entity, including a lawyer, accountant, or bank, who employs a manipulative device or makes a material misstatement (or omission) on which a purchaser or seller of securities relies may be liable as a primary violator under § 10b-5, assuming *all* of the requirements for primary liability under Rule 10b-5 are met. In any complex securities fraud, moreover, there are likely to be multiple violators; in this case, for example, respondents named four defendants as primary violators.

Respondents concede that Central Bank did not commit a manipulative or deceptive act within the meaning of § 10(b). Instead, in the words of the complaint, Central Bank was "secondarily liable under § 10(b) for its conduct in aiding and abetting the fraud." Because of our conclusion that there is no private aiding and abetting liability under § 10(b), Central Bank may not be held liable as an aider and abettor. The District Court's grant of summary judgment to Central Bank was proper, and the judgment of the Court of Appeals is

Reversed.

JUSTICE STEVENS, with whom JUSTICE BLACKMUN, JUSTICE SOUTER, and JUSTICE GINSBURG join, dissenting.

The main themes of the Court's opinion are that the text of § 10(b) of the Securities Exchange Act of 1934 does not expressly mention aiding and abetting liability, and that Congress knows how to legislate. Both propositions are unexceptionable, but neither is reason to eliminate the private right of action against aiders and abettors of violations of § 10(b) and the Securities and Exchange Commission's Rule 10b-5. Because the majority gives short shrift to a long history of aider and abettor liability under § 10(b) and Rule 10b-5, and because its rationale imperils other well-established forms of secondary liability not expressly addressed in the securities laws, I respectfully dissent.

In *hundreds* of judicial and administrative proceedings in every circuit in the federal system, the courts and the SEC have concluded that aiders and abettors are subject to liability under § 10(b) and Rule 10b-5. While we have reserved decision on the legitimacy of the theory in two cases that did not present it, all 11 Courts of Appeals to have considered the question have recognized a private cause of action against aiders and abettors under § 10(b) and Rule 10b-5. The early aiding and abetting decisions relied upon principles borrowed from tort law; in those cases, judges closer to the times and climate of the 73d Congress than we concluded that holding aiders and abettors liable was consonant with the 1934 Act's purpose to strengthen the antifraud remedies of the common law....

... If indeed there has been "continuing confusion" concerning the private right of action against aiders and abettors, that confusion has not concerned its basic structure, still less its "existence." Indeed, in this case, petitioner *assumed* the existence of a right of action against aiders and abettors, and sought review only of the subsidiary questions whether an indenture trustee could be found liable as an aider and abettor absent a breach of an indenture agreement or other duty under state law, and whether it could be liable as an aider and abettor based only on a showing of recklessness. These questions, it is true, have engendered genuine disagreement in the Courts of Appeals. But instead of simply addressing the questions presented by the parties, on which the law really was unsettled, the Court *sua sponte* directed the parties to address a question on which even the petitioner justifiably thought the law was settled, and reaches out to overturn a most considerable body of precedent.

Many of the observations in the majority's opinion would be persuasive if we were considering whether to recognize a private right of action based upon a securities statute enacted recently. Our approach to implied causes of action, as to other matters of statutory construction, has changed markedly since the Exchange Act's passage in 1934. At that time, and indeed until quite recently, courts regularly assumed, in accord with the traditional common law presumption, that a statute enacted for the benefit of a particular class conferred on members of that class the right to sue violators of that statute. Moreover, shortly before the Exchange Act was passed, this Court instructed that such "remedial" legislation should receive "a broader and more liberal interpretation than that to be drawn from mere dictionary definitions of the words employed by Congress." There is a risk of anachronistic error in applying our current approach to implied causes of action to a statute enacted when courts commonly read statutes of this kind broadly to accord with their remedial purposes and regularly approved rights to sue despite statutory silence.

Even had § 10(b) not been enacted against a backdrop of liberal construction of remedial statutes and judicial favor toward implied rights of action, I would still disagree with the majority for the simple reason that a "settled construction of an important federal statute should not be disturbed unless and until Congress so decides.". . . A policy of respect for consistent judicial and administrative interpretations leaves it to elected representatives to assess settled law and to evaluate the merits and demerits of changing it. Even when there is no affirmative evidence of ratification, the Legislature's failure to reject a consistent judicial or administrative construction counsels hesitation from a court asked to invalidate it. Here, however, the available evidence suggests congressional approval of aider and abettor liability in private § 10(b) actions. In its comprehensive revision of the Exchange Act in 1975, Congress left untouched the sizeable body of case law approving aiding and abetting liability in private actions under § 10(b) and Rule 10b-5. The case for leaving aiding and abetting liability intact draws further strength from the fact that the SEC itself has consistently understood § 10(b) to impose aider and abettor liability since shortly after the rule's promulgation. In short, one need not agree as an original matter with the many decisions recognizing the private right against aiders and abettors to concede that the right fits comfortably within the statutory scheme, and that it has become a part of the established system of private enforcement. We should leave it to Congress to alter that scheme.

The Court would be on firmer footing if it had been shown that aider and abettor liability "detracts from the effectiveness of the 10b-5 implied action or interferes with the effective operation of the securities laws." However, the line of decisions recognizing aider and abettor liability suffers from no such infirmities. The language of both § 10(b) and Rule 10b-5 encompasses "any person" who violates the Commission's anti-fraud rules, whether "directly or indirectly"; we have read this "broad" language "not technically and restrictively, but flexibly to effectuate its remedial purposes." In light of the encompassing language of § 10(b), and its acknowledged purpose to strengthen the anti-fraud remedies of the common law, it was certainly no wild extrapolation for courts to conclude that aiders and abettors should be subject to the private action under § 10(b). Allowing aider and abettor claims in private § 10(b) actions can hardly be said to impose unfair legal duties on those whom Congress has opted to leave unregulated: Aiders and abettors of § 10(b) and Rule 10b-5 violations have always been subject to criminal liability under 18 U.S.C. § 2. Although the Court canvasses policy arguments against aider and abettor liability, it does not suggest that the aiding and abetting theory has had such deleterious consequences that we should dispense with it on those grounds. The agency charged with primary responsibility for enforcing the securities laws does not perceive such drawbacks, and urges retention of the private right to sue aiders and abettors.

As framed by the Court's order redrafting the questions presented, this case concerns only the existence and scope of aiding and abetting liability in suits brought by private parties under § 10(b) and Rule 10b-5. The majority's rationale, however, sweeps far beyond even those important issues. The majority leaves little doubt that the Exchange Act does not even permit the *Commission* to pursue aiders and abettors in civil enforcement actions under § 10b and Rule 10b-5. Aiding and abetting liability has a long pedigree in civil proceedings brought by the SEC under § 10(b) and Rule 10b-5, and has become an important part of the Commission's enforcement arsenal. Moreover, the majority's approach to aiding and abetting at the very least casts serious doubt, both for private and SEC actions, on *other* forms of secondary liability that, like the aiding and abetting theory, have long been recognized by the SEC and the courts but are not expressly spelled out in the securities statutes. The principle the Court espouses today—that liability may not be imposed on parties who are not within the scope of § 10(b)'s plain language—is inconsistent with long-established Commission and judicial precedent.

As a general principle, I agree, "the creation of new rights ought to be left to legislatures, not courts." But judicial restraint does not always favor the narrowest possible interpretation of rights derived from federal statutes. While we are now properly reluctant to recognize private rights of action without an instruction from Congress, we should also be reluctant to lop off rights of action that have been recognized for decades, even if the judicial methodology that gave them birth is now out of favor. Caution is particularly appropriate here, because the judicially recognized right in question accords with the longstanding construction of the agency Congress has assigned to enforce the securities laws. . . .

I respectfully dissent.

□□□

No. 92-1239

J. E. B., Petitioner v. Alabama ex rel. T. B.

On writ of certiorari to the Court of Civil Appeals of Alabama

[April 19, 1994]

JUSTICE BLACKMUN delivered the opinion of the Court.

In *Batson* v. *Kentucky* (1986), this Court held that the Equal Protection Clause of the Fourteenth Amendment governs the exercise of peremptory challenges by a prosecutor in a criminal trial. The Court explained that although a defendant has "no right to a 'petit jury composed in whole or in part of persons of his own race,' " the "defendant does have the right to be tried by a jury whose members are selected pursuant to nondiscriminatory criteria." Since *Batson,* we have reaffirmed repeatedly our commitment to jury selection procedures that are fair and nondiscriminatory. We have recognized that whether the trial is criminal or civil, potential jurors, as well as litigants, have an equal protection right to jury selection procedures that are free from state-sponsored group stereotypes rooted in, and reflective of, historical prejudice. See *Powers* v. *Ohio* (1991); *Edmonson* v. *Leesville Concrete Co.* (1991); *Georgia* v. *McCollum* (1992).

Although premised on equal protection principles that apply equally to gender discrimination, all our recent cases defining the scope of *Batson* involved alleged racial discrimination in the exercise of peremptory challenges. Today we are faced with the question whether the Equal Protection Clause forbids intentional discrimination on the basis of gender, just as it prohibits discrimination on the basis of race. We hold that gender, like race, is an unconstitutional proxy for juror competence and impartiality.

I

On behalf of relator T. B., the mother of a minor child, respondent State of Alabama filed a complaint for paternity and child support against petitioner J. E. B. in the District Court of Jackson County, Alabama. On October 21, 1991, the matter was called for trial and jury selection began. The trial court assembled a panel of 36 potential jurors, 12 males and 24 females. After the court excused three jurors for cause, only 10 of the remaining 33 jurors were male. The State then used 9 of its 10 peremptory strikes to remove male jurors; petitioner used all but one of his strikes to remove female jurors. As a result, all the selected jurors were female.

Before the jury was empaneled, petitioner objected to the State's peremptory challenges on the ground that they were exercised against male jurors solely on the basis of gender, in violation of the Equal Protection Clause of the Fourteenth Amendment. Petitioner argued that the logic and reasoning of *Batson* v. *Kentucky,* which prohibits peremptory strikes solely on the basis of race, similarly forbids intentional discrimination on the basis of gender. The court rejected petitioner's claim and empaneled the all-female jury. The jury found petitioner to be the father of the child and the court entered an order directing him to pay child support. On post-judgment motion, the court reaffirmed its ruling that *Batson* does not extend to gender-based peremptory challenges. The Alabama Court of Civil Appeals affirmed. . . . The Supreme Court of Alabama denied certiorari.

We granted certiorari to resolve a question that has created a conflict of authority—whether the Equal Protection Clause forbids peremptory challenges on the basis of gender as well as on the basis of race. Today we reaffirm what, by now, should be axiomatic: Intentional discrimination on the basis of gender by state actors violates the Equal Protection Clause, particularly where, as here, the discrimination serves to ratify and perpetuate invidious, archaic, and overbroad stereotypes about the relative abilities of men and women.

II

Discrimination on the basis of gender in the exercise of peremptory challenges is a relatively recent phenomenon. Gender-based peremptory strikes were hardly practicable for most of our country's existence, since, until the 19th century, women were completely excluded from jury service. So well-entrenched was this exclusion of women that in 1880 this Court, while finding that the exclusion of African-American men from juries violated the Fourteenth Amendment, expressed no doubt that a

State "may confine the selection [of jurors] to males." *Strauder* v. *West Virginia* [1880].

Many States continued to exclude women from jury service well into the present century, despite the fact that women attained suffrage upon ratification of the Nineteenth Amendment in 1920. States that did permit women to serve on juries often erected other barriers, such as registration requirements and automatic exemptions, designed to deter women from exercising their right to jury service. . . .

This Court in *Ballard* v. *United States* (1946) first questioned the fundamental fairness of denying women the right to serve on juries. Relying on its supervisory powers over the federal courts, it held that women may not be excluded from the venire in federal trials in States where women were eligible for jury service under local law. . . .

Fifteen years later, however, the Court . . . found it reasonable, "despite the enlightened emancipation of women," to exempt women from mandatory jury service by statute, allowing women to serve on juries only if they volunteered to serve. The Court justified the differential exemption policy on the ground that women, unlike men, occupied a unique position "as the center of home and family life." [*Hoyt* v. *Florida* (1961).]

In 1975, the Court finally repudiated the reasoning of *Hoyt* and struck down, under the Sixth Amendment, an affirmative registration statute nearly identical to the one at issue in *Hoyt*. See *Taylor* v. *Louisiana* (1975). We explained: "Restricting jury service to only special groups or excluding identifiable segments playing major roles in the community cannot be squared with the constitutional concept of jury trial." The diverse and representative character of the jury must be maintained "partly as assurance of a diffused impartiality and partly because sharing in the administration of justice is a phase of civic responsibility.". . .

III

Taylor relied on Sixth Amendment principles, but the opinion's approach is consistent with the heightened equal protection scrutiny afforded gender-based classifications. Since *Reed* v. *Reed* (1971), this Court consistently has subjected gender-based classifications to heightened scrutiny in recognition of the real danger that government policies that professedly are based on reasonable considerations in fact may be reflective of "archaic and overbroad" generalizations about gender or based on "outdated misconceptions concerning the role of females in the home rather than in the 'marketplace and world of ideas.' ". . .

Despite the heightened scrutiny afforded distinctions based on gender, respondent argues that gender discrimination in the selection of the petit jury should be permitted, though discrimination on the basis of race is not. Respondent suggests that "gender discrimination in this country . . . has never reached the level of discrimination" against African-Americans, and therefore gender discrimination, unlike racial discrimination, is tolerable in the courtroom.

While the prejudicial attitudes toward women in this country have not been identical to those held toward racial minorities, the similarities between the experiences of racial minorities and women, in some contexts, "overpower those differences." . . . Certainly, with respect to jury service, African-Americans and women share a history of total exclusion, a history which came to an end for women many years after the embarrassing chapter in our history came to an end for African-Americans.

We need not determine, however, whether women or racial minorities have suffered more at the hands of discriminatory state actors during the decades of our Nation's history. It is necessary only to acknowledge that "our Nation has had a long and unfortunate history of sex discrimination," a history which warrants the heightened scrutiny we afford all gender-based classifications today. Under our equal protection jurisprudence, gender-based classifications require "an exceedingly persuasive justification" in order to survive constitutional scrutiny. Thus, the only question is whether discrimination on the basis of gender in jury selection substantially furthers the State's legitimate interest in achieving a fair and impartial trial. In making this assessment, we do not weigh the value of peremptory challenges as an institution against our asserted commitment to eradicate invidious discrimination from the courtroom. Instead, we consider whether peremptory challenges based on gender stereotypes provide substantial aid to a litigant's effort to secure a fair and impartial jury.

Far from proffering an exceptionally persuasive justification for its gender-based peremptory challenges, respondent maintains that its decision to strike virtually all the males from the jury in this case "may reasonably have been based upon the perception, supported by history, that men otherwise totally qualified to serve upon a jury might be more sympathetic and receptive to the arguments of a man alleged in a paternity action to be the father of an out-of-wedlock child, while women equally qualified to serve upon a jury might be more sympathetic and receptive to the arguments of the complaining witness who bore the child."

We shall not accept as a defense to gender-based peremptory challenges "the very stereotype the law condemns." Respondent's rationale, not unlike those regularly expressed for gender-based strikes, is reminiscent of the arguments advanced to justify the total exclusion of women from juries. Respondent offers virtually no support for the conclusion that gender alone is an accurate predictor of juror's attitudes; yet it urges this Court to condone the same stereotypes that justified the wholesale exclusion of women from juries and the ballot box. Respondent seems to assume that gross generalizations that would be deemed impermissible if made on the basis of race are somehow permissible when made on the basis of gender.

Discrimination in jury selection, whether based on race or on gender, causes harm to the litigants, the community, and the individual jurors who are wrongfully excluded from participation in the judicial process. The litigants are harmed by the risk that the prejudice which motivated the discriminatory selection of the jury will infect the entire proceedings. . . . The community is harmed by the State's participation in the perpetuation of invidious group stereotypes and the inevitable loss of confidence in our judicial system that state-sanctioned discrimination in the courtroom engenders.

When state actors exercise peremptory challenges in reliance on gender stereotypes, they ratify and reinforce prejudicial views of the relative abilities of men and women. Because these stereotypes have wreaked injustice in so many other spheres of our country's public life, active discrimination by litigants on the basis of gender during jury selection "invites cynicism respecting the jury's neutrality and its obligation to adhere to the law." The potential for cynicism is particularly acute in cases where gender-related issues are prominent, such as cases involving rape, sexual harassment, or paternity. Discriminatory use of peremptory challenges may create the impression that the judicial system has acquiesced in suppressing full participation by one gender or that the "deck has been stacked" in favor of one side. . . .

In recent cases we have emphasized that individual jurors themselves have a right to nondiscriminatory jury selection procedures. Contrary to respondent's suggestion, this right extends to both men and women. . . . All persons, when granted the opportunity to serve on a jury, have the right not to be excluded summarily because of discriminatory and stereotypical presumptions that reflect and reinforce patterns of historical discrimination. Striking individual jurors on the assumption that they hold particular views simply because of their gender . . . denigrates the dignity of the excluded juror, and, for a woman, reinvokes a history of exclusion from political participation. The message it sends to all those in the courtroom, and all those who may later learn of the discriminatory act, is that certain individuals, for no reason other than gender, are presumed unqualified by state actors to decide important questions upon which reasonable persons could disagree.

IV

Our conclusion that litigants may not strike potential jurors solely on the basis of gender does not imply the elimination of all peremptory challenges. Neither does it conflict with a State's legitimate interest in using such challenges in its effort to secure a fair and impartial jury. Parties still may remove jurors whom they feel might be less acceptable than others on the panel; gender simply may not serve as a proxy for bias. Parties may also exercise their peremptory challenges to remove from the venire any group or class of individuals normally subject to "rational basis" review. Even strikes based on characteristics that are disproportionately associated with one gender could be appropriate, absent a showing of pretext. . . .

The experience in the many jurisdictions that have barred gender-based challenges belies the claim that litigants and trial courts are incapable of complying with a rule barring strikes based on gender. As with race-based *Batson* claims, a party alleging gender discrimination must make a prima facie showing of intentional discrimination before the party exercising the challenge is required to explain the basis for the strike. When an explanation is required, it need not rise to the level of a "for cause" challenge; rather, it merely must be based on a juror characteristic other than gender, and the proffered explanation may not be pretextual. . . .

V

Equal opportunity to participate in the fair administration of justice is fundamental to our democratic system. It not only furthers the goals of the jury system. It reaffirms the promise of equality under the law " that all citizens, regardless of race, ethnicity, or gender, have the chance to take part directly in our democracy. . . . When persons are excluded from participation in our democratic processes solely because of race or gender, this promise of equality dims, and the integrity of our judicial system is jeopardized.

In view of these concerns, the Equal Protection Clause prohibits discrimination in jury selection on the basis of gender, or on the assumption that an individual will be biased in a particular case for no reason other than the fact that the person happens to be a woman or happens to be a man. . . .

The judgment of the Court of Civil Appeals of Alabama is reversed and the case is remanded to that court for further proceedings not inconsistent with this opinion.

It is so ordered.

JUSTICE O'CONNOR, concurring.

I agree with the Court that the Equal Protection Clause prohibits the government from excluding a person from jury service on account of that person's gender. . . . I therefore join the Court's opinion in this case. But today's important blow against gender discrimination is not costless. I write separately to discuss some of these costs, and to express my belief that today's holding should be limited to the *government's* use of gender-based peremptory strikes.

Batson v. *Kentucky* (1986) itself was a significant intrusion into the jury selection process. *Batson* mini-hearings are now routine in state and federal trial courts, and *Batson* appeals have proliferated as well. Demographics indicate that today's holding may have an even greater impact than did *Batson* itself. In further constitutionalizing jury selection procedures, the Court increases the number of cases in which jury selection—once a sideshow—will become part of the main event.

For this same reason, today's decision further erodes the role of the peremptory challenge. . . . The principal value of the peremptory is that it helps produce fair and impartial juries. . . . The peremptory's importance is confirmed by its persistence: it was well-established at the time of *Blackstone* and continues to endure in all the States.

. . . [A]s we add, layer by layer, additional constitutional restraints on the use of the peremptory, we force lawyers to articulate what we know is often inarticulable.

In so doing we make the peremptory challenge less discretionary and more like a challenge for cause. We also increase the possibility that biased jurors will be allowed onto the jury, because sometimes a lawyer will be unable to provide an acceptable gender-neutral explanation even though the lawyer is in fact correct that the juror is unsympathetic. Similarly, in jurisdictions where lawyers exercise their strikes in open court, lawyers may be deterred from using their peremptories, out of the fear that if they are unable to justify the strike the court will seat a juror who knows that the striking party thought him unfit. Because I believe the peremptory remains an important litigator's tool and a fundamental part of the process of selecting impartial juries, our increasing limitation of it gives me pause.

Nor is the value of the peremptory challenge to the litigant diminished when the peremptory is exercised in a gender-based manner. We know that like race, gender matters. A plethora of studies make clear that in rape cases, for example, female jurors are somewhat more likely to vote to convict than male jurors. . . . Moreover, though there have been no similarly definitive studies regarding, for example, sexual harassment, child custody, or spousal or child abuse, one need not be a sexist to share the intuition that in certain cases a person's gender and resulting life experience will be relevant to his or her view of the case. . . .

Today's decision severely limits a litigant's ability to act on this intuition, for the import of our holding is that any correlation between a juror's gender and attitudes is irrelevant as a matter of constitutional law. But to say that gender makes no difference as a matter of law is not to say that gender makes no difference as a matter of fact. . . . Though we gain much from this statement, we cannot ignore what we lose. In extending *Batson* to gender we have added an additional burden to the state and federal trial process, taken a step closer to eliminating the peremptory challenge, and diminished the ability of litigants to act on sometimes accurate gender-based assumptions about juror attitudes.

These concerns reinforce my conviction that today's decision should be limited to a prohibition on the government's use of gender-based peremptory challenges. The Equal Protection Clause prohibits only discrimination by state actors. In *Edmonson*, we made the mistake of concluding that private civil litigants were state actors when they exercised peremptory challenges; in *Georgia* v. *McCollum*, we compounded the mistake by holding that criminal defendants were also state actors. Our commitment to eliminating discrimination from the legal process should not allow us to forget that not all that occurs in the courtroom is state action. Private civil litigants are just that—*private* litigants. . . .

Clearly, criminal defendants are not state actors. . . . Limiting the accused's use of the peremptory is "a serious misordering of our priorities," for it means "we have exalted the right of citizens to sit on juries over the rights of the criminal defendant, even though it is the defendant, not the jurors, who faces imprisonment or even death." *McCollum* (THOMAS, J., concurring in judgment).

Accordingly, I adhere to my position that the Equal Protection Clause does not limit the exercise of peremptory challenges by private civil litigants and criminal defendants. This case itself presents no state action dilemma, for here the State of Alabama itself filed the paternity suit on behalf of petitioner. But what of the next case? Will we, in the name of fighting gender discrimination, hold that the battered wife—on trial for wounding her abusive husband—is a state actor? Will we preclude her from using her peremptory challenges to ensure that the jury of her peers contains as many women members as possible? I assume we will, but I hope we will not.

JUSTICE KENNEDY, concurring in the judgment.

I am in full agreement with the Court that the Equal Protection Clause prohibits gender discrimination in the exercise of peremptory challenges. I write to explain my understanding of why our precedents lead to that conclusion. . . .

. . . In over 20 cases beginning in 1971, we have subjected government classifications based on sex to heightened scrutiny. Neither the State nor any Member of the Court questions that principle here. And though the intermediate scrutiny test we have applied may not provide a very clear standard in all instances, our case law does reveal a strong presumption that gender classifications are invalid.

There is no doubt under our precedents, therefore, that the Equal Protection Clause prohibits sex discrimination in the selection of jurors. The only question is whether the Clause also prohibits peremptory challenges based on sex. The Court is correct to hold that it does. The Equal Protection Clause and our constitutional tradition are based on the theory that an individual possesses rights that are protected against lawless action by the government.... For purposes of the Equal Protection Clause, an individual denied jury service because of a peremptory challenge exercised against her on account of her sex is no less injured than the individual denied jury service because of a law banning members of her sex from serving as jurors. The injury is to personal dignity and to the individual's right to participate in the political process. The neutrality of the Fourteenth Amendment's guarantee is confirmed by the fact that the Court has no difficulty in finding a constitutional wrong in this case, which involves males excluded from jury service because of their gender.

The importance of individual rights to our analysis prompts a further observation concerning what I conceive to be the intended effect of today's decision. We do not prohibit racial and gender bias in jury selection only to encourage it in jury deliberations. Once seated, a juror should not give free rein to some racial or gender bias of his or her own....

In this regard, it is important to recognize that a juror sits not as a representative of a racial or sexual group but as an individual citizen.... The jury pool must be representative of the community, but that is a structural mechanism for preventing bias, not enfranchising it.... Thus, the Constitution guarantees a right only to an impartial jury, not to a jury composed of members of a particular race or gender....

CHIEF JUSTICE REHNQUIST, dissenting.

I agree with the dissent of JUSTICE SCALIA, which I have joined. I add these words in support of its conclusion. Accepting *Batson* v. *Kentucky* (1986) as correctly decided, there are sufficient differences between race and gender discrimination such that the principle of *Batson* should not be extended to peremptory challenges to potential jurors based on sex.

That race and sex discrimination are different is acknowledged by our equal protection jurisprudence, which accords different levels of protection to the two groups. Classifications based on race are inherently suspect, triggering "strict scrutiny," while gender-based classifications are judged under a heightened, but less searching standard of review. *Mississippi Univ. for Women* v. *Hogan* (1982). Racial groups comprise numerical minorities in our society, warranting in some situations a greater need for protection, whereas the population is divided almost equally between men and women. Furthermore, while substantial discrimination against both groups still lingers in our society, racial equality has proved a more challenging goal to achieve on many fronts than gender equality.

Batson, which involved a black defendant challenging the removal of black jurors, announced a sea-change in the jury selection process. In balancing the dictates of equal protection and the historical practice of peremptory challenges, long recognized as securing fairness in trials, the Court concluded that the command of the Equal Protection Clause was superior. . . .

Under the Equal Protection Clause, . . . the balance should tilt in favor of peremptory challenges when sex, not race, is the issue. Unlike the Court, I think the State has shown that jury strikes on the basis of gender "substantially further" the State's legitimate interest in achieving a fair and impartial trial through the venerable practice of peremptory challenges. . . . The two sexes differ, both biologically and, to a diminishing extent, in experience. It is not merely "stereotyping" to say that these differences may produce a difference in outlook which is brought to the jury room. Accordingly, use of peremptory challenges on the basis of sex is generally not the sort of derogatory and invidious act which peremptory challenges directed at black jurors may be.

JUSTICE O'CONNOR's concurrence recognizes several of the costs associated with extending *Batson* to gender-based peremptory challenges—lengthier trials, an increase in the number and complexity of appeals addressing jury selection, and a "diminished . . . ability of litigants to act on sometimes accurate gender-based assumptions about juror attitudes." These costs are, in my view, needlessly imposed by the Court's opinion, because the Constitution simply does not require the result which it reaches.

JUSTICE SCALIA, with whom THE CHIEF JUSTICE and JUSTICE THOMAS join, dissenting.

Today's opinion is an inspiring demonstration of how thoroughly up-to-date and right-thinking we Justices are in matters pertaining to the sexes (or as the Court would have it, the genders), and how sternly we disapprove the male chauvinist attitudes of our predecessors. The price to be paid for this display "a modest price, surely" is that most of the opinion is quite irrelevant to the case at hand. The hasty reader will be surprised to learn, for example, that this lawsuit involves a complaint about the use of peremptory challenges to exclude men from a petit jury. To be sure, petitioner, a man, used all but one of *his* peremptory strikes to remove *women* from the jury (he used his last challenge to strike the sole remaining male from the pool), but the validity of *his* strikes is not before us. Nonetheless, the Court treats itself to an extended discussion of the historic exclusion of women not only from jury service, but also from service at the bar (which is rather like jury service, in that it involves going to the courthouse a lot). All this, as I say, is irrelevant, since the case involves state action that allegedly discriminates against men. . . .

The Court also spends time establishing that the use of sex as a proxy for particular views or sympathies is unwise and perhaps irrational. The opinion stresses the lack of statistical evidence to support the widely held belief that, at least in certain types of cases, a juror's sex has some statistically significant predictive value as to how the juror will behave. . . . Personally, I am less inclined to demand statistics, and more inclined to credit the perceptions of experienced litigators who have had money on the line. But it does not matter. . . . Even if sex was a remarkably good predictor in certain cases, the Court would find its use in peremptories unconstitutional. . . .

The core of the Court's reasoning is that peremptory challenges on the basis of any group characteristic subject to heightened scrutiny are inconsistent with the guarantee of the Equal Protection Clause. That conclusion can be reached only by focusing unrealistically upon individual exercises of the peremptory challenge, and ignoring the totality of the practice. Since all groups are subject to the peremptory challenge (and will be made the object of it, depending upon the nature of the particular case) it is hard to see how any group is denied equal protection. That explains why peremptory challenges coexisted with the Equal Protection Clause for 120 years. This case is a perfect example of how the system as a whole is even-handed. While the only claim before the Court is petitioner's complaint that the prosecutor struck male jurors, for every man struck by the government petitioner's own lawyer struck a woman. To say that men were singled out for discriminatory treatment in this process is preposterous. . . .

Although the Court's legal reasoning in this case is largely obscured by anti-male-chauvinist oratory, to the extent such reasoning is discernible it invalidates much more than sex-based strikes. After identifying unequal treatment (by separating individual exercises of peremptory challenge from the process as a whole), the Court applies the "heightened scrutiny" mode of equal-protection analysis used for sex-based discrimination, and concludes that the strikes fail heightened scrutiny because they do not substantially further an important government interest. The Court says that the only important government interest that could be served by peremptory strikes is "securing a fair and impartial jury." It refuses to accept respondent's argument that these strikes further that interest by eliminating a group (men) which may be partial to male defendants, because it will not accept any argument based on " 'the very stereotype the law condemns.' " This analysis, entirely eliminating the only allowable argument, implies that sex-based strikes do not even rationally further a legitimate government interest, let alone pass heightened scrutiny. That places *all* peremptory strikes based on *any* group characteristic at risk, since they can all be denominated "stereotypes." . . .

Even if the line of our later cases guaranteed by today's decision limits the theoretically boundless *Batson* principle to race, sex, and perhaps other classifications subject to heightened scrutiny (which presumably would include religious belief), much damage has been done. It has been done, first and foremost, to the peremptory challenge system, which loses its whole character when (in order to defend against "impermissible stereotyping" claims) "reasons" for strikes must be given. . . . The loss of the real peremptory will be felt most keenly by the criminal defendant. . . . And make no mistake about it: there really is no substitute for the peremptory. Voir dire (though it can be expected to expand as a consequence of today's decision) cannot fill the gap. The biases that go along with group characteristics tend to be biases that the juror himself does not perceive, so that it is no use asking about them. It is fruitless to inquire of a male juror whether he harbors any subliminal prejudice in favor of unwed fathers.

And damage has been done, secondarily, to the entire justice system, which will bear the burden of the expanded quest for "reasoned peremptories" that the Court demands. The extension of *Batson* to sex, and almost certainly beyond, will provide the basis for extensive collateral litigation, which especially the criminal defendant (who litigates full-time and cost-free) can be expected to pursue. While demographic reality places some limit on the number of cases in which race-based challenges will be an issue, every case contains a potential sex-based claim. Another consequence, as I have mentioned, is a lengthening of the voir dire process that already burdens trial courts. . . .

In order, it seems to me, not to eliminate any real denial of equal protection, but simply to pay conspicuous obeisance to the equality of the sexes, the Court imperils a practice that has been considered an essential part of fair jury trial since the dawn of the common law. The Constitution of the United States neither requires nor permits this vandalizing of our people's traditions.

For these reasons, I dissent.

□□□

No. 93-644

Honda Motor Co., Ltd., et al., Petitioners v. Karl L. Oberg

On writ of certiorari to the Supreme Court of Oregon

[June 24, 1994]

JUSTICE STEVENS delivered the opinion of the Court.

An amendment to the Oregon Constitution prohibits judicial review of the amount of punitive damages awarded by a jury "unless the court can affirmatively say there is no evidence to support the verdict." The question presented is whether that prohibition is consistent with the Due Process Clause of the Fourteenth Amendment. We hold that it is not.

I

Petitioner manufactured and sold the three-wheeled all-terrain vehicle that overturned while respondent was driving it, causing him severe and permanent injuries. Respondent brought suit alleging that petitioner knew or should have known that the vehicle had an inherently and unreasonably dangerous design. The jury found petitioner liable and awarded respondent $919,390.39 in compensatory damages and punitive damages of $5,000,000. The compensatory damages, however, were reduced by 20% to $735,512.31, because respondent's own negligence contributed to the accident. On appeal, relying on our then recent decision in *Pacific Mut. Life Ins. Co.* v. *Haslip* (1991), petitioner argued that the award of punitive damages violated the Due Process Clause of the Fourteenth Amendment, because the punitive damages were excessive and because Oregon courts lacked the power to correct excessive verdicts.

The Oregon Court of Appeals affirmed, as did the Oregon Supreme Court. The latter court relied heavily on the fact that the Oregon statute governing the award of punitive damages in product liability actions and the jury instructions in this case contain substantive criteria that provide at least as much guidance to the factfinders as the Alabama statute and jury instructions that we upheld in *Haslip*. The Oregon Supreme Court also noted that Oregon law provides an additional protection by requiring the plaintiff to prove entitlement to punitive damages by clear and convincing evidence rather than a mere preponderance. Recognizing that other state courts had interpreted *Haslip* as including a "clear constitutional mandate for meaningful judicial scrutiny of punitive damage awards," the Court nevertheless declined to "interpret *Haslip* to hold that an award of punitive damages, to comport with the requirements of the Due Process

Clause, always must be subject to a form of post-verdict or appellate review that includes the possibility of remittitur." It also noted that trial and appellate courts were "not entirely powerless" because a judgment may be vacated if "there is no evidence to support the jury's decision," and because "appellate review is available to test the sufficiency of the jury instructions."

We granted certiorari (1994) to consider whether Oregon's limited judicial review of the size of punitive damage awards is consistent with our decision in *Haslip*.

II

Our recent cases have recognized that the Constitution imposes a substantive limit on the size of punitive damage awards. *Pacific Mut. Life Ins. Co.* v. *Haslip; TXO Production Corp.* v. *Alliance Resources Corp.* (1993). Although they fail to "draw a mathematical bright line between the constitutionally acceptable and the constitutionally unacceptable," a majority of the Justices agreed that the Due Process Clause imposes a limit on punitive damage awards. . . . In the case before us today we are not directly concerned with the character of the standard that will identify unconstitutionally excessive awards; rather we are confronted with the question of what procedures are necessary to ensure that punitive damages are not imposed in an arbitrary manner. More specifically, the question is whether the Due Process Clause requires judicial review of the amount of punitive damage awards.

The opinions in both *Haslip* and *TXO* strongly emphasized the importance of the procedural component of the Due Process Clause. In *Haslip,* the Court held that the common law method of assessing punitive damages did not violate procedural due process. In so holding, the Court stressed the availability of both "meaningful and adequate review by the trial court" and subsequent appellate review. Similarly, in *TXO,* the plurality opinion found that the fact that the "award was reviewed and upheld by the trial judge" and unanimously affirmed on appeal gave rise "to a strong presumption of validity." Concurring in the judgment, JUSTICE SCALIA (joined by JUSTICE THOMAS) considered it sufficient that traditional common law procedures were followed. In particular, he noted that " 'procedural due process' requires judicial review of punitive damages awards for reasonableness. . . ."

All of those opinions suggest that our analysis in this case should focus on Oregon's departure from traditional procedures. We therefore first contrast the relevant common law practice with Oregon's procedure, which that State's Supreme Court once described as "a system of trial by jury in which the judge is reduced to the status of a mere monitor." We then examine the constitutional implications of Oregon's deviation from established common law procedures.

III

Judicial review of the size of punitive damage awards has been a safeguard against excessive verdicts for as long as punitive damages have been awarded. One of the earliest reported cases involving exemplary damages, *Huckle* v. *Money* (1763), arose out of King George III's attempt to punish the publishers of the allegedly seditious *North Briton,* No. 45. The King's agents arrested the plaintiff, a journeyman printer, in his home and detained him for six hours. Although the defendants treated the plaintiff rather well, feeding him "beef-steaks and beer, so that he suffered very little or no damages," the jury awarded him £300, an enormous sum almost three hundred times the plaintiff's weekly wage. The defendant's lawyer requested a new trial, arguing that the jury's award was excessive. Plaintiff's counsel, on the other hand, argued that "in cases of tort . . . the Court will never interpose in setting aside verdicts for excessive damages." While the court denied the motion for new trial, the Chief Justice explicitly rejected plaintiff's absolute rule against review of damages amounts. Instead, he noted that when the damages are "outrageous" and "all mankind at first blush must think so," a court may grant a new trial "for excessive damages." In accord with his view that the amount of an award was relevant to the motion for a new trial, the Chief Justice noted that "[u]pon the whole, I am of opinion the damages are not excessive."

Subsequent English cases, while generally deferring to the jury's determination of damages, steadfastly upheld the court's power to order new trials solely on the basis that the damages were too high. . . .

Common law courts in the United States followed their English predecessors in providing judicial review of the size of damage awards. They too emphasized the deference ordinarily afforded jury verdicts, but they recognized that juries sometimes awarded damages so high as to require correction. . . .

In the 19th century, both before and after the ratification of the Fourteenth Amendment, many American courts reviewed damages for "partiality" or "passion and prejudice." Nevertheless, because of the difficulty of probing juror reasoning, passion and prejudice review was, in fact, review of the amount of awards. Judges would infer passion, prejudice, or partiality from the size of the award. . . .

Nineteenth century treatises similarly recognized judges' authority to award new trials on the basis of the size of damage awards. . . .

Modern practice is consistent with these earlier authorities. In the federal courts and in every State, except Oregon, judges review the size of damage awards. . . .

IV

There is a dramatic difference between the judicial review of punitive damages awards under the common law and the scope of review available in Oregon. An Oregon trial judge, or an Oregon Appellate Court, may order a new trial if the jury was not properly instructed, if error occurred during the trial, or if there is no evidence to support any punitive damages at all. But if the defendant's only basis for relief is the amount of punitive damages the jury awarded, Oregon provides no procedure for reducing or setting aside that award. This has been the law in Oregon at least since 1949 when the State Supreme Court announced its opinion in *Van Lom* v. *Schneiderman*, definitively construing the 1910 Amendment to the Oregon Constitution.

In that case the court held that it had no power to reduce or set aside an award of both compensatory and punitive damages that was admittedly excessive. It recognized that the constitutional amendment placing a limitation on its power was a departure from the traditional common law approach. . . . Every other State in the Union affords post-verdict judicial review of the amount of a punitive damages award, and subsequent decisions have reaffirmed Oregon judges' lack of authority to order new trials or other relief to remedy excessive damages. . . .

Respondent argues that Oregon's procedures do not deviate from common law practice, because Oregon judges have the power to examine the size of the award to determine whether the jury was influenced by passion and prejudice. This is simply incorrect. The earliest Oregon cases interpreting the 1910 amendment squarely held that Oregon courts lack precisely that power. . . . No Oregon court for more than half a century has inferred passion and prejudice from the size of a damages award, and no court in more than a decade has even hinted that courts might possess the power to do so. Finally, if Oregon courts could evaluate the excessiveness of punitive damage awards through passion and prejudice review, the Oregon Supreme Court would have mentioned that power in this very case. Petitioner argued that Oregon procedures were unconstitutional precisely because they failed to provide judicial review of the size of punitive damage awards. The Oregon Supreme Court responded by rejecting the idea that judicial review of the size of punitive damage awards was required by *Haslip*. . . . If, as respondent claims, Oregon law provides passion and prejudice review of excessive verdicts, the Oregon Supreme Court would have had a more obvious response to petitioner's argument.

Respondent also argues that Oregon provides adequate review, because the trial judge can overturn a punitive damage award if there is no substantial evidence to support an award of punitive damages. This argument is unconvincing, because the review provided by Oregon courts ensures only that there is evidence to support *some* punitive damages, not that there is evidence to support the amount actually awarded.... Oregon, unlike the common law, provides no assurance that those whose conduct is sanctionable by punitive damages are not subjected to punitive damages of arbitrary amounts. What we are concerned with is the possibility that a guilty defendant may be unjustly punished; evidence of guilt warranting some punishment is not a substitute for evidence providing at least a rational basis for the particular deprivation of property imposed by the State to deter future wrongdoing.

V

Oregon's abrogation of a well-established common law protection against arbitrary deprivations of property raises a presumption that its procedures violate the Due Process Clause. As this Court has stated from its first Due Process cases, traditional practice provides a touchstone for constitutional analysis. Because the basic procedural protections of the common law have been regarded as so fundamental, very few cases have arisen in which a party has complained of their denial. In fact, most of our Due Process decisions involve arguments that traditional procedures provide too little protection and that additional safeguards are necessary to ensure compliance with the Constitution.

Nevertheless, there are a handful of cases in which a party has been deprived of liberty or property without the safeguards of common law procedure. When the absent procedures would have provided protection against arbitrary and inaccurate adjudication, this Court has not hesitated to find the proceedings violative of Due Process....

Punitive damages pose an acute danger of arbitrary deprivation of property. Jury instructions typically leave the jury with wide discretion in choosing amounts, and the presentation of evidence of a defendant's net worth creates the potential that juries will use their verdicts to express biases against big businesses, particularly those without strong local presences. Judicial review of the amount awarded was one of the few procedural safeguards which the common law provided against that danger. Oregon has removed that safeguard without providing any substitute procedure and without any indication that the danger of arbitrary awards has in any way subsided over time. For these reasons, we hold that Oregon's denial of judicial review of the size of punitive damage awards violates the Due Process Clause of the Fourteenth Amendment.

VI

Respondent argues that Oregon has provided other safeguards against arbitrary awards and that, in any event, the exercise of this unreviewable power by the jury is consistent with the jury's historic role in our judicial system.

Respondent points to four safeguards provided in the Oregon courts: the limitation of punitive damages to the amount specified in the complaint, the clear and convincing standard of proof, pre-verdict determination of maximum allowable punitive damages, and detailed jury instructions. The first, limitation of punitive damages to the amount specified, is hardly a constraint at all, because there is no limit to the amount the plaintiff can request, and it is unclear whether an award exceeding the amount requested could be set aside. . . . The second safeguard, the clear and convincing standard of proof, is an important check against unwarranted imposition of punitive damages, but, like the "no substantial evidence" review discussed above, it provides no assurance that those whose conduct is sanctionable by punitive damages are not subjected to punitive damages of arbitrary amounts. Regarding the third purported constraint, respondent cites no cases to support the idea that Oregon courts do or can set maximum punitive damage awards in advance of the verdict. Nor are we aware of any court which implements that procedure. Respondent's final safeguard, proper jury instruction, is a well-established and, of course, important check against excessive awards. The problem that concerns us, however, is the possibility that a jury will not follow those instructions and may return a lawless, biased, or arbitrary verdict.

In support of his argument that there is a historic basis for making the jury the final arbiter of the amount of punitive damages, respondent calls our attention to early civil and criminal cases in which the jury was allowed to judge the law as well as the facts. As we have already explained, in civil cases, the jury's discretion to determine the amount of damages was constrained by judicial review. The criminal cases do establish—as does our practice today—that a jury's arbitrary decision to acquit a defendant charged with a crime is completely unreviewable. There is, however, a vast difference between arbitrary grants of freedom and arbitrary deprivations of liberty or property. The Due Process Clause has nothing to say about the former, but its whole purpose is to prevent the latter. A decision to punish a tortfeasor by means of an exaction of exemplary damages is an exercise of state power that must comply with the Due Process Clause of the Fourteenth Amendment. The common law practice, the procedures applied by every other State, the strong presumption favoring judicial review that we have applied in other areas of the law, and elementary considerations of justice, all support the conclusion that such a decision should not be committed to the unreviewable discretion of a jury.

The judgment is reversed, and the case is remanded to the Oregon Supreme Court for further proceedings not inconsistent with this opinion.

It is so ordered.

JUSTICE SCALIA, concurring.

I join the opinion of the Court, but a full explanation of why requires that I supplement briefly the description of what has occurred here.

Before the 1910 Amendment to Article VII, § 3 of the Oregon Constitution, Oregon courts had developed and were applying common-law standards that limited the size of damage awards. The 1910 Amendment, by its terms, did not eliminate those substantive standards but altered the procedures of judicial review: *"no fact tried by a jury shall be otherwise re-examined in any court of this state, unless the court can affirmatively say there is no evidence to support the verdict"* (emphasis added). The Oregon courts appear to believe that a state-law "reasonable-ness" limit upon the amount of punitive damages subsists, but cannot be enforced through the process of judicial review. . . .

The Court's opinion establishes that the right of review eliminated by the Amendment was a procedure traditionally accorded at common law. The deprivation of property without observing (or providing a reasonable substitute for) an important traditional procedure for enforcing state-prescribed limits upon such deprivation violates the Due Process Clause.

JUSTICE GINSBURG, with whom the CHIEF JUSTICE joins, dissenting.

In product liability cases, Oregon guides and limits the factfinder's discretion on the availability and amount of punitive damages. The plaintiff must establish entitlement to punitive damages, under specific substantive criteria, by clear and convincing evidence. Where the factfinder is a jury, its decision is subject to judicial review to this extent: the trial court, or an appellate court, may nullify the verdict if reversible error occurred during the trial, if the jury was improperly or inadequately instructed, or if there is no evidence to support the verdict. Absent trial error, and if there is evidence to support the award of punitive damages, however, Oregon's Constitution, Article VII, § 3, provides that a properly instructed jury's verdict shall not be reexamined. Oregon's procedures, I conclude, are adequate to pass the Constitution's due process threshold. I therefore dissent from the Court's judgment upsetting Oregon's disposition in this case.

I

A

To assess the constitutionality of Oregon's scheme, I turn first to this Court's recent opinions in *Pacific Mut. Life Ins. Co.* v. *Haslip* (1991) and *TXO Production Corp.* v. *Alliance Resources Corp.* (1993). The Court upheld punitive damage awards in both cases, but indicated that due process imposes an outer limit on remedies of this type. Significantly, neither decision declared any specific procedures or substantive criteria essential to satisfy due process. In *Haslip,* the Court expressed concerns about "unlimited jury discretion—or unlimited judicial discretion for that matter—in the fixing of punitive damages," but refused to "draw a mathematical bright line between the constitutionally acceptable and the constitutionally unacceptable." Regarding the components of "the constitutional calculus," the Court simply referred to "general concerns of reasonableness and [the need for] adequate guidance from the court when the case is tried to a jury."

And in *TXO,* a majority agreed that a punitive damage award may be so grossly excessive as to violate the Due Process Clause. In the plurality's view, however, "a judgment that is a product" of "fair procedures . . . is entitled to a strong presumption of validity"; this presumption, "persuasive reasons" indicated, "should be irrebuttable, . . . or virtually so." . . .

B

The procedures Oregon's courts followed in this case satisfy the due process limits indicated in *Haslip* and *TXO;* the jurors were adequately guided by the trial court's instructions, and Honda has not maintained, in its full presentation to this Court, that the award in question was "so 'grossly excessive' as to violate the Federal Constitution."

1

Several preverdict mechanisms channeled the jury's discretion more tightly in this case than in either *Haslip* or *TXO.* First, providing at least some protection against unguided, utterly arbitrary jury awards, respondent Karl Oberg was permitted to recover no more than the amounts specified in the complaint, $919,390.39 in compensatory damages and $5 million in punitive damages. . . . No provision of Oregon law appears to preclude the defendant from seeking an instruction setting a lower cap, if the evidence at trial cannot support an award in the amount demanded. Additionally, if the trial judge relates the incorrect maximum amount, a defendant who timely objects may gain modification or nullification of the verdict.

Second, Oberg was not allowed to introduce evidence regarding Honda's wealth until he "presented evidence sufficient to justify to the court a prima facie claim of punitive damages.". . . This evidentiary rule is designed to lessen the risk "that juries will use their verdicts to express biases against big businesses."

Third, and more significant, as the trial court instructed the jury, Honda could not be found liable for punitive damages unless Oberg established by "clear and convincing evidence" that Honda "show[ed] wanton disregard for the health, safety and welfare of others.". . . "[T]he clear-and-convincing evidence requirement," which is considerably more rigorous than the standards applied by Alabama in *Haslip* and West Virginia in *TXO*, "constrain[s] the jury's discretion, limiting punitive damages to the more egregious cases." Nothing in Oregon law appears to preclude a new trial order if the trial judge, informed by the jury's verdict, determines that his charge did not adequately explain what the "clear and convincing" standard means.

Fourth, and perhaps most important, in product liability cases, Oregon requires that punitive damages, if any, be awarded based on seven substantive criteria. . . . These substantive criteria, and the precise instructions detailing them, gave the jurors "adequate guidance" in making their award, far more guidance than their counterparts in *Haslip* and *TXO* received. In *Haslip*, for example, the jury was told only the purpose of punitive damages (punishment and deterrence) and that an award was discretionary, not compulsory. We deemed those instructions, notable for their generality, constitutionally sufficient.

. . . Because Oregon requires the factfinder to apply objective criteria, . . . its procedures are perhaps more likely to prompt rational and fair punitive damage decisions than are the *post hoc* checks employed in jurisdictions following Alabama's pattern. . . . As the Oregon court concluded, "application of objective criteria ensures that sufficiently definite and meaningful constraints are imposed on the finder of fact." The Oregon court also concluded that the statutory criteria, by adequately guiding the jury, worked to "ensur[e] that the resulting award is not disproportionate to a defendant's conduct and to the need to punish and deter."

2

The Supreme Court of Oregon's conclusions are buttressed by the availability of at least some postverdict judicial review of punitive damage awards. Oregon's courts ensure that there is evidence to support the verdict. . . . The State's courts have shown no reluctance to strike punitive damage awards in cases where punitive liability is not established, so that defendant qualifies for judgment on that issue as a matter of law.

In addition, punitive damage awards may be set aside because of flaws in jury instructions. As the Court acknowledges, "proper jury instructio[n] is a well-established and, of course, important check against excessive awards."

II

In short, Oregon has enacted legal standards confining punitive damage awards in product liability cases. These state standards are judicially enforced by means of comparatively comprehensive preverdict procedures but markedly limited postverdict review, for Oregon has elected to make factfinding, once supporting evidence is produced, the province of the jury. The Court today invalidates this choice, largely because it concludes that English and early American courts generally provided judicial review of the size of punitive damage awards. The Court's account of the relevant history is not compelling.

A

I am not as confident as the Court about either the clarity of early American common law, or its import. Tellingly, the Court barely acknowledges the large authority exercised by American juries in the 18th and 19th centuries. In the early years of our Nation, juries "usually possessed the power to determine both law and fact." And at the time trial by jury was recognized as the constitutional right of parties "[i]n [s]uits at common law," U. S. Const., Amdt. 7, the assessment of "uncertain damages" was regarded, generally, as exclusively a jury function.

More revealing, the Court notably contracts the scope of its inquiry. It asks: Did common law judges claim the power to overturn jury verdicts they viewed as excessive? But full and fair historical inquiry ought to be wider. The Court should inspect, comprehensively and comparatively, the procedures employed—at trial *and* on appeal—to fix the amount of punitive damages. Evaluated in this manner, Oregon's scheme affords defendants like Honda more procedural safeguards than 19th-century law provided.

. . . Oregon instructs juries to decide punitive damage issues based on seven substantive factors and a clear and convincing evidence standard. When the Fourteenth Amendment was adopted in 1868, in contrast, "no particular procedures were deemed necessary to circumscribe a jury's discretion regarding the award of [punitive] damages, or their amount." The responsibility entrusted to the jury surely was not guided by instructions of the kind Oregon has enacted. . . .

Furthermore, common-law courts reviewed punitive damage verdicts extremely deferentially, if at all. . . . True, 19th-century judges occasionally asserted that they had authority to overturn damage awards upon concluding, from the size of an award, that the jury's decision must have been based on "partiality" or "passion and prejudice." But courts rarely *exercised* this authority.

B

Because Oregon's procedures assure "adequate guidance from the court when the case is tried to a jury," this Court has no cause to disturb the judgment in this instance, for Honda presses here only a *procedural* due process claim. True, in a footnote to its petition for certiorari, not repeated in its briefs, Honda attributed to this Court an "assumption that procedural due process requires [judicial] review of both federal substantive due process and state-law excessiveness challenges to the size of an award." But the assertion regarding "state-law excessiveness challenges" is extraordinary, for this Court has never held that the Due Process Clause requires a State's courts to police jury factfindings to ensure their conformity with state law. And, as earlier observed, the plurality opinion in *TXO* disavowed the suggestion that a defendant has a federal due process right to a correct determination under state law of the "reasonableness" of a punitive damages award.

... If ... in some future case, a plea is plausibly made that a particular punitive damage award is not merely excessive, but "so 'grossly excessive' as to violate the Federal Constitution," and Oregon's judiciary nevertheless insists that it is powerless to consider the plea, this Court might have cause to grant review. No such case is before us today, nor does Honda, in this Court, maintain otherwise.

To summarize: Oregon's procedures adequately guide the jury charged with the responsibility to determine a plaintiff's qualification for, and the amount of, punitive damages, and on that account do not deny defendants procedural due process; Oregon's Supreme Court correctly refused to rule that "an award of punitive damages, to comport with the requirements of the Due Process Clause, *always* must be subject to a form of post-verdict or appellate review" for excessiveness (emphasis added); the verdict in this particular case, considered in light of this Court's decisions in *Haslip* and *TXO*, hardly appears "so 'grossly excessive' as to violate the substantive component of the Due Process Clause." Accordingly, the Court's procedural directive to the state court is neither necessary nor proper. The Supreme Court of Oregon has not refused to enforce federal law, and I would affirm its judgment.

□□□

No. 93-518

Florence Dolan, Petitioner v. City of Tigard

On writ of certiorari to the Supreme Court of Oregon

[June 24, 1994]

CHIEF JUSTICE REHNQUIST delivered the opinion of the Court.

Petitioner challenges the decision of the Oregon Supreme Court which held that the city of Tigard could condition the approval of her building permit on the dedication of a portion of her property for flood control and traffic improvements. We granted certiorari to resolve a question left open by our decision in *Nollan* v. *California Coastal Comm'n* (1987) of what is the required degree of connection between the exactions imposed by the city and the projected impacts of the proposed development.

I

The State of Oregon enacted a comprehensive land use management program in 1973. The program required all Oregon cities and counties to adopt new comprehensive land use plans that were consistent with the statewide planning goals. The plans are implemented by land use regulations which are part of an integrated hierarchy of legally binding goals, plans, and regulations. Pursuant to the State's requirements, the city of Tigard, a community of some 30,000 residents on the southwest edge of Portland, developed a comprehensive plan and codified it in its Community Development Code (CDC). The CDC requires property owners in the area zoned Central Business District to comply with a 15% open space and landscaping requirement, which limits total site coverage, including all structures and paved parking, to 85% of the parcel. After the completion of a transportation study that identified congestion in the Central Business District as a particular problem, the city adopted a plan for a pedestrian/bicycle pathway intended to encourage alternatives to automobile transportation for short trips. The CDC requires that new development facilitate this plan by dedicating land for pedestrian pathways where provided for in the pedestrian/bicycle pathway plan.

The city also adopted a Master Drainage Plan. The Drainage Plan noted that flooding occurred in several areas along Fanno Creek, including areas near petitioner's property. The Drainage Plan also established that the increase in impervious surfaces associated with continued urbanization would exacerbate these flooding problems. To combat these risks, the Drainage Plan suggested a series of improvements to the Fanno Creek Basin, including channel excavation in the area next to petitioner's property. Other recommendations included ensuring that the floodplain remains free of structures and that it be preserved as greenways to minimize flood damage to structures. The Drainage Plan concluded that the cost of these improvements should be shared based on both direct and indirect benefits, with property owners along the waterways paying more due to the direct benefit that they would receive.

Petitioner Florence Dolan owns a plumbing and electric supply store located on Main Street in the Central Business District of the city. The store covers approximately 9,700 square feet on the eastern side of a 1.67-acre parcel, which includes a gravel parking lot. Fanno Creek flows through the southwestern corner of the lot and along its western boundary. . . .

Petitioner applied to the city for a permit to redevelop the site. Her proposed plans called for nearly doubling the size of the store to 17,600 square feet, and paving a 39-space parking lot. The existing store, located on the opposite side of the parcel, would be razed in sections as construction progressed on the new building. In the second phase of the project, petitioner proposed to build an additional structure on the northeast side of the site for complementary businesses, and to provide more parking. . . .

The City Planning Commission granted petitioner's permit application subject to conditions imposed by the city's CDC. The CDC establishes the following standard for site development review approval:

> "Where landfill and/or development is allowed within and adjacent to the 100-year floodplain, the city shall require the dedication of sufficient open land area for greenway adjoining and within the floodplain. This area shall include portions at a suitable elevation for the construction of a pedestrian/bicycle pathway within the floodplain in accordance with the adopted pedestrian/bicycle plan."

Thus, the Commission required that petitioner dedicate the portion of her property lying within the 100-year floodplain for improvement of a storm drainage system along Fanno Creek and that she dedicate an additional 15-foot strip of land adjacent to the floodplain as a pedestrian/bicycle pathway. The dedication required by that condition encompasses approximately 7,000 square feet, or roughly 10% of the property. . . .

Petitioner requested variances from the CDC standards. . . . Petitioner . . . argued that her proposed development would not conflict with the policies of the comprehensive plan. The Commission denied the request.

The Commission made a series of findings concerning the relationship between the dedicated conditions and the projected impacts of petitioner's project. First, the Commission noted that "[i]t is reasonable to assume that customers and employees of the future uses of this site could utilize a pedestrian/bicycle pathway adjacent to this development for their transportation and recreational needs." The Commission noted that the site plan has provided for bicycle parking in a rack in front of the proposed building and "[i]t is reasonable to expect that some of the users of the bicycle parking provided for by the site plan will use the pathway adjacent to Fanno Creek if it is constructed." In addition, the Commission found that creation of a convenient, safe pedestrian/bicycle pathway system as an alternative means of transportation "could offset some of the traffic demand on [nearby] streets and lessen the increase in traffic congestion."

The Commission went on to note that the required floodplain dedication would be reasonably related to petitioner's request to intensify the use of the site given the increase in the impervious surface. The Commission stated that the "anticipated increased storm water flow from the subject property to an already strained creek and drainage basin can only add to the public need to manage the stream channel and floodplain for drainage purposes." Based on this anticipated increased storm water flow, the Commission concluded that "the requirement of dedication of the floodplain area on the site is related to the applicant's plan to intensify development on the site." The Tigard City Council approved the Commission's final order, subject to one minor modification. . . .

Petitioner appealed to the Land Use Board of Appeals (LUBA) on the ground that the city's dedication requirements were not related to the proposed development, and, therefore, those requirements constituted an uncompensated taking of their property under the Fifth Amendment. In evaluating the federal taking claim, LUBA assumed that the city's findings about the impacts of the proposed development were supported by substantial evidence. Given the undisputed fact that the proposed larger building and paved parking area would increase the amount of impervious surfaces and the runoff into Fanno Creek, LUBA concluded that "there is a 'reasonable relationship' between the proposed development and the requirement to dedicate land along Fanno Creek for a greenway." With respect to the pedestrian/bicycle pathway, LUBA noted the Commission's finding that a significantly larger retail sales building and parking lot would attract larger numbers of customers and employees and their vehicles. It again found a "reasonable relationship" between alleviating the impacts of increased traffic from the development and facilitating the provision of a pedestrian/bicycle pathway as an alternative means of transportation.

The Oregon Court of Appeals affirmed, rejecting petitioner's contention that in *Nollan* v. *California Coastal Comm'n* we had abandoned the "reasonable relationship" test in favor of a stricter "essential nexus" test. The Oregon Supreme Court affirmed. The court also disagreed with petitioner's contention that the *Nollan* Court abandoned the "reasonably related" test. Instead, the court read *Nollan* to mean that an "exaction is reasonably related to an impact if the exaction serves the same purpose that a denial of the permit would serve." The court decided that both the pedestrian/bicycle pathway condition and the storm drainage dedication had an essential nexus to the development of the proposed site. Therefore, the court found the conditions to be reasonably related to the impact of the expansion of petitioner's business. We granted certiorari (1993), because of an alleged conflict between the Oregon Supreme Court's decision and our decision in *Nollan*.

II

The Takings Clause of the Fifth Amendment of the United States Constitution, made applicable to the States through the Fourteenth Amendment, *Chicago, B. & Q. R. Co.* v. *Chicago* (1897), provides: "[N]or shall private property be taken for public use, without just compensation." One of the principal purposes of the Takings Clause is "to bar Government from forcing some people alone to bear public burdens which, in all fairness and justice, should be borne by the public as a whole." Without question, had the city simply required petitioner to dedicate a strip of land along Fanno Creek for public use, rather than conditioning the grant of her permit to redevelop her property on such a dedication, a taking would have occurred. Such public access would deprive petitioner of the right to exclude others, "one of the most essential sticks in the bundle of rights that are commonly characterized as property."

On the other side of the ledger, the authority of state and local governments to engage in land use planning has been sustained against constitutional challenge as long ago as our decision in *Euclid* v. *Ambler Realty Co.* (1926). . . . A land use regulation does not effect a taking if it "substantially advance[s] legitimate state interests" and does not "den[y] an owner economically viable use of his land."

The sort of land use regulations discussed in the cases just cited, however, differ in two relevant particulars from the present case. First, they involved essentially legislative determinations classifying entire areas of the city, whereas here the city made an adjudicative decision to condition petitioner's application for a building permit on an individual parcel. Second, the conditions imposed were not simply a limitation on the use petitioner might make of her own parcel, but a requirement that she deed portions of the property to the city. In *Nollan*, we held that governmental authority to exact such a condition was circumscribed by the Fifth and Fourteenth Amendments. Under the well-settled doctrine of "unconstitutional conditions," the government may not require a person to give up a constitutional right—here the right to receive just compensation when property is taken for a public use—in exchange for a discretionary benefit conferred by the government where the property sought has little or no relationship to the benefit.

Petitioner contends that the city has forced her to choose between the building permit and her right under the Fifth Amendment to just compensation for the public easements. Petitioner does not quarrel with the city's authority to exact some forms of dedication as a condition for the grant of a building permit, but challenges the showing made by the city to justify these exactions. She argues that the city has identified "no special benefits" conferred on her, and has not identified any "special quantifiable burdens" created by her new store that would justify the particular dedications required from her which are not required from the public at large.

III

In evaluating petitioner's claim, we must first determine whether the "essential nexus" exists between the "legitimate state interest" and the permit condition exacted by the city. If we find that a nexus exists, we must then decide the required degree of connection between the exactions and the projected impact of the proposed development. . . .

A

. . . Undoubtedly, the prevention of flooding along Fanno Creek and the reduction of traffic congestion in the Central Business District qualify as the type of legitimate public purposes we have upheld. It seems equally obvious that a nexus exists between preventing flooding along Fanno Creek and limiting development within the creek's 100-year flood-plain. . . .

The same may be said for the city's attempt to reduce traffic congestion by providing for alternative means of transportation. In theory, a pedestrian/bicycle pathway provides a useful alternative means of transportation for workers and shoppers. . . .

B

The second part of our analysis requires us to determine whether the degree of the exactions demanded by the city's permit conditions bear the required relationship to the projected impact of petitioner's proposed development. . . .

The city required that petitioner dedicate "to the city as Greenway all portions of the site that fall within the existing 100-year floodplain [of Fanno Creek] ... and all property 15 feet above [the floodplain] boundary." In addition, the city demanded that the retail store be designed so as not to intrude into the greenway area. The city relies on the Commission's rather tentative findings that increased stormwater flow from petitioner's property "can only add to the public need to manage the [floodplain] for drainage purposes" to support its conclusion that the "requirement of dedication of the floodplain area on the site is related to the applicant's plan to intensify development on the site."

The city made the following specific findings relevant to the pedestrian/bicycle pathway:

> "In addition, the proposed expanded use of this site is anticipated to generate additional vehicular traffic thereby increasing congestion on nearby collector and arterial streets. Creation of a convenient, safe pedestrian/bicycle pathway system as an alternative means of transportation could offset some of the traffic demand on these nearby streets and lessen the increase in traffic congestion."

The question for us is whether these findings are constitutionally sufficient to justify the conditions imposed by the city on petitioner's building permit. Since state courts have been dealing with this question a good deal longer than we have, we turn to representative decisions made by them.

In some States, very generalized statements as to the necessary connection between the required dedication and the proposed development seem to suffice. ... We think this standard is too lax to adequately protect petitioner's right to just compensation if her property is taken for a public purpose.

Other state courts require a very exacting correspondence, described as the "specifi[c] and uniquely attributable" test. ... Under this standard, if the local government cannot demonstrate that its exaction is directly proportional to the specifically created need, the exaction becomes "a veiled exercise of the power of eminent domain and a confiscation of private property behind the defense of police regulations." We do not think the Federal Constitution requires such exacting scrutiny, given the nature of the interests involved.

A number of state courts have taken an intermediate position, requiring the municipality to show a "reasonable relationship" between the required dedication and the impact of the proposed development. ...

We think the "reasonable relationship" test adopted by a majority of the state courts is closer to the federal constitutional norm than either of those previously discussed. But we do not adopt it as such, partly because the term "reasonable relationship" seems confusingly similar to the term "rational basis" which describes the minimal level of scrutiny under the

Equal Protection Clause of the Fourteenth Amendment. We think a term such as "rough proportionality" best encapsulates what we hold to be the requirement of the Fifth Amendment. No precise mathematical calculation is required, but the city must make some sort of individualized determination that the required dedication is related both in nature and extent to the impact of the proposed development.

JUSTICE STEVENS' dissent relies upon a law review article for the proposition that the city's conditional demands for part of petitioner's property are "a species of business regulation that heretofore warranted a strong presumption of constitutional validity." But simply denominating a governmental measure as a "business regulation" does not immunize it from constitutional challenge on the grounds that it violates a provision of the Bill of Rights. . . . We see no reason why the Takings Clause of the Fifth Amendment, as much a part of the Bill of Rights as the First Amendment or Fourth Amendment, should be relegated to the status of a poor relation in these comparable circumstances. We turn now to analysis of whether the findings relied upon by the city here, first with respect to the floodplain easement, and second with respect to the pedestrian/bicycle path, satisfied these requirements.

It is axiomatic that increasing the amount of impervious surface will increase the quantity and rate of stormwater flow from petitioner's property. Therefore, keeping the floodplain open and free from development would likely confine the pressures on Fanno Creek created by petitioner's development. In fact, because petitioner's property lies within the Central Business District, the Community Development Code already required that petitioner leave 15% of it as open space and the undeveloped floodplain would have nearly satisfied that requirement. But the city demanded more—it not only wanted petitioner not to build in the floodplain, but it also wanted petitioner's property along Fanno Creek for its Greenway system. The city has never said why a public greenway, as opposed to a private one, was required in the interest of flood control.

The difference to petitioner, of course, is the loss of her ability to exclude others. . . . It is difficult to see why recreational visitors trampling along petitioner's floodplain easement are sufficiently related to the city's legitimate interest in reducing flooding problems along Fanno Creek, and the city has not attempted to make any individualized determination to support this part of its request.

The city contends that recreational easement along the Greenway is only ancillary to the city's chief purpose in controlling flood hazards. It further asserts that unlike the residential property at issue in *Nollan*, petitioner's property is commercial in character and therefore, her right to exclude others is compromised. . . .

Admittedly, petitioner wants to build a bigger store to attract members of the public to her property. She also wants, however, to be able to control the time and manner in which they enter. . . . [T]he city wants to impose a permanent recreational easement upon petitioner's property that borders Fanno Creek. Petitioner would lose all rights to regulate the time in which the public entered onto the Greenway, regardless of any interference it might pose with her retail store. Her right to exclude would not be regulated, it would be eviscerated.

If petitioner's proposed development had somehow encroached on existing greenway space in the city, it would have been reasonable to require petitioner to provide some alternative greenway space for the public either on her property or elsewhere. . . . But that is not the case here. We conclude that the findings upon which the city relies do not show the required reasonable relationship between the floodplain easement and the petitioner's proposed new building.

With respect to the pedestrian/bicycle pathway, we have no doubt that the city was correct in finding that the larger retail sales facility proposed by petitioner will increase traffic on the streets of the Central Business District. The city estimates that the proposed development would generate roughly 435 additional trips per day. Dedications for streets, sidewalks, and other public ways are generally reasonable exactions to avoid excessive congestion from a proposed property use. But on the record before us, the city has not met its burden of demonstrating that the additional number of vehicle and bicycle trips generated by the petitioner's development reasonably relate to the city's requirement for a dedication of the pedestrian/bicycle pathway easement. The city simply found that the creation of the pathway "could offset some of the traffic demand . . . and lessen the increase in traffic congestion."

As Justice Peterson of the Supreme Court of Oregon explained in his dissenting opinion, however, "[t]he findings of fact that the bicycle pathway system 'could offset some of the traffic demand' is a far cry from a finding that the bicycle pathway system will, or is likely to, offset some of the traffic demand." No precise mathematical calculation is required, but the city must make some effort to quantify its findings in support of the dedication for the pedestrian/bicycle pathway beyond the conclusory statement that it could offset some of the traffic demand generated.

IV

Cities have long engaged in the commendable task of land use planning, made necessary by increasing urbanization particularly in metropolitan areas such as Portland. The city's goals of reducing flooding hazards and traffic congestion, and providing for public greenways, are laudable, but there are outer limits to how this may be done. "A strong public desire to improve the public condition [will not] warrant achieving the desire by a shorter cut than the constitutional way of paying for the change." *Pennsylvania Coal* [*Co.* v. *Mahon* (1922)].

The judgment of the Supreme Court of Oregon is reversed, and the case is remanded for further proceedings consistent with this opinion.

It is so ordered.

JUSTICE STEVENS, with whom JUSTICE BLACKMUN and JUSTICE GINSBURG join, dissenting.

The record does not tell us the dollar value of petitioner Florence Dolan's interest in excluding the public from the greenway adjacent to her hardware business. The mountain of briefs that the case has generated nevertheless makes it obvious that the pecuniary value of her victory is far less important than the rule of law that this case has been used to establish. It is unquestionably an important case. . . .

The Court is correct in concluding that the city may not attach arbitrary conditions to a building permit or to a variance even when it can rightfully deny the application outright. I also agree that state court decisions dealing with ordinances that govern municipal development plans provide useful guidance in a case of this kind. Yet the Court's description of the doctrinal underpinnings of its decision, the phrasing of its fledgling test of "rough proportionality," and the application of that test to this case run contrary to the traditional treatment of these cases and break considerable and unpropitious new ground.

I

Candidly acknowledging the lack of federal precedent for its exercise in rulemaking, the Court purports to find guidance in 12 "representative" state court decisions. To do so is certainly appropriate. The state cases the Court consults, however, either fail to support or decidedly undermine the Court's conclusions in key respects.

First, although discussion of the state cases permeates the Court's analysis of the appropriate test to apply in this case, the test on which the Court settles is not naturally derived from those courts' decisions. . . .

Not one of the state cases cited by the Court announces anything akin to a "rough proportionality" requirement. For the most part, moreover, those cases that invalidated municipal ordinances did so on state law or unspecified grounds roughly equivalent to *Nollan*'s "essential nexus" requirement. . . . Although 4 of the 12 opinions mention the Federal Constitution—two of those only in passing—it is quite obvious that neither the courts nor the litigants imagined they might be participating in the development of a new rule of federal law. Thus, although these state cases do lend support to the Court's reaffirmance of *Nollan*'s reasonable nexus requirement, the role the Court accords them in the announcement of its newly minted second phase of the constitutional inquiry is remarkably inventive.

In addition, the Court ignores the state courts' willingness to consider what the property owner gains from the exchange in question. . . . In this case . . . Dolan's acceptance of the permit, with its attached conditions, would provide her with benefits that may well go beyond any advantage she gets from expanding her business. As the United States pointed out at oral argument, the improvement that the city's drainage plan contemplates would widen the channel and reinforce the slopes to increase the carrying capacity during serious floods, "confer[ring] considerable benefits on the property owners immediately adjacent to the creek."

The state court decisions also are enlightening in the extent to which they required that the entire parcel be given controlling importance. All but one of the cases involve challenges to provisions in municipal ordinances requiring developers to dedicate either a percentage of the entire parcel . . . or an equivalent value in cash . . . to help finance the construction of roads, utilities, schools, parks and playgrounds. In assessing the legality of the conditions, the courts gave no indication that the transfer of an interest in realty was any more objectionable than a cash payment. None of the decisions identified the surrender of the fee owner's "power to exclude" as having any special significance. Instead, the courts uniformly examined the character of the entire economic transaction.

II

It is not merely state cases, but our own cases as well, that require the analysis to focus on the impact of the city's action on the entire parcel of private property. . . .

The Court's narrow focus on one strand in the property owner's bundle of rights is particularly misguided in a case involving the development of commercial property. . . . The exactions associated with the development of a retail business are likewise a species of business regulation that heretofore warranted a strong presumption of constitutional validity.

. . . The city of Tigard has demonstrated that its plan is rational and impartial and that the conditions at issue are "conducive to fulfillment of authorized planning objectives." Dolan, on the other hand, has offered no evidence that her burden of compliance has any impact at all on the value or profitability of her planned development. Following the teaching of the cases on which it purports to rely, the Court should not isolate the burden associated with the loss of the power to exclude from an evaluation of the benefit to be derived from the permit to enlarge the store and the parking lot.

The Court's assurances that its "rough proportionality" test leaves ample room for cities to pursue the "commendable task of land use planning"—even twice avowing that "[n]o precise mathematical calculation is required"—are wanting given the result that test compels here. Under the Court's approach, a city must not only "quantify its findings" and make "individualized determination[s]" with respect to the nature *and* the extent of the relationship between the conditions and the impact, but also demonstrate "proportionality." The correct inquiry should instead concentrate on whether the required nexus is present and venture beyond considerations of a condition's nature or germaneness only if the developer establishes that a concededly germane condition is so grossly disproportionate to the proposed development's adverse effects that it manifests motives other than land use regulation on the part of the city. The heightened requirement the Court imposes on cities is even more unjustified when all the tools needed to resolve the questions presented by this case can be garnered from our existing case law.

III

Applying its new standard, the Court finds two defects in the city's case. First, while the record would adequately support a requirement that Dolan maintain the portion of the floodplain on her property as undeveloped open space, it does not support the additional requirement that the floodplain be dedicated to the city. Second, while the city adequately established the traffic increase that the proposed development would generate, it failed to quantify the offsetting decrease in automobile traffic that the bike path will produce. Even under the Court's new rule, both defects are, at most, nothing more than harmless error.

In her objections to the floodplain condition, Dolan made no effort to demonstrate that the dedication of that portion of her property would be any more onerous than a simple prohibition against any development on that portion of her property. Given the commercial character of both the existing and the proposed use of the property as a retail store, it seems likely that potential customers "trampling along petitioner's floodplain" are more valuable than a useless parcel of vacant land. Moreover, the duty to pay taxes and the responsibility for potential tort liability may well make ownership of the fee interest in useless land a liability rather than an asset. That may explain why Dolan never conceded that she could be prevented from building on the floodplain. The City Attorney also pointed out that absent a dedication, property owners would be required to "build on their own land" and "with their own money" a storage facility for the water runoff. Dolan apparently "did have that option," but chose not to seek it. If Dolan might have been entitled to a variance confining the city's condition in a manner this Court would accept, her failure to seek that narrower form of relief at any stage of the state administrative and judicial proceedings clearly should preclude that relief in this Court now.

The Court's rejection of the bike path condition amounts to nothing more than a play on words. Everyone agrees that the bike path "could" offset some of the increased traffic flow that the larger store will generate, but the findings do not unequivocally state that it *will* do so, or tell us just how many cyclists will replace motorists. Predictions on such matters are inherently nothing more than estimates. Certainly the assumption that there will be an offsetting benefit here is entirely reasonable and should suffice whether it amounts to 100 percent, 35 percent, or only 5 percent of the increase in automobile traffic that would otherwise occur. If the Court proposes to have the federal judiciary micromanage state decisions of this kind, it is indeed extending its welcome mat to a significant new class of litigants. Although there is no reason to believe that state courts have failed to rise to the task, property owners have surely found a new friend today.

IV

The Court has made a serious error by abandoning the traditional presumption of constitutionality and imposing a novel burden of proof on a city implementing an admittedly valid comprehensive land use plan. Even more consequential than its incorrect disposition of this case, however, is the Court's resurrection of a species of substantive due process analysis that it firmly rejected decades ago.

The Court begins its constitutional analysis by citing *Chicago, B. & Q. R. Co.* v. *Chicago* (1897) for the proposition that the Takings Clause of the Fifth Amendment is "applicable to the States through the Fourteenth Amendment." That opinion, however, contains no mention of either the Takings Clause or the Fifth Amendment; it held that the protection afforded by the Due Process Clause of the Fourteenth Amendment extends to matters of substance as well as procedure, and that the substance of "the due process of law enjoined by the Fourteenth Amendment requires compensation to be made or adequately secured to the owner of private property taken for public use under the authority of a State." It applied the same kind of substantive due process analysis more frequently identified with a better known case that accorded similar substantive protection to a baker's liberty interest in working 60 hours a week and 10 hours a day. See *Lochner* v. *New York* (1905).

Later cases have interpreted the Fourteenth Amendment's substantive protection against uncompensated deprivations of private property by the States as though it incorporated the text of the Fifth Amendment's Takings Clause. . . . Justice Holmes charted a significant new course, however, when he opined that a state law making it "commercially impracticable to mine certain coal" had "very nearly the same effect for constitutional purposes as appropriating or destroying it." *Pennsylvania Coal Co.* v. *Mahon* (1922). The so-called "regulatory takings" doctrine that the Holmes dictum kindled has an obvious kinship with the line of substantive due process cases that *Lochner* exemplified. Besides having similar ancestry, both doctrines are potentially open-ended sources of judicial power to invalidate state economic regulations that Members of this Court view as unwise or unfair.

This case inaugurates an even more recent judicial innovation than the regulatory takings doctrine: the application of the "unconstitutional conditions" label to a mutually beneficial transaction between a property owner and a city. The Court tells us that the city's refusal to grant Dolan a discretionary benefit infringes her right to receive just compensation for the property interests that she has refused to dedicate to the city "where the property sought has little or no relationship to the benefit." Although it is well settled that a government cannot deny a benefit on a basis that infringes constitutionally protected interests—especially [one's] interest in freedom of speech," *Perry* v. *Sindermann* (1972)—the "unconstitutional conditions" doctrine provides an inadequate framework in which to analyze this case.

Dolan has no right to be compensated for a taking unless the city acquires the property interests that she has refused to surrender. Since no taking has yet occurred, there has not been any infringement of her constitutional right to compensation. . . .

Even if Dolan should accept the city's conditions in exchange for the benefit that she seeks, it would not necessarily follow that she had been denied "just compensation" since it would be appropriate to consider the receipt of that benefit in any calculation of "just compensation.". . . Particularly in the absence of any evidence on the point, we should not presume that the discretionary benefit the city has offered is less valuable than the property interests that Dolan can retain or surrender at her option. But even if that discretionary benefit were so trifling that it could not be considered just compensation when it has "little or no relationship" to the property, the Court fails to explain why the same value would suffice when the required nexus is present. In this respect, the Court's reliance on the "unconstitutional conditions" doctrine is assuredly novel, and arguably incoherent. The city's conditions are by no means immune from constitutional scrutiny. The level of scrutiny, however, does not approximate the kind of review that would apply if the city had insisted on a surrender of Dolan's First Amendment rights in exchange for a building permit. One can only hope that the Court's reliance today on

First Amendment cases and its candid disavowal of the term "rational basis" to describe its new standard of review do not signify a reassertion of the kind of superlegislative power the Court exercised during the *Lochner* era. . . .

In our changing world one thing is certain: uncertainty will characterize predictions about the impact of new urban developments on the risks of floods, earthquakes, traffic congestion, or environmental harms. When there is doubt concerning the magnitude of those impacts, the public interest in averting them must outweigh the private interest of the commercial entrepreneur. If the government can demonstrate that the conditions it has imposed in a land-use permit are rational, impartial and conducive to fulfilling the aims of a valid land-use plan, a strong presumption of validity should attach to those conditions. The burden of demonstrating that those conditions have unreasonably impaired the economic value of the proposed improvement belongs squarely on the shoulders of the party challenging the state action's constitutionality. That allocation of burdens has served us well in the past. The Court has stumbled badly today by reversing it.

I respectfully dissent.

JUSTICE SOUTER, dissenting.

This case, like *Nollan* v. *California Coastal Comm'n* (1987), invites the Court to examine the relationship between conditions imposed by development permits, requiring landowners to dedicate portions of their land for use by the public, and governmental interests in mitigating the adverse effects of such development. *Nollan* declared the need for a nexus between the nature of an exaction of an interest in land (a beach easement) and the nature of governmental interests. The Court treats this case as raising a further question, not about the nature, but about the degree, of connection required between such an exaction and the adverse effects of development. The Court's opinion announces a test to address this question, but as I read the opinion, the Court does not apply that test to these facts, which do not raise the question the Court addresses.

First, as to the floodplain and Greenway, the Court acknowledges that an easement of this land for open space (and presumably including the five feet required for needed creek channel improvements) is reasonably related to flood control, but argues that the "permanent recreational easement" for the public on the Greenway is not so related. . . . It seems to me such incidental recreational use can stand or fall with the bicycle path, which the city justified by reference to traffic congestion. As to the relationship the Court examines, between the recreational easement and a purpose never put forth as a justification by the city, the Court unsurprisingly finds a recreation area to be unrelated to flood control.

Second, as to the bicycle path, the Court again acknowledges the "theor[etically]" reasonable relationship between "the city's attempt to reduce traffic congestion by providing [a bicycle path] for alternative means of transportation" and the "correct" finding of the city that "the larger retail sales facility proposed by petitioner will increase traffic on the streets of the Central Business District." The Court only faults the city for saying that the bicycle path "could" rather than "would" offset the increased traffic from the store. . . .

I cannot agree that the application of *Nollan* is a sound one here, since it appears that the Court has placed the burden of producing evidence of relationship on the city, despite the usual rule in cases involving the police power that the government is presumed to have acted constitutionally. Having thus assigned the burden, the Court concludes that the City loses based on one word ("could" instead of "would"), and despite the fact that this record shows the connection the Court looks for. . . .

In any event, on my reading, the Court's conclusions about the city's vulnerability carry the Court no further than *Nollan* has gone already, and I do not view this case as a suitable vehicle for taking the law beyond that point. The right case for the enunciation of takings doctrine seems hard to spot.

□□□

Nos. 93-517, 93-527 and 93-539

Board of Education of Kiryas Joel Village School District, Petitioner v. Louis Grumet et al.

Board of Education of Monroe-Woodbury Central School District, Petitioner v. Louis Grumet et al.

Attorney General of New York, Petitioner v. Louis Grumet et al.

On writs of certiorari to the Court of Appeals of New York

[June 27, 1994]

JUSTICE SOUTER delivered the opinion of the Court.

The Village of Kiryas Joel in Orange County, New York, is a religious enclave of Satmar Hasidim, practitioners of a strict form of Judaism. The village fell within the Monroe-Woodbury Central School District until a special state statute passed in 1989 carved out a separate district, following village lines, to serve this distinctive population. The question is whether the Act creating the separate school district violates the Establishment Clause of the First Amendment, binding on the States through the Fourteenth Amendment. Because this unusual act is tantamount to an allocation of political power on a religious criterion and neither presupposes nor requires governmental impartiality toward religion, we hold that it violates the prohibition against establishment.

I

The Satmar Hasidic sect takes its name from the town near the Hungarian and Romanian border where, in the early years of this century, Grand Rebbe Joel Teitelbaum molded the group into a distinct community. After World War II and the destruction of much of European Jewry, the Grand Rebbe and most of his surviving followers moved to the Williamsburg section of Brooklyn, New York. Then, 20 years ago, the Satmars purchased an approved but undeveloped subdivision in the town of Monroe and began assembling the community that has since become the Village of Kiryas Joel. When a zoning dispute arose in the course of settlement, the Satmars presented the Town Board of Monroe with a petition to form a new village within the town. . . . Neighbors who did not wish to secede with the Satmars objected strenuously, and after arduous negotiations the proposed boundaries of the Village of Kiryas Joel were drawn to include just the 320 acres owned and inhabited entirely by Satmars. The village, incorporated in 1977, has a population of about 8,500 today. Rabbi Aaron Teitelbaum, eldest son of the current Grand Rebbe, serves as the village rov (chief rabbi) and rosh yeshivah (chief authority in the parochial schools).

The residents of Kiryas Joel are vigorously religious people who make few concessions to the modern world and go to great lengths to avoid assimilation into it. They interpret the Torah strictly; segregate the sexes outside the home; speak Yiddish as their primary language; eschew television, radio, and English-language publications; and dress in distinctive ways that include headcoverings and special garments for boys and modest dresses for girls. Children are educated in private religious schools, most boys at the United Talmudic Academy where they receive a thorough grounding in the Torah and limited exposure to secular subjects, and most girls at Bais Rochel, an affiliated school with a curriculum designed to prepare girls for their roles as wives and mothers.

These schools do not, however, offer any distinctive services to handicapped children, who are entitled under state and federal law to special education services even when enrolled in private schools. Starting in 1984 the Monroe-Woodbury Central School District provided such services for the children of Kiryas Joel at an annex to Bais Rochel, but a year later ended that arrangement in response to our decisions in *Aguilar* v. *Felton* (1985) and *School Dist. of Grand Rapids* v. *Ball* (1985). Children from Kiryas Joel who needed special education (including the deaf, the mentally retarded, and others suffering from a range of physical, mental, or emotional disorders) were then forced to attend public schools outside the village, which their families found highly unsatisfactory. Parents of most of these children withdrew them from the Monroe-Woodbury secular schools, citing "the panic, fear and trauma [the children] suffered in leaving their own community and being with people whose ways were so different," and some sought administrative review of the public-school placements.

Monroe-Woodbury ... sought a declaratory judgment in state court that New York law barred the district from providing special education services outside the district's regular public schools. The New York Court of Appeals disagreed, holding that state law left Monroe-Woodbury free to establish a separate school in the village because it gives educational authorities broad discretion in fashioning an appropriate program. . . .

By 1989, only one child from Kiryas Joel was attending Monroe-Woodbury's public schools; the village's other handicapped children received privately funded special services or went without. It was then that the New York Legislature passed the statute at issue in this litigation, which provided that the Village of Kiryas Joel "is constituted a separate school district, . . . and shall have and enjoy all the powers and duties of a union free school district. . . ." . . . In signing the bill into law, Governor Cuomo recognized that the residents of the new school district were "all members of the same religious sect," but said that the bill was "a good faith effort to solve th[e] unique problem" associated with providing special education services to handicapped children in the village.

Although it enjoys plenary legal authority over the elementary and secondary education of all school-aged children in the village, the Kiryas Joel Village School District currently runs only a special education program for handicapped children. The other village children have stayed in their parochial schools, relying on the new school district only for transportation, remedial education, and health and welfare services. If any child without handicap in Kiryas Joel were to seek a public-school education, the district would pay tuition to send the child into Monroe-Woodbury or another school district nearby. Under like arrangements, several of the neighboring districts send their handicapped Hasidic children into Kiryas Joel, so that two thirds of the full-time students in the village's public school come from outside. In all, the new district serves just over 40 full-time students, and two or three times that many parochial school students on a part-time basis.

Several months before the new district began operations, the New York State School Boards Association and respondents Grumet and Hawk brought this action . . . challenging Chapter 748 under the national and state constitutions as an unconstitutional establishment of religion. . . . On cross-motions for summary judgment, the trial court ruled for the plaintiffs (respondents here), finding that the statute failed all three prongs of the test in *Lemon* v. *Kurtzman* (1971) and was thus unconstitutional under both the National and State Constitutions.

A divided Appellate Division affirmed on the ground that Chapter 748 had the primary effect of advancing religion, in violation of both constitutions, and the state Court of Appeals affirmed on the federal question, while expressly reserving the state constitutional issue. . . .

We stayed the mandate of the Court of Appeals (1993) and granted certiorari (1993).

II

"A proper respect for both the Free Exercise and the Establishment Clauses compels the State to pursue a course of 'neutrality' toward religion," *Committee for Public Ed. & Religious Liberty* v. *Nyquist* (1973), favoring neither one religion over others nor religious adherents collectively over nonadherents. Chapter 748, the statute creating the Kiryas Joel Village School District, departs from this constitutional command by delegating the State's discretionary authority over public schools to a group defined by its character as a religious community, in a legal and historical context that gives no assurance that governmental power has been or will be exercised neutrally.

Larkin v. *Grendel's Den, Inc.* (1982) provides an instructive comparison with the litigation before us. There, the Court was requested to strike down a Massachusetts statute granting religious bodies veto power over applications for liquor licenses. . . . In spite of the State's valid interest in protecting churches, schools, and like institutions from " 'the hurly-burly' associated with liquor outlets," the Court found that in two respects the statute violated "the wholesome 'neutrality' of which this Court's cases speak." The Act brought about a " 'fusion of governmental and religious functions' " by delegating "important, discretionary governmental powers" to religious bodies, thus impermissibly entangling government and religion. . . . [S]ee also *Lemon* v. *Kurtzman*. And it lacked "any 'effective means of guaranteeing' that the delegated power '[would] be used exclusively for secular, neutral, and nonideological purposes' "; this, along with the "significant symbolic benefit to religion" associated with "the mere appearance of a joint exercise of legislative authority by Church and State," led the Court to conclude that the statute had a " 'primary' and 'principal' effect of advancing religion." . . . [S]ee also *Lemon* v. *Kurtzman*. Comparable constitutional problems inhere in the statute before us.

A

Larkin presented an example of united civic and religious authority, an establishment rarely found in such straightforward form in modern America, and a violation of "the core rationale underlying the Establishment Clause.". . .

The Establishment Clause problem presented by Chapter 748 is more subtle, but it resembles the issue raised in *Larkin* to the extent that the earlier case teaches that a State may not delegate its civic authority to a group chosen according to a religious criterion. Authority over public schools belongs to the State and cannot be delegated to a local school district defined by the State in order to grant political control to a religious group. What makes this litigation different from *Larkin* is the delegation here of civic power to the "qualified voters of the village of Kiryas Joel," as distinct from a religious leader such as the village rov, or an institution of religious government like the formally constituted parish council in *Larkin*. In light of the circumstances of this case, however, this distinction turns out to lack constitutional significance.

It is, first, not dispositive that the recipients of state power in this case are a group of religious individuals united by common doctrine, not the group's leaders or officers. Although some school district franchise is common to all voters, the State's manipulation of the franchise for this district limited it to Satmars, giving the sect exclusive control of the political subdivision. In the circumstances of this case, the difference between thus vesting state power in the members of a religious group as such instead of the officers of its sectarian organization is one of form, not substance. . . . If New York were to delegate civic authority to "the Grand Rebbe," *Larkin* would obviously require invalidation . . . and the same is true if New York delegates political authority by reference to religious belief. Where "fusion" is an issue, the difference lies in the distinction between a government's purposeful delegation on the basis of religion and a delegation on principles neutral to religion, to individuals whose religious identities are incidental to their receipt of civic authority.

Of course, Chapter 748 delegates power not by express reference to the religious belief of the Satmar community, but to residents of the "territory of the village of Kiryas Joel." Thus the second (and arguably more important) distinction between this case and *Larkin* is the identification here of the group to exercise civil authority in terms not expressly religious. But our analysis does not end with the text of the statute at issue, and the context here persuades us that Chapter 748 effectively identifies these recipients of governmental authority by reference to doctrinal adherence, even though it does not do so expressly. We find this to be the better view of the facts because of the way the boundary lines of the school district divide residents according to religious affiliation, under the terms of an unusual and special legislative act.

It is undisputed that those who negotiated the village boundaries when applying the general village incorporation statute drew them so as to exclude all but Satmars, and that the New York Legislature was well aware that the village remained exclusively Satmar in 1989 when it adopted Chapter 748. The significance of this fact to the state legislature is indicated by the further fact that carving out the village school district ran counter to customary districting practices in the State. Indeed, the trend in New York is not toward dividing school districts but toward consolidating them. The thousands of small common school districts laid out in the early 19th century have been combined and recombined, first into union free school districts and then into larger central school districts, until only a tenth as many remain today. Most of these cover several towns, many of them cross county boundaries, and only one remains precisely coterminous with an incorporated village. The object of the State's practice of consolidation is the creation of districts large enough to provide a comprehensive education at affordable cost, which is thought to require at least 500 pupils for a combined junior-senior high school. The Kiryas Joel Village School District, in contrast, has only 13 local, full-time students in all (even including out-of-area and part-time students leaves the number under 200), and in offering only special education and remedial programs it makes no pretense to be a full-service district.

The origin of the district in a special act of the legislature, rather than the State's general laws governing school district reorganization, is likewise anomalous. Although the legislature has established some 20 existing school districts by special act, all but one of these are districts in name only, having been designed to be run by private organizations serving institutionalized children. They have neither tax bases nor student populations of their own but serve children placed by other school districts or public agencies. . . . The one school district petitioners point to that was formed by special act of the legislature to serve a whole community, as this one was, is a district formed for a new town, much larger and more heterogeneous than this village, being built on land that straddled two existing districts. Thus the Kiryas Joel Village School District is exceptional to the point of singularity, as the only district coming to our notice that the legislature carved from a single existing district to serve local residents. . . .

Because the district's creation ran uniquely counter to state practice, following the lines of a religious community where the customary and neutral principles would not have dictated the same result, we have good reasons to treat this district as the reflection of a religious criterion for identifying the recipients of civil authority. Not even the special needs of the children in this community can explain the legislature's unusual Act, for the State could have responded to the concerns of the Satmar parents without implicating the Establishment Clause, as we explain in some detail further on. We therefore find the legislature's Act to be substantially equivalent to defining a political subdivision and hence the qualification for its franchise by a religious test, resulting in a purposeful and forbidden "fusion of governmental and religious functions." *Larkin* v. *Grendel's Den.*

B

The fact that this school district was created by a special and unusual Act of the legislature also gives reason for concern whether the benefit received by the Satmar community is one that the legislature will provide equally to other religious (and nonreligious) groups. This is the second malady the *Larkin* Court identified in the law before it, the absence of an "effective means of guaranteeing" that governmental power will be and has been neutrally employed. But whereas in *Larkin* it was religious groups the Court thought might exercise civic power to advance the interests of religion (or religious adherents), here the threat to neutrality occurs at an antecedent stage.

The fundamental source of constitutional concern here is that the legislature itself may fail to exercise governmental authority in a religiously neutral way. The anomalously case-specific nature of the legislature's exercise of state authority in creating this district for a religious community leaves the Court without any direct way to review such state action for the purpose of safeguarding a principle at the heart of the Establishment Clause, that government should not prefer one religion to another, or religion to irreligion. Because the religious community of Kiryas Joel did not receive its new governmental authority simply as one of many communities eligible for equal treatment under a general law, we have no assurance that the next similarly situated group seeking a school district of its own will receive one; unlike an administrative agency's denial of an exemption from a generally applicable law, which "would be entitled to a judicial audience," a legislature's failure to enact a special law is itself unreviewable. Nor can the historical context in this case furnish us with any reason to suppose that the Satmars are merely one in a series of communities receiving the benefit of special school district laws. Early on in the development of public education in New York, the State rejected highly localized school districts for New York City when they were promoted as a way to allow separate schooling for Roman Catholic children. And in more recent history, the special Act in this case stands alone.

The general principle that civil power must be exercised in a manner neutral to religion is one the *Larkin* Court recognized, although it did not discuss the specific possibility of legislative favoritism along religious lines because the statute before it delegated state authority to any religious group assembled near the premises of an applicant for a liquor license as well as to a further category of institutions not identified by religion. But the principle is well grounded in our case law, as we have frequently relied explicitly on the general availability of any benefit provided religious groups or individuals in turning aside Establishment Clause challenges. In *Walz* v. *Tax Comm'n of New York City* (1970), for example, the Court sustained a property tax exemption for religious properties in part because the State had "not singled out one particular church or religious group or even churches as such," but had exempted "a broad class of property owned by nonprofit, quasi-public corporations." And *Bowen* v. *Kendrick* (1988) upheld a statute enlisting a "wide spectrum of organizations" in addressing adolescent sexuality because the law was "neutral with respect to the grantee's status as a sectarian or purely secular institution." See also *Texas Monthly, Inc.* v. *Bullock* (1989) (striking down sales tax exemption exclusively for religious publications). . . . Here the benefit flows only to a single sect, but aiding this single, small religious group causes no less a constitutional problem than would follow from aiding a sect with more members or religion as a whole, and we are forced to conclude that the State of New York has violated the Establishment Clause.

C

In finding that Chapter 748 violates the requirement of governmental neutrality by extending the benefit of a special franchise, we do not deny that the Constitution allows the state to accommodate religious needs by alleviating special burdens. Our cases leave no doubt that in commanding neutrality the Religion Clauses do not require the government to be oblivious to impositions that legitimate exercises of state power may place on religious belief and practice. Rather, there is "ample room under the Establishment Clause for 'benevolent neutrality which will permit religious exercise to exist without sponsorship and without interference,'" *Corporation of Presiding Bishop of Church of Jesus Christ of Latter-Day Saints* v. *Amos* (1987). . . . The fact that Chapter 748 facilitates the practice of religion is not what renders it an unconstitutional establishment. . . .

But accommodation is not a principle without limits, and what petitioners seek is an adjustment to the Satmars' religiously grounded preferences that our cases do not countenance. Prior decisions have allowed religious communities and institutions to pursue their own interests free from governmental interference, . . . but we have never hinted that an otherwise unconstitutional delegation of political power to a religious group could be saved as a religious accommodation. Petitioners' proposed accommodation singles out a particular religious sect for special treatment, and whatever the limits of permissible legislative accommodations may be, ... it is clear that neutrality as among religions must be honored. ...

This conclusion does not, however, bring the Satmar parents, the Monroe-Woodbury school district, or the State of New York to the end of the road in seeking ways to respond to the parents' concerns. Just as the Court in *Larkin* observed that the State's interest in protecting religious meeting places could be "readily accomplished by other means," there are several alternatives here for providing bilingual and bicultural special education to Satmar children. Such services can perfectly well be offered to village children through the Monroe-Woodbury Central School District. Since the Satmars do not claim that separatism is religiously mandated, their children may receive bilingual and bicultural instruction at a public school already run by the Monroe-Woodbury district. Or if the educationally appropriate offering by Monroe-Woodbury should turn out to be a separate program of bilingual and bicultural education at a neutral site near one of the village's parochial schools, this Court has already made it clear that no Establishment Clause difficulty would inhere in such a scheme, administered in accordance with neutral principles that would not necessarily confine special treatment to Satmars.

To be sure, the parties disagree on whether the services Monroe-Woodbury actually provided in the late 1980's were appropriately tailored to the needs of Satmar children, but this dispute is of only limited relevance to the question whether such services could have been provided, had adjustments been made. As we understand New York law, parents who are dissatisfied with their handicapped child's program have recourse through administrative review proceedings ... and if the New York Legislature should remain dissatisfied with the responsiveness of the local school district, it could certainly enact general legislation tightening the mandate to school districts on matters of special education or bilingual and bicultural offerings.

III

Justice Cardozo once cast the dissenter as "the gladiator making a last stand against the lions." JUSTICE SCALIA's dissent is certainly the work of a gladiator, but he thrusts at lions of his own imagining. We do not disable a religiously homogeneous group from exercising political power conferred on it without regard to religion. Unlike the states of Utah and New Mexico (which were laid out according to traditional political methodologies taking account of lines of latitude and longitude and topographical features . . .), the reference line chosen for the Kiryas Joel Village School District was one purposely drawn to separate Satmars from non-Satmars. Nor do we impugn the motives of the New York Legislature, which no doubt intended to accommodate the Satmar community without violating the Establishment Clause; we simply refuse to ignore that the method it chose is one that aids a particular religious community, as such, . . . rather than all groups similarly interested in separate schooling. The dissent protests it is novel to insist "up front" that a statute not tailor its benefits to apply only to one religious group, but if this were so, *Texas Monthly, Inc.* would have turned out differently, . . . and language in *Walz* v. *Tax Comm'n of New York City* and *Bowen* v. *Kendrick* purporting to rely on the breadth of the statutory schemes would have been mere surplusage. Indeed, under the dissent's theory, if New York were to pass a law providing school buses only for children attending Christian day schools, we would be constrained to uphold the statute against Establishment Clause attack until faced by a request from a non-Christian family for equal treatment under the patently unequal law. And to end on the point with which JUSTICE SCALIA begins, the license he takes in suggesting that the Court holds the Satmar sect to be New York's established church is only one symptom of his inability to accept the fact that this Court has long held that the First Amendment reaches more than classic, 18th century establishments.

Our job, of course, would be easier if the dissent's position had prevailed with the Framers and with this Court over the years. An Establishment Clause diminished to the dimensions acceptable to JUSTICE SCALIA could be enforced by a few simple rules, and our docket would never see cases requiring the application of a principle like neutrality toward religion as well as among religious sects. But that would be as blind to history as to precedent, and the difference between JUSTICE SCALIA and the Court accordingly turns on the Court's recognition that the Establishment Clause does comprehend such a principle and obligates courts to exercise the judgment necessary to apply it.

In this case we are clearly constrained to conclude that the statute before us fails the test of neutrality. It delegates a power this Court has said "ranks at the very apex of the function of a State" to an electorate defined by common religious belief and practice, in a manner that fails to foreclose religious favoritism. It therefore crosses the line from permissible accommodation to impermissible establishment. The judgment of the Court of Appeals of the State of New York is accordingly

Affirmed.

JUSTICE BLACKMUN, concurring.

For the reasons stated by JUSTICE SOUTER and JUSTICE STEVENS, whose opinions I join, I agree that the New York statute under review violates the Establishment Clause of the First Amendment. I write separately only to note my disagreement with any suggestion that today's decision signals a departure from the principles described in *Lemon* v. *Kurtzman* (1971). The opinion of the Court (and of the plurality with respect to Part II-A) relies upon several decisions, including *Larkin* v. *Grendel's Den, Inc.* (1982), that explicitly rested on the criteria set forth in *Lemon*. Indeed, the two principles on which the opinion bases its conclusion that the legislative act is constitutionally invalid essentially are the second and third *Lemon* criteria. . . .

I have no quarrel with the observation of JUSTICE O'CONNOR that the application of constitutional principles, including those articulated in *Lemon,* must be sensitive to particular contexts. But I remain convinced of the general validity of the basic principles stated in *Lemon,* which have guided this Court's Establishment Clause decisions in over 30 cases.

JUSTICE STEVENS, with whom JUSTICE BLACKMUN and JUSTICE GINSBURG join, concurring.

New York created a special school district for the members of the Satmar religious sect in response to parental concern that children suffered "panic, fear and trauma" when "leaving their own community and being with people whose ways were so different." To meet those concerns, the State could have taken steps to alleviate the children's fear by teaching their schoolmates to be tolerant and respectful of Satmar customs. Action of that kind would raise no constitutional concerns and would further the strong public interest in promoting diversity and understanding in the public schools.

Instead, the State responded with a solution that affirmatively supports a religious sect's interest in segregating itself and preventing its children from associating with their neighbors. The isolation of these children, while it may protect them from "panic, fear and trauma," also unquestionably increased the likelihood that they would remain within the fold, faithful adherents of their parents' religious faith. By creating a school district that is specifically intended to shield children from contact with others who have "different ways," the State provided official support to cement the attachment of young adherents to a particular faith. It is telling, in this regard, that two thirds of the school's full-time students are Hasidic handicapped children from outside the village; the Kiryas Joel school thus serves a population far wider than the village—one defined less by geography than by religion.

Affirmative state action in aid of segregation of this character is unlike the evenhanded distribution of a public benefit or service, a "release time" program for public school students involving no public premises or funds, or a decision to grant an exemption from a burdensome general rule. It is, I believe, fairly characterized as establishing, rather than merely accommodating, religion. For this reason, as well as the reasons set out in JUSTICE SOUTER's opinion, I am persuaded that the New York law at issue in these cases violates the Establishment Clause of the First Amendment.

JUSTICE O'CONNOR, concurring in part and concurring in the judgment.

[I, II omitted]

III

I join Parts I, II-B, II-C, and III of the Court's opinion because I think this law, rather than being a general accommodation, singles out a particular religious group for favorable treatment. The Court's analysis of the history of this law and of the surrounding statutory scheme persuades me of this.

On its face, this statute benefits one group—the residents of Kiryas Joel. Because this benefit was given to this group based on its religion, it seems proper to treat it as a legislatively drawn religious classification. I realize this is a close question, because the Satmars may be the only group who currently need this particular accommodation. The legislature may well be acting without any favoritism, so that if another group came to ask for a similar district, the group might get it on the same terms as the Satmars. But the nature of the legislative process makes it impossible to be sure of this. A legislature, unlike the judiciary or many administrative decisionmakers, has no obligation to respond to any group's requests. A group petitioning for a law may never get a definite response, or may get a "no" based not on the merits but on the press of other business or the lack of an influential sponsor. Such a legislative refusal to act would not normally be reviewable by a court. Under these circumstances, it seems dangerous to validate what appears to me a clear religious preference.

Our invalidation of this statute in no way means that the Satmars' needs cannot be accommodated. There is nothing improper about a legislative intention to accommodate a religious group, so long as it is implemented through generally applicable legislation. New York may, for instance, allow all villages to operate their own school districts. If it does not want to act so broadly, it may set forth neutral criteria that a village must meet to have a school district of its own; these criteria can then be applied by a state agency, and the decision would then be reviewable by the judiciary. A district created under a generally applicable scheme would be acceptable even though it coincides with a village which was consciously created by its voters as an enclave for their religious group. I do not think the Court's opinion holds the contrary.

I also think there is one other accommodation that would be entirely permissible: the 1984 scheme, which was discontinued because of our decision in *Aguilar* [v. *Felton* (1985)]. The Religion Clauses prohibit the government from favoring religion, but they provide no warrant for discriminating against religion. All handicapped children are entitled by law to government-funded special education. If the government provides this education on-site at public schools and at nonsectarian private schools, it is only fair that it provide it on-site at sectarian schools as well.

I thought this to be true in *Aguilar,* and I still believe it today. The Establishment Clause does not demand hostility to religion, religious ideas, religious people, or religious schools. It is the Court's insistence on disfavoring religion in *Aguilar* that led New York to favor it here. The Court should, in a proper case, be prepared to reconsider *Aguilar,* in order to bring our Establishment Clause jurisprudence back to what I think is the proper track—government impartiality, not animosity, towards religion.

IV

One aspect of the Court's opinion in this case is worth noting: Like the opinions in two recent cases, *Lee* v. *Weisman* (1992); *Zobrest* v. *Catalina Foothills School Dist.* (1993); and the case I think is most relevant to this one, *Larson* v. *Valente* (1982), the Court's opinion does not focus on the Establishment Clause test we set forth in *Lemon* v. *Kurtzman* (1971).

It is always appealing to look for a single test, a Grand Unified Theory that would resolve all the cases that may arise under a particular clause. There is, after all, only one Establishment Clause, one Free Speech Clause, one Fourth Amendment, one Equal Protection Clause.

But the same constitutional principle may operate very differently in different contexts. . . .

And setting forth a unitary test for a broad set of cases may sometimes do more harm than good. Any test that must deal with widely disparate situations risks being so vague as to be useless. . . .

Moreover, shoehorning new problems into a test that does not reflect the special concerns raised by those problems tends to deform the language of the test. Relatively simple phrases like "primary effect . . . that neither advances nor inhibits religion" and "entanglement" acquire more and more complicated definitions which stray ever further from their literal meaning. Distinctions are drawn between statutes whose effect is to advance religion and statutes whose effect is to allow religious organizations to advance religion. Assertions are made that authorizing churches to veto liquor sales in surrounding areas "can be seen as having a 'primary' and 'principal' effect of advancing religion." *Larkin* v. *Grendel's Den, Inc.* (1982). "Entanglement" is discovered in public employers monitoring the performance of public employees—surely a proper enough function—on parochial school premises, and in the public employees cooperating with the school on class scheduling and other administrative details. *Aguilar* v. *Felton*. Alternatives to *Lemon* suffer from a similar failing when they lead us to find "coercive pressure" to pray when a school asks listeners—with no threat of legal sanctions—to stand or remain silent during a graduation prayer. *Lee* v. *Weisman* (1992). Some of the results and perhaps even some of the reasoning in these cases may have been right. I joined two of the cases cited above, *Larkin* and *Lee,* and continue to believe they were correctly decided. But I think it is more useful to recognize the relevant concerns in each case on their own terms, rather than trying to squeeze them into language that does not really apply to them.

Finally, another danger to keep in mind is that the bad test may drive out the good. Rather than taking the opportunity to derive narrower, more precise tests from the case law, courts tend to continually try to patch up the broad test, making it more and more amorphous and distorted. This, I am afraid, has happened with *Lemon.*

Experience proves that the Establishment Clause, like the Free Speech Clause, cannot easily be reduced to a single test. There are different categories of Establishment Clause cases, which may call for different approaches. Some cases, like this one, involve government actions targeted at particular individuals or groups, imposing special duties or giving special benefits. Cases involving government speech on religious topics seem to me to fall into a different category and to require an analysis focusing on whether the speech endorses or disapproves of religion, rather than on whether the government action is neutral with regard to religion.

Another category encompasses cases in which the government must make decisions about matters of religious doctrine and religious law. These cases, which often arise in the application of otherwise neutral property or contract principles to religious institutions, involve complicated questions not present in other situations. . . . Government delegations of power to religious bodies may make up yet another category. As *Larkin* itself suggested, government impartiality towards religion may not be enough in such situations: A law that bars all alcohol sales within some distance of a church, school, or hospital may be valid, but an equally evenhanded law that gives each institution discretionary power over the sales may not be. Of course, there may well be additional categories, or more opportune places to draw the lines between the categories.

As the Court's opinion today shows, the slide away from *Lemon*'s unitary approach is well under way. A return to *Lemon,* even if possible, would likely be futile, regardless of where one stands on the substantive Establishment Clause questions. I think a less unitary approach provides a better structure for analysis. If each test covers a narrower and more homogeneous area, the tests may be more precise and therefore easier to apply. There may be more opportunity to pay attention to the specific nuances of each area. There might also be, I hope, more consensus on each of the narrow tests than there has been on a broad test. And abandoning the *Lemon* framework need not mean abandoning some of the insights that the test reflected, nor the insights of the cases that applied it.

Perhaps eventually under this structure we may indeed distill a unified, or at least a more unified, Establishment Clause test from the cases. But it seems to me that the case law will better be able to evolve towards this if it is freed from the *Lemon* test's rigid influence. The hard questions would, of course, still have to be asked; but they will be asked within a more carefully tailored and less distorted framework. . . .

JUSTICE KENNEDY, concurring in the judgment.

The Court's ruling that the Kiryas Joel Village School District violates the Establishment Clause is in my view correct, but my reservations about what the Court's reasoning implies for religious accommodations in general are sufficient to require a separate writing. As the Court recognizes, a legislative accommodation that discriminates among religions may become an establishment of religion. But the Court's opinion can be interpreted to say that an accommodation for a particular religious group is invalid because of the risk that the legislature will not grant the same accommodation to another religious group suffering some similar burden. This rationale seems to me without grounding in our precedents and a needless restriction upon the legislature's ability to respond to the unique problems of a particular religious group. The real vice of the school district, in my estimation, is that New York created it by drawing political boundaries on the basis of religion. I would decide the issue we confront upon this narrower theory, though in accord with many of the Court's general observations about the State's actions in this case.

[I omitted]

II

The Kiryas Joel Village School District . . . does not suffer any of the typical infirmities that might invalidate an attempted legislative accommodation. In the ordinary case, the fact that New York has chosen to accommodate the burdens unique to one religious group would raise no constitutional problems. Without further evidence that New York has denied the same accommodation to religious groups bearing similar burdens, we could not presume from the particularity of the accommodation that the New York Legislature acted with discriminatory intent.

This particularity takes on a different cast, however, when the accommodation requires the government to draw political or electoral boundaries.... [I]n my view ... government may not use religion as a criterion to draw political or electoral lines. Whether or not the purpose is accommodation and whether or not the government provides similar gerrymanders to people of all religious faiths, the Establishment Clause forbids the government to use religion as a line-drawing criterion. In this respect, the Establishment Clause mirrors the Equal Protection Clause. Just as the government may not segregate people on account of their race, so too it may not segregate on the basis of religion. The danger of stigma and stirred animosities is no less acute for religious line-drawing than for racial.... I agree with the Court insofar as it invalidates the school district for being drawn along religious lines. As the plurality observes, the New York Legislature knew that everyone within the village was Satmar when it drew the school district along the village lines, and it determined who was to be included in the district by imposing, in effect, a religious test. There is no serious question that the legislature configured the school district, with purpose and precision, along a religious line. This explicit religious gerrymandering violates the First Amendment Establishment Clause.

It is important to recognize the limits of this principle. We do not confront the constitutionality of the Kiryas Joel Village itself, and the formation of the village appears to differ from the formation of the school district in one critical respect. As the Court notes, the village was formed pursuant to a religion-neutral self-incorporation scheme. Under New York law, a territory with at least 500 residents and not more than five square miles may be incorporated upon petition by at least 20 percent of the voting residents of that territory or by the owners of more than 50 percent of the territory's real property. Aside from ensuring that the petition complies with certain procedural requirements, the supervisor of the town in which the territory is located has no discretion to reject the petition.... The residents of the town then vote upon the incorporation petition in a special election. By contrast, the Kiryas Joel Village School District was created by state legislation. The State of New York had complete discretion not to enact it. The State thus had a direct hand in accomplishing the religious segregation.

As the plurality indicates, the Establishment Clause does not invalidate a town or a state "whose boundaries are derived according to neutral historical and geographic criteria, but whose population happens to comprise coreligionists." People who share a common religious belief or lifestyle may live together without sacrificing the basic rights of self-governance that all American citizens enjoy, so long as they do not use those rights to establish their religious faith. Religion flourishes in community, and the Establishment Clause must not be construed as some sort of homogenizing solvent that forces unconventional religious groups to choose between assimilating to mainstream American culture or losing their political rights. There is more than a fine line, however, between the voluntary association that leads to a political community comprised of people who share a common religious faith, and the forced separation that occurs when the government draws explicit political boundaries on the basis of people's faith. In creating the Kiryas Joel Village School District, New York crossed that line, and so we must hold the district invalid.

III

This is an unusual case, for it is rare to see a State exert such documented care to carve out territory for people of a particular religious faith. It is also unusual in that the problem to which the Kiryas Joel Village School District was addressed is attributable in no small measure to what I believe were unfortunate rulings by this Court.

Before 1985, the handicapped Satmar children of Kiryas Joel attended the private religious schools within the village that the other Satmar children attended. Because their handicaps were in some cases acute (ranging from mental retardation and deafness to spina bifida and cerebral palsy), the State of New York provided public funds for special education of these children at annexes to the religious schools. Then came the companion cases of *School Dist. of Grand Rapids* v. *Ball* (1985) and *Aguilar* v. *Felton* (1985). In *Grand Rapids,* the Court invalidated a program in which public school teachers would offer supplemental classes at private schools, including religious schools, at the end of the regular school day. And in *Aguilar,* the Court invalidated New York City's use of Title I funding to pay the salaries of public school teachers who taught educationally deprived children of low-income families at parochial schools in the city. After these cases, the Monroe-Woodbury School District suspended its special education program at the Kiryas Joel religious schools, and the Kiryas Joel parents were forced to enroll their handicapped children at the Monroe-Woodbury public schools in order for the children to receive special education. The ensuing difficulties, as the Court recounts, led to the creation of the Kiryas Joel Village School District.

The decisions in *Grand Rapids* and *Aguilar* may have been erroneous. In light of the case before us, and in the interest of sound elaboration of constitutional doctrine, it may be necessary for us to reconsider them at a later date. A neutral aid scheme, available to religious and nonreligious alike, is the preferable way to address problems such as the Satmar handicapped children have suffered. But for *Grand Rapids* and *Aguilar,* the Satmars would have had no need to seek special accommodations or their own school district. Our decisions led them to choose that unfortunate course, with the deficiencies I have described.

One misjudgment is no excuse, however, for compounding it with another. We must confront this case as it comes before us, without bending rules to free the Satmars from a predicament into which we put them. The Establishment Clause forbids the government to draw political boundaries on the basis of religious faith. For this reason, I concur in the judgment of the Court.

JUSTICE SCALIA, with whom THE CHIEF JUSTICE and JUSTICE THOMAS join, dissenting.

The Court today finds that the Powers That Be, up in Albany, have conspired to effect an establishment of the Satmar Hasidim. I do not know who would be more surprised at this discovery: the Founders of our Nation or Grand Rebbe Joel Teitelbaum, founder of the Satmar. The Grand Rebbe would be astounded to learn that after escaping brutal persecution and coming to America with the modest hope of religious toleration for their ascetic form of Judaism, the Satmar had become so powerful, so closely allied with Mammon, as to have become an "establishment" of the Empire State. And the Founding Fathers would be astonished to find that the Establishment Clause—which they designed "to insure that no one powerful sect or combination of sects could use political or governmental power to punish dissenters"—has been employed to prohibit characteristically and admirably American accommodation of the religious practices (or more precisely, cultural peculiarities) of a tiny minority sect. *I,* however, am *not* surprised. Once this Court has abandoned text and history as guides, nothing prevents it from calling religious toleration the establishment of religion.

I

Unlike most of our Establishment Clause cases involving education, these cases involve no public funding, however slight or indirect, to private religious schools. They do not involve private schools at all. The school under scrutiny is a public school specifically designed to provide a public secular education to handicapped students. The superintendent of the school, who is not Hasidic, is a 20-year veteran of the New York City public school system, with expertise in the area of bilingual, bicultural, special education. The teachers and therapists at the school all live outside the village of Kiryas Joel. While the village's private schools are profoundly religious and strictly segregated by sex, classes at the public school are co-ed and the curriculum secular. The school building has the bland appearance of a public school, unadorned by religious symbols or markings; and the school complies with the laws and regulations governing all other New York State public schools. There is no suggestion, moreover, that this public school has gone too far in making special adjustments to the religious needs of its students. . . . In sum, these cases involve only public aid to a school that is public as can be. The only thing distinctive about the school is that all the students share the same religion.

None of our cases has ever suggested that there is anything wrong with that. In fact, the Court has specifically *approved* the education of students of a single religion on a neutral site adjacent to a private religious school. See *Wolman* v. *Walter* (1977). In that case, the Court rejected the argument that "any program that isolates the sectarian pupils is impermissible" and held that, "[t]he fact that a unit on a neutral site on occasion may serve only sectarian pupils does not provoke [constitutional] concerns." And just last Term, the Court held that the State could permit public employees to assist students in a Catholic school. See *Zobrest* v. *Catalina Foothills School Dist.* (1993) (sign-language translator for deaf student). If a State can furnish services to a group of sectarian students on a neutral site adjacent to a private religious school, or even *within* such a school, how can there be any defect in educating those same students in a public school? As the Court noted in *Wolman,* the constitutional dangers of establishment arise "from the nature of the institution, not from the nature of the pupils." There is no danger in educating religious students in a public school.

For these very good reasons, JUSTICE SOUTER's opinion does not focus upon the school, but rather upon the school district and the New York Legislature that created it. His arguments, though sometimes intermingled, are two: that reposing governmental power in the Kiryas Joel School District is the same as reposing governmental power in a religious group; and that in enacting the statute creating the district, the New York State Legislature was discriminating on the basis of religion, *i.e.,* favoring the Satmar Hasidim over others. I shall discuss these arguments in turn.

II

For his thesis that New York has unconstitutionally conferred governmental authority upon the Satmar sect, JUSTICE SOUTER relies extensively, and virtually exclusively, upon *Larkin* v. *Grendel's Den, Inc.* (1982). JUSTICE SOUTER believes that the present case "resembles"

Grendel's Den because that case "teaches that a state may not delegate its civic authority *to a group chosen according to a religious criterion*" (emphasis added). That misdescribes both what that case taught (which is that a state may not delegate its civil authority *to a church*), and what this case involves (which is a group chosen according to cultural characteristics). The statute at issue there gave churches veto power over the State's authority to grant a liquor license to establishments in the vicinity of the church. The Court had little difficulty finding the statute unconstitutional. . . .

. . . The uniqueness of the case stemmed from the grant of governmental power directly to a religious institution, and the Court's opinion focused on that fact. . . . Astonishingly, however, JUSTICE SOUTER dismisses the difference between a transfer of government power to citizens who share a common religion as opposed to "the officers of its sectarian organization"—the critical factor that made *Grendel's Den* unique and "rar[e]—as being "one of form, not substance."

JUSTICE SOUTER's steamrolling of the difference between civil authority held by a church, and civil authority held by members of a church, is breathtaking. To accept it, one must believe that large portions of the civil authority exercised during most of our history were unconstitutional, and that much more of it than merely the Kiryas Joel School District is unconstitutional today. The history of the populating of North America is in no small measure the story of groups of people sharing a common religious and cultural heritage striking out to form their own communities. It is preposterous to suggest that the civil institutions of these communities, separate from their churches, were constitutionally suspect. And if they were, surely JUSTICE SOUTER cannot mean that the inclusion of one or two nonbelievers in the community would have been enough to eliminate the constitutional vice. If the conferral of governmental power upon a religious institution *as such* (rather than upon American citizens who belong to the religious institution) is not the test of *Grendel's Den* invalidity, there is no reason why giving power to a body that is overwhelmingly dominated by the members of one sect would not suffice to invoke the Establishment Clause. That might have made the entire States of Utah and New Mexico unconstitutional at the time of their admission to the Union, and would undoubtedly make many units of local government unconstitutional today.

JUSTICE SOUTER's position boils down to the quite novel proposition that any group of citizens (say, the residents of Kiryas Joel) can be invested with political power, but not if they all belong to the same religion. Of course such *disfavoring* of religion is positively antagonistic to the purposes of the Religion Clauses, and we have rejected it before. In *McDaniel* v. *Paty* (1978), we invalidated a state constitutional amendment that would have permitted all persons to participate in political conventions, except ministers. . . . I see no reason why it is any less pernicious to deprive a group rather than an individual of its rights simply because of its religious beliefs.

Perhaps appreciating the startling implications for our constitutional jurisprudence of collapsing the distinction between religious institutions and their members, JUSTICE SOUTER tries to limit his "unconstitutional conferral of civil authority" holding by pointing out several features supposedly unique to the present case: that the "boundary lines of the school district divide residents *according* to religious affiliation" (emphasis added); that the school district was created by "a special act of the legislature"; and that the formation of the school district ran counter to the legislature's trend of consolidating districts in recent years. Assuming all these points to be true (and they are not), they would certainly bear upon whether the legislature had an impermissible religious motivation in creating the district (which is JUSTICE SOUTER's *next* point, in the discussion of which I shall reply to these arguments). But they have nothing to do with whether conferral of power upon a group of citizens can be the conferral of power upon a religious institution. It cannot. Or if it can, our Establishment Clause jurisprudence has been transformed.

III

I turn, next, to JUSTICE SOUTER's second justification for finding an establishment of religion: his facile conclusion that the New York Legislature's creation of the Kiryas Joel School District was religiously motivated. But in the Land of the Free, democratically adopted laws are not so easily impeached by unelected judges. To establish the unconstitutionality of a facially neutral law on the mere basis of its asserted religiously preferential (or discriminatory) effects—or at least to establish it in conformity with our precedents—JUSTICE SOUTER "must be able to show the absence of a neutral, secular basis" for the law. . . .

There is of course no possible doubt of a secular basis here. The New York Legislature faced a unique problem in Kiryas Joel: a community in which all the nonhandicapped children attend private schools, and the physically and mentally disabled children who attend public school suffer the additional handicap of cultural distinctiveness. It would be troublesome enough if these peculiarly dressed, handicapped students were sent to the next town, accompanied by their similarly clad but unimpaired classmates. But all the unimpaired children of Kiryas Joel attend private school. The handicapped children suffered sufficient emotional trauma from their predicament that their parents kept them home from school. Surely the legislature could target this problem, and provide a public education for these students, in the same way it addressed, *by a similar law,* the unique needs of children institutionalized in a hospital.

Since the obvious presence of a neutral, secular basis renders the asserted preferential effect of this law inadequate to invalidate it, JUSTICE SOUTER is required to come forward with direct evidence that religious preference was the objective. His case could scarcely be weaker. It consists, briefly, of this: The People of New York created the Kiryas Joel Village School District in order to further the Satmar religion, rather than for any proper secular purpose, because (1) they created the district in an extraordinary manner—by special Act of the legislature, rather than under the State's general laws governing school-district reorganization; (2) the creation of the district ran counter to a State trend towards consolidation of school districts; and (3) the District includes only adherents of the Satmar religion.

On this indictment, no jury would convict.

One difficulty with the first point is that it is not true. There was really nothing so "special" about the formation of a school district by an Act of the New York Legislature. The State has created both large school districts and small specialized school districts for institutionalized children through these special Acts. But in any event all that the first point proves, and the second point as well (countering the trend toward consolidation), is that New York regarded Kiryas Joel as a special case, requiring special measures. I should think it *obvious* that it did, and obvious that it *should have.* But even if the New York Legislature had never before created a school district by special statute (which is not true), and even if it had done nothing but consolidate school districts for over a century (which is not true), how could the departure from those past practices possibly demonstrate that the legislature had religious favoritism in mind? It could not. . . .

JUSTICE SOUTER's case against the statute comes down to nothing more, therefore, than his third point: the fact that all the residents of the Kiryas Joel Village School District are Satmars. But all its residents also wear unusual dress, have unusual civic customs, and have not much to do with people who are culturally different from them. . . . On what basis does JUSTICE SOUTER conclude that it is the theological distinctiveness rather than the cultural distinctiveness that was the basis for New York State's decision? The normal assumption would be that it was the latter, since it was not theology but dress, language, and cultural alienation that posed the educational problem for the children. JUSTICE SOUTER not only does not adopt the logical assumption, he does not even give the New York Legislature the benefit of the doubt. The following is the level of his analysis:

"Not even the special needs of the children in this community can explain the legislature's unusual Act, for the State could have responded to the concerns of the Satmar parents [by other means]."

In other words, we know the legislature must have been motivated by the desire to favor the Satmar Hasidim religion, because it *could* have met the needs of these children by a method that did not place the Satmar Hasidim in a separate school district. This is not a rational argument proving religious favoritism; it is rather a novel Establishment Clause principle to the effect that no secular objective may be pursued by a means that might also be used for religious favoritism if some other means is available.

I have little doubt that JUSTICE SOUTER would laud this humanitarian legislation if all of the distinctiveness of the students of Kiryas Joel were attributable to the fact that their parents were nonreligious commune-dwellers, or American Indians, or gypsies. The creation of a special, one-culture school district for the benefit of those children would pose no problem. The neutrality demanded by the Religion Clauses requires the same indulgence towards cultural characteristics that are accompanied by religious belief. . . .

Even if JUSTICE SOUTER could successfully establish that the cultural distinctiveness of the Kiryas Joel students (which is the problem the New York Legislature addressed) was an *essential part* of their religious belief rather than merely an *accompaniment* of their religious belief, that would not discharge his heavy burden. In order to invalidate a facially neutral law, JUSTICE SOUTER would have to show not only that legislators were aware that religion caused the problems addressed, but also that the legislature's proposed solution was motivated by a desire to disadvantage or benefit a religious group (*i.e.* to disadvantage or benefit them *because of their religion*). . . . Here a facially neutral statute extends an educational benefit to the one area where it was not effectively distributed. Whether or not the reason for the ineffective distribution had anything to do with religion, it is a remarkable stretch to say that the Act was motivated by a desire to favor or disfavor a particular religious group. The proper analogy to Chapter 748 is not the Court's hypothetical law providing school buses only to Christian students, but a law providing extra buses to rural school districts (which happen to be predominantly Southern Baptist).

At various times JUSTICE SOUTER intimates, though he does not precisely say, that the boundaries of the school district were intentionally drawn on the basis of religion. He refers, for example, to "[t]he State's manipulation of the franchise for this district . . . , giving the sect exclusive control of the political subdivision"—implying that the "giving" of political power to the religious sect was the object of the "manipulation." There is no evidence of that. The special district was created to meet the special educational needs of distinctive handicapped children, and the geographical boundaries selected for that district were (quite logically) those that already existed for the village. It sometimes appears as though the shady "manipulation" JUSTICE SOUTER has in mind is that which occurred when the village was formed, so that the drawing of its boundaries infected the coterminous boundaries of the district. He says, for example, that "[i]t is undisputed that those who negotiated the village boundaries when applying the general village incorporation statute drew them so as to exclude all but Satmars." It is indeed. But non-Satmars were excluded, not (as he intimates) because of their religion, but . . . because of their lack of desire for the high-density zoning that Satmars favored. It was a classic drawing of lines on the basis of communality of *secular governmental desires,* not communality of religion. What happened in the creation of the village is in fact precisely what happened in the creation of the school district, so that the former cannot possibly infect the latter, as JUSTICE SOUTER tries to suggest. Entirely secular reasons (zoning for the village, cultural alienation of students for the school district) produced a political unit whose members happened to share the same religion. There is no evidence (indeed, no plausible suspicion) of the legislature's desire to favor the Satmar religion, as opposed to meeting distinctive secular needs or desires of citizens who happened to be Satmars. If there were, JUSTICE SOUTER would say so; instead, he must merely insinuate.

IV

But even if Chapter 748 were intended to create a special arrangement for the Satmars *because of* their religion (not including, as I have shown in Part I, any conferral of governmental power upon a religious entity), it would be a permissible accommodation. . . .

This Court has also long acknowledged the permissibility of legislative accommodation. In one of our early Establishment Clause cases, we upheld New York City's early release program, which allowed students to be released from public school during school hours to attend religious instruction or devotional exercises. *Zorach* [v. *Clauson* (1952)]. . . . In *Walz* [v. *Tax Comm'n of N.Y. City* (1970)], we upheld a property tax exemption for religious organizations, observing that it was part of a salutary tradition of "permissible state accommodation to religion." And in [*Corporation for*] *Presiding Bishop* [of *Church of Jesus of Latter-Day Saints* v. *Amos* (1987)], we upheld a section of the Civil Rights Act of 1964 exempting religious groups from the antidiscrimination provisions of Title VII. . . .

In today's opinion, however, the Court seems uncomfortable with this aspect of our constitutional tradition. Although it acknowledges the concept of accommodation, it quickly points out that it is "not a principle without limits" and then gives reasons why the present case exceeds those limits, reasons which simply do not hold water. "[W]e have never hinted," the Court says, "that an otherwise unconstitutional delegation of political power to a religious group could be saved as a religious accommodation." Putting aside the circularity inherent in referring to a delegation as "otherwise unconstitutional" when its constitutionality turns on whether there is an accommodation, if this statement is true, it is only because we have never hinted that delegation of political power to citizens who share a particular religion could be unconstitutional. This is simply a replay of the argument we rejected in Part II.

The second and last reason the Court finds accommodation impermissible is, astoundingly, the mere risk that the State will not offer accommodation to a similar group in the future, and that neutrality will therefore not be preserved. . . .

At bottom, the Court's "no guarantee of neutrality" argument is an assertion of *this Court's* inability to control the New York Legislature's future denial of comparable accommodation. We have "no assurance," the Court says, "that the next similarly situated group seeking a school district of its own will receive one," since "a legislature's failure to enact a special law is . . . unreviewable." . . . That is true only in the technical (and irrelevant) sense that the later group denied an accommodation may need to challenge the grant of the first accommodation in light of the later denial, rather than challenging the denial directly. . . .

The Court's demand for "up front" assurances of a neutral system is at war with both traditional accommodation doctrine and the judicial role. . . . [M]ost efforts at accommodation seek to solve a problem that applies to members of only one or a few religions. Not every religion uses wine in its sacraments, but that does not make an exemption from Prohibition for sacramental wine-use impermissible, nor does it require the State granting such an exemption to explain in advance how it will treat every other claim for dispensation from its controlled-substances laws. Likewise, not every religion uses peyote in its services, but we have suggested that legislation which exempts the sacramental use of peyote from generally applicable drug laws is not only permissible, but desirable, without any suggestion that some "up front" legislative guarantee of equal treatment for sacramental substances used by other sects must be provided. The record is clear that the necessary guarantee can and will be provided, after the fact, *by the courts.* . . .

Contrary to the Court's suggestion, I do not think that the Establishment Clause prohibits formally established "state" churches and nothing more. I have always believed, and all my opinions are consistent with the view, that the Establishment Clause prohibits the favoring of one religion over others. In this respect, it is the Court that attacks lions of straw.

What I attack is the Court's imposition of novel "up front" procedural requirements on state legislatures. Making law (and making exceptions) one case at a time, whether through adjudication or through highly particularized rulemaking or legislation, violates, *ex ante,* no principle of fairness, equal protection, or neutrality, simply because it does not announce in advance how all future cases (and all future exceptions) will be disposed of. If it did, the manner of proceeding of this Court itself would be unconstitutional. It is presumptuous for this Court to impose— out of nowhere—an unheard-of prohibition against proceeding in this manner upon the Legislature of New York State. I never heard of such a principle, nor has anyone else, nor will it ever be heard of again. Unlike what the New York Legislature has done, this is a special rule to govern only the Satmar Hasidim.

[V omitted]

The Court's decision today is astounding. Chapter 748 involves no public aid to private schools and does not mention religion. In order to invalidate it, the Court casts aside, on the flimsiest of evidence, the strong presumption of validity that attaches to facially neutral laws, and invalidates the present accommodation because it does not trust New York to be as accommodating toward other religions (presumably those less powerful than the Satmar Hasidim) in the future. This is unprecedented—except that it continues, and takes to new extremes, a recent tendency in the opinions of this Court to turn the Establishment Clause into a repealer of our Nation's tradition of religious toleration. I dissent.

□□□

No. 93-44

Turner Broadcasting System, Inc., et al., Appellants v. Federal Communications Commission et al.

On appeal from the United States District Court for the District of Columbia

[June 27, 1994]

JUSTICE KENNEDY announced the judgment of the Court and delivered the opinion of the Court, except as to Part III-B.

Sections 4 and 5 of the Cable Television Consumer Protection and Competition Act of 1992 require cable television systems to devote a portion of their channels to the transmission of local broadcast television stations. This case presents the question whether these provisions abridge the freedom of speech or of the press, in violation of the First Amendment.

The United States District Court for the District of Columbia granted summary judgment for the United States, holding that the challenged provisions are consistent with the First Amendment. Because issues of material fact remain unresolved in the record as developed thus far, we vacate the District Court's judgment and remand the case for further proceedings.

I

A

The role of cable television in the Nation's communications system has undergone dramatic change over the past 45 years. Given the pace of technological advancement and the increasing convergence between cable and other electronic media, the cable industry today stands at the center of an ongoing telecommunications revolution with still undefined potential to affect the way we communicate and develop our intellectual resources.

The earliest cable systems were built in the late 1940's to bring clear broadcast television signals to remote or mountainous communities. The purpose was not to replace broadcast television but to enhance it. Modern cable systems do much more than enhance the reception of nearby broadcast television stations. With the capacity to carry dozens of channels and import distant programming signals via satellite or microwave relay, today's cable systems are in direct competition with over-the-air broadcasters as an independent source of television programming.

Broadcast and cable television are distinguished by the different technologies through which they reach viewers. Broadcast stations radiate electromagnetic signals from a central transmitting antenna. These signals can be captured, in turn, by any television set within the antenna's range. Cable systems, by contrast, rely upon a physical, point-to-point connection between a transmission facility and the television sets of individual subscribers. Cable systems make this connection much like telephone companies, using cable or optical fibers strung aboveground or buried in ducts to reach the homes or businesses of subscribers. The construction of this physical infrastructure entails the use of public rights-of-way and easements and often results in the disruption of traffic on streets and other public property. As a result, the cable medium may depend for its very existence upon express permission from local governing authorities. . . .

Cable technology affords two principal benefits over broadcast. First, it eliminates the signal interference sometimes encountered in over-the-air broadcasting and thus gives viewers undistorted reception of broadcast stations. Second, it is capable of transmitting many more channels than are available through broadcasting, giving subscribers access to far greater programming variety. More than half of the cable systems in operation today have a capacity to carry between 30 and 53 channels. And about 40 percent of cable subscribers are served by systems with a capacity of more than 53 channels. Newer systems can carry hundreds of channels, and many older systems are being upgraded with fiber optic rebuilds and digital compression technology to increase channel capacity.

The cable television industry includes both cable operators (those who own the physical cable network and transmit the cable signal to the viewer) and cable programmers (those who produce television programs and sell or license them to cable operators). In some cases, cable operators have acquired ownership of cable programmers, and vice versa. Although cable operators may create some of their own programming, most of their programming is drawn from outside sources. These outside sources include not only local or distant broadcast stations, but also the many national and regional cable programming networks that have emerged in recent years, such as CNN, MTV, ESPN, TNT, C-Span, The Family Channel, Nickelodeon, Arts and Entertainment, Black Entertainment Television, CourtTV, The Discovery Channel, American Movie Classics, Comedy Central, The Learning Channel, and The Weather Channel. Once the cable operator has selected the programming sources, the cable system functions, in essence, as a conduit for the speech of others, transmitting it on a continuous and unedited basis to subscribers. . . .

In contrast to commercial broadcast stations, which transmit signals at no charge to viewers and generate revenues by selling time to advertisers, cable systems charge subscribers a monthly fee for the right to receive cable programming and rely to a lesser extent on advertising. . . .

B

On October 5, 1992, Congress overrode a Presidential veto to enact the Cable Television Consumer Protection and Competition Act of 1992. Among other things, the Act subjects the cable industry to rate regulation by the Federal Communications Commission (FCC) and by municipal franchising authorities; prohibits municipalities from awarding exclusive franchises to cable operators; imposes various restrictions on cable programmers that are affiliated with cable operators; and directs the FCC to develop and promulgate regulations imposing minimum technical standards for cable operators. At issue in this case is the constitutionality of the so-called must-carry provisions, contained in §§ 4 and 5 of the Act, which require cable operators to carry the signals of a specified number of local broadcast television stations.

Section 4 requires carriage of "local commercial television stations," defined to include all full power television broadcasters, other than those qualifying as "noncommercial educational" stations under § 5, that operate within the same television market as the cable system. . . .

. . . [S]ubject to a few exceptions, a cable operator may not charge a fee for carrying broadcast signals in fulfillment of its must-carry obligations.

Section 5 of the Act imposes similar requirements regarding the carriage of local public broadcast television stations, referred to in the Act as local "noncommercial educational television stations." . . . As with commercial broadcast stations, § 5 requires cable system operators to carry the program schedule of the public broadcast station in its entirety and at its same over-the-air channel position.

Taken together, therefore, §§ 4 and 5 subject all but the smallest cable systems nationwide to must-carry obligations, and confer must-carry privileges on all full power broadcasters operating within the same television market as a qualified cable system.

C

Congress enacted the 1992 Cable Act after conducting three years of hearings on the structure and operation of the cable television industry. The conclusions Congress drew from its factfinding process are recited in the text of the Act itself. See §§ 2(a)(1)-(21). In brief, Congress found that the physical characteristics of cable transmission, compounded by the increasing concentration of economic power in the cable industry, are endangering the ability of over-the-air broadcast television stations to compete for a viewing audience and thus for necessary operating revenues. Congress determined that regulation of the market for video programming was necessary to correct this competitive imbalance.

In particular, Congress found that over 60 percent of the households with television sets subscribe to cable, and for these households cable has replaced over-the-air broadcast television as the primary provider of video programming. . . . In addition, Congress concluded that due to "local franchising requirements and the extraordinary expense of constructing more than one cable television system to serve a particular geographic area," the overwhelming majority of cable operators exercise a monopoly over cable service. "The result," Congress determined, "is undue market power for the cable operator as compared to that of consumers and video programmers."

According to Congress, this market position gives cable operators the power and the incentive to harm broadcast competitors. The power derives from the cable operator's ability, as owner of the transmission facility, to "terminate the retransmission of the broadcast signal, refuse to carry new signals, or reposition a broadcast signal to a disadvantageous channel position." The incentive derives from the economic reality that "[c]able television systems and broadcast television stations increasingly compete for television advertising revenues." By refusing carriage of broadcasters' signals, cable operators, as a practical matter, can reduce the number of households that have access to the broadcasters' programming, and thereby capture advertising dollars that would otherwise go to broadcast stations.

Congress found, in addition, that increased vertical integration in the cable industry is making it even harder for broadcasters to secure carriage on cable systems, because cable operators have a financial incentive to favor their affiliated programmers. Congress also determined that the cable industry is characterized by horizontal concentration, with many cable operators sharing common ownership. This has resulted in greater "barriers to entry for new programmers and a reduction in the number of media voices available to consumers."

In light of these technological and economic conditions, Congress concluded that unless cable operators are required to carry local broadcast stations, "[t]here is a substantial likelihood that . . . additional local broadcast signals will be deleted, repositioned, or not carried"; the "marked shift in market share" from broadcast to cable will continue to erode the advertising revenue base which sustains free local broadcast television; and that, as a consequence, "the economic viability of free local broadcast television and its ability to originate quality local programming will be seriously jeopardized."

D

Soon after the Act became law, appellants filed these five consolidated actions in the United States District Court for the District of Columbia against the United States and the Federal Communications Commission (hereinafter referred to collectively as the Government), challenging the constitutionality of the must-carry provisions. Appellants, plaintiffs below, are numerous cable programmers and cable operators. After additional parties intervened, a three-judge District Court convened . . . to hear the actions. . . . [T]he District Court, in a divided opinion, granted summary judgment in favor of the Government and the other intervenor-defendants, ruling that the must-carry provisions are consistent with the First Amendment.

The court . . . said that the must-carry requirements "are essentially economic regulation designed to create competitive balance in the video industry as a whole, and to redress the effects of cable operators' anti-competitive practices." The court rejected appellants' contention that the must-carry requirements warrant strict scrutiny as a content-based regulation. . . . The court proceeded to sustain the must-carry provisions under the intermediate standard of scrutiny set forth in *United States* v. *O'Brien* (1968), concluding that the preservation of local broadcasting is an important governmental interest, and that the must-carry provisions are sufficiently tailored to serve that interest.

Judge Williams dissented. . . . In his view, the must-carry rules are content based, and thus subject to strict scrutiny, because they require cable operators to carry speech they might otherwise choose to exclude, and because Congress' decision to grant favorable access to broadcast programmers rested "in part, but quite explicitly, on a finding about their content." Applying strict scrutiny, Judge Williams determined that the interests advanced in support of the law are inadequate to justify it. . . . Likewise, he concluded that the rules are insufficiently tailored to the asserted interest in programming diversity because cable operators "now carry the vast majority of local stations," and thus to the extent the rules have any effect at all, "it will be only to replace the mix chosen by cablecasters—whose livelihoods depend largely on satisfying audience demand—with a mix derived from congressional dictate."

This direct appeal followed, . . . and we noted probable jurisdiction (1993).

II

There can be no disagreement on an initial premise: Cable programmers and cable operators engage in and transmit speech, and they are entitled to the protection of the speech and press provisions of the First Amendment. *Leathers* v. *Medlock* (1991). . . . By requiring cable systems to set aside a portion of their channels for local broadcasters, the must-carry rules regulate cable speech in two respects: The rules reduce the number of channels over which cable operators exercise unfettered control, and they render it more difficult for cable programmers to compete for carriage on the limited channels remaining. Nevertheless, because not every interference with speech triggers the same degree of scrutiny under the First Amendment, we must decide at the outset the level of scrutiny applicable to the must-carry provisions.

A

We address first the Government's contention that regulation of cable television should be analyzed under the same First Amendment standard that applies to regulation of broadcast television. . . . [T]he inherent physical limitation on the number of speakers who may use the broadcast medium has been thought to require some adjustment in traditional First Amendment analysis to permit the Government to place limited content restraints, and impose certain affirmative obligations, on broadcast licensees. *Red Lion* [*Broadcasting Co.* v. *FCC* (1969)]. . . .

. . . The broadcast cases are inapposite in the present context because cable television does not suffer from the inherent limitations that characterize the broadcast medium. Indeed, given the rapid advances in fiber optics and digital compression technology, soon there may be no practical limitation on the number of speakers who may use the cable medium. Nor is there any danger of physical interference between two cable speakers attempting to share the same channel. In light of these fundamental technological differences between broadcast and cable transmission, application of the more relaxed standard of scrutiny adopted in *Red Lion* and the other broadcast cases is inapt when determining the First Amendment validity of cable regulation. . . .

This is not to say that the unique physical characteristics of cable transmission should be ignored when determining the constitutionality of regulations affecting cable speech. They should not. But whatever relevance these physical characteristics may have in the evaluation of particular cable regulations, they do not require the alteration of settled principles of our First Amendment jurisprudence.

Although the Government acknowledges the substantial technological differences between broadcast and cable, it advances a second argument for application of the *Red Lion* framework to cable regulation. It asserts that the foundation of our broadcast jurisprudence is not the physical limitations of the electromagnetic spectrum, but rather the "market dysfunction" that characterizes the broadcast market. Because the cable market is beset by a similar dysfunction, the Government maintains, the *Red Lion* standard of review should also apply to cable. While we agree that the cable market suffers certain structural impediments, the Government's argument is flawed in two respects. First, as discussed above, the special physical characteristics of broadcast transmission, not the economic characteristics of the broadcast market, are what underlie our broadcast jurisprudence. Second, the mere assertion of dysfunction or failure in a speech market, without more, is not sufficient to shield a speech regulation from the First Amendment standards applicable to nonbroadcast media. . . .

By a related course of reasoning, the Government and some appellees maintain that the must-carry provisions are nothing more than industry-specific antitrust legislation, and thus warrant rational basis scrutiny under this Court's "precedents governing legislative efforts to correct market failure in a market whose commodity is specch.". . . [W]hile the enforcement of a generally applicable law may or may not be subject to heightened scrutiny under the First Amendment, . . . laws that single out the press, or certain elements thereof, for special treatment "pose a particular danger of abuse by the State," and so are always subject to at least some degree of heightened First Amendment scrutiny.... Because the must-carry provisions impose special obligations upon cable operators and special burdens upon cable programmers, some measure of heightened First Amendment scrutiny is demanded....

B

At the heart of the First Amendment lies the principle that each person should decide for him or herself the ideas and beliefs deserving of expression, consideration, and adherence.... Government action that stifles speech on account of its message, or that requires the utterance of a particular message favored by the Government, contravenes this essential right....

For these reasons, the First Amendment, subject only to narrow and well-understood exceptions, does not countenance governmental control over the content of messages expressed by private individuals. Our precedents thus apply the most exacting scrutiny to regulations that suppress, disadvantage, or impose differential burdens upon speech because of its content. Laws that compel speakers to utter or distribute speech bearing a particular message are subject to the same rigorous scrutiny. In contrast, regulations that are unrelated to the content of speech are subject to an intermediate level of scrutiny....

C

Insofar as they pertain to the carriage of full power broadcasters, the must-carry rules, on their face, impose burdens and confer benefits without reference to the content of speech. Although the provisions interfere with cable operators' editorial discretion by compelling them to offer carriage to a certain minimum number of broadcast stations, the extent of the interference does not depend upon the content of the cable operators' programming. The rules impose obligations upon all operators, save those with fewer than 300 subscribers, regardless of the programs or stations they now offer or have offered in the past. Nothing in the Act imposes a restriction, penalty, or burden by reason of the views, programs, or stations the cable operator has selected or will select....

The must-carry provisions also burden cable programmers by reducing the number of channels for which they can compete. But, again, this burden is unrelated to content, for it extends to all cable programmers irrespective of the programming they choose to offer viewers.... And finally, the privileges conferred by the must-carry provisions are also unrelated to content. The rules benefit all full power broadcasters who request carriage—be they commercial or noncommercial, independent or network-affiliated, English or Spanish language, religious or secular. The aggregate effect of the rules is thus to make every full power commercial and noncommercial broadcaster eligible for must-carry, provided only that the broadcaster operates within the same television market as a cable system.

It is true that the must-carry provisions distinguish between speakers in the television programming market. But they do so based only upon the manner in which speakers transmit their messages to viewers, and not upon the messages they carry: Broadcasters, which transmit over the airwaves, are favored, while cable programmers, which do not, are disfavored. Cable operators, too, are burdened by the carriage obligations, but only because they control access to the cable conduit. So long as they are not a subtle means of exercising a content preference, speaker distinctions of this nature are not presumed invalid under the First Amendment.

That the must-carry provisions, on their face, do not burden or benefit speech of a particular content does not end the inquiry. Our cases have recognized that even a regulation neutral on its face may be content-based if its manifest purpose is to regulate speech because of the message it conveys. . . .

Appellants contend, in this regard, that the must-carry regulations are content-based because Congress' purpose in enacting them was to promote speech of a favored content. We do not agree. Our review of the Act and its various findings persuades us that Congress' overriding objective in enacting must-carry was not to favor programming of a particular subject matter, viewpoint, or format, but rather to preserve access to free television programming for the 40 percent of Americans without cable. . . .

. . . This overriding congressional purpose is unrelated to the content of expression disseminated by cable and broadcast speakers. . . .

The design and operation of the challenged provisions confirm that the purposes underlying the enactment of the must-carry scheme are unrelated to the content of speech. The rules, as mentioned, confer must-carry rights on all full power broadcasters, irrespective of the content of their programming. They do not require or prohibit the carriage of particular ideas or points of view. They do not penalize cable operators or programmers because of the content of their programming. They do not compel cable operators to affirm points of view with which they disagree. They do not produce any net decrease in the amount of available speech. And they leave cable operators free to carry whatever programming they wish on all channels not subject to must-carry requirements.

Appellants and the dissent make much of the fact that, in the course of describing the purposes behind the Act, Congress referred to the value of broadcast programming. . . . We do not think, however, that such references cast any material doubt on the content-neutral character of must-carry. That Congress acknowledged the local orientation of broadcast programming and the role that noncommercial stations have played in educating the public does not indicate that Congress regarded broadcast programming as more valuable than cable programming. Rather, it reflects nothing more than the recognition that the services provided by broadcast television have some intrinsic value and, thus, are worth preserving against the threats posed by cable. . . .

The operation of the Act further undermines the suggestion that Congress' purpose in enacting must-carry was to force programming of a "local" or "educational" content on cable subscribers. The provisions, as we have stated, benefit all full power broadcasters irrespective of the nature of their programming. In fact, if a cable system were required to bump a cable programmer to make room for a broadcast station, nothing would stop a cable operator from displacing a cable station that provides all local or education-oriented programming with a broadcaster that provides very little. . . .

In short, Congress' acknowledgment that broadcast television stations make a valuable contribution to the Nation's communications system does not render the must-carry scheme content-based. The scope and operation of the challenged provisions make clear, in our view, that Congress designed the must-carry provisions not to promote speech of a particular content, but to prevent cable operators from exploiting their economic power to the detriment of broadcasters, and thereby to ensure that all Americans, especially those unable to subscribe to cable, have access to free television programming—whatever its content.

We likewise reject the suggestion, advanced by appellants and by Judge Williams in dissent, that the must-carry rules are content-based because the preference for broadcast stations "*automatically* entails content requirements." It is true that broadcast programming, unlike cable programming, is subject to certain limited content restraints imposed by statute and FCC regulation. But it does not follow that Congress mandated cable carriage of broadcast television stations as a means of ensuring that particular programs will be shown, or not shown, on cable systems.

As an initial matter, the argument exaggerates the extent to which the FCC is permitted to intrude into matters affecting the content of broadcast programming. The FCC is forbidden by statute from engaging in "censorship" or from promulgating any regulation "which shall interfere with the [broadcasters'] right of free speech." . . . [T]he FCC's oversight responsibilities do not grant it the power to ordain any particular type of programming that must be offered by broadcast stations. . . .

Stations licensed to broadcast over the special frequencies reserved for "noncommercial educational" stations are subject to no more intrusive content regulation than their commercial counterparts. . . . [N]oncommercial licensees are not required by statute or regulation to carry any specific quantity of "educational" or any particular "educational" programs. Noncommercial licensees, like their commercial counterparts, need only adhere to the general requirement that their programming serve "the public interest, convenience or necessity.". . .

In addition, although federal funding provided through the Corporation for Public Broadcasting (CPB) supports programming on noncommercial stations, the Government is foreclosed from using its financial support to gain leverage over any programming decisions. . . .

Indeed, our cases have recognized that Government regulation over the content of broadcast programming must be narrow, and that broadcast licensees must retain abundant discretion over programming choices. Thus, given the minimal extent to which the FCC and Congress actually influence the programming offered by broadcast stations, it would be difficult to conclude that Congress enacted must-carry in an effort to exercise content control over what subscribers view on cable television. . . .

In short, the must-carry provisions are not designed to favor or disadvantage speech of any particular content. Rather, they are meant to protect broadcast television from what Congress determined to be unfair competition by cable systems. In enacting the provisions, Congress sought to preserve the existing structure of the Nation's broadcast television medium while permitting the concomitant expansion and development of cable television, and, in particular, to ensure that broadcast television remains available as a source of video programming for those without cable. Appellants' ability to hypothesize a content-based purpose for these provisions rests on little more than speculation and does not cast doubt upon the content-neutral character of must-carry. . . .

D

Appellants advance three additional arguments to support their view that the must-carry provisions warrant strict scrutiny. In brief, appellants contend that the provisions (1) compel speech by cable operators, (2) favor broadcast programmers over cable programmers, and (3) single out certain members of the press for disfavored treatment. None of these arguments suffices to require strict scrutiny in the present case.

1

Appellants maintain that the must-carry provisions trigger strict scrutiny because they compel cable operators to transmit speech not of their choosing. Relying principally on *Miami Herald Publishing Co.* v. *Tornillo* (1974), appellants say this intrusion on the editorial control of cable operators amounts to forced speech which, if not *per se* invalid, can be justified only if narrowly tailored to a compelling government interest.

Tornillo affirmed an essential proposition: The First Amendment protects the editorial independence of the press. The right-of-reply statute at issue in *Tornillo* required any newspaper that assailed a political candidate's character to print, upon request by the candidate and without cost, the candidate's reply in equal space and prominence. Although the statute did not censor speech in the traditional sense—it only required newspapers to grant access to the messages of others—we found that it imposed an impermissible content-based burden on newspaper speech. . . .

The same principles led us to invalidate a similar content-based access regulation in *Pacific Gas & Electric* [*Co. v. Public Utilities Comm'n of Cal.* (1986)]. At issue was a rule requiring a privately-owned utility, on a quarterly basis, to include with its monthly bills an editorial newsletter published by a consumer group critical of the utility's ratemaking practices. . . . Like the statute in *Tornillo,* the regulation conferred benefits to speakers based on viewpoint, giving access only to a consumer group opposing the utility's practices. . . .

Tornillo and *Pacific Gas & Electric* do not control this case for the following reasons. First, unlike the access rules struck down in those cases, the must-carry rules are content-neutral in application. They are not activated by any particular message spoken by cable operators and thus exact no content-based penalty. Likewise, they do not grant access to broadcasters on the ground that the content of broadcast programming will counterbalance the messages of cable operators. Instead, they confer benefits upon all full power, local broadcasters, whatever the content of their programming.

Second, appellants do not suggest, nor do we think it the case, that must-carry will force cable operators to alter their own messages to respond to the broadcast programming they are required to carry. . . . Given cable's long history of serving as a conduit for broadcast signals, there appears little risk that cable viewers would assume that the broadcast stations carried on a cable system convey ideas or messages endorsed by the cable operator. . . . Moreover, in contrast to the statute at issue in *Tornillo,* no aspect of the must-carry provisions would cause a cable operator or cable programmer to conclude that "the safe course is to avoid controversy," and by so doing diminish the free flow of information and ideas.

Finally, the asserted analogy to *Tornillo* ignores an important technological difference between newspapers and cable television. Although a daily newspaper and a cable operator both may enjoy monopoly status in a given locale, the cable operator exercises far greater control over access to the relevant medium. A daily newspaper, no matter how secure its local monopoly, does not possess the power to obstruct readers' access to other competing publications—whether they be weekly local newspapers, or daily newspapers published in other cities. Thus, when a newspaper asserts exclusive control over its own news copy, it does not thereby prevent other newspapers from being distributed to willing recipients in the same locale.

The same is not true of cable. When an individual subscribes to cable, the physical connection between the television set and the cable network gives the cable operator bottleneck, or gatekeeper, control over most (if not all) of the television programming that is channeled into the subscriber's home. Hence, simply by virtue of its ownership of the essential pathway for cable speech, a cable operator can prevent its subscribers from obtaining access to programming it chooses to exclude. A cable operator, unlike speakers in other media, can thus silence the voice of competing speakers with a mere flick of the switch.

The potential for abuse of this private power over a central avenue of communication cannot be overlooked. . . . The First Amendment's command that government not impede the freedom of speech does not disable the government from taking steps to ensure that private interests not restrict, through physical control of a critical pathway of communication, the free flow of information and ideas. . . .

2

Second, appellants urge us to apply strict scrutiny because the must-carry provisions favor one set of speakers (broadcast programmers) over another (cable programmers). Appellants maintain that as a consequence of this speaker preference, some cable programmers who would have secured carriage in the absence of must-carry may now be dropped. Relying on language in *Buckley* v. *Valeo* (1976), appellants contend that such a regulation is presumed invalid under the First Amendment because the government may not "restrict the speech of some elements of our society in order to enhance the relative voice of others."

To the extent appellants' argument rests on the view that all regulations distinguishing between speakers warrant strict scrutiny, it is mistaken. At issue in *Buckley* was a federal law prohibiting individuals from spending more than $1,000 per year to support or oppose a particular political candidate. . . .

Our holding in *Buckley* . . . stands for the proposition that speaker-based laws demand strict scrutiny when they reflect the Government's preference for the substance of what the favored speakers have to say (or aversion to what the disfavored speakers have to say). Because the expenditure limit in *Buckley* was designed to ensure that the political speech of the wealthy not drown out the speech of others, we found that it was concerned with the communicative impact of the regulated speech. . . .

The question here is whether Congress preferred broadcasters over cable programmers based on the content of programming each group offers. The answer, as we explained above, is no. Congress granted must-carry privileges to broadcast stations on the belief that the broadcast television industry is in economic peril due to the physical characteristics of cable transmission and the economic incentives facing the cable industry. Thus, the fact that the provisions benefit broadcasters and not cable programmers does not call for strict scrutiny under our precedents.

3

Finally, appellants maintain that strict scrutiny applies because the must-carry provisions single out certain members of the press—here, cable operators—for disfavored treatment. In support, appellants point out that Congress has required cable operators to provide carriage to broadcast stations, but has not imposed like burdens on analogous video delivery systems, such as multichannel multipoint distribution (MMDS) systems and satellite master antenna television (SMATV) systems. Relying upon our precedents invalidating discriminatory taxation of the press, see, *e.g., Arkansas Writers' Project, Inc.* v. *Ragland* (1987); *Minneapolis Star & Tribune Co.* v. *Minnesota Comm'r of Revenue* (1983) . . ., appellants contend that this sort of differential treatment poses a particular danger of abuse by the government and should be presumed invalid. . . .

It would be error to conclude, however, that the First Amendment mandates strict scrutiny for any speech regulation that applies to one medium (or a subset thereof) but not others. In *Leathers* v. *Medlock* (1991), for example, we upheld against First Amendment challenge the application of a general state tax to cable television services, even though the print media and scrambled satellite broadcast television services were exempted from taxation. . . .

The must-carry provisions, as we have explained above, are justified by special characteristics of the cable medium: the bottleneck monopoly power exercised by cable operators and the dangers this power poses to the viability of broadcast television. Appellants do not argue, nor does it appear, that other media—in particular, media that transmit video programming such as MMDS and SMATV—are subject to bottleneck monopoly control, or pose a demonstrable threat to the survival of broadcast television. It should come as no surprise, then, that Congress decided to impose the must-carry obligations upon cable operators only.

In addition, the must-carry provisions are not structured in a manner that carries the inherent risk of undermining First Amendment interests. The regulations are broad-based, applying to almost all cable systems in the country, rather than just a select few. As a result, the provisions do not pose the same dangers of suppression and manipulation that were posed by the more narrowly targeted regulations in *Minneapolis Star* and *Arkansas Writers' Project*. For these reasons, the must-carry rules do not call for strict scrutiny. . . .

III

A

In sum, the must-carry provisions do not pose such inherent dangers to free expression, or present such potential for censorship or manipulation, as to justify application of the most exacting level of First Amendment scrutiny. We agree with the District Court that the appropriate standard by which to evaluate the constitutionality of must-carry is the intermediate level of scrutiny applicable to content-neutral restrictions that impose an incidental burden on speech. See *Ward* v. *Rock Against Racism* (1989); *United States* v. *O'Brien* (1968).

Under *O'Brien,* a content-neutral regulation will be sustained if

> "it furthers an important or substantial governmental interest; if the governmental interest is unrelated to the suppression of free expression; and if the incidental restriction on alleged First Amendment freedoms is no greater than is essential to the furtherance of that interest."

To satisfy this standard, a regulation need not be the least speech-restrictive means of advancing the Government's interests. "Rather, the requirement of narrow tailoring is satisfied 'so long as the . . . regulation promotes a substantial government interest that would be achieved less effectively absent the regulation.' " *Ward*. Narrow tailoring in this context requires, in other words, that the means chosen do not "burden substantially more speech than is necessary to further the government's legitimate interests."

Congress declared that the must-carry provisions serve three interrelated interests: (1) preserving the benefits of free, over-the-air local broadcast television, (2) promoting the widespread dissemination of information from a multiplicity of sources, and (3) promoting fair competition in the market for television programming. None of these interests is related to the "suppression of free expression," or to the content of any speakers' messages. And viewed in the abstract, we have no difficulty concluding that each of them is an important governmental interest.

In the Communications Act of 1934, Congress created a system of free broadcast service and directed that communications facilities be licensed across the country in a "fair, efficient, and equitable" manner. . . . The interest in maintaining the local broadcasting structure does not evaporate simply because cable has come upon the scene. Although cable and other technologies have ushered in alternatives to broadcast television, nearly 40 percent of American households still rely on broadcast stations as their exclusive source of television programming. And as we said in *Capital Cities Cable, Inc.* v. *Crisp* [1984], "protecting noncable households from loss of regular television broadcasting service due to competition from cable systems" is an important federal interest.

Likewise, assuring that the public has access to a multiplicity of information sources is a governmental purpose of the highest order, for it promotes values central to the First Amendment. . . . Finally, the Government's interest in eliminating restraints on fair competition is always substantial, even when the individuals or entities subject to particular regulations are engaged in expressive activity protected by the First Amendment.

B

That the Government's asserted interests are important in the abstract does not mean, however, that the must-carry rules will in fact advance those interests. When the Government defends a regulation on speech as a means to redress past harms or prevent anticipated harms, it . . . must demonstrate that the recited harms are real, not merely conjectural, and that the regulation will in fact alleviate these harms in a direct and material way. . . .

Thus, in applying *O'Brien* scrutiny we must ask first whether the Government has adequately shown that the economic health of local broadcasting is in genuine jeopardy and in need of the protections afforded by must-carry. Assuming an affirmative answer to the foregoing question, the Government still bears the burden of showing that the remedy it has adopted does not "burden substantially more speech than is necessary to further the government's legitimate interests." On the state of the record developed thus far, and in the absence of findings of fact from the District Court, we are unable to conclude that the Government has satisfied either inquiry.

In defending the factual necessity for must-carry, the Government relies in principal part on Congress' legislative finding that, absent mandatory carriage rules, the continued viability of local broadcast television would be "seriously jeopardized." § 2(a)(16). The Government contends that this finding, though predictive in nature, must be accorded great weight in the First Amendment inquiry, especially when, as here, Congress has sought to "address the relationship between two technical, rapidly changing, and closely interdependent industries—broadcasting and cable."

We agree that courts must accord substantial deference to the predictive judgments of Congress. . . . Sound policymaking often requires legislators to forecast future events and to anticipate the likely impact of these events based on deductions and inferences for which complete empirical support may be unavailable. As an institution, moreover, Congress is far better equipped than the judiciary to "amass and evaluate the vast amounts of data" bearing upon an issue as complex and dynamic as that presented here. And Congress is not obligated, when enacting its statutes, to make a record of the type that an administrative agency or court does to accommodate judicial review.

That Congress' predictive judgments are entitled to substantial deference does not mean, however, that they are insulated from meaningful judicial review altogether. On the contrary, we have stressed in First Amendment cases that the deference afforded to legislative findings does "not foreclose our independent judgment of the facts bearing on an issue of constitutional law." *Sable Communications of Cal., Inc.* v. *FCC.* (1989) . . . This obligation to exercise independent judgment when First Amendment rights are implicated is not a license to reweigh the evidence *de novo,* or to replace Congress' factual predictions with our own. Rather, it is to assure that, in formulating its judgments, Congress has drawn reasonable inferences based on substantial evidence. . . .

The Government's assertion that the must-carry rules are necessary to protect the viability of broadcast television rests on two essential propositions: (1) that unless cable operators are compelled to carry broadcast stations, significant numbers of broadcast stations will be refused carriage on cable systems; and (2) that the broadcast stations denied carriage will either deteriorate to a substantial degree or fail altogether.

As support for the first proposition, the Government relies upon a 1988 FCC study showing, at a time when no must-carry rules were in effect, that approximately 20 percent of cable systems reported dropping or refusing carriage to one or more local broadcast stations on at least one occasion. The record does not indicate, however, the time frame within which these drops occurred, or how many of these stations were dropped for only a temporary period and then restored to carriage. The same FCC study indicates that about 23 percent of the cable operators reported shifting the channel positions of one or more local broadcast stations, and that, in most cases, the repositioning was done for "marketing" rather than "technical" reasons. . . .

The parties disagree about the significance of these statistics. But even if one accepts them as evidence that a large number of broadcast stations would be dropped or repositioned in the absence of must-carry, the Government must further demonstrate that broadcasters so affected would suffer financial difficulties as a result. Without a more substantial elaboration in the District Court of the predictive or historical evidence upon which Congress relied, or the introduction of some additional evidence to establish that the dropped or repositioned broadcasters would be at serious risk of financial difficulty, we cannot determine whether the threat to broadcast television is real enough to overcome the challenge to the provisions made by these appellants. We think it significant, for instance, that the parties have not presented any evidence that local broadcast stations have fallen into bankruptcy, turned in their broadcast licenses, curtailed their broadcast operations, or suffered a serious reduction in operating revenues as a result of their being dropped from, or otherwise disadvantaged by, cable systems.

The paucity of evidence indicating that broadcast television is in jeopardy is not the only deficiency in this record. Also lacking are any findings concerning the actual effects of must-carry on the speech of cable operators and cable programmers—*i.e.,* the extent to which cable operators will, in fact, be forced to make changes in their current or anticipated programming selections; the degree to which cable programmers will be dropped from cable systems to make room for local broadcasters; and the extent to which cable operators can satisfy their must-carry obligations by devoting previously unused channel capacity to the carriage of local broadcasters. The answers to these and perhaps other questions are critical to the narrow tailoring step of the *O'Brien* analysis, for unless we know the extent to which the must-carry provisions in fact interfere with protected speech, we cannot say whether they suppress "substantially more speech than . . . necessary" to ensure the viability of broadcast television. Finally, the record fails to provide any judicial findings concerning the availability and efficacy of "constitutionally acceptable less restrictive means" of achieving the Government's asserted interests. . . .

In sum, because there are genuine issues of material fact still to be resolved on this record, we hold that the District Court erred in granting summary judgment in favor of the Government. . . . Because of the unresolved factual questions, the importance of the issues to the broadcast and cable industries, and the conflicting conclusions that the parties contend are to be drawn from the statistics and other evidence presented, we think it necessary to permit the parties to develop a more thorough factual record, and to allow the District Court to resolve any factual disputes remaining, before passing upon the constitutional validity of the challenged provisions.

The judgment below is vacated, and the case is remanded for further proceedings consistent with this opinion.

It is so ordered.

JUSTICE BLACKMUN, concurring.

I join JUSTICE KENNEDY's opinion, which aptly identifies and analyzes the First Amendment concerns and principles that should guide consideration of free speech issues in the expanding cable industry. I write to emphasize the paramount importance of according substantial deference to the predictive judgments of Congress, particularly where, as here, that legislative body has compiled an extensive record in the course of reaching its judgment. Nonetheless, the standard for summary judgment is high, and no less so when First Amendment values are at stake and the issue is of far-reaching importance. Because in this case there remain a few unresolved issues of material fact, a remand is appropriate. The Government had occasion to submit to the District Court only portions of the record developed by Congress. In light of the Court's opinion today, those portions, which were submitted to defeat a motion for summary judgment, are not adequate to support one. The record before the District Court no doubt will benefit from any additional evidence the Government and the other parties now see fit to present.

JUSTICE STEVENS, concurring in part and concurring in the judgment. . . .

While I agree with most of Justice Kennedy's reasoning, and join Parts I, II(C), II(D), and III(A) of his opinion, I part ways with him on the appropriate disposition of this case. In my view the District Court's judgment sustaining the must-carry provisions should be affirmed. The District Court majority evaluated §§ 4 and 5 as content-neutral regulations of protected speech according to the same standard that JUSTICE KENNEDY's opinion instructs it to apply on remand. In my view, the District Court reached the correct result the first time around. Economic measures are always subject to second-guessing; they rest on inevitably provisional and uncertain forecasts about the future effect of legal rules in complex conditions. Whether *Congress* might have accomplished its goals more efficiently through other means; whether it correctly interpreted emerging trends in the protean communications industry; and indeed whether must-carry is actually imprudent as a matter of policy will remain matters of debate long after the 1992 Act has been repealed or replaced by successor legislation. But the question for us is merely whether Congress could fairly conclude that cable operators' monopoly position threatens the continued viability of broadcast television and that must-carry is an appropriate means of minimizing that risk.

As JUSTICE KENNEDY recognizes, findings by the Congress, particularly those emerging from such sustained deliberations, merit special respect from this Court. Accorded proper deference, the findings in § 2 are sufficient to sustain the must-carry provisions against facial attack. . . .

An industry need not be in its death throes before Congress may act to protect it from economic harm threatened by a monopoly. The mandatory access mechanism that Congress fashioned in §§ 4 and 5 of the

1992 Act is a simple and direct means of dealing with the dangers posed by cable operators' exclusive control of what is fast becoming the preeminent means of transferring video signals to homes. . . . Moreover, Congress did not have to find that all broadcasters were at risk before acting to protect vulnerable ones, for the interest in preserving access to free television is valid throughout the Nation. Indeed, the Act is well tailored to assist those broadcasters who are most in jeopardy. Because thriving commercial broadcasters will likely avail themselves of the remunerative "retransmission consent" procedure of § 6, those broadcasters who gain access via the § 4 must-carry route are apt to be the most economically vulnerable ones. . . .

JUSTICE KENNEDY asks the three-judge panel to take additional evidence on such matters as whether the must-carry provisions really respond to threatened harms to broadcasters, whether §§ 4-5 "will in fact alleviate these harms in a direct and material way," and "the extent to which cable operators will, in fact, be forced to make changes in their current or anticipated programming selections." While additional evidence might cast further light on the efficacy and wisdom of the must-carry provisions, additional evidence is not necessary to resolve the question of their facial constitutionality.

To predicate the facial validity of the must-carry provisions upon forecasts of the ultimate consequences of their implementation is to ask the District Court to address questions that are not at present susceptible of reliable answers. Some of the matters the lead opinion singles out for further review—for example, "the degree to which cable programmers will be dropped from cable systems to make room for local broadcasters"—depend upon predictions about the future voluntary actions of entities who are parties to this case. At best, a remand for consideration of such factors will require the District Court to engage in speculation; it may actually invite the parties to adjust their conduct in an effort to affect the result of this litigation (perhaps by opting to drop cable programs rather than seeking to increase total channel capacity). The must-carry provisions may ultimately prove an ineffective or needlessly meddlesome means of achieving Congress' legitimate goals. However, such a conclusion could be confidently drawn, if ever, only after the must-carry scheme has been tested by experience. On its face, that scheme is rationally calculated to redress the dangers that Congress discerned after its lengthy investigation of the relationship between the cable and broadcasting industries.

It is thus my view that we should affirm the judgment of the District Court. Were I to vote to affirm, however, no disposition of this appeal would command the support of a majority of the Court. An accommodation is therefore necessary. Accordingly, because I am in substantial agreement with JUSTICE KENNEDY's analysis of the case, I concur in the judgment vacating and remanding for further proceedings.

JUSTICE O'CONNOR, with whom JUSTICE SCALIA and JUSTICE GINSBURG join, and with whom JUSTICE THOMAS joins as to Parts I and III, concurring in part and dissenting in part.

There are only so many channels that any cable system can carry. If there are fewer channels than programmers who want to use the system, some programmers will have to be dropped. In the must-carry provisions of the Cable Television Consumer Protection and Competition Act of 1992, Congress made a choice: By reserving a little over one-third of the channels on a cable system for broadcasters, it ensured that in most cases it will be a cable programmer who is dropped and a broadcaster who is retained. The question presented in this case is whether this choice comports with the commands of the First Amendment.

I

A

The 1992 Cable Act implicates the First Amendment rights of two classes of speakers. First, it tells cable operators which programmers they must carry, and keeps cable operators from carrying others that they might prefer. Though cable operators do not actually originate most of the programming they show, the Court correctly holds that they are, for First Amendment purposes, speakers. Selecting which speech to retransmit is, as we know from the example of publishing houses, movie theaters, bookstores, and *Reader's Digest,* no less communication than is creating the speech in the first place.

Second, the Act deprives a certain class of video programmers—those who operate cable channels rather than broadcast stations—of access to over one-third of an entire medium. Cable programmers may compete only for those channels that are not set aside by the must-carry provisions. A cable programmer that might otherwise have been carried may well be denied access in favor of a broadcaster that is less appealing to the viewers but is favored by the must-carry rules. It is as if the government ordered all movie theaters to reserve at least one-third of their screening for films made by American production companies, or required all bookstores to devote one-third of their shelf space to nonprofit publishers. As the Court explains in Parts I, II-A and II-B of its opinion, which I join, cable programmers and operators stand in the same position under the First Amendment as do the more traditional media.

Under the First Amendment, it is normally not within the government's power to decide who may speak and who may not, at least on private property or in traditional public fora. The government does have the power to impose content-neutral time, place, and manner restrictions, but this is in large part precisely because such restrictions apply to all speakers. Laws that treat all speakers equally are relatively poor tools for controlling public debate, and their very generality creates a substantial political check that prevents them from being unduly burdensome. Laws that single out particular speakers are substantially more dangerous, even when they do not draw explicit content distinctions. . . .

I agree with the Court that some speaker-based restrictions—those genuinely justified without reference to content—need not be subject to strict scrutiny. But looking at the statute at issue, I cannot avoid the conclusion that its preference for broadcasters over cable programmers is justified with reference to content. The findings, enacted by Congress as § 2 of the Act, . . . make this clear. "There is a substantial governmental and First Amendment interest in promoting a diversity of views provided through multiple technology media." § 2(a)(6). "[P]ublic television provides educational and informational programming to the Nation's citizens, thereby advancing the Government's compelling interest in educating its citizens." § 2(a)(8)(A). "A primary objective and benefit of our Nation's system of regulation of television broadcasting is the local origination of programming. There is a substantial governmental interest in ensuring its continuation." § 2(a)(10). "Broadcast television stations continue to be an important source of local news and public affairs programming and other local broadcast services critical to an informed electorate." § 2(a)(11).

Similar justifications are reflected in the operative provisions of the Act. In determining whether a broadcast station should be eligible for must-carry in a particular market, the FCC must "afford particular attention to the value of localism by taking into account such factors as . . . whether any other [eligible station] provides news coverage of issues of concern to such community or provides carriage or coverage of sporting and other events of interest to the community." In determining whether a low-power station is eligible for must-carry, the FCC must ask whether the station "would address local news and informational needs which are not being adequately served by full power television broadcast stations." Moreover, the Act distinguishes between commercial television stations and noncommercial educational television stations, giving special benefits to the latter. These provisions may all be technically severable from the statute, but they are still strong evidence of the statute's justifications.

Preferences for diversity of viewpoints, for localism, for educational programming, and for news and public affairs all make reference to content. They may not reflect hostility to particular points of view, or a desire to suppress certain subjects because they are controversial or offensive. They may be quite benignly motivated. But benign motivation, we have consistently held, is not enough to avoid the need for strict scrutiny of content-based justifications. The First Amendment does more than just bar government from intentionally suppressing speech of which it disapproves. It also generally prohibits the government from excepting certain kinds of speech from regulation because it thinks the speech is especially valuable.

This is why the Court is mistaken in concluding that the interest in diversity—in "access to a multiplicity" of "diverse and antagonistic sources"—is content neutral. Indeed, the interest is not "related to the *suppression* of free expression," (emphasis added and internal quotation marks omitted), but that is not enough for content neutrality.... The interest in ensuring access to a multiplicity of diverse and antagonistic sources of information, no matter how praiseworthy, is directly tied to the content of what the speakers will likely say.

B

The Court dismisses the findings quoted above by speculating that they do not reveal a preference for certain kinds of content; rather, the Court suggests, the findings show "nothing more than the recognition that the services provided by broadcast television have some intrinsic value and, thus, are worth preserving against the threats posed by cable." I cannot agree. It is rare enough that Congress states, in the body of the statute itself, the findings underlying its decision. When it does, it is fair to assume that those findings reflect the basis for the legislative decision, especially when the thrust of the findings is further reflected in the rest of the statute.

Moreover, it does not seem likely that Congress would make extensive findings merely to show that broadcast television is valuable. The controversial judgment at the heart of the statute is not that broadcast television has some value—obviously it does—but that broadcasters should be preferred over cable programmers. The best explanation for the findings, it seems to me, is that they represent Congress' reasons for adopting this preference; and, according to the findings, these reasons rest in part on the content of broadcasters' speech....

It may well be that Congress also had other, content-neutral, purposes in mind when enacting the statute. But we have never held that the presence of a permissible justification lessens the impropriety of relying in part on an impermissible justification.... [W]hen a content-based justification appears on the statute's face, we cannot ignore it because another, content-neutral justification is present.

C

Content-based speech restrictions are generally unconstitutional unless they are narrowly tailored to a compelling state interest. This is an exacting test. It is not enough that the goals of the law be legitimate, or reasonable, or even praiseworthy. There must be some pressing public necessity, some essential value that has to be preserved; and even then the law must restrict as little speech as possible to serve the goal.

The interest in localism, either in the dissemination of opinions held by the listeners' neighbors or in the reporting of events that have to do with the local community, cannot be described as "compelling" for the purposes of the compelling state interest test. It is a legitimate interest, perhaps even an important one—certainly the government can foster it by, for instance, providing subsidies from the public fisc—but it does not rise to the level necessary to justify content-based speech restrictions. It is for private speakers and listeners, not for the government, to decide what fraction of their news and entertainment ought to be of a local character and what fraction ought to be of a national (or international) one. And the same is true of the interest in diversity of viewpoints: While the government may subsidize speakers that it thinks provide novel points of view, it may not restrict other speakers on the theory that what they say is more conventional. . . .

The interests in public affairs programming and educational programming seem somewhat weightier, though it is a difficult question whether they are compelling enough to justify restricting other sorts of speech. We have never held that the Government could impose educational content requirements on, say, newsstands, bookstores, or movie theaters; and it is not clear that such requirements would in any event appreciably further the goals of public education.

But even assuming *arguendo* that the Government could set some channels aside for educational or news programming, the Act is insufficiently tailored to this goal. To benefit the educational broadcasters, the Act burdens more than just the cable entertainment programmers. It equally burdens CNN, C-SPAN, the Discovery Channel, the New Inspirational Network, and other channels with as much claim as PBS to being educational or related to public affairs.

Even if the Government can restrict entertainment in order to benefit supposedly more valuable speech, I do not think the restriction can extend to other speech that is as valuable as the speech being benefited. In the rare circumstances where the government may draw content-based distinctions to serve its goals, the restrictions must serve the goals a good deal more precisely than this. . . .

Finally, my conclusion that the must-carry rules are content based leads me to conclude that they are an impermissible restraint on the cable operators' editorial discretion as well as on the cable programmers' speech. For reasons related to the content of speech, the rules restrict the ability of cable operators to put on the programming they prefer, and require them to include programming they would rather avoid. This, it seems to me, puts this case squarely within the rule of *Pacific Gas & Electric Co.* [*v. Public Utilities Comm'n of Cal.* (1986)].

II

Even if I am mistaken about the must-carry provisions being content based, however, in my view they fail content-neutral scrutiny as well. Assuming *arguendo* that the provisions are justified with reference to the content-neutral interests in fair competition and preservation of free television, they nonetheless restrict too much speech that does not implicate these interests. Sometimes, a cable system's choice to carry a cable programmer rather than a broadcaster may be motivated by anticompetitive impulses, or might lead to the broadcaster going out of business. That some speech within a broad category causes harm, however, does not justify restricting the whole category. If Congress wants to protect those stations that are in danger of going out of business, or bar cable operators from preferring programmers in which the operators have an ownership stake, it may do that. But it may not, in the course of advancing these interests, restrict cable operators and programmers in circumstances where neither of these interests is threatened. . . .

The must-carry provisions are fatally overbroad, even under a content-neutral analysis: They disadvantage cable programmers even if the operator has no anticompetitive motives, and even if the broadcaster that would have to be dropped to make room for the cable programmer would survive without cable access. None of the factfinding that the District Court is asked to do on remand will change this. The Court does not suggest that either the antitrust interest or the loss of free television interest are implicated in all, or even most, of the situations in which must-carry makes a difference. Perhaps on remand the District Court will find out just how many broadcasters will be jeopardized, but the remedy for this jeopardy will remain the same: Protect those broadcasters that are put in danger of bankruptcy, without unnecessarily restricting cable programmers in markets where free broadcasting will thrive in any event.

III

Having said all this, it is important to acknowledge one basic fact: The question is not whether there will be control over who gets to speak over cable—the question is who will have this control. Under the FCC's view, the answer is Congress, acting within relatively broad limits. Under my view, the answer is the cable operator. Most of the time, the cable operator's decision will be largely dictated by the preferences of the viewers; but because many cable operators are indeed monopolists, the viewers' preferences will not always prevail. Our recognition that cable operators are speakers is bottomed in large part on the very fact that the cable operator has editorial discretion.

I have no doubt that there is danger in having a single cable operator decide what millions of subscribers can or cannot watch. And I have no doubt that Congress can act to relieve this danger. In other provisions of the Act, Congress has already taken steps to foster competition among cable systems. Congress can encourage the creation of new media, such as inexpensive satellite broadcasting, or fiber-optic networks with virtually unlimited channels, or even simple devices that would let people easily switch from cable to over-the-air broadcasting. And of course Congress can subsidize broadcasters that it thinks provide especially valuable programming.

Congress may also be able to act in more mandatory ways. If Congress finds that cable operators are leaving some channels empty—perhaps for ease of future expansion—it can compel the operators to make the free channels available to programmers who otherwise would not get carriage.... Congress might also conceivably obligate cable operators to act as common carriers for some of their channels, with those channels being open to all through some sort of lottery system or timesharing arrangement. Setting aside any possible Takings Clause issues, it stands to reason that if Congress may demand that telephone companies operate as common carriers, it can ask the same of cable companies; such an approach would not suffer from the defect of preferring one speaker to another.

But the First Amendment as we understand it today rests on the premise that it is government power, rather than private power, that is the main threat to free expression; and as a consequence, the Amendment imposes substantial limitations on the Government even when it is trying to serve concededly praiseworthy goals. Perhaps Congress can to some extent restrict, even in a content-based manner, the speech of cable operators and cable programmers. But it must do so in compliance with the constitutional requirements, requirements that were not complied with here. Accordingly, I would reverse the judgment below.

JUSTICE GINSBURG, concurring in part and dissenting in part.

Substantially for the reasons stated by Circuit Judge Williams in his opinion dissenting from the three-judge District Court's judgment, I conclude that Congress' "must-carry" regime, which requires cable operators to set aside just over one-third of their channels for local broadcast stations, reflects an unwarranted content-based preference and hypothesizes a risk to local stations that remains imaginary. I therefore concur in Parts I, II-A, and II-B of the Court's opinion, and join JUSTICE O'CONNOR's opinion concurring in part and dissenting in part. . . .

□□□

Nos. 92-519, 92-593 and 92-767

Bolley Johnson, Speaker of the Florida House of Representatives, et al., Appellants v. Miguel De Grandy et al.*

On appeals from the United States District Court
for the Northern District of Florida

[June 30, 1994]

JUSTICE SOUTER delivered the opinion of the Court.

These consolidated cases are about the meaning of vote dilution and the facts required to show it, when § 2 of the Voting Rights Act of 1965 [42 U.S.C. § 1973] is applied to challenges to single-member legislative districts. We hold that no violation of § 2 can be found here, where, in spite of continuing discrimination and racial bloc voting, minority voters form effective voting majorities in a number of districts roughly proportional to the minority voters' respective shares in the voting-age population. While such proportionality is not dispositive in a challenge to single-member districting, it is a relevant fact in the totality of circumstances to be analyzed when determining whether members of a minority group have "less opportunity than other members of the electorate to participate in the political process and to elect representatives of their choice."

I

On the first day of Florida's 1992 legislative session, a group of Hispanic voters including Miguel De Grandy (De Grandy plaintiffs) complained in the United States District Court against the speaker of Florida's House of Representatives, the president of its Senate, the Governor, and other state officials (State). The complainants alleged that the districts from which Florida voters had chosen their state senators and representatives since 1982 were malapportioned, failing to reflect changes

---

* Together with *De Grandy et al.* v. *Johnson, Speaker of the Florida House of Representatives, et al.,* and *United States* v. *Florida,* also on appeal from the same court.

in the State's population during the ensuing decade. The State Conference of NAACP Branches and individual black voters (NAACP plaintiffs) filed a similar suit, which the three-judge District Court consolidated with the De Grandy case.

Several months after the first complaint was filed, on April 10, 1992, the state legislature adopted Senate Joint Resolution 2-G (SJR 2-G), providing the reapportionment plan currently at issue. The plan called for dividing Florida into 40 single-member Senate, and 120 single-member House, districts based on population data from the 1990 census. . . .

The De Grandy and NAACP plaintiffs responded to SJR 2-G by amending their federal complaints to charge the new reapportionment plan with violating § 2. They claimed that SJR 2-G "unlawfully fragments cohesive minority communities and otherwise impermissibly submerges their right to vote and to participate in the electoral process," and they pointed to areas around the State where black or Hispanic populations could have formed a voting majority in a politically cohesive, reasonably compact district (or in more than one), if SJR 2-G had not fragmented each group among several districts or packed it into just a few.

The Department of Justice filed a similar complaint, naming the State of Florida and several elected officials as defendants and claiming that SJR 2-G diluted the voting strength of blacks and Hispanics in two parts of the State in violation of § 2. The Government alleged that SJR 2-G diluted the votes of the Hispanic population in an area largely covered by Dade County (including Miami). . . . The District Court consolidated this action with the other two and held a 5-day trial, followed immediately by an hours-long hearing on remedy.

At the end of the hearing, on July 1, 1992, the District Court ruled from the bench. It held the plan's provisions for state House districts to be in violation of § 2 because "more than [SJR 2-G's] nine Hispanic districts may be drawn without having or creating a regressive effect upon black voters," and it imposed a remedial plan offered by the De Grandy plaintiffs calling for 11 majority-Hispanic House districts. As to the Senate, the court found that a fourth majority-Hispanic district could be drawn in addition to the three provided by SJR 2-G, but only at the expense of black voters in the area. The court was of two minds about the implication of this finding, once observing that it meant the legislature's plan for the Senate was a violation of § 2 but without a remedy, once saying the Plan did not violate § 2 at all. In any event, it ordered elections to be held using SJR 2-G's senatorial districts.

In a later, expanded opinion the court reviewed the totality of circumstances as required by § 2 and *Thornburg* v. *Gingles* (1986). In explaining Dade County's "tripartite politics," in which "ethnic factors . . . predominate over all other[s] . . .," the court found political cohesion within each of the Hispanic and black populations but none between the two, and a tendency of non-Hispanic whites to vote as a bloc to bar minority groups from electing their chosen candidates except in a district where a given minority makes up a voting majority. The court further found that the nearly one million Hispanics in the Dade County area could be combined into 4 Senate and 11 House districts, each one relatively compact and with a functional majority of Hispanic voters, whereas SJR 2-G created fewer majority-Hispanic districts; and that one more Senate district with a black voting majority could have been drawn. Noting that Florida's minorities bore the social, economic, and political effects of past discrimination, the court concluded that SJR 2-G impermissibly diluted the voting strength of Hispanics in its House districts and of both Hispanics and blacks in its Senate districts. The findings of vote dilution in the senatorial districts had no practical effect, however, because the court held that remedies for the blacks and the Hispanics were mutually exclusive; it consequently deferred to the state legislature's work as the "fairest" accommodation of all the ethnic communities in South Florida.

We stayed the judgment of the District Court (1992), and noted probable jurisdiction (1993).

[II omitted]

III

On the merits of the vote dilution claims covering the House districts, the crux of the State's argument is the power of Hispanics under SJR 2-G to elect candidates of their choice in a number of districts that mirrors their share of the Dade County area's voting-age population (*i.e.*, 9 out of 20 House districts); this power, according to the State, bars any finding that the plan dilutes Hispanic voting strength. The District Court is said to have missed that conclusion by mistaking our precedents to require the plan to maximize the number of Hispanic-controlled districts.

The State's argument takes us back to ground covered last Term in two cases challenging single-member districts. See *Voinovich* v. *Quilter* (1993); *Growe* v. *Emison* (1993). In *Growe,* we held that a claim of vote dilution in a single-member district requires proof meeting the same three threshold conditions for a dilution challenge to a multimember district: that a minority group be "sufficiently large and geographically compact to constitute a majority in a single-member district"; that it be "politically cohesive"; and that "the white majority vot[e] sufficiently as a bloc to enable it ... usually to defeat the minority's preferred candidate." (Quoting *Thornburg* v. *Gingles*). Of course, as we reflected in *Voinovich* and amplify later in this opinion, "the *Gingles* factors cannot be applied mechanically and without regard to the nature of the claim.". . .

Plaintiffs in *Growe* and *Voinovich* failed to show vote dilution because the former did not prove political cohesiveness of the minority group, and the latter showed no significant white bloc voting. Here, on the contrary, the District Court found, and the State does not challenge, the presence of both these *Gingles* preconditions. The dispute in this litigation centers on two quite different questions: whether Hispanics are sufficiently numerous and geographically compact to be a majority in additional single-member districts, as required by the first *Gingles* factor; and whether, even with all three *Gingles* conditions satisfied, the circumstances in totality support a finding of vote dilution when Hispanics can be expected to elect their chosen representatives in substantial proportion to their percentage of the area's population.

A

When applied to a claim that single-member districts dilute minority votes, the first *Gingles* condition requires the possibility of creating more than the existing number of reasonably compact districts with a sufficiently large minority population to elect candidates of its choice. The District Court found the condition satisfied by contrasting SJR 2-G with the De Grandy plan for the Dade County area, which provided for 11 reasonably compact districts, each with a voting-age population at least 64 percent Hispanic. . . .

B

We . . . part company from the District Court in assessing the totality of circumstances. The District Court found that the three *Gingles* preconditions were satisfied, and that Hispanics had suffered historically from official discrimination, the social, economic, and political effects of which they generally continued to feel. Without more, and on the apparent assumption that what could have been done to create additional Hispanic super-majority districts should have been done, the District Court found a violation of § 2. But the assumption was erroneous, and more is required, as a review of *Gingles* will show.

1

Thornburg v. *Gingles* prompted this Court's first reading of § 2 of the Voting Rights Act after its 1982 amendment. Section 2(a) of the amended Act prohibits any "standard, practice, or procedure . . . which results in a denial or abridgement of the right of any citizen of the United States to vote on account of race or color [or membership in a language minority group]. . . ." Section 2(b) provides that a denial or abridgment occurs where,

> "based on the totality of circumstances, it is shown that the political processes leading to nomination or election in the State or political subdivision are not equally open to participation by members of a class of citizens protected by subsection (a) in that its members have less opportunity than other members of the electorate to participate in the political process and to elect representatives of their choice. The extent to which members of a protected class have been elected to office in the State or political subdivision is one circumstance which may be considered: *Provided*, That nothing in this section establishes a right to have members of a protected class elected in numbers equal to their proportion in the population."

Gingles provided some structure to the statute's "totality of circumstances" test in a case challenging multimember legislative districts. . . . The Court . . . summarized the three now-familiar *Gingles* factors (compactness/numerousness, minority cohesion or bloc voting, and majority bloc voting) as "necessary preconditions" for establishing vote dilution by use of a multimember district.

But if *Gingles* so clearly identified the three as generally necessary to prove a § 2 claim, it just as clearly declined to hold them sufficient in combination, either in the sense that a court's examination of relevant circumstances was complete once the three factors were found to exist, or in the sense that the three in combination necessarily and in all circumstances demonstrated dilution. . . . Lack of electoral success is evidence of vote dilution, but courts must also examine other evidence in the totality of circumstances, including the extent of the opportunities minority voters enjoy to participate in the political processes. . . .

2

If the three *Gingles* factors may not be isolated as sufficient, standing alone, to prove dilution in every multimember district challenge, *a fortiori* they must not be when the challenge goes to a series of single-member districts, where dilution may be more difficult to grasp. Plaintiffs challenging single-member districts may claim not total submergence, but partial submergence; not the chance for some electoral success in place of none, but the chance for more success in place of some. When the question thus comes down to the reasonableness of drawing a series of district lines in one combination of places rather than another, judgments about inequality may become closer calls. . . .

The cases now before us, of course, fall on this more complex side of the divide, requiring a court to determine whether provision for somewhat fewer majority-minority districts than the number sought by the plaintiffs was dilution of the minority votes. The District Court was accordingly required to assess the probative significance of the *Gingles* factors critically after considering the further circumstances with arguable bearing on the issue of equal political opportunity. We think that in finding dilution here the District Court misjudged the relative importance of the *Gingles* factors and of historical discrimination, measured against evidence tending to show that in spite of these facts, SJR 2-G would provide minority voters with an equal measure of political and electoral opportunity.

The District Court did not, to be sure, commit the error of treating the three *Gingles* conditions as exhausting the enquiry required by § 2. Consistently with *Gingles,* the court received evidence of racial relations outside the immediate confines of voting behavior and found a history of discrimination against Hispanic voters continuing in society generally to the present day. But the District Court was not critical enough in asking whether a history of persistent discrimination reflected in the larger society and its bloc-voting behavior portended any dilutive effect from a newly proposed districting scheme, whose pertinent features were majority-minority districts in substantial proportion to the minority's share of voting-age population. The court failed to ask whether the totality of facts, including those pointing to proportionality, showed that the new scheme would deny minority voters equal political opportunity.

Treating equal political opportunity as the focus of the enquiry, we do not see how these district lines, apparently providing political effectiveness in proportion to voting-age numbers, deny equal political opportunity. The record establishes that Hispanics constitute 50 percent of the voting-age population in Dade County and under SJR 2-G would make up super-majorities in 9 of the 18 House districts located primarily within the county. Likewise, if one considers the 20 House districts located at least in part within Dade County, the record indicates that Hispanics would be an effective voting majority in 45 percent of them (*i.e.,* nine), and would constitute 47 percent of the voting-age population in the area. In other words, under SJR 2-G Hispanics in the Dade County area would enjoy substantial proportionality. On this evidence, we think the State's scheme would thwart the historical tendency to exclude Hispanics, not encourage or perpetuate it. Thus in spite of that history and its legacy, including the racial cleavages that characterize Dade County politics today, we see no grounds for holding in this case that SJR 2-G's district lines diluted the votes cast by Hispanic voters.

The De Grandy plaintiffs urge us to put more weight on the District Court's findings of packing and fragmentation, allegedly accomplished by the way the State drew certain specific lines.... We would agree that where a State has split (or lumped) minority neighborhoods that would have been grouped into a single district (or spread among several) if the State had employed the same line-drawing standards in minority neighborhoods as it used elsewhere in the jurisdiction, the inconsistent treatment might be significant evidence of a § 2 violation, even in the face of proportionality. The District Court, however, made no such finding. Indeed, the propositions the Court recites on this point are not even phrased as factual findings, but merely as recitations of testimony offered by plaintiffs' expert witness. While the District Court may well have credited the testimony, the court was apparently wary of adopting the witness's conclusions as findings. But even if one imputed a greater significance to the accounts of testimony, they would boil down to findings that several of SJR 2-G's district lines separate portions of Hispanic neighborhoods, while another district line draws several Hispanic neighborhoods into a single district. This, however, would be to say only that lines could have been drawn elsewhere, nothing more. But some dividing by district lines and combining within them is virtually inevitable and befalls any population group of substantial size. Attaching the labels "packing" and "fragmenting" to these phenomena, without more, does not make the result vote dilution when the minority group enjoys substantial proportionality.

3

It may be that the significance of the facts under § 2 was obscured by the rule of thumb apparently adopted by the District Court, that anything short of the maximum number of majority-minority districts consistent with the *Gingles* conditions would violate § 2, at least where societal discrimination against the minority had occurred and continued to occur. But reading the first *Gingles* condition in effect to define dilution as a failure to maximize in the face of bloc voting (plus some other incidents of societal bias to be expected where bloc voting occurs) causes its own dangers, and they are not to be courted.

Assume a hypothetical jurisdiction of 1,000 voters divided into 10 districts of 100 each, where members of a minority group make up 40 percent of the voting population and voting is totally polarized along racial lines. With the right geographic dispersion to satisfy the compactness requirement, and with careful manipulation of district lines, the minority voters might be placed in control of as many as 7 of the 10 districts. Each such district could be drawn with at least 51 members of the minority group, and whether the remaining minority voters were added to the groupings of 51 for safety or scattered in the other three districts, minority voters would be able to elect candidates of their choice in all seven districts. The point of the hypothetical is not, of course, that any given district is likely to be open to such extreme manipulation, or that bare majorities are likely to vote in full force and strictly along racial lines, but that reading § 2 to define dilution as any failure to maximize tends to obscure the very object of the statute and to run counter to its textually stated purpose. One may suspect vote dilution from political famine, but one is not entitled to suspect (much less infer) dilution from mere failure to guarantee a political feast. However prejudiced a society might be, it would be absurd to suggest that the failure of a districting scheme to provide a minority group with effective political power 75 percent above its numerical strength indicates a denial of equal participation in the political process. Failure to maximize cannot be the measure of § 2.

4

. . . [T]he State seeks to impart a measure of determinacy by applying a definitive rule of its own: that as a matter of law no dilution occurs whenever the percentage of single-member districts in which minority voters form an effective majority mirrors the minority voters' percentage of the relevant population. Proportionality so defined would thus be a safe harbor for any districting scheme.

The safety would be in derogation of the statutory text and its considered purpose, however, and of the ideal that the Voting Rights Act attempts to foster. An inflexible rule would run counter to the textual command of § 2, that the presence or absence of a violation be assessed "based on the totality of circumstances." The need for such "totality" review springs from the demonstrated ingenuity of state and local governments in hobbling minority voting power. . . . In modifying § 2, Congress . . . endorsed our view in *White* v. *Regester* (1973) that "whether the political processes are 'equally open' depends upon a searching practical evaluation of the 'past and present reality.'" In a substantial number of voting jurisdictions, that past reality has included such reprehensible practices as ballot box stuffing, outright violence, discretionary registration, property requirements, the poll tax, and the white primary; and other practices censurable when the object of their use is discriminatory, such as at-large elections, runoff requirements, anti-single-shot devices, gerrymandering, the impeachment of officeholders, the annexation or deannexation of territory, and the creation or elimination of elective offices. Some of those expedients could occur even in a jurisdiction with numerically demonstrable proportionality; the harbor safe for States would thus not be safe for voters. It is, in short, for good reason that we have been, and remain, chary of entertaining a simplification of the sort the State now urges upon us. . . .

Even if the State's safe harbor were open only in cases of alleged dilution by the manipulation of district lines, however, it would rest on an unexplored premise of highly suspect validity: that in any given voting jurisdiction (or portion of that jurisdiction under consideration), the rights of some minority voters under § 2 may be traded off against the rights of other members of the same minority class. Under the State's view, the most blatant racial gerrymandering in half of a county's single member districts would be irrelevant under § 2 if offset by political gerrymandering in the other half, so long as proportionality was the bottom line. . . .

Finally, we reject the safe harbor rule because of a tendency the State would itself certainly condemn, a tendency to promote and perpetuate efforts to devise majority-minority districts even in circumstances where they may not be necessary to achieve equal political and electoral opportunity. Because in its simplest form the State's rule would shield from § 2 challenge a districting scheme in which the number of majority-minority districts reflected the minority's share of the relevant population, the conclusiveness of the rule might be an irresistible inducement to create such districts. It bears recalling, however, that for all the virtues of majority-minority districts as remedial devices, they rely on a quintessentially race-conscious calculus aptly described as the "politics of second best.". . . If the lesson of *Gingles* is that society's racial and ethnic cleavages sometimes necessitate majority-minority districts to ensure equal political and electoral opportunity, that should not obscure the fact that there are communities in which minority citizens are able to form coalitions with voters from other racial and ethnic groups, having no need to be a majority within a single district in order to elect candidates of their choice. Those candidates may not represent perfection to every minority voter, but minority voters are not immune from the obligation to pull, haul, and trade to find common political ground, the virtue of which is not to be slighted in applying a statute meant to hasten the waning of racism in American politics.

It is enough to say that, while proportionality in the sense used here is obviously an indication that minority voters have an equal opportunity, in spite of racial polarization, "to participate in the political process and to elect representatives of their choice," the degree of probative value assigned to proportionality may vary with other facts. No single statistic provides courts with a short-cut to determine whether a set of single-member districts unlawfully dilutes minority voting strength.

5

While the United States concedes the relevance of proportionality to a § 2 claim, it would confine proportionality to an affirmative defense, and one to be made only on a statewide basis in cases that challenge districts for electing a body with statewide jurisdiction. In this case, the United States would have us treat any claim that evidence of proportionality supports the State's plan as having been waived because the State made no argument in the District Court that the proportion of districts statewide in which Hispanics constitute an effective voting majority mirrors the proportion of statewide Hispanic population.

The argument has two flaws. There is, first, no textual reason to segregate some circumstances from the statutory totality, to be rendered insignificant unless the defendant pleads them by way of affirmative defense. Second, and just as importantly, the argument would recast these cases as they come to us, in order to bar consideration of proportionality except on statewide scope, whereas up until now the dilution claims have been litigated on a smaller geographical scale. It is, indeed, the plaintiffs themselves, including the United States, who passed up the opportunity to frame their dilution claim in statewide terms.... Thus we have no occasion to decide which frame of reference should have been used if the parties had not apparently agreed in the District Court on the appropriate geographical scope for analyzing the alleged § 2 violation and devising its remedy.

6

In sum, the District Court's finding of dilution did not address the statutory standard of unequal political and electoral opportunity, and reflected instead a misconstruction of § 2 that equated dilution with failure to maximize the number of reasonably compact majority-minority districts. Because the ultimate finding of dilution in districting for the Florida House was based on a misreading of the governing law, we hold it to be clearly erroneous.

IV

Having found insufficient evidence of vote dilution in the drawing of House districts in the Dade County area, we look now to the comparable districts for the state Senate. As in the case of House districts, we understand the District Court to have misapprehended the legal test for vote dilution when it found a violation of § 2 in the location of the Senate district lines. Because the court did not modify the State's plan, however, we hold the ultimate result correct in this instance.

SJR 2-G creates 40 single-member Senate districts, five of them wholly within Dade County. Of these five, three have Hispanic super-majorities of at least 64 percent, and one has a clear majority of black voters. Two more Senate districts crossing county lines include substantial numbers of Dade County voters, and in one of these, black voters, although not close to a majority, are able to elect representatives of their choice with the aid of cross-over votes.

Within this seven-district Dade County area, both minority groups enjoy rough proportionality. The voting-age population in the seven-district area is 44.8 percent Hispanic and 15.8 percent black. Hispanics predominate in 42.9 percent of the districts (three out of seven), as do blacks in 14.3 percent of them (one out of seven). While these numbers indicate something just short of perfect proportionality (42.9 percent against 44.8; 14.3 percent against 15.8), the opposite is true of the five districts located wholly within Dade County.

The District Court concentrated not on these facts but on whether additional districts could be drawn in which either Hispanics or blacks would constitute an effective majority. The court found that indeed a fourth senatorial district with an Hispanic super-majority could be drawn, or that an additional district could be created with a black majority, in each case employing reasonably compact districts. Having previously established that each minority group was politically cohesive, that each labored under a legacy of official discrimination, and that whites voted as a bloc, the District Court believed it faced "two independent, viable Section 2 claims." Because the court did not, however, think it was possible to create both another Hispanic district and another black district on the same map, it concluded that no remedy for either violation was practical and, deferring to the State's plan as a compromise policy, imposed SJR 2-G's senatorial districts.

We affirm the District Court's decision to leave the State's plan for Florida State Senate districts undisturbed. As in the case of the House districts, the totality of circumstances appears not to support a finding of vote dilution here, where both minority groups constitute effective voting majorities in a number of state Senate districts substantially proportional to their share in the population, and where plaintiffs have not produced evidence otherwise indicating that under SJR 2-G voters in either minority group have "less opportunity than other members of the electorate to participate in the political process and to elect representatives of their choice."

V

There being no violation of the Voting Rights Act shown, we have no occasion to review the District Court's decisions going to remedy. The judgment of the District Court is accordingly affirmed in part and reversed in part.

It is so ordered.

JUSTICE O'CONNOR, concurring.

The critical issue in this case is whether § 2 of the Voting Rights Act of 1965 requires courts to "maximize" the number of districts in which minority voters may elect their candidates of choice....

... [T]he Court's carefully crafted approach treats proportionality as relevant evidence, but does not make it the only relevant evidence. In doing this the Court makes clear that § 2 does not require maximization of minority voting strength, yet remains faithful to § 2's command that minority voters be given equal opportunity to participate in the political process and to elect representatives of their choice. With this understanding, I join the opinion of the Court.

JUSTICE KENNEDY, concurring in part and concurring in the judgment.

At trial, the plaintiffs alleged that the State violated § 2 of the Voting Rights Act of 1965 by not creating as many majority-minority districts as was feasible. The District Court agreed and found a violation of § 2, thus equating impermissible vote dilution with the failure to maximize the number of majority-minority districts. I agree with the Court that the District Court's maximization theory was an erroneous application of § 2.

A more difficult question is whether proportionality, ascertained by comparing the number of majority-minority districts to the minority group's proportion of the relevant population, is relevant in deciding whether there has been vote dilution under § 2 in a challenge to election district lines. . . .

Although the statutory text does not speak in precise terms to the issue, our precedents make clear that proportionality, or the lack thereof, has some relevance to a vote dilution claim under § 2. In a unanimous decision last Term, we recognized that single-member districts were subject to vote dilution challenges under § 2, and further that "[d]ividing [a politically cohesive] minority group among various [single-member] districts so that it is a majority in none" is one "device for diluting minority voting power" within the meaning of the statute. *Voinovich* v. *Quilter* (1993). If "the fragmentation of a minority group among various districts" is an acknowledged dilutive device, it follows that analysis under § 2 takes some account of whether the number of majority-minority districts falls short of a statistical norm. . . .

To be sure, placing undue emphasis upon proportionality risks defeating the goals underlying the Voting Rights Act of 1965, as amended. As today's decision provides, a lack of proportionality is "never dispositive" proof of vote dilution, just as the presence of proportionality "is not a safe harbor for States [and] does not immunize their election schemes from § 2 challenge." But given our past construction of the statute, I would hesitate to conclude that proportionality has no relevance to the § 2 inquiry.

It is important to emphasize that the precedents to which I refer, like today's decision, only construe the statute, and do not purport to assess its constitutional implications. See *Chisom* v. *Roemer* (1991) (KENNEDY, J., dissenting). Operating under the constraints of a statutory regime in which proportionality has some relevance, States might consider it lawful and proper to act with the explicit goal of creating a proportional number of majority-minority districts in an effort to avoid § 2 litigation. Likewise, a court finding a § 2 violation might believe that the only appropriate remedy is to order the offending State to engage in race-based redistricting and create a minimum number of districts in which minorities constitute a voting majority. The Department of Justice might require (in effect) the same as a condition of granting preclearance, under § 5 of the Act, to a State's proposed legislative redistricting. Those governmental actions, in my view, tend to entrench the very practices and stereotypes the Equal Protection Clause is set against. As a general matter, the sorting of persons with an intent to divide by reason of race raises the most serious constitutional questions. . . .

Our decision in *Shaw* [v. *Reno* (1993)] alluded to, but did not resolve, the broad question whether "the intentional creation of majority-minority districts, without more, always gives rise to an equal protection claim." . . . Given our decision in *Shaw,* there is good reason for state and federal officials with responsibilities related to redistricting, as well as reviewing courts, to recognize that explicit race-based districting embarks us on a most dangerous course. It is necessary to bear in mind that redistricting must comply with the overriding demands of the Equal Protection Clause. But no constitutional claims were brought here, and the Court's opinion does not address any constitutional issues.

With these observations, I concur in all but Parts III-B-2, III-B-4 and IV of the Court's opinion and in its judgment.

JUSTICE THOMAS, with whom JUSTICE SCALIA joins, dissenting.

For the reasons I explain in *Holder* v. *Hall,* I would vacate the judgment of the District Court and remand with instructions to dismiss the actions consolidated in these cases for failure to state a claim under § 2 of the Voting Rights Act of 1965. Each of the actions consolidated in these cases asserted that Florida's apportionment plan diluted the vote of a minority group. In accordance with the views I express in *Holder,* I would hold that an apportionment plan is not a "standard, practice, or procedure" that may be challenged under § 2. I therefore respectfully dissent.

□□□

No. 91-2012

Jackie Holder, etc., et al., Petitioners v. E. K. Hall, Sr., et al.

On writ of certiorari to the United States Court of Appeals for the Eleventh Circuit

[June 30, 1994]

JUSTICE KENNEDY announced the judgment of the Court and delivered an opinion, in which THE CHIEF JUSTICE joined, and in all but Part II-B of which JUSTICE O'CONNOR joined.

This case presents the question whether the size of a governing authority is subject to a vote dilution challenge under § 2 of the Voting Rights Act of 1965, 42 U.S.C. § 1973.

I

The State of Georgia has 159 counties, one of which is Bleckley County, a rural county in central Georgia. Black persons make up nearly 20% of the eligible voting population in Bleckley County. Since its creation in 1912, the county has had a single-commissioner form of government for the exercise of "county governing authority." Under this system, the Bleckley County Commissioner performs all of the executive and legislative functions of the county government, including the levying of general and special taxes, the directing and controlling of all county property, and the settling of all claims. In addition to Bleckley County, about 10 other Georgia counties use the single-commissioner system; the rest have multimember commissions.

In 1985, the Georgia Legislature authorized Bleckley County to adopt a multimember commission consisting of five commissioners elected from single-member districts and a single chairman elected at large. In a referendum held in 1986, however, the electorate did not adopt the change to a multimember commission. (In a similar referendum four years earlier, county voters had approved a five-member district plan for the election of the county school board.)

In 1985, respondents (six black registered voters from Bleckley County and the Cochran/Bleckley County Chapter of the National Association for the Advancement of Colored People) challenged the single-commissioner system in a suit filed against petitioners (Jackie Holder, the incumbent county commissioner, and Probate Judge Robert Johnson, the superintendent of elections). The complaint raised both a constitutional and a statutory claim.

In their constitutional claim, respondents alleged that the county's single-member commission was enacted or maintained with an intent to exclude or to limit the political influence of the county's black community in violation of the Fourteenth and Fifteenth Amendments. At the outset, the District Court made extensive findings of fact about the political history and dynamics of Bleckley County. The court found, for example, that when the county was formed in 1912, few if any black citizens could vote. Indeed, until passage of federal civil rights laws, Bleckley County "enforced racial segregation in all aspects of local government—courthouse, jails, public housing, governmental services—and deprived its black citizens of the opportunity to participate in local government." And even today, though legal segregation no longer exists, "more black than white residents of Bleckley County continue to endure a depressed socioeconomic status." No black person has run for or been elected to the office of Bleckley County Commissioner, and the District Judge stated that, having run for public office himself, he "wouldn't run if [he] were black in Bleckley County."

The court rejected respondents' constitutional contention, however, concluding that respondents "ha[d] failed to provide any evidence that Bleckley County's single member county commission [wa]s the product of original or continued racial animus or discriminatory intent." . . .

In their statutory claim, respondents asserted that the county's single-member commission violated § 2 of the Voting Rights Act of 1965. Under the statute, the suit contended, Bleckley County must have a county commission of sufficient size that, with single-member election districts, the county's black citizens would constitute a majority in one of the single-member districts. Applying the § 2 framework established in *Thornburg* v. *Gingles* (1986), the District Court found that respondents satisfied the first of the three *Gingles* preconditions because black voters were sufficiently numerous and compact that they could have constituted a majority in one district of a multimember commission. In particular, the District Court found that "[i]f the county commission were increased in number to six commissioners to be elected from five single member districts and if the districts were the same as the present school board election districts, a black majority 'safe' district . . . would result." The court found, however, that respondents failed to satisfy the second and third *Gingles* preconditions—that whites vote as a bloc in a manner sufficient to defeat the black-preferred candidate and that blacks were politically cohesive.

The Court of Appeals for the Eleventh Circuit reversed on the statutory claim. . . . [T]he court first held that a challenge to the single-commissioner system was subject to the same analysis as that used in *Gingles*. Applying that analysis, the Court of Appeals agreed with the District Court that respondents had satisfied the first *Gingles* precondition by showing that blacks could constitute a majority of the electorate in one of five single-member districts. . . . The Court of Appeals further found that the District Court had erred in concluding that the second and third *Gingles* preconditions were not met.... The court ... concluded that respondents had proved a violation of § 2, and it remanded for formulation of a remedy, which, it suggested, "could well be modeled" after the system used to elect the Bleckley County school board. Because of its statutory ruling, the Court of Appeals did not consider the District Court's ruling on respondents' constitutional claim.

We granted certiorari to review the statutory holding of the Court of Appeals (1993).

II

A

Section 2 of the Voting Rights Act of 1965 provides that "[n]o voting qualification or prerequisite to voting, or standard, practice, or procedure shall be imposed or applied by any State or political subdivision in a manner which results in a denial or abridgement of the right of any citizen of the United States to vote on account of race or color." In a § 2 vote dilution suit, along with determining whether the *Gingles* preconditions are met and whether the totality of the circumstances supports a finding of liability, a court must find a reasonable alternative practice as a benchmark against which to measure the existing voting practice....

In certain cases, the benchmark for comparison in a § 2 dilution suit is obvious. The effect of an anti-single-shot voting rule, for instance, can be evaluated by comparing the system with that rule to the system without that rule. But where there is no objective and workable standard for choosing a reasonable benchmark by which to evaluate a challenged voting practice, it follows that the voting practice cannot be challenged as dilutive under § 2....

As the facts of this case well illustrate, the search for a benchmark is quite problematic when a § 2 dilution challenge is brought to the size of a government body. There is no principled reason why one size should be picked over another as the benchmark for comparison. Respondents here argue that we should compare Bleckley County's sole commissioner system to a hypothetical five-member commission in order to determine whether the current system is dilutive. Respondents and the United States as *amicus curiae* give three reasons why the single commissioner structure should be compared to a five-member commission (instead of, say, a 3-, 10-, or 15-member body): (1) because the five-member commission is a common form of governing authority in the State; (2) because the state legislature had authorized Bleckley County to adopt a five-member commission if it so chose (it did not); and (3) because the county had moved from a single superintendent of education to a school board with five members elected from single-member districts.

These referents do not bear upon dilution. It does not matter, for instance, how popular the single-member commission system is in Georgia in determining whether it dilutes the vote of a minority racial group in Bleckley County. That the single-member commission is uncommon in the State of Georgia, or that a five-member commission is quite common, tells us nothing about its effects on a minority group's voting strength. The sole commissioner system has the same impact regardless of whether it is shared by none, or by all, of the other counties in Georgia. It makes little sense to say (as do respondents and the United States) that the sole commissioner system should be subject to a dilution challenge if it is rare—but immune if it is common.

That Bleckley County was authorized by the State to expand its commission, and that it adopted a five-member school board, are likewise irrelevant considerations in the dilution inquiry. At most, those facts indicate that Bleckley County could change the size of its commission with minimal disruption. But the county's failure to do so says nothing about the effects the sole commissioner system has on the voting power of Bleckley County's citizens. . . . One gets the sense that respondents and the United States have chosen a benchmark for the sake of having a benchmark. But it is one thing to say that a benchmark can be found, quite another to give a convincing reason for finding it in the first place.

B

To bolster their argument, respondents point out that our § 5 cases may be interpreted to indicate that covered jurisdictions may not change the size of their government bodies without obtaining preclearance from the Attorney General or the federal courts. Respondents contend that these § 5 cases, together with the similarity in language between §§ 2 and 5 of the Act, compel the conclusion that the size of a government body must be subject to a dilution challenge under § 2. . . . [W]e do not think that the fact that a change in a voting practice must be precleared under § 5 necessarily means that the voting practice is subject to challenge in a dilution suit under § 2.

To be sure, if the structure and purpose of § 2 mirrored that of § 5, then the case for interpreting § 2 and § 5 to have the same application in all cases would be convincing. But the two sections differ in structure, purpose, and application. Section § 5 applies only in certain jurisdictions specified by Congress and "only to proposed changes in voting procedures." . . . Under § 5, . . . the proposed voting practice is measured against the existing voting practice to determine whether retrogression would result from the proposed change. . . .

Retrogression is not the inquiry in § 2 dilution cases. Unlike in § 5 cases, therefore, a benchmark does not exist by definition in § 2 dilution cases. And as explained above, with some voting practices, there in fact may be no appropriate benchmark to determine if an existing voting practice is dilutive under § 2. For that reason, a voting practice that is subject to the preclearance requirements of § 5 is not necessarily subject to a dilution challenge under § 2. . . .

III

With respect to challenges to the size of a governing authority, respondents fail to explain where the search for reasonable alternative benchmarks should begin and end, and they provide no acceptable principles for deciding future cases. The wide range of possibilities makes the choice "inherently standardless" (O'CONNOR, J., concurring in part and concurring in judgment), and we therefore conclude that a plaintiff cannot maintain a § 2 challenge to the size of a government body, such as the Bleckley County Commission. The judgment of the Court of Appeals is reversed, and the case is remanded for consideration of respondents' constitutional claim.

It is so ordered.

JUSTICE O'CONNOR, concurring in part and concurring in the judgment.

I agree with JUSTICES KENNEDY and THOMAS that a plaintiff cannot maintain a § 2 vote dilution challenge to the size of a governing authority, though I reach that conclusion by a somewhat different rationale. JUSTICE THOMAS rejects the notion that § 2 covers *any* dilution challenges, and would hold that § 2 is limited to "state enactments that regulate citizens' access to the ballot or the processes for counting a ballot." As JUSTICE STEVENS points out, however, *stare decisis* concerns weigh heavily here. . . . These concerns require me to reject JUSTICE THOMAS' suggestion that we overhaul our established reading of § 2.

I also agree with JUSTICE BLACKMUN that our precedents compel the conclusion that the size of the Bleckley County Commission is both a "standard, practice, or procedure" under § 2 and a "standard, practice, or procedure with respect to voting" under § 5. . . .

But determining the threshold scope of coverage does not end the inquiry, at least so far as § 2 dilution challenges are concerned. . . . Section 2 vote dilution plaintiffs must establish that the challenged practice is dilutive. In order for an electoral system to dilute a minority group's voting power, there must be an alternative system that would provide greater electoral opportunity to minority voters. . . .

Accordingly, to determine whether voters possess the potential to elect representatives of choice in the absence of the challenged structure, courts must choose an objectively reasonable alternative practice as a benchmark for the dilution comparison. . . .

. . . This case presents the question whether, in a § 2 dilution challenge to size, there can ever be an objective alternative benchmark for comparison. And I agree with JUSTICE KENNEDY that there cannot be. . . .

In a dilution challenge to the size of a governing authority, choosing the alternative for comparison—a hypothetical larger (or smaller) governing authority—is extremely problematic. The wide range of possibilities makes the choice inherently standardless. Here, for example, respondents argued that the single-member commission structure was dilutive in comparison to a five-member structure, in which African-Americans would probably have been able to elect one representative of their choice. Some groups, however, will not be able to constitute a majority in one of five districts. Once a court accepts respondents' reasoning, it will have to allow a plaintiff group insufficiently large or geographically compact to form a majority in one of five districts to argue that the jurisdiction's failure to establish a 10-, 15-, or 25-commissioner structure is dilutive. . . .

Respondents argue that this concern with arbitrary and standardless intrusions into the size of local governing authority is overstated. Respondents' principal support for this conclusion is that a five-member commission is the *most* common size for Georgia. But a five-member commission is not the *only* common size in Georgia: 22 Georgia counties have three-member commissions (and one county has an 11-member commission). Moreover, there is no good reason why the search for benchmarks should be limited to Georgia. Expanding the search nationwide produces many 20-person county commissions in Tennessee, and 40-member commissions in Wisconsin. . . . In sum, respondents do not explain how common an alternative practice must be before it can be a reliable alternative benchmark for the dilution comparison, nor do they explain where the search for alternative benchmarks should begin and end.

Respondents' failure to provide any meaningful principles for deciding future cases demonstrates the difficulty with allowing dilution challenges to the size of a governing authority. Under respondents' open-ended test, a wide range of state governmental bodies may be subject to a dilution challenge. Within each State there are many forms of government, including county commissions that range dramatically in size. . . .

Nor are deviations from the norm limited to counties. Statewide governing authorities also range dramatically in size, and often do not correlate to the size of the State. For example, Texas has only 31 members in its State Senate, while tiny Rhode Island has 50. The Texas Senate is smaller than the national average and the Rhode Island Senate is larger.

Similarly, California has an unusually small 80-person Assembly, while New Hampshire has a 400-person House.

The discrepancies in size among state and local governing authorities reinforce my concern that the limiting principle offered by respondents will in practice limit very little. Though respondents purport to present Bleckley County as unique, it is not. County commissions throughout New Jersey, South Carolina, Tennessee, and Wisconsin, and the State Legislatures of Texas, Rhode Island, California, and New Hampshire are ripe for a dilution challenge under respondents' theory, since they do not fit the norm for their State. Moreover, though my examples are some of the more extreme ones, they are not alone. In these cases, and perhaps in many more, the potential reach of allowing dilution challenges to size will not be meaningfully circumscribed by the open-ended requirement that the alternative benchmark be "reasonable and workable." (BLACK-MUN, J., dissenting).

For these reasons, I concur in the conclusion that respondents' dilution challenge to the size of the Bleckley County Commission cannot be maintained under § 2 of the Voting Rights Act, and I join Parts I, II-A, and III of JUSTICE KENNEDY's opinion. Because the Court appropriately reverses the judgment below and remands for consideration of respondents' constitutional claim of intentional discrimination, I also concur in the judgment.

JUSTICE THOMAS, with whom JUSTICE SCALIA joins, concurring in the judgment.

We are asked in this case to determine whether the size of a local governing body is subject to challenge under § 2 of the Voting Rights Act as a "dilutive" practice. . . .

. . . Only a "voting qualification or prerequisite to voting or standard, practice, or procedure" can be challenged under § 2. I would hold that the size of a governing body is not a "standard, practice, or procedure" within the terms of the Act. In my view, however, the only principle limiting the scope of the terms "standard, practice, or procedure" that can be derived from the text of the Act would exclude, not only the challenge to size advanced today, but also challenges to allegedly dilutive election methods that we have considered within the scope of the Act in the past.

I believe that a systematic reassessment of our interpretation of § 2 is required in this case. The broad reach we have given the section might suggest that the size of a governing body, like an election method that has the potential for diluting the vote of a minority group, should come within the terms of the Act. But the gloss we have placed on the words "standard, practice, or procedure" in cases alleging dilution is at odds with the terms of the statute and has proved utterly unworkable in practice. A review of the current state of our cases shows that by construing the Act to cover potentially dilutive electoral mechanisms, we have immersed the federal courts in a hopeless project of weighing questions of political theory— questions judges must confront to establish a benchmark concept of an "undiluted" vote. Worse, in pursuing the ideal measure of voting strength, we have devised a remedial mechanism that encourages federal courts to segregate voters into racially designated districts to ensure minority electoral success. In doing so, we have collaborated in what may aptly be termed the racial "balkaniz[ation]" of the Nation. *Shaw* v. *Reno* (1993).

I can no longer adhere to a reading of the Act that does not comport with the terms of the statute and that has produced such a disastrous misadventure in judicial policymaking. I would hold that the size of a government body is not a "standard, practice, or procedure" because, properly understood, those terms reach only state enactments that limit citizens' access to the ballot.

I

If one surveys the history of the Voting Rights Act, one can only be struck by the sea change that has occurred in the application and enforcement of the Act since it was passed in 1965. The statute was originally perceived as a remedial provision directed specifically at eradicating discriminatory practices that restricted blacks' ability to register and vote in the segregated South. Now, the Act has grown into something entirely different. In construing the Act to cover claims of vote dilution, we have converted the Act into a device for regulating, rationing, and apportioning political power among racial and ethnic groups. In the process, we have read the Act essentially as a grant of authority to the federal judiciary to develop theories on basic principles of representative government, for it is only a resort to political theory that can enable a court to determine which electoral systems provide the "fairest" levels of representation or the most "effective" or "undiluted" votes to minorities. . . .

A

As it was enforced in the years immediately following its enactment, the Voting Rights Act of 1965 was perceived primarily as legislation directed at eliminating literacy tests and similar devices that had been used to prevent black voter registration in the segregated South. . . .

The Court's decision in *Allen* v. *State Bd. of Elections* (1969), however, marked a fundamental shift in the focal point of the Act. In an opinion dealing with four companion cases, the *Allen* Court determined that the Act should be given "the broadest possible scope." Thus, in

Fairley v. *Patterson,* the Court decided that a covered jurisdiction's switch from a districting system to an at-large system for election of county supervisors was a "standard, practice, or procedure with respect to voting," subject to preclearance under § 5. Stating that the Act "was aimed at the subtle, as well as the obvious, state regulations which have the effect of denying citizens their right to vote because of their race," the Court reasoned that § 5's preclearance provisions should apply, not only to changes in electoral laws that pertain to registration and access to the ballot, but to provisions that might "dilute" the force of minority votes that were duly cast and counted. The decision in *Allen* thus ensured that the terms "standard, practice, or procedure" would extend to encompass a wide array of electoral practices or voting systems that might be challenged for reducing the potential impact of minority votes.

As a consequence, *Allen* also ensured that courts would be required to confront a number of complex and essentially political questions in assessing claims of vote dilution under the Voting Rights Act. The central difficulty in any vote dilution case, of course, is determining a point of comparison against which dilution can be measured. . . . But in setting the benchmark of what "undiluted" or fully "effective" voting strength should be, a court must necessarily make some judgments based purely on an assessment of principles of political theory. . . .

Perhaps the most prominent feature of the philosophy that has emerged in vote dilution decisions since *Allen* has been the Court's preference for single-member districting schemes, both as a benchmark for measuring undiluted minority voting strength and as a remedial mechanism for guaranteeing minorities undiluted voting power. . . .

It should be apparent, however, that there is no principle inherent in our constitutional system, or even in the history of the Nation's electoral practices, that makes single-member districts the "proper" mechanism for electing representatives to governmental bodies or for giving "undiluted" effect to the votes of a numerical minority. On the contrary, from the earliest days of the Republic, multimember districts were a common feature of our political systems. . . . Today, . . . multimember district systems continue to be a feature on the American political landscape, especially in municipal governments. . . .

The obvious advantage the Court has perceived in single-member districts, of course, is their tendency to enhance the ability of any numerical minority in the electorate to gain control of seats in a representative body. But in choosing single-member districting as a benchmark electoral plan on that basis the Court has made a political decision. . . . [T]he Court has determined that the purpose of the vote—or of the fully "effective" vote—is controlling seats. In other words, in an effort to develop standards for assessing claims of dilution, the Court has adopted the view that members of any numerically significant minority are denied a fully effective use of the franchise unless they are able to control seats in an elected body. Under this theory, votes that do not control a representative are essentially wasted; those who cast them go unrepresented and are just as surely disenfranchised as if they had been barred from registering. . . .

. . . [T]he the assumptions that have guided the Court reflect only one possible understanding of effective exercise of the franchise. . . . [I]t is certainly possible to construct a theory of effective political participation that would accord greater importance to voters' ability to influence, rather than control, elections. And especially in a two-party system such as ours, the influence of a potential "swing" group of voters composing 10%-20% of the electorate in a given district can be considerable. Even such a focus on practical influence, however, is not a necessary component of the definition of the "effective" vote. Some conceptions of representative government may primarily emphasize the formal value of the vote as a mechanism for participation in the electoral process, whether it results in control of a seat or not. Under such a theory, minorities unable to control elected posts would not be considered essentially without a vote; rather, a vote duly cast and counted would be deemed just as "effective" as any other. If a minority group is unable to control seats, that result may plausibly be attributed to the inescapable fact that, in a majoritarian system, numerical minorities lose elections.

In short, there are undoubtedly an infinite number of theories of effective suffrage, representation, and the proper apportionment of political power in a representative democracy that could be drawn upon to answer the questions posed in *Allen*. . . . [S]uch matters of political theory are beyond the ordinary sphere of federal judges. . . . The matters the Court has set out to resolve in vote dilution cases are questions of political philosophy, not questions of law. As such, they are not readily subjected to any judicially manageable standards that can guide courts in attempting to select between competing theories.

But the political choices the Court has had to make do not end with the determination that the primary purpose of the "effective" vote is controlling seats or with the selection of single-member districting as the mechanism for providing that control. . . . Single-member districting tells a court "how" members of a minority are to control seats, but not "how many" seats they should be allowed to control.

But "how many" is the critical issue. Once one accepts the proposition that the effectiveness of votes is measured in terms of the control of seats, the core of any vote dilution claim is an assertion that the group in question is unable to control the "proper" number of seats—that is, the number of seats that the minority's percentage of the population would enable it to control in the benchmark "fair" system. The claim is inherently based on ratios between the numbers of the minority in the population and the numbers of seats controlled. . . . As a result, only a mathematical calculation can answer the fundamental question posed by a claim of vote dilution. And once again, in selecting the proportion that will be used to define the undiluted strength of a minority—the ratio that will provide the principle for decision in a vote dilution case—a court must make a political choice.

The ratio for which this Court has opted, and thus the mathematical principle driving the results in our cases, is undoubtedly direct proportionality. . . . While in itself that choice may strike us intuitively as the fairest or most just rule to apply, opting for proportionality is still a political choice, not a result required by any principle of law.

B

The dabbling in political theory that dilution cases have prompted, however, is hardly the worst aspect of our vote dilution jurisprudence. Far more pernicious has been the Court's willingness to accept the one underlying premise that must inform every minority vote dilution claim: the assumption that the group asserting dilution is not merely a racial or ethnic group, but a group having distinct political interests as well. Of necessity, in resolving vote dilution actions we have given credence to the view that race defines political interest. We have acted on the implicit assumption that members of racial and ethnic groups must all think alike on important matters of public policy and must have their own "minority preferred" representatives holding seats in elected bodies if they are to be considered represented at all. . . .

The assumptions upon which our vote dilution decisions have been based should be repugnant to any nation that strives for the ideal of a color-blind Constitution. . . . [O]ur voting rights decisions are rapidly progressing towards a system that is indistinguishable in principle from a scheme under which members of different racial groups are divided into separate electoral registers and allocated a proportion of political power on the basis of race. Under our jurisprudence, rather than requiring registration on racial rolls and dividing power purely on a population basis, we have simply resorted to the somewhat less precise expedient of drawing geographic district lines to capture minority populations and to ensure the existence of the "appropriate" number of "safe minority seats."

That distinction in the practical implementation of the concept, of course, is immaterial. The basic premises underlying our system of safe minority districts and those behind the racial register are the same: that members of the racial group must think alike and that their interests are so distinct that the group must be provided a separate body of representatives in the legislature to voice its unique point of view. . . . [F]ew devices could be better designed to exacerbate racial tensions than the consciously segregated districting system currently being constructed in the name of the Voting Rights Act.

As a practical political matter, our drive to segregate political districts by race can only serve to deepen racial divisions by destroying any need for voters or candidates to build bridges between racial groups or to form voting coalitions. "Black-preferred" candidates are assured election in "safe black districts"; "white-preferred" candidates are assured election in "safe white districts." Neither group needs to draw on support from the other's constituency to win on election day. . . .

C

. . . [W]e should recognize that our approach to splintering the electorate into racially designated single-member districts does not by any means mark a limit on the authority federal judges may wield to rework electoral systems under our Voting Rights Act jurisprudence. On the contrary, in relying on single-member districting schemes as a touchstone, our cases so far have been somewhat arbitrarily limited to addressing the interests of minority voters who are sufficiently geographically compact to form a majority in a single-member district. There is no reason *a priori*, however, that our focus should be so constrained. The decision to rely on single-member geographic districts as a mechanism for conducting elections is merely a political choice—and one that we might reconsider in the future. . . .

But as the destructive effects of our current penchant for majority-minority districts become more apparent, courts will undoubtedly be called upon to reconsider adherence to geographic districting as a method for ensuring minority voting power. Already, some advocates have criticized the current strategy of creating majority-minority districts and have urged the adoption of other voting mechanisms—for example, cumulative voting or a system using transferable votes—that can produce proportional results without requiring division of the electorate into racially segregated districts. . . .

Such changes may seem radical departures from the electoral systems with which we are most familiar. Indeed, they may be unwanted by the people in the several States who purposely have adopted districting systems in their electoral laws. But nothing in our present understanding of the Voting Rights Act places a principled limit on the authority of federal courts that would prevent them from instituting a system of cumulative voting as a remedy under § 2, or even from establishing a more elaborate mechanism for securing proportional representation based on transferable votes. . . . [G]eographic districting is not a requirement inherent in our political system. . . .

... [A]ll that is required for districting to fall out of favor is for Members of this Court to further develop their political thinking. We should not be surprised if voting rights advocates encourage us to "revive our political imagination" and to consider "innovative and nontraditional remedies" for vote dilution, for under our Voting Rights Act jurisprudence, it is only the limits on our "political imagination" that place restraints on the standards we may select for defining undiluted voting systems. Once we candidly recognize that geographic districting and other aspects of electoral systems that we have so far placed beyond question are merely political choices, those practices, too, may fall under suspicion of having a dilutive effect on minority voting strength. ... In principle, cumulative voting and other non-district-based methods of effecting proportional representation are simply more efficient and straightforward mechanisms for achieving what has already become our tacit objective: roughly proportional allocation of political power according to race.

At least one court, in fact, has already abandoned districting and has opted instead for cumulative voting on a county-wide basis as a remedy for a Voting Rights Act violation. ... If such a system can be ordered on a county-wide basis, we should recognize that there is no limiting principle under the Act that would prevent federal courts from requiring it for elections to state legislatures as well.

D

... We would be mighty Platonic guardians indeed if Congress had granted us the authority to determine the best form of local government for every county, city, village, and town in America. But under our constitutional system, this Court is not a centralized politburo appointed for life to dictate to the provinces the "correct" theories of democratic representation, the "best" electoral systems for securing truly "representative" government, the "fairest" proportions of minority political influence, or, as respondents would have us hold today, the "proper" sizes for local governing bodies. We should be cautious in interpreting any Act of Congress to grant us power to make such determinations.

JUSTICE BLACKMUN suggests that, if we were to interpret the Act to allow challenges to the size of governmental bodies under § 2, the Court's power to determine the structure that local governing bodies must take would be bounded by the constraints that local customs provide in the form of benchmarks. But as JUSTICE O'CONNOR rightly points out, such benchmarks are themselves arbitrarily selected and would provide no assured limits on judicial power. In my view, the local standards to which JUSTICE BLACKMUN points today are little different from the various standards to which the Court has resorted in the past as touchstones of undiluted voting systems. The appeal to such standards, which are necessarily arbitrarily chosen, should not serve to obscure the assumption in the Court's vote dilution jurisprudence of a sweeping authority to select the electoral systems to be used by every governing body in each of the 50 States, and to do so based upon little more than the passing preference of five Members of this Court for one political theory over another. . . .

II

Section 2(a) of the Voting Rights Act provides that "[n]o voting qualification or prerequisite to voting or standard, practice, or procedure shall be imposed or applied by any State or political subdivision in a manner which results in a denial or abridgement of the right of any citizen of the United States to vote" on account of race, color, or membership in one of the language minority groups defined in the Act. . . . Properly understood, the terms "standard, practice, or procedure" in § 2(a) refer only to practices that affect minority citizens' access to the ballot. Districting systems and electoral mechanisms that may affect the "weight" given to a ballot duly cast and counted are simply beyond the purview of the Act. . . .

A

. . . Reading the words in context strongly suggests that § 2(a) must be understood as referring to any standard, practice, or procedure *with respect to voting*. And thus understood, the terms of the section would not extend to the size of a governmental body; we would not usually describe the size or form of a governing authority as a "practice" or "procedure" concerning voting.

But under our precedents, we have already stretched the terms "standard, practice, or procedure" beyond the limits of ordinary meaning. We have concluded, for example, that the choice of a certain set of district lines is a "procedure," or perhaps a "practice," concerning voting subject to challenge under the Act, even though the drawing of a given set of district lines has nothing to do with the basic process of allowing a citizen to vote—that is, the process of registering, casting a ballot, and having it counted. Similarly, we have determined that the use of multimember districts, rather than single-member districts, can be challenged under the Act. . . . [I]f *how* districts are drawn is a "practice" concerning voting, why not conclude that *how many* districts are drawn is a "practice" as well? . . .

If we return to the Act to reexamine the terms setting out the actions regulated by § 2, a careful reading of the statutory text will reveal a good deal more about the limitations on the scope of the section than suggested above. The terms "standard, practice, or procedure" appear to have been included in § 2 as a sort of catch-all provision. They seem phrased with an eye to eliminating the possibility of evasion. Nevertheless, they are catch-all terms that round out a list. . . .

Here, the specific items described in § 2(a) ("voting qualification[s]" and "prerequisite[s] to voting") indicate that Congress was concerned in this section with any procedure, however it might be denominated, that regulates citizens' access to the ballot—that is, any procedure that might erect a barrier to prevent the potential voter from casting his vote. . . . Simply by including general terms in § 2(a) to ensure the efficacy of the restriction imposed, Congress should not be understood to have expanded the scope of the restriction beyond the logical limits implied in the specific terms of the statute. . . .

While the terms of § 2(a) thus indicate that the section focuses only on securing access to the ballot, it might be argued that reenactment of § 2 in 1982 should be understood as an endorsement of the interpretation contained in cases such as *Allen* that the terms "standard, practice, or procedure" were meant to reach potentially dilutive practices. . . . But it was hardly well settled in 1982 that *Allen*'s broad reading of the terms "standard, practice, or procedure" in § 5 would set the scope of § 2 as a provision reaching claims of vote dilution. . . .

Finally, as our cases have shown, reading § 2(a) to reach beyond laws that regulate in some way citizens' access to the ballot turns the section into a command for courts to evaluate abstract principles of political theory in order to develop rules for deciding which votes are "diluted" and which are not. Common sense would suggest that we should not lightly interpret the Act to require courts to address such matters so far outside the normal bounds of judicial competence, and the mere use of three more general terms at the end of the list of regulated practices in § 2(a) cannot properly be understood to incorporate such an expansive command into the Act. . . .

Of course, this interpretation of the terms "standard, practice, or procedure" effectively means that § 2(a) does not provide for any claims of what we have called vote "dilution." But that is precisely the result suggested by the text of the statute. Section § 2(a) nowhere uses the term "vote dilution" or suggests that its goal is to ensure that votes are given their proper "weight." . . .

B

. . . We first considered the amended § 2 in *Thornburg* v. *Gingles.* Although the precise scope of the terms "standard, practice, or procedure" was not specifically addressed in that case, *Gingles* nevertheless established our current interpretation of the amended section as a provision that addresses vote dilution, and in particular it fixed our understanding that the results test in § 2(b) is intended to measure vote dilution in terms of electoral outcomes. . . .

In approaching § 2, the *Gingles* Court . . . bypassed a consideration of the text of the Act and proceeded to interpret the section based almost exclusively on its legislative history. It was from the legislative history that the Court culled its understanding that § 2 is a provision encompassing claims that an electoral system has diluted a minority group's vote and its understanding that claims of dilution are to be evaluated based upon how closely electoral outcomes under a given system approximate the outcomes that would obtain under an alternative, undiluted norm.

Contrary to the remarkable "legislative history first" method of statutory construction pursued in *Gingles,* however, I had thought it firmly established that the "authoritative source" for legislative intent was the text of the statute passed by both houses of Congress and presented to the President, not a series of partisan statements about purposes and objectives collected by congressional staffers and packaged into a Committee Report. . . . [H]ad the Court addressed the text, it would have concluded that the terms of the Act do not address matters of vote "dilution.". . .

. . . [W]e have arrived at our current understanding of the Act, with all of its attendant pitfalls, only by abandoning proper methods of statutory construction. Our errors in method in past cases ordinarily might not indicate a need to forsake an established line of precedent. But here they have produced an "inherent tension" between our interpretation of § 2 and the text of the Act and have yielded a construction of the statute that . . . is so unworkable in practice and destructive in its effects that it must be repudiated.

C

"*Stare decisis* is not an inexorable command," *Payne* v. *Tennessee* (1991). Indeed, "when governing decisions are unworkable or are badly reasoned, this Court has never felt constrained to follow precedent." The discussion above should make clear that our decision in *Gingles* interpreting the scope of § 2 was badly reasoned; it wholly substituted reliance on legislative history for analysis of statutory text. In doing so, it produced a far more expansive interpretation of § 2 than a careful reading of the language of the statute would allow.

Our interpretation of § 2 has also proved unworkable. . . . [I]t has mired the federal courts in an inherently political task—one that requires answers to questions that are ill-suited to principled judicial resolution. Under § 2, we have assigned the federal judiciary a project that involves, not the application of legal standards to the facts of various cases or even the elaboration of legal principles on a case-by-case basis, but rather the creation of standards from an abstract evaluation of political philosophy.

Worse, our interpretation of § 2 has required us to distort our decisions to obscure the fact that the political choice at the heart of our cases rests on precisely the principle the Act condemns: proportional allocation of political power according to race. Continued adherence to a line of decisions that necessitates such dissembling cannot possibly promote what we have perceived to be one of the central values of the policy of *stare decisis:* the preservation of "the actual and perceived integrity of the judicial process."

I have endeavored to explain above that the core of any vote dilution claim is an assertion that the plaintiff group does not hold seats in the proportion that it should. There is no logical way to avoid reliance on a simple ratio in evaluating such a claim. And allocation of seats in direct proportion to the minority group's percentage in the population provides the most logical ratio to apply as an "undiluted" norm. But § 2 makes it clear that the Act does not create a right to proportional representation, and thus dictates that proportionality should not provide the rule of decision for § 2 claims. Nevertheless, despite the statutory command, in deciding claims of vote dilution we have turned to proportionality as a guide, simply for lack of any better alternative.

No formulation of the test for evaluating vote dilution claims has ever dispensed with the inevitable need to consult a mathematical formula to decide a case. The factors listed in *White* v. *Regester* [1973], resurrected in the Senate Report on the 1982 amendments to § 2, and finally reincorporated into our decision in *Gingles,* although praised in our cases as a multi-faceted test ensuring that vote dilution is determined based on the "totality of circumstances," in reality provide no rule for deciding a vote dilution claim based on anything other than a numerical principle....

... [T]he factors listed in *Gingles*—in their various incarnations and by whatever names they are known—are nothing but puffery used to fill out an impressive verbal formulation and to create the impression that the outcome in a vote dilution case rests upon a reasoned evaluation of a variety of relevant circumstances. The "totality of circumstances" test outlined in *Gingles* thus serves to obscure the inherent conflict between the text of the Act and an underlying reliance on proportionality....

Few words would be too strong to describe the dissembling that pervades the application of the "totality of circumstances" test under our interpretation of § 2. It is an empty incantation—a mere conjurer's trick that serves to hide the drive for proportionality that animates our decisions. As actions such as that brought in *Shaw* v. *Reno* (1993) have already started to show, what might euphemistically be termed the benign "creation of majority-minority single-member districts to enhance the opportunity of minority groups to elect representatives of their choice" might also more simply and more truthfully be termed "racial gerrymandering." Similarly, what we might call a "totality of circumstances" test to determine whether an electoral practice "interacts with social and historical conditions to cause an inequality in the opportunities enjoyed by black and white voters to elect their preferred representatives," might more accurately be called a test for ensuring proportional electoral results according to race.

In my view, our current practice should not continue. Not for another Term, not until the next case, not for another day. The disastrous implications of the policies we have adopted under the Act are too grave; the dissembling in our approach to the Act too damaging to the credibility of the federal judiciary. The "inherent tension"—indeed, I would call it an irreconcilable conflict—between the standards we have adopted for evaluating vote dilution claims and the text of the Voting Rights Act would itself be sufficient in my view to warrant overruling the interpretation of §2 set out in *Gingles*. When that obvious conflict is combined with the destructive effects our expansive reading of the Act has had in involving the federal judiciary in the project of dividing the Nation into racially segregated electoral districts, I can see no reasonable alternative to abandoning our current unfortunate understanding of the Act.

Stare decisis is a powerful concern, especially in the field of statutory construction. But "we have never applied *stare decisis* mechanically to prohibit overruling our earlier decisions determining the meaning of statutes." *Stare decisis* should not bind the Court to an interpretation of the Voting Rights Act that was based on a flawed method of statutory construction from its inception and that in every day of its continued existence involves the federal judiciary in attempts to obscure the conflict between our cases and the explicit commands of the Act. . . . I cannot subscribe to the view that in our decisions under the Voting Rights Act it is more important that we have a settled rule than that we have the right rule. When, under our direction, federal courts are engaged in methodically carving the country into racially designated electoral districts, it is imperative that we stop to reconsider whether the course we have charted for the Nation is the one set by the people through their representatives in Congress. I believe it is not. . . .

III

For the foregoing reasons, I agree with the Court's conclusion that the size of a governing body is not subject to challenge under § 2 of the Voting Rights Act. I therefore concur in the Court's judgment reversing the judgment below and remanding for consideration of respondents' constitutional claim of intentional discrimination.

JUSTICE BLACKMUN, with whom JUSTICE STEVENS, JUSTICE SOUTER, and JUSTICE GINSBURG join, dissenting.

Five Justices today agree that the size of a governing body is a "standard, practice, or procedure" under § 2 of the Voting Rights Act of 1965, as amended. A different five Justices decide, under three separate theories, that voting rights plaintiffs cannot bring § 2 dilution challenges based on size. I, however, believe that the Act, its history, and our own precedent require us to conclude not only that the size of a governing body is a "standard, practice, or procedure" under § 2, but also that minority voters may challenge the dilutive effects of this practice by demonstrating their potential to elect representatives under an objectively reasonable alternative practice. Accordingly, I dissent from the Court's decision that minority voters cannot bring § 2 vote dilution challenges based on the size of an existing government body.

I

Section 2(a) of the Act prohibits the imposition or application of any "voting qualification or prerequisite to voting, or *standard, practice, or procedure*" that "results in a denial or abridgement of the right of any citizen of the United States to vote on account or race or color." Section 5 parallels § 2 by requiring certain jurisdictions to preclear with the Attorney General a change in "any voting qualification or prerequisite to voting, or *standard, practice, or procedure* with respect to voting." Under the broad interpretation that this Court, Congress, and the Attorney General consistently have given the Act in general and § 5 in particular, the practice of electing a single commissioner, as opposed to a multimember commission, constitutes a "standard, practice, or procedure" under § 2.

Nearly 30 years of precedent admonish us that the Act, which was adopted "for the broad remedial purpose of 'rid[ding] the country of racial discrimination in voting,' " should be given "the broadest possible scope." *Allen* v. *State Board of Elections* (1969). . . .

Consistent with the Act's remedial purposes, this Court has held that a wide variety of election- and voting-related practices fit within the term "standard, practice, or procedure." Among the covered practices are the annexation of land to enlarge city boundaries; a rule requiring employees to take leaves of absence while they campaign for elective office; candidate filing dates and other procedural requirements. . . .

Specifically, this Court long has treated a change in the size of a governing authority as a change in a "standard, practice, or proce-dure" with respect to voting. In *City of Rome* [v. *United States* (1980)], it noted that it "is not disputed" that an expansion in the size of a Board of Education was "within the purview of the Act" and subject to preclearance under § 5. In *Lockhart* v. *United States* (1983), it stated that a change from a three-member commission to a five-member commission was subject to § 5 preclearance. And, most recently, it said that the term "standard, practice, or procedure with respect to voting" included a change in the size of a governing authority or an increase or decrease in the number of elected offices. *Presley* v. *Etowah County Comm'n* (1992).

This conclusion flowed naturally from the holding in *Bunton* v. *Patterson* (1969) that a change from an elected to an appointed office was a "standard, practice, or procedure with respect to voting." In *Bunton,* the Court reasoned that the power of a citizen's vote is affected by the change because the citizen has been "prohibited from electing an officer formerly subject to the approval of the voters." The reverse is also true: a change from an appointed to an elected office affects a citizen's voting power by increasing the number of officials for whom he may vote. . . . And, as the Court recognized in *Presley,* a change in the size of a governing authority is a "standard, practice, or procedure with respect to voting" because the change "increase[s] or diminish[es] the number of officials for whom the electorate may vote; this change bears "on the substance of voting power" and has "a direct relation to voting and the election process."

To date, our precedent has dealt with § 5 challenges to a change in the size of a governing authority, rather than § 2 challenges to the existing size of a governing body. I agree with JUSTICE O'CONNOR, that, as a textual matter, "standard, practice, or procedure" under § 2 is at least as broad as "standard, practice, or procedure with respect to voting" under § 5. . . .

Congress repeatedly has endorsed the broad construction this Court has given the Act in general and § 5 in particular. Significantly, when Congress considered the 1982 amendments to the Voting Rights Act, it made no effort to curtail the application of § 5 to changes in size, in the face of the longstanding practice of submitting such changes for preclearance, and on the heels of this Court's recognition just two years earlier that it was "not disputed" that a change in the size of a governing body was covered under § 5. . . . Similarly, the Attorney General, whose construction of the Act "is entitled to con-siderable deference," *NAACP* v. *Hampton County Election Comm'n* (1985), for years has required § 5 preclearance of the expansion or reduction of a governing body. It is not surprising that no party to this case argued that the size of a governing authority is not a "standard, practice, or procedure." . . .

. . . [T]he Act's "all-inclusive" definition of "standard, practice, or procedure," cannot be read to exclude threshold coverage of challenges to the size of a governing authority. . . .

II

Although five Justices agree that the size of a governing body is a "standard, practice, or procedure" under § 2, a like number of Justices conclude, under varying rationales, that Voting Rights plaintiffs nonetheless cannot bring size challenges under 2. This conclusion is inconsistent with our precedent giving the Act " 'the broadest possible scope' in combatting racial discrimination" and with the vote-dilution analysis prescribed in *Thornburg* v. *Gingles* (1986).

To prevail in a vote-dilution challenge, minority voters must show that they "possess the *potential* to elect representatives *in the absence of the challenged structure* or practice." There is widespread agreement that minority voters' potential "in the absence of" the allegedly dilutive mechanism must be measured against the benchmark of an alternative structure or practice that is reasonable and workable under the facts of the specific case.

By all objective measures, the proposed five-member Bleckley County Commission presents a reasonable, workable benchmark against which to measure the practice of electing a sole commissioner. First, the Georgia Legislature specifically authorized a five-member commission for Bleckley County. Moreover, a five-member commission is the most common form of governing authority in Georgia. . . . Bleckley County, as one of a small and dwindling number of counties in Georgia still employing a sole commissioner, markedly departs from practices elsewhere in Georgia. This marked "depart[ure] . . . from practices elsewhere in the jurisdiction . . . bears on the fairness of [the sole commissioner's] impact." Finally, the county itself has moved from a single superintendent of education to a school board with five members elected from single-member districts, providing a workable and readily available model for commission districts. Thus, the proposed five-member baseline is reasonable and workable.

In this case, identifying an appropriate baseline against which to measure dilution is not difficult. In other cases, it may be harder. But the need to make difficult judgments does not "justify a judicially created limitation on the coverage of the broadly worded statute, as enacted and amended by Congress." Vote dilution is inherently a relative concept, requiring a highly "flexible, fact-intensive" inquiry and calling for an exercise of the "court's overall judgment, based on the totality of the circumstances and guided by those relevant factors in the particular case," as mandated by Congress. Certainly judges who engage in the complex task of evaluating reapportionment plans and examining district lines will be able to determine whether a proposed baseline is an appropriate one against which to measure a claim of vote dilution based on the size of a county commission.

There are, to be sure, significant constraints on size challenges. Minority plaintiffs, who bear the burden of demonstrating dilution, also bear the burden of demonstrating that their proposed benchmark is reasonable and workable. One indication of benchmark's reasonableness is its grounding in history, custom, or practice. This consideration will discourage size challenges to traditional single-member executive offices, such as governors and mayors, or even sheriffs or clerks of court. By tradition and practice, these executive positions are occupied by one person, so plaintiffs could rarely point to an objectively reasonable alternative size that has any foundation in the past or present. . . . The sole commissioner, by contrast, holds plenary legislative, as well as executive, power. A one-member legislature, far from being the norm, is an anomaly. Accordingly, the Eleventh Circuit, while permitting § 2 challenges to the practice of electing a sole commissioner, has held that this provision cannot be used to alter the practice of electing a single person to offices such as lieutenant governor, sheriff, probate judge, and tax collector.

Additionally, every successful vote-dilution challenge will be based on the "totality of the circumstances," often including the lingering effects of past discrimination. Not every racial or language minority that constitutes 5% of the population has a claim to have a governing authority expanded to 20 members in order to give them an opportunity to elect a representative. Instead, the voters would have to prove that a 20-member governing authority was a reasonable benchmark—which, of course, respondents could not do here—and that their claim satisfied the three *Gingles* preconditions and was warranted under the totality of the circumstances.

With these limitations, successful vote-dilution challenges to the size of a governing authority always will be based not on abstract manipulation of numbers, but on a "searching practical evaluation of 'past and present reality.' " These limitations protect against a proliferation of vote-dilution challenges premised on eccentric or impracticable alternative methods of redistricting.

III

The Voting Rights Act of 1965 was bold and ambitious legislation, designed to eradicate the vestiges of past discrimination and to make members of racial and language minorities full participants in American political life. Nearly 30 years after the passage of this landmark civil rights legislation, its goals remain unfulfilled. Today, the most blatant forms of discrimination—including poll taxes, literacy tests, and "white" primaries—have been eliminated. But subtler, more complex means of infringing minority voting strength—including submergence or dispersion of minority voters—are still present and indeed prevalent. We have recognized over the years that seemingly innocuous and even well-intentioned election practices may impede minority voters' ability not only to vote, but to have their votes count. It is clear that the practice of electing a single-member county commission can be one such dilutive practice. It is equally clear that a five-member commission is an appropriate benchmark against which to measure the alleged dilutive effects of Bleckley County's practice of electing a sole commissioner. I respectfully dissent.

JUSTICE GINSBURG, dissenting.

I join the dissenting opinion by JUSTICE BLACKMUN and the separate opinion of JUSTICE STEVENS, and add a further observation about the responsibility Congress has given to the judiciary.

Section 2 of the Voting Rights Act calls for an inquiry into "[t]he extent to which members of a protected class have been elected to office," but simultaneously disclaims any "right to have members of a protected class elected in numbers equal to their proportion in the population." . . . Tension of this kind is hardly unique to the Voting Rights Act, for when Congress acts on issues on which its constituents are divided, sometimes bitterly, the give-and-take of legislative compromise can yield statutory language that fails to reconcile conflicting goals and purposes. . . .

When courts are confronted with congressionally-crafted compromises of this kind, it is "not an easy task" to remain "faithful to the balance Congress struck." *Thornburg* v. *Gingles* [1986] (O'CONNOR, J., joined by Burger, C. J., Powell, and REHNQUIST, JJ., concurring in judgment). The statute's broad remedial purposes, as well as the constraints on the courts' remedial powers, need to be carefully considered in light of the particular circumstances of each case to arrive at an appropriate resolution of the competing congressional concerns. However difficult this task may prove to be, it is one that courts must undertake because it is their mission to effectuate Congress' multiple purposes as best they can. . . .

Separate opinion of JUSTICE STEVENS, in which JUSTICE BLACKMUN, JUSTICE SOUTER, and JUSTICE GINSBURG join.

JUSTICE THOMAS has written a separate opinion proposing that the terms "standard, practice, or procedure" as used in the Voting Rights Act should henceforth be construed to refer only to practices that affect minority citizens' access to the ballot. Specifically, JUSTICE THOMAS would no longer interpret the Act to forbid practices that dilute minority voting strength. To the extent that his opinion advances policy arguments in favor of that interpretation of the statute, it should be addressed to Congress, which has ample power to amend the statute. To the extent that the opinion suggests that federal judges have an obligation to subscribe to the proposed narrow reading of statutory language, it is appropriate to supplement JUSTICE THOMAS' writing with a few words of history.

[I omitted]

II

JUSTICE THOMAS' narrow interpretation of the words "voting qualification ... standard, practice, or procedure," if adopted, would require us to overrule *Allen* [v. *State Bd. of Elections* (1969)] and the cases that have adhered to its reading of the critical statutory language. ... The *Allen* interpretation of the Act has also been followed in a host of cases decided in later years. ... In addition, JUSTICE THOMAS' interpretation would call into question the numerous other cases since 1978 that have assumed the broad coverage of the Voting Rights Act that JUSTICE THOMAS would now have us reject.

The large number of decisions that we would have to overrule or reconsider, as well as the congressional reenactments ... , suggests that JUSTICE THOMAS' radical reinterpretation of the Voting Rights Act is barred by the well-established principle that *stare decisis* has special force in the statutory arena. ...

Throughout his opinion, JUSTICE THOMAS argues that this case is an exception to *stare decisis,* because *Allen* and its progeny have "immersed the federal courts in a hopeless project of weighing questions of political theory." There is no question that the Voting Rights Act has required the courts to resolve difficult questions, but that is no reason to deviate from an interpretation that Congress has thrice approved. Statutes frequently require courts to make policy judgments. The Sherman Act, for example, requires courts to delve deeply into the theory of economic organization. Similarly, Title VII of the Civil Rights Act has required the courts to formulate a theory of equal opportunity. Our work would certainly be much easier if every case could be resolved by consulting a dictionary, but when Congress has legislated in general terms, judges may not invoke judicial modesty to avoid difficult questions.

III

When a statute has been authoritatively, repeatedly, and consistently construed for more than a quarter century, and when Congress has reenacted and extended the statute several times with full awareness of that construction, judges have an especially clear obligation to obey settled law. Whether JUSTICE THOMAS is correct that the Court's settled construction of the Voting Rights Act has been "a disastrous misadventure" should not affect the decision in this case. It is therefore inappropriate for me to comment on the portions of his opinion that are best described as an argument that the statute be repealed or amended in important respects.

□□□

No. 93-6497

Frank B. McFarland, Petitioner v. Wayne Scott, Director, Texas Department of Criminal Justice, Institutional Division

On writ of certiorari to the United States Court of Appeals for the Fifth Circuit

[June 30, 1994]

JUSTICE BLACKMUN delivered the opinion of the Court.

In establishing a federal death penalty for certain drug offenses under the Anti-Drug Abuse Act of 1988, 21 U.S.C. § 848(e), Congress created a statutory right to qualified legal representation for capital defendants in federal habeas corpus proceedings. § 848(q)(4)(B). This case presents the question whether a capital defendant must file a formal habeas corpus petition in order to invoke this statutory right and to establish a federal court's jurisdiction to enter a stay of execution.

I

Petitioner Frank Basil McFarland was convicted of capital murder on November 13, 1989, in the State of Texas and sentenced to death. The Texas Court of Criminal Appeals affirmed the conviction and sentence, and on June 7, 1993, this Court denied certiorari. Two months later, on August 16, 1993, the Texas trial court scheduled McFarland's execution for September 23, 1993. On September 19, McFarland filed a *pro se* motion requesting that the trial court stay or withdraw his execution date to allow the Texas Resource Center an opportunity to recruit volunteer counsel for his state habeas corpus proceeding. Texas opposed a stay of execution, arguing that McFarland had not filed an application for writ of habeas corpus and that the court thus lacked jurisdiction to enter a stay. The trial court declined to appoint counsel, but modified McFarland's execution date to October 27, 1993.

On October 16, 1993, the Resource Center informed the trial court that it had been unable to recruit volunteer counsel and asked the court to appoint counsel for McFarland. Concluding that Texas law did not authorize the appointment of counsel for state habeas corpus proceedings, the trial court refused either to appoint counsel or to modify petitioner's execution date. McFarland then filed a *pro se* motion in the Texas Court of Criminal Appeals requesting a stay and a remand for appointment of counsel. The court denied the motion without comment.

Having failed to obtain either the appointment of counsel or a modification of his execution date in state court, McFarland, on October 22, 1993, commenced the present action in the United States District Court for the Northern District of Texas by filing a *pro se* motion stating that he "wish[ed] to challenge [his] conviction and sentence under [the federal habeas corpus statute,] 28 U. S. C. § 2254." McFarland requested the appointment of counsel under 21 U.S.C. § 848(q)(4)(B) and a stay of execution to give that counsel time to prepare and file a habeas corpus petition.

The District Court denied McFarland's motion on October 25, 1993, concluding that because no "post conviction proceeding" had been initiated pursuant to 28 U.S.C. § 2254 or § 2255, petitioner was not entitled to appointment of counsel and the court lacked jurisdiction to enter a stay of execution. The court later denied a certificate of probable cause to appeal.

On October 26, the eve of McFarland's scheduled execution, the Court of Appeals for the Fifth Circuit denied his application for stay. The court noted that federal law expressly authorizes federal courts to stay state proceedings while a federal habeas corpus proceeding is pending, 28 U.S.C. § 2251, but held that no such proceeding was pending, because a "motion for stay and for appointment of counsel [is not] the equivalent of an application for habeas relief." The court concluded that any other federal judicial interference in state court proceedings was barred by the Anti-Injunction Act, 28 U.S.C. § 2283.

Shortly before the Court of Appeals ruled, a federal magistrate judge located an attorney willing to accept appointment in McFarland's case and suggested that if the attorney would file a skeletal document entitled "petition for writ of habeas corpus," the District Court might be willing to appoint him and grant McFarland a stay of execution. The attorney accordingly drafted and filed a *pro forma* habeas petition, together with a motion for stay of execution and appointment of counsel. . . . [D]espite the fact that Texas did not oppose a stay, the District Court found the petition to be insufficient and denied the motion for stay on the merits.

On October 27, 1993, this Court granted a stay of execution in McFarland's original suit pending consideration of his petition for certiorari. The Court later granted certiorari to resolve an apparent conflict with *Brown* v. *Vasquez* (CA9 1991).

II

A

Section 848(q)(4)(B) of Title 21 provides:

"In any *post conviction proceeding* under section 2254 or 2255 of title 28, seeking to vacate or set aside a death sentence, any defendant who is or becomes financially unable to obtain adequate representation or investigative, expert, or other reasonably necessary services *shall be entitled* to the appointment of one or more attorneys and the furnishing of such other services in accordance with paragraphs (5), (6), (7), (8), and (9)" (emphasis added).

On its face, this statute grants indigent capital defendants a mandatory right to qualified legal counsel and related services "[i]n any [federal] post conviction proceeding." The express language does not specify, however, how a capital defendant's right to counsel in such a proceeding shall be invoked.

Neither the federal habeas corpus statute, 28 U.S.C. § 2241 *et seq.*, nor the rules governing habeas corpus proceedings define a "post conviction proceeding" under § 2254 or § 2255 or expressly state how such a proceeding shall be commenced. Construing § 848(q)(4)(B) in light of its related provisions, however, indicates that the right to appointed counsel adheres prior to the filing of a formal, legally sufficient habeas corpus petition. Section § 848(q)(4)(B) expressly incorporates 21 U.S.C. § 848(q)(9), which entitles capital defendants to a variety of expert and investigative services upon a showing of necessity:

"Upon a finding in ex parte proceedings that investigative, expert or other services are reasonably necessary for the representation of the defendant, ... the court *shall authorize* the defendant's attorneys to obtain such services on behalf of the defendant and shall order the payment of fees and expenses therefore" (emphasis added).

The services of investigators and other experts may be critical in the preapplication phase of a habeas corpus proceeding, when possible claims and their factual bases are researched and identified. Section § 848(q)(9) clearly anticipates that capital defense counsel will have been appointed under § 848(q)(4)(B) before the need for such technical assistance arises, since the statute requires "the defendant's attorneys to obtain such services" from the court. In adopting § 848(q)(4)(B), Congress thus established a right to preapplication legal assistance for capital defendants in federal habeas corpus proceedings.

This interpretation is the only one that gives meaning to the statute as a practical matter. Congress' provision of a right to counsel under § 848(q)(4)(B) reflects a determination that quality legal representation is necessary in capital habeas corpus proceedings in light of "the seriousness of the possible penalty and ... the unique and complex nature of the litigation." An attorney's assistance prior to the filing of a capital defendant's habeas corpus petition is crucial, because "[t]he complexity of our jurisprudence in this area . . . makes it unlikely that capital defendants will be able to file successful petitions for collateral relief without the assistance of persons learned in the law." *Murray* v. *Giarratano* (1989) (KENNEDY, J., joined by O'CONNOR, J., concurring in judgment). . . .

Habeas corpus petitions must meet heightened pleading requirements and comply with this Court's doctrines of procedural default and waiver. Federal courts are authorized to dismiss summarily any habeas petition that appears legally insufficient on its face, and to deny a stay of execution where a habeas petition fails to raise a substantial federal claim. Moreover, should a defendant's *pro se* petition be summarily dismissed, any petition subsequently filed by counsel could be subject to dismissal as an abuse of the writ. Requiring an indigent capital petitioner to proceed without counsel in order to obtain counsel thus would expose him to the substantial risk that his habeas claims never would be heard on the merits. Congress legislated against this legal backdrop in adopting § 848(q)(4)(B), and we safely assume that it did not intend for the express requirement of counsel to be defeated in this manner.

The language and purposes of § 848(q)(4)(B) and its related provisions establish that the right to appointed counsel includes a right to legal assistance in the preparation of a habeas corpus application. We therefore conclude that a "post conviction proceeding" within the meaning of § 848(q)(4)(B) is commenced by the filing of a death row defendant's motion requesting the appointment of counsel for his federal habeas corpus proceeding. McFarland filed such a motion and was entitled to the appointment of a lawyer.

B

Even if the District Court had granted McFarland's motion for appointment of counsel and had found an attorney to represent him, this appointment would have been meaningless unless McFarland's execution also was stayed. We therefore turn to the question whether the District Court had jurisdiction to grant petitioner's motion for stay.

Federal courts cannot enjoin state court proceedings unless the intervention is authorized expressly by federal statute or falls under one of two other exceptions to the Anti-Injunction Act. The federal habeas corpus statute grants any federal judge "before whom a *habeas corpus proceeding is pending*" power to stay a state court action "for any matter involved in the habeas corpus proceeding." 28 U.S.C. § 2251 (emphasis added). McFarland argues that his request for counsel in a "post conviction proceeding" under § 848(q)(4)(B) initiated a "habeas corpus proceeding" within the meaning of § 2251, and that the District Court thus had jurisdiction to enter a stay. Texas contends, in turn, that even if a "post conviction proceeding" under § 848(q)(4)(B) can be triggered by a death row defendant's request for appointment of counsel, no "habeas corpus proceeding" is "pending" under § 2251, and thus no stay can be entered, until a legally sufficient habeas petition is filed.

The language of these two statutes indicates that the sections refer to the same proceeding. Section 848(q)(4)(B) expressly applies to "any post conviction proceeding under section 2254 or 2255—the precise "habeas corpus proceeding[s]" that § 2251 involves. The terms "post conviction" and "habeas corpus" also are used interchangeably in legal parlance to refer to proceedings under § 2254 and § 2255. We thus conclude that the two statutes must be read *in pari materia* to provide that once a capital defendant invokes his right to appointed counsel, a federal court also has jurisdiction under § 2251 to enter a stay of execution. Because § 2251 expressly authorizes federal courts to stay state court proceedings "for any matter involved in the habeas corpus proceeding," the exercise of this authority is not barred by the Anti-Injunction Act.

This conclusion by no means grants capital defendants a right to an automatic stay of execution. Section § 2251 does not mandate the entry of a stay, but dedicates the exercise of stay jurisdiction to the sound discretion of a federal court. Under ordinary circumstances, a capital defendant presumably will have sufficient time to request the appointment of counsel and file a formal habeas petition prior to his scheduled execution. But the right to counsel necessarily includes a right for that counsel meaningfully to research and present a defendant's habeas claims. Where this opportunity is not afforded, "[a]pproving the execution of a defendant before his [petition] is decided on the merits would clearly be improper." On the other hand, if a dilatory capital defendant inexcusably ignores this opportunity and flouts the available processes, a federal court presumably would not abuse its discretion in denying a stay of execution.

III

A criminal trial is the "main event" at which a defendant's rights are to be determined, and the Great Writ is an extraordinary remedy that should not be employed to "relitigate state trials." At the same time, criminal defendants are entitled by federal law to challenge their conviction and sentence in habeas corpus proceedings. By providing indigent capital defendants with a mandatory right to qualified legal counsel in these proceedings, Congress has recognized that federal habeas corpus has a particularly important role to play in promoting fundamental fairness in the imposition of the death penalty.

We conclude that a capital defendant may invoke this right to a counseled federal habeas corpus proceeding by filing a motion requesting the appointment of habeas counsel, and that a district court has jurisdiction to enter a stay of execution where necessary to give effect to that statutory right. McFarland filed a motion for appointment of counsel and for stay of execution in this case, and the District Court had authority to grant the relief he sought.

The judgment of the Court of Appeals is reversed.

It is so ordered.

JUSTICE O'CONNOR, concurring in the judgment in part and dissenting in part.

I agree with the Court's conclusion that 21 U.S.C. § 848 entitles capital defendants pursuing federal habeas corpus relief to a properly trained attorney. I also agree that this right includes legal assistance in preparing a habeas petition. Thus, the Court correctly holds that a defendant need not file a habeas petition to invoke the right to counsel. I write separately, however, because I disagree with the Court's conclusion that 28 U. S. C. § 2251 allows a district court to stay an execution pending counsel's preparation of an application for a writ of habeas corpus.

In my view, . . . petitioner is not entitled under present law to a stay of execution while counsel prepares a habeas petition. The habeas statute provides in relevant part that "[a] justice or judge of the United States before whom a habeas corpus proceeding is pending, may . . . stay any proceeding against the person detained in any State court." 28 U.S.C. § 2251. While this provision authorizes a stay in the habeas context, it does not explicitly allow a stay prior to the filing of a petition, and our cases have made it clear that capital defendants must raise at least some colorable federal claim before a stay of execution may be entered. . . .

Petitioner has not filed anything describing the nature of his claims, if any. As a consequence, the Court's approach, which permits a stay of execution in the absence of any showing of a constitutional claim, conflicts with the sound principle underlying our precedents that federal habeas review exists only to review errors of constitutional dimension, and that the habeas procedures may be invoked only when necessary to resolve a constitutional claim.

Congress knows how to give courts the broad authority to stay proceedings of the sort urged by the petitioner. . . . The absence of such explicit authority in the habeas statute is evidence that Congress did not intend federal courts to enter stays of execution in the absence of some showing on the merits. . . .

JUSTICE THOMAS, with whom THE CHIEF JUSTICE and JUSTICE SCALIA join, dissenting.

Today the Court holds that a state prisoner under sentence of death may invoke a federal district court's jurisdiction to obtain appointed counsel under 21 U.S.C. § 848(q)(4)(B) and to obtain a stay of execution under 28 U.S.C. § 2251 simply by filing a motion for appointment of counsel. In my view, the Court's conclusion is at odds with the terms of both statutory provisions. Each statute allows a federal district court to take action (appointing counsel under § 848(q)(4)(B) or granting a stay under § 2251) only after a habeas proceeding has been commenced. As JUSTICE O'CONNOR points out, such a proceeding is initiated under the habeas corpus statute, 28 U.S.C. § 2241 *et seq.*, only with the filing of an application for a writ of habeas corpus. I therefore agree with JUSTICE O'CONNOR that a district court lacks jurisdiction to grant a stay under § 2251 until such an application has been filed. But because § 848(q)(4)(B), like § 2251, conditions a court's power to act upon the existence of a habeas proceeding, I would also hold that a district court cannot appoint counsel until an application for habeas relief has been filed. I therefore respectfully dissent.

I

In its attempt to discern Congress' intent regarding the point at which § 848(q)(4)(B) makes counsel available, the Court spends a good deal of time considering how, as a "practical matter," the provision of counsel can be made meaningful. But here, as in any case of statutory interpretation, our primary guide to Congress' intent should be the text of the statute. The relevant terms of § 848(q)(4)(B) state that an indigent prisoner shall be entitled to an attorney and "investigative, expert, or other reasonably necessary services" only "[i]n any post conviction proceeding under section 2254 . . . seeking to vacate or set aside a death sentence." The clear import of the provision is that an indigent prisoner is not entitled to an attorney or to other services under the section *until* a "post conviction proceeding under section 2254" exists—that is, not until after such a proceeding has been commenced in district court. . . .

By providing that death-sentenced prisoners may obtain counsel "[i]n any post conviction proceeding under section 2254," Congress referred to a well-known form of action with established contours. We should therefore assume that Congress intended to incorporate into § 848(q)(4)(B) the settled understanding of what constitutes a "proceeding under section 2254" in the habeas statute. Indeed, the similarity between the language in §§ 848(q)(4)(B) and 2254(d) suggests that Congress used the phrase "[i]n any post conviction proceeding under section 2254" in the former provision as a shorthand form of the language "[i]n any proceeding instituted in a Federal court by an application for a writ of habeas corpus" contained in the latter. In short, the terms of § 848(q)(4)(B) indicate that Congress intended that legal assistance be made available under the provision only after a habeas proceeding has been commenced by the filing of an application for habeas relief.

The Court rejects this interpretation. Rather than turning to the habeas statute for guidance in determining when a "proceeding under section 2254" commences, the Court bases its examination of the question primarily on what it perceives to be the time at which legal assistance would be most useful to a death-sentenced prisoner. From this analysis, the Court concludes that a " 'post conviction proceeding' within the meaning of § 848(q)(4)(B) is commenced by the filing of a death row defendant's [preapplication] motion requesting the appointment of counsel." The only textual provision the Court cites in support of that conclusion is 21 U.S.C. § 848(q)(9), which states that

> "Upon a finding in ex parte proceedings that investigative, expert or other services are reasonably necessary for the representation of the defendant, whether in connection with issues relating to guilt or sentence, the court shall authorize the defendant's attorneys to obtain such services on behalf of the defendant and shall order the payment of fees and expenses therefore. . . ."

At bottom, the Court's textual argument amounts to the following: because investigative, expert, and other services described in § 848(q)(9) "may be critical in the preapplication phase of a habeas corpus proceeding," and because § 848(q)(9) provides that those services are to be obtained by the defendant's attorneys, an attorney must be appointed "before the need for such technical assistance arises"—that is, prior to the filing of an application for habeas relief. Thus, the sole textual source upon which the Court relies is the statement that "the defendant's attorneys" are "authorize[d]" to obtain services on the defendant's behalf.

In my view, such an oblique reference to "the defendant's attorneys" is a remarkably thin reed upon which to rest Congress' supposed intention to "establis[h] a right to preapplication legal assistance for capital defendants in federal habeas corpus proceedings.". . .

As for the policy concerns rehearsed by the Court, I agree that legal assistance prior to the filing of a federal habeas petition can be very valuable to a prisoner. That such assistance is valuable, however, does not compel the conclusion that Congress intended the Federal Government to *pay* for it under § 848(q). As the Ninth Circuit has aptly observed: "Section 848(q) is *a funding statute.* It provides for the appointment of attorneys and the furnishing of investigative services for [federal] defendants or habeas corpus petitioners seeking to vacate or set aside a death sentence." *Jackson* v. *Vasquez* (1993) (emphasis added). It might well be a wise and generous policy for the government to provide prisoners appointed counsel prior to the filing of a habeas petition, but that is not a policy declared by Congress in the terms of § 848(q)(4)(B).

Implicit in the Court's analysis is the assumption that it would be unthinkable for Congress to grant an entitlement to appointed counsel, but to have that entitlement attach only upon the filing of a habeas petition. The Court suggests that its interpretation is required because it is "the *only* one that gives meaning to the statute as a practical matter" (emphasis added). . . . Yet under the interpretation of § 848(q)(4)(B) I have outlined above, Congress has not required death-sentenced prisoners to proceed *without counsel* during the preapplication period; rather, it has merely concluded that such prisoners would proceed without counsel *funded under* § 848(q)(4)(B).

Moreover, leaving prisoners without counsel appointed under § 848(q)(4)(B) during the preapplication period would be fully reasonable. Congress was no doubt aware that alternative sources of funding for preapplication legal assistance exist for death-sentenced prisoners. Petitioner, for example, is represented by the Texas Resource Center, which has been "designated . . . a Community Defender Organization . . . for the purpose of providing representation, assistance, information, and other related services to eligible persons and appointed attorneys in connection with" federal habeas corpus cases arising from capital convictions. The Center, which is "funded primarily by a grant from the Administrative Office of the United States Courts," became involved in petitioner's case soon after his conviction was affirmed by the Texas Court of Criminal Appeals. Thus, although petitioner did not have preapplication assistance of counsel made available to him under § 848(q)(4)(B), he still could benefit from federally funded legal assistance.

In addition, it seems likely that Congress expected that the States would also shoulder some of the burden of providing preapplication legal assistance to indigent death-sentenced prisoners. . . . Defendants under a state-imposed sentence of death must exhaust state remedies by presenting their claims in state court prior to coming to federal court. Given this exhaustion requirement, it would have been logical for Congress, in drafting § 848(q)(4)(B), to assume that by the time a death-sentenced prisoner reaches federal court, "possible claims and their factual bases" will already have been "researched and identified." Indeed, if the claims have not been identified and presented to state courts, a prisoner cannot proceed on federal habeas. . . . Thus, it would not have been unreasonable for Congress to require prisoners to meet the ordinary requirement for invoking a federal court's habeas jurisdiction—namely, the filing of an adequate application for habeas corpus relief—prior to obtaining an attorney under § 848(q)(4)(B).

II

Had the Court ended its analysis with the ruling that an indigent death-sentenced prisoner is entitled to counsel under § 848(q)(4)(B) prior to filing an application for habeas relief, today's decision would have an impact on federal coffers, but would not expand the power of the federal courts to interfere with States' legitimate interests in enforcing the judgments of their criminal justice systems. The Court, however, does not stop with its decision on availability of counsel; rather, it goes on to hold that upon a motion for appointment of counsel, a death-sentenced prisoner is also able to obtain a stay of his execution in order to permit counsel "to research and present [his] habeas claims."

The Court reaches its decision through the sheerest form of bootstrapping. After reasoning that "a proceeding under section 2254" for purposes of § 848(q)(4)(B) commences with the filing of a motion for appointment of counsel, the Court imports that meaning of "proceeding" into 28 U.S.C. § 2251, which provides that a federal judge "before whom *a habeas corpus proceeding is pending*" may "stay any proceeding against the person detained in any State court." (emphasis added). . . . [T]he method the Court employs to impart meaning to the term "proceeding" in the two provisions is simply backwards. Section 848(q)(4)(B) was enacted as part of the Anti-Drug Abuse Act of 1988 long after the enactment of the habeas statute. . . . As a matter of basic statutory construction, then, we should look to the habeas statute to inform our construction of § 848(q)(4)(B), not *vice versa*.

The reason the Court pursues a different approach is clear: There is no basis in the habeas statute for reading "habeas corpus proceeding" in § 2251 to mean an action commenced by the filing of a motion for appointment of counsel. Thus, to avoid the conclusion that a "proceeding" in § 2251 is commenced by the filing of an application for habeas relief, the Court is forced to hold that by enacting § 848(q), Congress amended the habeas statute *sub silentio*. . . . Yet § 848(q)(4)(B) in no way suggests a connection between the availability of counsel and the stay power; indeed, the provision does not even mention the term "stay." . . .

In reaching its expansive interpretation of 2251, the Court ignores the fact that the habeas statute provides federal courts with exceptional powers. . . . We should not lightly assume that Congress intended to expand federal courts' habeas power; this is particularly true regarding their power directly to interfere with state proceedings through granting stays. . . .

Under the Court's interpretation of § 2251, a prisoner may obtain a stay of execution without presenting a single claim to a federal court. Indeed, under the Court's reading of the statute, a federal district court determining whether to enter a stay will no longer have to evaluate whether a prisoner has presented a potentially meritorious constitutional claim. Rather, the court's task will be to determine whether a "capital defendant" who comes to federal court shortly before his scheduled execution has been "dilatory" in pursuing his "right to counsel." If he has not been "dilatory," the district court presumably must enter a stay to preserve his "right to counsel" and his "right for that counsel meaningfully to research and present [his] habeas claims." In my view, simply by providing for the appointment of counsel in habeas cases, Congress did not intend to achieve such an extraordinary result.

Because petitioner had not filed an application for habeas relief prior to filing his motion for stay of execution and for appointment of counsel, the courts below correctly determined that they lacked jurisdiction to consider his motion. I respectfully dissent.

□□□

No. 93-880

Judy Madsen, et al., Petitioners
v. Women's Health Center, Inc., et al.

On writ of certiorari to the Supreme Court of Florida

[June 30, 1994]

CHIEF JUSTICE REHNQUIST delivered the opinion of the Court.

Petitioners challenge the constitutionality of an injunction entered by a Florida state court which prohibits antiabortion protestors from demonstrating in certain places and in various ways outside of a health clinic that performs abortions. We hold that the establishment of a 36-foot buffer zone on a public street from which demonstrators are excluded passes muster under the First Amendment, but that several other provisions of the injunction do not.

I

Respondents operate abortion clinics throughout central Florida. Petitioners and other groups and individuals are engaged in activities near the site of one such clinic in Melbourne, Florida. They picketed and demonstrated where the public street gives access to the clinic. In September 1992, a Florida state court permanently enjoined petitioners from blocking or interfering with public access to the clinic, and from physically abusing persons entering or leaving the clinic. Six months later, respondents sought to broaden the injunction, complaining that access to the clinic was still impeded by petitioners' activities and that such activities had also discouraged some potential patients from entering the clinic, and had deleterious physical effects on others. The trial court thereupon issued a broader injunction, which is challenged here.

The court found that, despite the initial injunction, protesters continued to impede access to the clinic by congregating on the paved portion of the street—Dixie Way—leading up to the clinic, and by marching in front of the clinic's driveways. It found that as vehicles heading toward the clinic slowed to allow the protesters to move out of the way, "sidewalk counselors" would approach and attempt to give the vehicle's occupants antiabortion literature. The number of people congregating varied from a handful to 400, and the noise varied from singing and chanting to the use of loudspeakers and bullhorns.

The protests, the court found, took their toll on the clinic's patients. A clinic doctor testified that, as a result of having to run such a gauntlet to enter the clinic, the patients "manifested a higher level of anxiety and hypertension causing those patients to need a higher level of sedation to undergo the surgical procedures, thereby increasing the risk associated with such procedures." The noise produced by the protestors could be heard within the clinic, causing stress in the patients both during surgical procedures and while recuperating in the recovery rooms. And those patients who turned away because of the crowd to return at a later date, the doctor testified, increased their health risks by reason of the delay.

Doctors and clinic workers, in turn, were not immune even in their homes. Petitioners picketed in front of clinic employees' residences; shouted at passersby; rang the doorbells of neighbors and provided literature identifying the particular clinic employee as a "baby killer." Occasionally, the protestors would confront minor children of clinic employees who were home alone.

This and similar testimony led the state court to conclude that its original injunction had proved insufficient "to protect the health, safety and rights of women in Brevard and Seminole County, Florida, and surrounding counties seeking access to [medical and counseling] services." The state court therefore amended its prior order, enjoining a broader array of activities. The amended injunction prohibits petitioners from engaging in the following acts:

> "(1) At all times on all days, from entering the premises and property of the Aware Woman Center for Choice [the Melbourne clinic]. . . .
> "(2) At all times on all days, from blocking, impeding, inhibiting, or in any other manner obstructing or interfering with access to, ingress into and egress from any building or parking lot of the Clinic.

"(3) At all times on all days, from congregating, picketing, patrolling, demonstrating or entering that portion of public right-of-way or private property within [36] feet of the property line of the Clinic. . . . An exception to the 36 foot buffer zone is the area immediately adjacent to the Clinic on the east. . . . The [petitioners] . . . must remain at least [5] feet from the Clinic's east line. Another exception to the 36 foot buffer zone relates to the record title owners of the property to the north and west of the Clinic. The prohibition against entry into the 36 foot buffer zones does not apply to such persons and their invitees. The other prohibitions contained herein do apply, if such owners and their invitees are acting in concert with the [petitioners]. . . .

"(4) During the hours of 7:30 a.m. through noon, on Mondays through Saturdays, during surgical procedures and recovery periods, from singing, chanting, whistling, shouting, yelling, use of bullhorns, auto horns, sound amplification equipment or other sounds or images observable to or within earshot of the patients inside the Clinic.

"(5) At all times on all days, in an area within [300] feet of the Clinic, from physically approaching any person seeking the services of the Clinic unless such person indicates a desire to communicate by approaching or by inquiring of the [petitioners]. . . .

"(6) At all times on all days, from approaching, congregating, picketing, patrolling, demonstrating or using bullhorns or other sound amplification equipment within [300] feet of the residence of any of the [respondents'] employees, staff, owners or agents, or blocking or attempting to block, barricade, or in any other manner, temporarily or otherwise, obstruct the entrances, exits or driveways of the residences of any of the [respondents'] employees, staff, owners or agents. The [petitioners] and those acting in concert with them are prohibited from inhibiting or impeding or attempting to impede, temporarily or otherwise, the free ingress or egress of persons to any street that provides the sole access to the street on which those residences are located.

"(7) At all times on all days, from physically abusing, grabbing, intimidating, harassing, touching, pushing, shoving, crowding or assaulting persons entering or leaving, working at or using services at the [respondents'] Clinic or trying to gain access to, or leave, any of the homes of owners, staff or patients of the Clinic.

"(8) At all times on all days, from harassing, intimidating or physically abusing, assaulting or threatening any present or former doctor, health care professional, or other staff member, employee or volunteer who assists in providing services at the [respondents'] Clinic.

"(9) At all times on all days, from encouraging, inciting, or securing other persons to commit any of the prohibited acts listed herein."

The Florida Supreme Court upheld the constitutionality of the trial court's amended injunction. That court recognized that the forum at issue, which consists of public streets, sidewalks, and rights-of-way, is a traditional public forum. It then determined that the restrictions are content neutral, and it accordingly refused to apply the heightened scrutiny dictated by *Perry Education Assn.* v. *Perry Local Educators' Assn.* (1983) (To enforce a content-based exclusion the State must show that its regulation is necessary to serve a compelling state interest and that it is narrowly drawn to achieve that end). Instead, the court analyzed the injunction to determine whether the restrictions are "narrowly tailored to serve a significant government interest, and leave open ample alternative channels of communication." It concluded that they were.

Shortly before the Florida Supreme Court's opinion was announced, the United States Court of Appeals for the Eleventh Circuit heard a separate challenge to the same injunction. The Court of Appeals struck down the injunction, characterizing the dispute as a clash "between an actual prohibition of speech and a potential hinderance to the free exercise of abortion rights." It stated that the asserted interests in public safety and order were already protected by other applicable laws and that these interests could be protected adequately without infringing upon the First Amendment rights of others. The Court of Appeals found the injunction to be content based and neither necessary to serve a compelling state interest nor narrowly drawn to achieve that end. We granted certiorari (1994) to resolve the conflict between the Florida Supreme Court and the Court of Appeals over the constitutionality of the state court's injunction.

II

We begin by addressing petitioners' contention that the state court's order, because it is an injunction that restricts only the speech of antiabortion protesters, is necessarily content or viewpoint based. Accordingly, they argue, we should examine the entire injunction under the strictest standard of scrutiny. We disagree. To accept petitioners' claim would be to classify virtually every injunction as content or viewpoint based. An injunction, by its very nature, applies only to a particular group (or individuals) and regulates the activities, and perhaps the speech, of that group. It does so, however, because of the group's past actions in the context of a specific dispute between real parties. The parties seeking the injunction assert a violation of their rights; the court hearing the action is charged with fashioning a remedy for a specific deprivation, not with the drafting of a statute addressed to the general public.

The fact that the injunction in the present case did not prohibit activities of those demonstrating in favor of abortion is justly attributable to the lack of any similar demonstrations by those in favor of abortion, and of any consequent request that their demonstrations be regulated by injunction. There is no suggestion in this record that Florida law would not equally restrain similar conduct directed at a target having nothing to do with abortion; none of the restrictions imposed by the court were directed at the contents of petitioner's message.

Our principal inquiry in determining content neutrality is whether the government has adopted a regulation of speech "without reference to the content of the regulated speech." We thus look to the government's purpose as the threshold consideration. Here, the state court imposed restrictions on petitioners incidental to their antiabortion message because they repeatedly violated the court's original order. That petitioners all share the same viewpoint regarding abortion does not in itself demonstrate that some invidious content- or viewpoint-based purpose motivated the issuance of the order. It suggests only that those in the group *whose conduct* violated the court's order happen to share the same opinion regarding abortions being performed at the clinic. In short, the fact that the injunction covered people with a particular viewpoint does not itself render the injunction content or viewpoint based. Accordingly, the injunction issued in this case does not demand the level of heightened scrutiny set forth in *Perry Education Assn.* And we proceed to discuss the standard which does govern.

III

If this were a content-neutral, generally applicable statute, instead of an injunctive order, its constitutionality would be assessed under the standard set forth in *Ward* v. *Rock Against Racism* [1989], and similar cases. Given that the forum around the clinic is a traditional public forum, we would determine whether the time, place, and manner regulations were "narrowly tailored to serve a significant governmental interest."

There are obvious differences, however, between an injunction and a generally applicable ordinance. Ordinances represent a legislative choice regarding the promotion of particular societal interests. Injunctions, by contrast, are remedies imposed for violations (or threatened violations) of a legislative or judicial decree. Injunctions also carry greater risks of censorship and discriminatory application than do general ordinances. . . . Injunctions, of course, have some advantages over generally applicable statutes in that they can be tailored by a trial judge to afford more precise relief than a statute where a violation of the law has already occurred.

We believe that these differences require a somewhat more stringent application of general First Amendment principles in this context. In past cases evaluating injunctions restricting speech, we have relied upon such general principles while also seeking to ensure that the injunction was no broader than necessary to achieve its desired goals. See *Carroll* v. *President and Comm'rs of Princess Anne* (1968); [*NAACP* v.] *Claiborne Hardware [Co.* (1982)]. Our close attention to the fit between the objectives of an injunction and the restrictions it imposes on speech is consistent with the general rule, quite apart from First Amendment considerations, "that injunctive relief should be no more burdensome to the defendants than necessary to provide complete relief to the plaintiffs." Accordingly, when evaluating a content-neutral injunction, we think that our standard time, place, and manner analysis is not sufficiently rigorous. We must ask instead whether the challenged provisions of the injunction burden no more speech than necessary to serve a significant government interest.

Both JUSTICE STEVENS and JUSTICE SCALIA disagree with the standard we announce, for policy reasons. JUSTICE STEVENS believes that "injunctive relief should be judged by a more lenient standard than legislation," "because injunctions are imposed on individuals or groups who have engaged in illegal activity." JUSTICE SCALIA, by contrast, believes that content-neutral injunctions are "*at least* as deserving of strict scrutiny as a statutory, content-based restriction." JUSTICE SCALIA bases his belief on the danger that injunctions, even though they might not "attack content *as content*," may be used to suppress particular ideas; that individual judges should not be trusted to impose injunctions in this context; and that an injunction is procedurally more difficult to challenge than a statute. We believe that consideration of *all* of the differences and similarities between statutes and injunctions supports, as a matter of policy, the standard we apply here.

JUSTICE SCALIA further contends that precedent compels the application of strict scrutiny in this case. Under that standard, we ask whether a restriction is "necessary to serve a compelling state interest and [is] narrowly drawn to achieve that end." JUSTICE SCALIA fails to cite a single case, and we are aware of none, in which we have applied this standard to a content-neutral injunction. He cites a number of cases in which we have struck down, with little or no elaboration, prior restraints on free expression. As we have explained, however, we do not believe that this injunction constitutes a prior restraint, and we therefore believe that the "heavy presumption" against its constitutionality does not obtain here.

JUSTICE SCALIA also relies on *Claiborne Hardware* and *Carroll* for support of his contention that our precedent requires the application of strict scrutiny in this context. In *Claiborne Hardware*, we stated simply that "precision of regulation" is demanded. JUSTICE SCALIA reads this case to require "surgical precision" of regulation, but that was not the adjective chosen by the author of the Court's opinion, JUSTICE STEVENS. We think a standard requiring that an injunction "burden no more speech than necessary" exemplifies "precision of regulation."

As for *Carroll*, JUSTICE SCALIA believes that the "standard" adopted in that case "is strict scrutiny," which "does not remotely resemble the Court's new proposal." Comparison of the language used in *Carroll* and the wording of the standard we adopt, however, belies JUSTICE SCALIA's exaggerated contention. *Carroll*, for example, requires that an injunction be "couched in the narrowest terms that will accomplish the pin-pointed objective" of the injunction. We require that the injunction "burden no more speech than necessary" to accomplish its objective. We fail to see a difference between the two standards.

The Florida Supreme Court concluded that numerous significant government interests are protected by the injunction. It noted that the State has a strong interest in protecting a woman's freedom to seek lawful medical or counseling services in connection with her pregnancy. See *Roe* v. *Wade* (1973). The State also has a strong interest in ensuring the public safety and order, in promoting the free flow of traffic on public streets and sidewalks, and in protecting the property rights of all its citizens. In addition, the court believed that the State's strong interest in residential privacy . . . applied by analogy to medical privacy. The court observed that while targeted picketing of the home threatens the psychological well-being of the "captive" resident, targeted picketing of a hospital or clinic threatens not only the psychological, but the physical well-being of the patient held "captive" by medical circumstance. We agree with the Supreme Court of Florida that the combination of these governmental interests is quite sufficient to justify an appropriately tailored injunction to protect them. We now examine each contested provision of the injunction to see if it burdens more speech than necessary to accomplish its goal.

A

1

We begin with the 36-foot buffer zone. The state court prohibited petitioners from "congregating, picketing, patrolling, demonstrating or entering" any portion of the public right-of-way or private property within 36 feet of the property line of the clinic as a way of ensuring access to the clinic. This speech-free buffer zone requires that petitioners move to the other side of Dixie Way and away from the driveway of the clinic, where the state court found that they repeatedly had interfered with the free access of patients and staff. . . . The buffer zone also applies to private property to the north and west of the clinic property. We examine each portion of the buffer zone separately.

We have noted a distinction between the type of focused picketing banned from the buffer zone and the type of generally disseminated communication that cannot be completely banned in public places, such as handbilling and solicitation. . . . Here the picketing is directed primarily at patients and staff of the clinic.

The 36-foot buffer zone protecting the entrances to the clinic and the parking lot is a means of protecting unfettered ingress to and egress from the clinic, and ensuring that petitioners do not block traffic on Dixie Way. The state court seems to have had few other options to protect access given the narrow confines around the clinic. As the Florida Supreme Court noted, Dixie Way is only 21 feet wide in the area of the clinic. The state court was convinced that allowing the petitioners to remain on the clinic's sidewalk and driveway was not a viable option in view of the failure of the first injunction to protect access. And allowing the petitioners to stand in the middle of Dixie Way would obviously block vehicular traffic.

The need for a complete buffer zone near the clinic entrances and driveway may be debatable, but some deference must be given to the state court's familiarity with the facts and the background of the dispute between the parties even under our heightened review. Moreover, one of petitioners' witnesses during the evidentiary hearing before the state court conceded that the buffer zone was narrow enough to place petitioners at a distance of no greater than 10 to 12 feet from cars approaching and leaving the clinic. Protesters standing across the narrow street from the clinic can still be seen and heard from the clinic parking lots. We also bear in mind the fact that the state court originally issued a much narrower injunction, providing no buffer zone, and that this order did not succeed in protecting access to the clinic. The failure of the first order to accomplish its purpose may be taken into consideration in evaluating the constitutionality of the broader order. On balance, we hold that the 36-foot buffer zone around the clinic entrances and driveway burdens no more speech than necessary to accomplish the governmental interest at stake.

JUSTICE SCALIA's dissent argues that a videotape made of demonstrations at the clinic represents "what one must presume to be the worst of the activity justifying the injunction." This seems to us a gratuitous assumption. The videotape was indeed introduced by respondents, presumably because they thought it supported their request for the second injunction. But witnesses also testified as to relevant facts in a 3-day evidentiary hearing, and the state court was therefore not limited to JUSTICE SCALIA's rendition of what he saw on the videotape to make its findings in support of the second injunction. Indeed, petitioners themselves studiously refrained from challenging the factual basis for the injunction both in the state courts and here. . . . We must therefore judge this case on the assumption that the evidence and testimony presented to the state court supported its findings that the presence of protesters standing, marching, and demonstrating near the clinic's entrance interfered with ingress to and egress from the clinic despite the issuance of the earlier injunction.

2

The inclusion of private property on the back and side of the clinic in the 36-foot buffer zone raises different concerns. The accepted purpose of the buffer zone is to protect access to the clinic and to facilitate the orderly flow of traffic on Dixie Way. Patients and staff wishing to reach the clinic do not have to cross the private property abutting the clinic property on the north and west, and nothing in the record indicates that petitioners' activities on the private property have obstructed access to the clinic. Nor was evidence presented that protestors located on the private property blocked vehicular traffic on Dixie Way. Absent evidence that petitioners standing on the private property have obstructed access to the clinic, blocked vehicular traffic, or otherwise unlawfully interfered with the clinic's operation, this portion of the buffer zone fails to serve the significant government interests relied on by the Florida Supreme Court. We hold that on the record before us the 36-foot buffer zone as applied to the private property to the north and west of the clinic burdens more speech than necessary to protect access to the clinic.

B

In response to high noise levels outside the clinic, the state court restrained the petitioners from "singing, chanting, whistling, shouting, yelling, use of bullhorns, auto horns, sound amplification equipment or other sounds or images observable to or within earshot of the patients inside the [c]linic" during the hours of 7:30 a.m. through noon on Mondays through Saturdays. We must, of course, take account of the place to which the regulations apply in determining whether these restrictions burden more speech than necessary. We have upheld similar noise restrictions in the past.... Noise control is particularly important around hospitals and medical facilities during surgery and recovery periods....

We hold that the limited noise restrictions imposed by the state court order burden no more speech than necessary to ensure the health and well-being of the patients at the clinic. The First Amendment does not demand that patients at a medical facility undertake Herculean efforts to escape the cacophony of political protests. "If overamplified loudspeakers assault the citizenry, government may turn them down." *Grayned* [v. *City of Rockford* (1972)]. That is what the state court did here, and we hold that its action was proper.

C

The same, however, cannot be said for the "images observable" provision of the state court's order. Clearly, threats to patients or their families, however communicated, are proscribable under the First Amendment.

But rather than prohibiting the display of signs that could be interpreted as threats or veiled threats, the state court issued a blanket ban on all "images observable." This broad prohibition on all "images observable" burdens more speech than necessary to achieve the purpose of limiting threats to clinic patients or their families. Similarly, if the blanket ban on "images observable" was intended to reduce the level of anxiety and hypertension suffered by the patients inside the clinic, it would still fail. The only plausible reason a patient would be bothered by "images observable" inside the clinic would be if the patient found the expression contained in such images disagreeable. But it is much easier for the clinic to pull its curtains than for a patient to stop up her ears, and no more is required to avoid seeing placards through the windows of the clinic. This provision of the injunction violates the First Amendment.

D

The state court ordered that petitioners refrain from physically approaching any person seeking services of the clinic "unless such person indicates a desire to communicate" in an area within 300 feet of the clinic. The state court was attempting to prevent clinic patients and staff from being "stalked" or "shadowed" by the petitioners as they approached the clinic. . . .

But it is difficult, indeed, to justify a prohibition on *all* uninvited approaches of persons seeking the services of the clinic, regardless of how peaceful the contact may be, without burdening more speech than necessary to prevent intimidation and to ensure access to the clinic. Absent evidence that the protesters' speech is independently proscribable (*i.e.,* "fighting words" or threats), or is so infused with violence as to be indistinguishable from a threat of physical harm, this provision cannot stand. . . . The "consent" requirement alone invalidates this provision; it burdens more speech than is necessary to prevent intimidation and to ensure access to the clinic.

E

The final substantive regulation challenged by petitioners relates to a prohibition against picketing, demonstrating, or using sound amplification equipment within 300 feet of the residences of clinic staff. The prohibition also covers impeding access to streets that provide the sole access to streets on which those residences are located. The same analysis applies to the use of sound amplification equipment here as that discussed above: the government may simply demand that petitioners turn down the volume if the protests overwhelm the neighborhood.

As for the picketing, our prior decision upholding a law banning targeted residential picketing remarked on the unique nature of the home, as "the last citadel of the tired, the weary, and the sick." *Frisby* [v. *Schultz* (1988)]. We stated that "[t]he State's interest in protecting the well-being, tranquility, and privacy of the home is certainly of the highest order in a free and civilized society."

But the 300-foot zone around the residences in this case is much larger than the zone provided for in the ordinance which we approved in *Frisby.* The ordinance at issue there made it "unlawful for any person to engage in picketing before or about the residence or dwelling of any individual." The prohibition was limited to "focused picketing taking place solely in front of a particular residence." By contrast, the 300-foot zone would ban "[g]eneral marching through residential neighborhoods, or even walking a route in front of an entire block of houses." The record before us does not contain sufficient justification for this broad a ban on picketing; it appears that a limitation on the time, duration of picketing, and number of pickets outside a smaller zone could have accomplished the desired result.

IV

Petitioners also challenge the state court's order as being vague and overbroad. They object to the portion of the injunction making it applicable to those acting "in concert" with the named parties. But petitioners themselves are named parties in the order, and they therefore lack standing to challenge a portion of the order applying to persons who are not parties. Nor is that phrase subject, at the behest of petitioners, to a challenge for "overbreadth"; the phrase itself does not prohibit any conduct, but is simply directed at unnamed parties who might later be found to be acting "in concert" with the named parties. . . .

Petitioners also contend that the "in concert" provision of the injunction impermissibly limits their freedom of association guaranteed by the First Amendment. . . . But petitioners are not enjoined from associating with others or from joining with them to express a particular viewpoint. The freedom of association protected by the First Amendment does not extend to joining with others for the purpose of depriving third parties of their lawful rights.

V

In sum, we uphold the noise restrictions and the 36-foot buffer zone around the clinic entrances and driveway because they burden no more speech than necessary to eliminate the unlawful conduct targeted by the state court's injunction. We strike down as unconstitutional the 36-foot buffer zone as applied to the private property to the north and west of the clinic, the "images observable" provision, the 300-foot no-approach zone around the clinic, and the 300-foot buffer zone around the residences, because these provisions sweep more broadly than necessary to accomplish the permissible goals of the injunction. Accordingly, the judgment of the Florida Supreme Court is

Affirmed in part, and reversed in part.

JUSTICE SOUTER, concurring.

I join the Court's opinion and write separately only to clarify two matters in the record. First, the trial judge made reasonably clear that the issue of who was acting "in concert" with the named defendants was a matter to be taken up in individual cases, and not to be decided on the basis of protesters' viewpoints. Second, petitioners themselves acknowledge that the governmental interests in protection of public safety and order, of the free flow of traffic, and of property rights are reflected in Florida law. . . .

JUSTICE STEVENS, concurring in part and dissenting in part.

The certiorari petition presented three questions, corresponding to petitioners' three major challenges to the trial court's injunction. The Court correctly and unequivocally rejects petitioners' argument that the injunction is a "content-based restriction on free speech," as well as their challenge to the injunction on the basis that it applies to persons acting "in concert" with them. I therefore join Parts II and IV of the Court's opinion, which properly dispose of the first and third questions presented. I part company with the Court, however, on its treatment of the second question presented, including its enunciation of the applicable standard of review.

I

I agree with the Court that a different standard governs First Amendment challenges to generally applicable legislation than the standard that measures such challenges to judicial remedies for proven wrongdoing. Unlike the Court, however, I believe that injunctive relief should be judged by a more lenient standard than legislation. As the Court notes, legislation is imposed on an entire community, regardless of individual culpability. By contrast, injunctions apply solely to an individual or a limited group of individuals who, by engaging in illegal conduct, have been judicially deprived of some liberty—the normal consequence of illegal activity. Given this distinction, a statute prohibiting demonstrations within 36 feet of an abortion clinic would probably violate the First Amendment, but an injunction directed at a limited group of persons who have engaged in unlawful conduct in a similar zone might well be constitutional.

The standard governing injunctions has two obvious dimensions. On the one hand, the injunction should be no more burdensome than necessary to provide complete relief. In a First Amendment context, as in any other, the propriety of the remedy depends almost entirely on the character of the violation and the likelihood of its recurrence. For this reason, standards fashioned to determine the constitutionality of statutes should not be used to evaluate injunctions.

On the other hand, even when an injunction impinges on constitutional rights, more than "a simple proscription against the precise conduct previously pursued" may be required; the remedy must include appropriate restraints on "future activities both to avoid a recurrence of the violation and to eliminate its consequences." Moreover, "[t]he judicial remedy for a proven violation of law will often include commands that the law does not impose on the community at large." As such, repeated violations may justify sanctions that might be invalid if applied to a first offender or if enacted by the legislature.

In this case, the trial judge heard three days of testimony and found that petitioners not only had engaged in tortious conduct, but also had repeatedly violated an earlier injunction. The injunction is thus twice removed from a legislative proscription applicable to the general public and should be judged by a standard that gives appropriate deference to the judge's unique familiarity with the facts.

II

The second question presented by the certiorari petition asks whether the "consent requirement before speech is permitted" within a 300-foot buffer zone around the clinic unconstitutionally infringes on free speech. Petitioners contend that these restrictions create a "no speech" zone in which they cannot speak unless the listener indicates a positive interest in their speech. And, in Part III-D of its opinion, the Court seems to suggest that, even in a more narrowly defined zone, such a consent requirement is constitutionally impermissible. Petitioners' argument and the Court's conclusion, however, are based on a misreading of paragraph (5) of the injunction.

That paragraph does not purport to prohibit speech; it prohibits a species of conduct. Specifically, it prohibits petitioners "from physically approaching any person seeking the services of the Clinic unless such person indicates a desire to communicate by approaching or by inquiring" of petitioners. The meaning of the term "physically approaching" is explained by the detailed prohibition that applies when the patient refuses to converse with, or accept delivery of literature from, petitioners. Absent such consent, the petitioners "shall not accompany such person, encircle, surround, harass, threaten or physically or verbally abuse those individuals who choose not to communicate with them." As long as petitioners do not physically approach patients in this manner, they remain free not only to communicate with the public but also to offer verbal or written advice on an individual basis to the clinic's patients through their "sidewalk counseling."

Petitioners' "counseling" of the clinic's patients is a form of expression analogous to labor picketing. It is a mixture of conduct and communication. . . . As with picketing, the principal reason why handbills containing the same message are so much less effective than "counseling" is that "the former depend entirely on the persuasive force of the idea." Just as it protects picketing, the First Amendment protects the speaker's right to offer "sidewalk counseling" to all passersby. That protection, however, does not encompass attempts to abuse an unreceptive or captive audience, at least under the circumstances of this case. . . .

The "physically approaching" prohibition entered by the trial court is no broader than the protection necessary to provide relief for the violations it found. The trial judge entered this portion of the injunction only after concluding that the injunction was necessary to protect the clinic's patients and staff from "uninvited contacts, shadowing and stalking" by petitioners. The protection is especially appropriate for the clinic patients given that the trial judge found that petitioners' prior conduct caused higher levels of "anxiety and hypertension" in the patients, increasing the risks associated with the procedures that the patients seek. Whatever the proper limits on a court's power to restrict a speaker's ability to physically approach or follow an unwilling listener, surely the First Amendment does not prevent a trial court from imposing such a restriction given the unchallenged findings in this case. . . .

[III, IV omitted]

JUSTICE SCALIA, with whom JUSTICE KENNEDY and JUSTICE THOMAS join, concurring in the judgment in part and dissenting in part.

The judgment in today's case has an appearance of moderation and Solomonic wisdom, upholding as it does some portions of the injunction while disallowing others. That appearance is deceptive. The entire injunction in this case departs so far from the established course of our jurisprudence that in any other context it would have been regarded as a candidate for summary reversal.

But the context here is abortion. A long time ago, in dissent from another abortion-related case, JUSTICE O'CONNOR, joined by then-JUSTICE REHNQUIST, wrote:

> This Court's abortion decisions have already worked a major distortion in the Court's constitutional jurisprudence. Today's decision goes further, and makes it painfully clear that no legal rule or doctrine is safe from ad hoc nullification

by this Court when an occasion for its application arises in a case involving state regulation of abortion. . . . *Thornburgh* v. *American College of Obstetricians and Gynecologists* (1986).

Today the ad hoc nullification machine claims its latest, greatest, and most surprising victim: the First Amendment.

Because I believe that the judicial creation of a 36-foot zone in which only a particular group, which had broken no law, cannot exercise its rights of speech, assembly, and association, and the judicial enactment of a noise prohibition, applicable to that group and that group alone, are profoundly at odds with our First Amendment precedents and traditions, I dissent.

I

The record of this case contains a videotape, with running caption of time and date, displaying what one must presume to be the worst of the activity justifying the injunction issued by Judge McGregor and partially approved today by this Court. The tape was shot by employees of, or volunteers at, the Aware Woman Clinic on three Saturdays in February and March 1993. . . . The tape was edited down (from approximately 6 to 8 hours of footage to ½ hour) by Ruth Arick, a management consultant employed by the clinic and by the Feminist Majority Foundation.

Anyone seriously interested in what this case was about must view that tape. And anyone doing so who is familiar with run-of-the-mine labor picketing, not to mention some other social protests, will be aghast at what it shows we have today permitted an individual judge to do. I will do my best to describe it.

On Saturday, March 6, 1993, a group of antiabortion protesters is gathered in front of the clinic, arrayed from east (camera-left) to west (camera-right) on the clinic side of Dixie Way, a small, nonartery street. Men, women, and children are also visible across the street, on the south side of Dixie Way; some hold signs and appear to be protesters, others may be just interested onlookers.

On the clinic side of the street, two groups confront each other across the line marking the south border of the clinic property. . . . On the clinic property . . . are a line of clinic and abortion-rights supporters. . . . Opposite them, and on the public right-of-way between the clinic property and Dixie Way itself, is a group of abortion opponents, some standing in place, others walking a picket line. . . . Melbourne police officers are visible at various times walking about in front of the clinic, and individuals can be seen crossing Dixie Way at various times.

Clinic supporters are more or less steadily chanting the following slogans: "Our right, our right, our right, to decide"; "Right to life is a lie, you don't care if women die." Then abortion opponents can be heard to sing: "Jesus loves the little children, all the children of the world, red and yellow, black and white, they are precious in His sight, Jesus loves the little children of the world." . . . On placards held by picketers and by stationary protestors on both sides of the line, the following slogans are visible: "Abortionists lie to women." "Choose Life: Abortion Kills." "N.O.W. Violence." "The God of Israel is Pro-life." "RU 486 Now." "She Is a Child, Not a Choice." "Abortion Kills Children." "Keep Abortion Legal." "Abortion: God Calls It Murder." Some abortion opponents wear T-shirts bearing the phrase "Choose Life."

. As the abortion opponents walk the picket line, they traverse portions of the public right-of-way that are crossed by paved driveways, on each side of the clinic, connecting the clinic's parking lot to the street. At one point an automobile moves west on Dixie Way and slows to turn into the westernmost driveway. There is a 3-to-4-second delay as the picketers, and then the clinic supporters, part to allow the car to enter. . . .

Later, at a point when the crowd appears to be larger and the picketers more numerous, a red car is delayed approximately 10 seconds as the picketers (and clinic supporters) move out of the driveway. Police are visible helping to clear a path for the vehicle to enter. As the car waits, two persons appearing to bear leaflets approach, respectively, the driver and front passenger doors. They appear to elicit no response from the car's occupants and the car passes safely onto clinic property. Later, a blue minivan enters the driveway and is also subject to the same delay. Still later a jeep-type vehicle leaves the clinic property and slows down slightly where the driveway crosses the public right-of-way. At no time is there any apparent effort to prevent entry or exit, or even to delay it, except for the time needed for the picketers to get out of the way. There is no sitting down, packing en masse, linking of hands or any other effort to blockade the clinic property. . . .

The second segment of the videotape displays a group of approximately 40 to 50 persons walking along the side of a major highway. It is Saturday, March 13, 1993, at 9:56 a.m. The demonstrators walk in an oval pattern, carrying no signs or other visible indicators of their purpose. According to Ruth Arick, this second portion was filmed in front of the condominium where clinic owner Ed Windle lived.

A third segment begins. The date-time register indicates that it is the morning of Saturday, February 20, 1993. A teenage girl faces the clinic and exclaims: "Please don't let them kill me, Mommy. Help me, Daddy, please." Clinic supporters chant, "We won't go back.". . . The videotape ends with a shot of an automobile moving eastbound on Dixie Way. As it slows to a stop at the intersection of U. S. 1, two leafletters approach the car and then pull back as it passes on.

The videotape and the rest of the record, including the trial court's findings, show that a great many forms of expression and conduct occurred in the vicinity of the clinic. These include singing, chanting, praying, shouting, the playing of music both from the clinic and from handheld boom boxes, speeches, peaceful picketing, communication of familiar political messages, handbilling, persuasive speech directed at opposing groups on the issue of abortion, efforts to persuade individuals not to have abortions, personal testimony, interviews with the press, and media efforts to report on the protest. What the videotape, the rest of the record, and the trial court's findings do not contain is any suggestion of violence near the clinic, nor do they establish any attempt to prevent entry or exit.

II

A

Under this Court's jurisprudence, there is no question that this public sidewalk area is a "public forum," where citizens generally have a First Amendment right to speak. The parties to this case invited the Court to employ one or the other of the two well established standards applied to restrictions upon this First Amendment right. Petitioners claimed the benefit of so-called "strict scrutiny," the standard applied to content-based restrictions: the restriction must be "necessary to serve a compelling state interest and ... narrowly drawn to achieve that end." *Perry Education Assn.* v. *Perry Local Educators' Assn.* (1983). Respondents, on the other hand, contended for what has come to be known as "intermediate scrutiny".... That standard, applicable to so-called "time, place and manner regulations" of speech, provides that the regulations are permissible so long as they "are content-neutral, are narrowly tailored to serve a significant government interest, and leave open ample alternative channels of communication." The Court adopts neither of these, but creates, brand-new for this abortion-related case, an additional standard that is (supposedly) "somewhat more stringent" than intermediate scrutiny, yet not as "rigorous" as strict scrutiny. The Court does not give this new standard a name, but perhaps we could call it intermediate-intermediate scrutiny. The difference between it and intermediate scrutiny (which the Court acknowledges is inappropriate for injunctive restrictions on speech) is frankly too subtle for me to describe, so I must simply recite it: whereas intermediate scrutiny requires that the restriction be "narrowly tailored to serve a significant government interest," the new standard requires that the restriction "burden no more speech than necessary to serve a significant government interest."

...The real question in this case is not whether intermediate scrutiny ... should be supplemented because of the distinctive characteristics of injunctions; but rather whether those distinctive characteristics are not, for reasons of both policy and precedent, fully as good a reason as "content-basis" for demanding strict scrutiny. That possibility is simply not considered. . . .

. . . The question should be approached, it seems to me, without any . . . artificial loading of the dice. And the central element of the answer is that a restriction upon speech imposed by injunction (whether nominally content-based or nominally content neutral) is *at least* as deserving of strict scrutiny as a statutory, content-based restriction.

That is so for several reasons: The danger of content-based statutory restrictions upon speech is that they may be designed and used precisely to suppress the ideas in question rather than to achieve any other proper governmental aim. But that same danger exists with injunctions. Although a speech-restricting injunction may not attack content *as content* (in the present case, as I shall discuss, even that is not true), it lends itself just as readily to the targeted suppression of particular ideas. When a judge, on the motion of an employer, enjoins picketing at the site of a labor dispute, he enjoins (and he *knows* he is enjoining) the expression of pro-union views. Such targeting of one or the other side of an ideological dispute cannot readily be achieved in speech-restricting general legislation except by making content the basis of the restriction; it is achieved in speech-restricting injunctions almost invariably. . . . The injunction was sought against a single-issue advocacy group by persons and organizations with a business or social interest in suppressing that group's point of view.

The second reason speech-restricting injunctions are at least as deserving of strict scrutiny is obvious enough: they are the product of individual judges rather than of legislatures—and often of judges who have been chagrined by prior disobedience of their orders. The right to free speech should not lightly be placed within the control of a single man or woman. And the third reason is that the injunction is a much more powerful weapon than a statute, and so should be subjected to greater safeguards. Normally, when injunctions are enforced through contempt proceedings, only the defense of factual innocence is available. The collateral bar rule of *Walker* v. *Birmingham* (1967) eliminates the defense that the injunction itself was unconstitutional. Thus, persons subject to a speech-restricting injunction who have not the money or not the time to lodge an immediate appeal face a Hobson's choice: they must remain silent, since if they speak their First Amendment rights are no defense in subsequent contempt proceedings. This is good reason to require the strictest standard for issuance of such orders.

The Court seeks to minimize the similarity between speech-restricting injunctions and content-based statutory proscriptions by observing that the fact that "petitioners all share the same viewpoint regarding abortion does not in itself demonstrate that some invidious content- or viewpoint-based purpose motivated the issuance of the order," but rather "suggests only that those in the group *whose conduct* violated the court's order happen to share the same opinion regarding abortions." But the Court errs in thinking that the vice of content-based statutes is that they necessarily have the invidious purpose of suppressing particular ideas. . . . The vice of content-based legislation—what renders it *deserving* of the high standard of strict scrutiny—is not that it is *always* used for invidious, thought-control purposes, but that it *lends itself* to use for those purposes. And, because of the unavoidable "targeting" discussed above, precisely the same is true of the speech-restricting injunction.

Finally, though I believe speech-restricting injunctions are dangerous enough to warrant strict scrutiny even when they are not technically content based, I think the injunction in the present case was content based (indeed, viewpoint based) to boot. The Court claims that it was directed, not at those who *spoke* certain things (anti-abortion sentiments), but at those who *did* certain things (violated the earlier injunction). If that were true, then the injunction's residual coverage of "all persons acting in concert or participation with [the named individuals and organizations], or on their behalf" would not include those who merely entertained the same beliefs and wished to express the same views as the named defendants. But the construction given to the injunction by the issuing judge . . . is to the contrary: all those who wish to express the same views as the named defendants are deemed to be "acting in concert or participation.". . .

B

I have discussed, in the prior subsection, the policy reasons for giving speech-restricting injunctions, even content-neutral ones, strict scrutiny. There are reasons of precedent as well, which are essentially ignored by the Court.

To begin with, an injunction against speech is the very prototype of the greatest threat to First Amendment values, the prior restraint. . . .

At oral argument neither respondents nor the Solicitor General, appearing as *amicus* for respondents, could identify a single speech-injunction case applying mere intermediate scrutiny (which differs little if at all from the Court's intermediate-intermediate scrutiny). We have, in our speech-injunction cases, affirmed both requirements that characterize strict scrutiny: compelling public need and surgical precision of restraint. Even when (unlike in the present case) the First Amendment activity is intermixed with *violent* conduct, "precision of regulation is demanded." *NAACP* v. *Claiborne Hardware Co.* (1982). . . .

The utter lack of support for the Court's test in our jurisprudence is demonstrated by the two cases the opinion relies upon. For the proposition that a speech restriction is valid when it "burden[s] no more speech than necessary to accomplish a significant government interest," the Court cites *NAACP* v. *Claiborne Hardware Co.* and *Carroll* v. *President and Commissioners of Princess Anne* [1968]. But . . . *Claiborne* applied a much more stringent test; and the very text of *Carroll* contradicts the Court. In the passage cited, *Carroll* says this: "An order issued in the area of First Amendment rights must be couched in the narrowest terms that will accomplish the pin-pointed objective permitted by constitutional mandate and the essential needs of the public order." That, of course, is strict scrutiny; and it does not remotely resemble the Court's new proposal, for which it is cited as precedential support. "Significant government interest[s]" (referred to in the Court's test) are general, innumerable, and omnipresent—at least one of them will be implicated by any activity set in a public forum. "Essential needs of the public order," on the other hand, are factors of *exceptional* application. And that an injunction "burden no more than necessary" is not nearly as demanding as the requirement that it be couched in the "narrowest terms that will accomplish [a] pin-pointed objective." That the Court should cite this case as its principal authority is an admission that what it announces rests upon no precedent at all.

III

[A omitted]

B

I turn now to the Court's performance in the present case. I am content to evaluate it under the lax (intermediate-intermediate scrutiny) standard that the Court has adopted, because even by that distorted light it is inadequate.

The first step under the Court's standard would be, one should think, to identify the "significant government interest" that justifies the portions of the injunction it upheld, namely, the enjoining of speech in the 36-foot zone, and the making (during certain times) of "sounds . . . within earshot of the patients inside the [c]linic." At one point in its opinion, the Court identifies a number of government interests: the "interest in protecting a woman's freedom to seek lawful medical or counseling services," the "interest in ensuring the public safety and order, in promoting the free flow of traffic on public streets and sidewalks, and in protecting the property rights of all its citizens," the "interest in . . . medical privacy," and the interest in "the psychological [and] physical well-being of the patient held 'captive' by medical circumstance." The Court says that "these governmental interests [are] quite sufficient to justify an appropriately tailored injunction to protect them." Unless, however, the Court has destroyed even more First Amendment law than I fear, this last statement must be read in conjunction with the Court's earlier acknowledgment that "[u]nder general equity principles, an injunction issues only if there is a showing that the defendant has violated, or imminently will violate, some provision of statutory or common law, and that there is a 'cognizable danger of recurrent violation.'" It is too much to believe, even of today's opinion, that it approves issuance of an injunction against speech "to promote the free flow of traffic" *even when there has been found no violation, or threatened violation, of a law relating to that interest.*

Assuming then that the "significant interests" the Court mentioned must in fact be significant enough to be protected by state law (a concept that includes a prior court order), which law has been, or is about to be, violated, the question arises: what state law is involved here? The only one even mentioned is the original September 30, 1992, injunction, which had been issued (quite rightly, in my judgment) in response to threats by the originally named parties (including petitioners here) that they would "'[p]hysically close down abortion mills,'" "bloc[k] access to clinics," "ignore the law of the State," and "shut down a clinic." That original injunction prohibited petitioners from:

> "1) trespassing on, sitting in, blocking, impeding or obstructing ingress into or egress from any facility at which abortions are performed in Brevard and Seminole County Florida;
> "2) pysically abusing persons entering, leaving, working, or using any services of any facility at which abortions are performed in Brevard and Seminole County, Florida; and
> "3) attempting or directing others to take any of the actions described in Paragraphs 1 and 2 above."

According to the Court, the state court imposed the later injunction's "restrictions on petitioner[s'] . . . antiabortion message because they repeatedly violated the court's original order." Surprisingly, the Court accepts this reason as valid, without asking whether the court's findings of fact support it—whether, that is, the acts of which the petitioners stood convicted *were* violations of the original injunction.

The Court simply takes this on faith—even though violation of the original injunction is an essential part of the reasoning whereby it approves portions of the amended injunction, even though petitioners denied any violation of the original injunction, even though the utter lack of proper basis for the other challenged portions of the injunction hardly inspires confidence that the lower courts knew what they were doing, and even though close examination of the factual basis for essential conclusions is the usual practice in First Amendment cases. Let us proceed, then, to the inquiry the Court neglected. . . .

On the basis of these findings [omitted] Judge McGregor concluded that "the actions of the respondents and those in concert with them in the street and driveway approaches to the clinic of the plaintiffs continue to impede and obstruct both staff and patients from entering the clinic. The paved surfaces of the public right-of-way must be kept open for the free flow of traffic."

These are the only findings and conclusions of the court that could conceivably be considered to relate to a violation of the original injunction. They all concern behavior by the protestors causing traffic on the street in front of the abortion clinic to slow down, and causing vehicles crossing the pedestrian right-of-way, between the street and the clinic's parking lot, to slow down or even, occasionally, to stop momentarily while pedestrians got out of the way. As far as appears from the court's findings, all of these results were produced, not by anyone intentionally seeking to block oncoming traffic, but as the incidental effect of persons engaged in the activities of walking a picket line and leafletting on public property in front of the clinic. There is no factual finding that petitioners engaged in *any* intentional or purposeful obstruction.

Now let us compare these activities with the earlier injunction, violation of which is the asserted justification for the speech-free zone. Walking the return leg of the picket line on the paved portion of Dixie Way (instead of on the sidewalk), and congregating on the unpaved portion of that street, may, for all we know, violate some municipal ordinance (though that was not alleged, and the municipal police evidently did not seek to prevent it); but it assuredly did not violate the earlier injunction, which made no mention of such a prohibition. Causing the traffic along Dixie Way to slow down "in response to the congestion" is also irrelevant; the injunction said nothing about slowing down traffic on public rights of way. It prohibited the doing (or urging) of *only three things:* 1) "physically abusing persons entering, leaving, working or using any services" of the abortion clinic (there is no allegation of that); 2) "trespassing on [or] sitting in" the abortion clinic (there is no allegation of that); and 3) "blocking, impeding or obstructing ingress into or egress from" the abortion clinic.

Only the last of these has any conceivable application here, and it seems to me that it must reasonably be read to refer to *intentionally* blocking, impeding or obstructing, and not to such temporary obstruction as may be the normal and incidental consequence of other protest activity. That is obvious, first of all, from the context in which the original injunction was issued—as a response to the petitioners' threatened actions of trespass and blockade, *i.e.,* the physical shutting down of the local clinics. Secondly, if that narrow meaning of intentional blockade, impediment or obstruction was not intended, and if it covered everything up to and including the incidental and "momentary" stopping of entering vehicles by persons leafletting and picketing, the original injunction would have failed the axiomatic requirement that its terms be drawn with precision.... And finally, if the original injunction did not have that narrow meaning it would assuredly have been unconstitutional, since it would have prevented speech-related activities that were, insofar as this record shows, neither criminally or civilly unlawful nor inextricably intertwined with unlawful conduct....

If the original injunction is read as it must be, there is nothing in the trial court's findings to suggest that it was violated. The Court today speaks of "the failure of the first injunction to protect access." But the first injunction did not broadly "protect access." It forbade particular acts that impeded access, to-wit, intentionally "blocking, impeding or obstructing." The trial court's findings identify none of these acts, but only a mild interference with access that is the incidental byproduct of leafletting and picketing. There was no sitting down, no linking of arms, no packing en masse in the driveway; the most that can be alleged (and the trial court did not even make this a finding) is that on one occasion protestors "took their time to get out of the way." If that is enough to support this one-man proscription of free speech, the First Amendment is in grave peril.

I almost forgot to address the facts showing prior violation of law (including judicial order) with respect to the other portion of the injunction the Court upholds: the no-noise-within-earshot-of-patients provision. That is perhaps because, amazingly, neither the Florida courts *nor this Court* makes the slightest attempt to link that provision to prior violations of law. The relevant portion of the Court's opinion, Part II-B, simply reasons that hospital patients should not have to be bothered with noise, from political protests or anything else (which is certainly true), and that therefore the noise restrictions could be imposed *by injunction* (which is certainly false). Since such a law is reasonable, in other words, it can be enacted by a single man to bind only a single class of social protesters. The pro-abortion demonstrators who were often making (if respondents' videotape is accurate) *more* noise than the petitioners, can continue to shout their chants at their opponents exiled across the street to their hearts' content. The Court says that "[w]e have upheld similar noise restrictions in the past," citing *Grayned* v. *City of Rockford* (1972). But *Grayned* involved an *ordinance,* and not an *injunction;* it applied to *everyone.* The only other authority the Court invokes is *NLRB* v. *Baptist Hospital, Inc.* (1979), which it describes as "evaluating another injunction involving a medical facility," but which evaluated no such thing. *Baptist Hospital,* like *Grayned,* involved a restriction of general application, adopted by the hospital itself—and the case in any event dealt not with whether the government had violated the First Amendment by restricting noise, but with whether the hospital had violated the National Labor Relations Act by restricting solicitation (including solicitation of union membership).

Perhaps there is a local ordinance in Melbourne, Florida, prohibiting loud noise in the vicinity of hospitals and abortion clinics. Or perhaps even a Florida common-law prohibition applies, rendering such noisemaking tortious. But the record in this case shows (and, alas, the Court's opinion today demands) neither indication of the existence of any such law nor a finding that it had been violated. The fact that such a law would be reasonable is enough, according to the Court, to justify a single judge in imposing it upon these protesters alone. The First Amendment (and even the common law of injunctions . . .) reels in disbelief.

. . . My point does not rely, as the Court's response suggests, upon my earlier description of the videotape. That was set forth just for context, to show the reader what suppression of normal and peaceful social protest is afoot here. Nor is it relevant to my point that "petitioners themselves studiously refrained from challenging the factual basis for the injunction." I accept the facts as the Florida court found them; I deny that those facts support its *conclusion* . . . that the original injunction had been violated. . . . The earlier injunction did not, and could not, prohibit all "interference—for example, the minor interference incidentally produced by lawful picketing and leafletting. What the Court needs, and cannot come up with, is a finding that the petitioners interfered *in a manner prohibited by the earlier injunction*. A conclusion that they "block[ed], imped[ed] or obstruct[ed] ingress . . . or egress" (the terminology of the original injunction) within the only fair, and indeed the only permissible, meaning of that phrase cannot be supported by the facts found.

To sum up: The interests assertedly protected by the supplementary injunction did not include any interest whose impairment was a violation of Florida law or of a Florida-court injunction. Unless the Court intends today to overturn long-settled jurisprudence, that means that the interests cannot possibly qualify as "significant interests" under the Court's new standard.

C

Finally, I turn to the Court's application of the second part of its test: whether the provisions of the injunction "burden no more speech than necessary" to serve the significant interest protected.

This test seems to me amply and obviously satisfied with regard to the noise restriction that the Court approves: it is only such noise as would reach the patients in the abortion clinic that is forbidden—and not even at all times, but only during certain fixed hours and "during surgical procedures and recovery periods.". . . With regard to the 36-foot speech-free zone, however, it seems to me just as obvious that the test which the Court sets for itself has not been met.

Assuming a "significant state interest" of the sort cognizable for injunction purposes (*i.e.*, one protected by a law that has been or is threatened to be violated) in both (1) keeping pedestrians off the paved portion of Dixie Way, and (2) enabling cars to cross the public sidewalk at the clinic's driveways without having to slow down or come to even a "momentary" stop, there are surely a number of ways to protect those interests short of banishing the entire protest demonstration from the 36-foot zone. For starters, the Court could have (for the first time) ordered the demonstrators to stay out of the street (the original injunction did not remotely require that). It could have limited the number of demonstrators permitted on the clinic side of Dixie Way. And it could have forbidden the pickets to walk on the driveways. The Court's only response to these options is that "[t]he state court was convinced that [they would not work] in view of the failure of the first injunction to protect access." But must we accept that conclusion as valid—when the original injunction contained no command (or at the very least no *clear* command) that had been disobeyed, and contained nothing even *related* to staying out of the street? If the "burden no more speech than necessary" requirement can be avoided by merely opining that (for some reason) no lesser restriction than *this* one will be obeyed, it is not much of a requirement at all.

But I need not engage in such precise analysis, since the Court itself admits that the requirement is not to be taken seriously. "The need for a complete buffer zone," it says, "*may be debatable,* but some deference must be given to the state court's familiarity with the facts and the background of the dispute between the parties even under our heightened review" (emphasis added). In application, in other words, the "burden no *more* speech than is necessary" test has become an "arguably burden no more speech than is necessary" test. This renders the Court's intermediate-intermediate scrutiny not only no more stringent than plain old intermediate scrutiny, but considerably less stringent. . . .

In his dissent in *Korematsu* v. *United States* (1944), the case in which this Court permitted the wartime military internment of Japanese-Americans, Justice Jackson wrote the following:

> "A military order, however unconstitutional, is not apt to last longer than the military emergency. . . . But once a judicial opinion . . . rationalizes the Constitution to show that the Constitution sanctions such an order, the Court for all time has validated the principle of racial discrimination in criminal procedure and of transplanting American citizens. The principle then lies about like a loaded weapon ready for the hand of any authority that can bring forward a plausible claim of an urgent need."

What was true of a misguided military order is true of a misguided trial-court injunction. And the Court has left a powerful loaded weapon lying about today.

What we have decided seems to be, and will be reported by the media as, an abortion case. But it will go down in the lawbooks, it will be cited, as a free-speech injunction case—and the damage its novel principles produce will be considerable. The proposition that injunctions against speech are subject to a standard indistinguishable from (unless perhaps more lenient in its application than) the "intermediate scrutiny" standard we have used for "time, place, and manner" legislative restrictions; the notion that injunctions against speech need not be closely tied to any violation of law, but may simply implement sound social policy; and the practice of accepting trial-court conclusions permitting injunctions without considering whether those conclusions are supported by any findings of fact—these latest byproducts of our abortion jurisprudence ought to give all friends of liberty great concern.

For these reasons, I dissent from that portion of the judgment upholding parts of the injunction. . . .

5 | *Preview of the 1994-1995 Term*

"Throw the bums out" has long been the rallying cry for voters fed up with the people they have elected to government office. As a practical matter, however, political incumbents often enjoy advantages—such as superior name recognition and fund-raising abilities—that can help them beat opposing candidates or even discourage potential challengers from running at all.

Members of Congress are particularly adept at using their offices to shore up their electoral support. Partly as a result, the reelection rate for representatives and senators has risen in recent years well past 90 percent. Critics complained that Congress had become an "automatic reelection machine." And some of these critics began pushing a powerfully appealing mechanism for throwing members of Congress out of office: term limits.

In 1990 and 1992 voters in fifteen states approved measures to limit the terms of their members of Congress—typically, twelve years for senators and six to twelve years for representatives. From its inception, however, the term limits movement ran up against strong doubts about the constitutionality of restricting the tenure of federal lawmakers. Congressional leaders, some citizens' groups, and many legal experts argued that states cannot impose any qualifications for election to Congress other than those mentioned in the Constitution: age, residence, and citizenship. But supporters said term limits were authorized under another constitutional provision (Art. I, sec. 4) that gives states the power to regulate the "Times, Places, and Manner of holding Elections for Senators and Representatives."

In two cases challenging term limit measures, a federal court in Washington State and the Arkansas Supreme Court sided with opponents. Supporters and opponents alike looked to the Supreme Court to resolve the legal issue. In June 1994 the Court agreed by granting review in companion cases involving the Arkansas term limits measure and putting them on its calendar for the 1994-1995 term. (*U.S. Term Limits, Inc. v. Thornton; Bryant v. Hill.*)

The politically charged term limits dispute was by far the most newsworthy of the cases that the Court carried over for the start of its new term. Many familiar and controversial topics—including abortion and separation of church and state—were nowhere to be seen. The Court did have three death penalty cases, but none raised broad questions about the validity of capital punishment. And the Court had no cases seeking to expand its new precedents helping property owners to contest land-use policies or business defendants to challenge punitive damage awards.

A few of the Court's cases raised provocative new questions. The justices agreed to decide whether a new law making it a federal offense to possess a firearm near a school violated states' rights. Federal civil servants wanted the Court to strike down an ethics law prohibiting them from being paid for giving speeches or writing articles, even on topics unrelated to their duties. And the federal government sought to overturn a ruling that exposed the Veterans Administration to no-fault liability for medical injuries suffered by veterans in VA hospitals.

On the whole, however, the Court's calendar was dominated by cases raising relatively technical questions of limited interest except to the parties and legal specialists. The number of cases carried over for the start of the new term (forty) was once again unusually low. Four years earlier the Court opened its 1990-1991 term with seventy cases on its calendar.

The small number of cases granted review as of June apparently prompted the Court to adopt, for the second year in a row, an unusual procedure to fill out its docket. One week before the justices were to reconvene for the start of the 1994-1995 term, the justices announced on September 26 that they had granted review in eight additional cases for the new term. Before the 1993-1994 term the Court had waited until its first formal session—on the first Monday in October—to announce which cases it had decided to hear.

The eight additional cases included two important civil rights disputes involving school desegregation and affirmative action.

In *Missouri v. Jenkins* the Court agreed to decide whether federal courts could keep jurisdiction over a school desegregation case against the Kansas City, Missouri, school system because achievement scores for black students remained below national norms. The state of Missouri asked the Court to lift the decree, saying the order went beyond previous desegregation rulings. The state had a financial stake in the outcome: it had paid about two-thirds of the cost of $1.3 billion in court-ordered remedial education programs. The school system opposed the state's appeal and asked to keep the remedial programs alive. The justices were familiar with the desegregation case. In 1990 the Court upheld, 5-4, an earlier decision ordering the school district to raise property taxes to pay for the remedial programs *(Supreme Court Yearbook, 1989-1990, pp. 20-21)*.

In the other case, *Adarand Constructors, Inc. v. Pena,* the Court was to rule on the constitutionality of Department of Transportation regulations benefiting minority-owned contractors. The regulations, which were issued under provisions of the Small Business Act aimed at increasing government contracts for "disadvantaged business enterprises," gave prime contractors additional compensation for subcontracting work to a minority-owned business. The program was challenged by a nonminority contractor that submitted a low bid on a federal highway contract but lost a subcontract to a minority-owned company.

Skip Cook, left, and Tim Jacob of Arkansans for Governmental Reform spoke at a news conference on a 1992 ballot measure to limit the terms of the members of the Arkansas congressional delegation. The Supreme Court agreed to hear a constitutional challenge to the measure in its 1994-1995 term.

Term Limits

Despite the thin caseload, the Court could expect close attention during the new term from its coequal branch of government, Congress. With seven additional states due to vote on term limits in the fall, the Court appeared to be Congress's only hope to thwart the movement. Ironically, lawmakers' hope to quash term limits depended in large part on a ruling by the Court twenty-five years earlier that had limited Congress's own power to decide who could serve in the House or the Senate.

The Court's 1969 ruling in *Powell v. McCormack* came after lengthy criminal and ethics investigations of Rep. Adam Clayton Powell, a veteran Democratic lawmaker from New York City. Powell won reelection in 1966 despite a conviction for criminal contempt and a record of misuse of public funds. The House voted twice in 1967 to "exclude" Powell, who challenged the action in court. In an 8-1 decision the Supreme Court ruled the House's action illegal, saying that neither chamber of Congress can add to the qualifications for membership listed in the Constitution. Term limit opponents pointed to the Court's ruling as proof that the measures are invalid because they add a new qualification for serving in Congress.

Term limits supporters had their own precedents to cite, however. They pointed to two cases in which the Court upheld state laws limiting who could run for Congress. In one case, *Storer v. Brown*, the Court in 1974 upheld a state law barring a candidate from seeking office as an independent if the candidate had been defeated in a party primary for the same office. In the other, *Clements v. Fashing*, the Court in 1982 upheld so-called resign-to-run laws that require an official to quit a current post to run for another. Supporters argued term limits were an equally valid exercise of states' power to run elections.

To try to circumvent the constitutional doubts, term limits supporters developed an alternative approach. Most later term limits measures barred members of Congress from the ballot after the specified number of terms but still allowed voters to cast write-in ballots for them. Opponents, however, said the ballot-access approach amounted to the same thing: an unconstitutional new qualification for serving in Congress.

The legal arguments had virtually no effect on the political battles over term limits. Nationwide, polls showed that the public supported term limits by substantial majorities. Supporters hammered away at Congress as a bloated institution, guilty of wasteful spending and pork-barrel politics but effectively immunized from voter retaliation. Opponents countered that term limits would increase the power of the president vis-à-vis Congress and increase the influence of unelected legislative staff and lobbyists over the legislative process. They also said voters could already impose term limits on their own by voting against members of Congress at the ballot box.

The opponents' arguments failed to sway voters, who approved term limits measures in every state where they appeared on the ballot. Typically, the measures also included term limits for state legislators, and state courts rejected constitutional attacks on those provisions.

The Arkansas measure limited ballot access for House members after six years in office and for senators after twelve years. Voters approved the measure, Amendment 73, in November 1992 by a 3-2 margin. A suit challenging the measure was promptly filed in the name of Bobbie Hill, a former president of the state's League of Women Voters, which opposed term limits as did the national organization. Term limits supporters, including the national group U.S. Term Limits, intervened to support the measure.

The Arkansas Supreme Court considered the two cases together and on March 7, 1994, voted 5-2 to strike down the congressional term limits. The court agreed with opponents that voters cannot add to the qualifications for Congress listed in the Constitution. The justices said that limiting incumbents from the ballot amounted to the same thing. "The intent and the effect of Amendment 73 are to disqualify incumbents from further congressional service," the court said.

Term limits opponents, such as House Speaker Thomas S. Foley, the Democratic lawmaker who led the legal challenge against the measure in his home state of Washington, were pleased with the U.S. Supreme Court's decision to take on the issue. "The Speaker has long felt this represents one of the major constitutional issues of the decade," a Foley spokesman said, adding that he believed the debate would "benefit from an expedited review" by the Court.

Supporters recognized they had an uphill argument to persuade the Supreme Court to permit term limits. "We're going to use our best efforts in putting together the best court case we can," said Norman Leahy, research director for U.S. Term Limits. "The Court decision is a necessary step along the way to getting term limits on Congress. It's not the end of the line, but it's a step along the way."

Drew S. Days III,
U.S. Solicitor General

In August, the Clinton administration moved to join the legal fight against term limits. In a motion filed with the Court, Solicitor General Drew S. Days III called the state term limit measures "a particular threat to the federal system in that it makes membership in the Congress dependent on regulation by the States." Days asked for time to argue against the term limits along with Arkansas opponents; the Court granted the motion in September.

Leahy said supporters were already discussing alternative strategies in the event of a loss in the Supreme Court case. One option, he said, was to try to elect people to Congress who would back a constitutional amendment on the issue. Supporters of women's suffrage and Prohibition had followed that route to win passage of constitutional amendments in the early twentieth century. That strategy, however, could be expensive and protracted, Leahy acknowledged.

Paradoxically, a Court ruling for term limits could backfire. The constitutional provision giving states power to regulate elections also gives Congress the power to "make or alter such regulations." Leahy said some term limits supporters feared that Congress might react to a decision upholding term limits by passing a uniform law that allowed longer service than the six-year limit for House members specified in most of the later state measures.

Most Court watchers, however, expected the Court to strike down term limit measures. "I would be very surprised if it did anything different," said Dennis Hutchinson, a law professor at the University of Chicago and editor of the *Supreme Court Review*. Term limit supporters disagree. "You can't study this issue without realizing that this is really a case of first impression," says Cleta Mitchell of the Term Limits Legal

Institute. "If it were so clear, the Court wouldn't have accepted it in the first place."

Following are some of the other major cases on the Supreme Court calendar as it began its 1994-1995 term:

Business Law

Frequent flyers. In the competitive climate fostered by deregulation, airlines created "frequent flyer" programs to maintain customer loyalty. But the programs, giving passengers credits to accumulate for free or reduced-rate travel later, proved so popular that airlines had to tinker with the details to avoid having full-fare passengers displaced by nonpaying customers.

When American Airlines altered its AAdvantage program in 1988 by reducing the number of seats available to frequent flyers and restricting travel on certain dates, some of its loyal customers turned hostile. A group of forty AAdvantage Club members—claiming to represent a class of 4 million passengers—filed a breach-of-contract suit in state court in Illinois. But the airlines argued that the suit was barred by the Airline Deregulation Act, which supersedes any local or state laws "relating to [airlines'] rates, routes, or services."

The Supreme Court boosted American's argument in 1992 by ruling, in *Morales v. Trans World Airlines, Inc.*, that the deregulation law did preclude states from regulating advertising of airline fares. But the Illinois Supreme Court said the Court's decision did not prevent the frequent flyers from recovering monetary damages for a violation of their contract with the airlines.

In urging the Court to review the case, American said state court suits over frequent-flyer programs would be "highly disruptive" and could ultimately force airlines to drop them altogether. But the plaintiffs' attorneys argued that Congress never intended "to give the airlines immunity from suits narrowly based on their private agreements."

The Air Transport Association and United Airlines filed briefs supporting American's position. But the Clinton administration agreed with the plaintiffs that the deregulation law did not preclude contract suits in state courts. It warned that a ruling for the airlines would either leave frequent-flyer passengers with no legal recourse or require federal courts or the Department of Transportation to handle the disputes. (*American Airlines, Inc. v. Wolens*)

Securities law. The Court was asked to limit the scope of a powerful antifraud remedy under federal securities law. The provision—section 12(2) of the Securities Act of 1933—allows an investor to recover damages or rescind a stock transaction altogether if there was any "false or misleading information" in connection with the sale. Investors who bought up the stock in a small manufacturing company in Chicago filed suit under the provision. But the former owners said the section applied only to initial public sales of stock and not to the privately negotiated resale of all the stock in a corporation. (*Gustafson v. Alloyd Co., Inc.*)

In another securities case the Court will try again to decide whether Congress can reinstate some federal securities suits dismissed because of a 1991 Court ruling that changed the time limit for bringing such cases. In a case this term, *Morgan Stanley & Co., Inc. v. Pacific Mutual Life Insurance Co.*, the justices were divided 4-4 on whether the law, passed six months after the Court's ruling, violated the doctrine of separation of powers; Justice O'Connor recused herself. In the new case investors in a Kentucky-based horse farm are seeking to use the law to revive a stock fraud suit. (*Plaut v. Spendthrift Farm, Inc.*)

Banks and insurance. The banking industry and the federal government joined in asking the Court to uphold a regulation that allowed banks to sell certain types of life insurance. Federal banking law generally prohibits banks in towns with populations of more than 5,000 from selling insurance. But the Comptroller of the Currency ruled in 1990 that banks could sell annuities, insurance-like contracts that provide purchasers with annual payments beginning at some time in the future. The Fifth U.S. Circuit Court of Appeals struck down the regulation in a suit brought by an insurance concern. The comptroller's office and the North Carolina bank named as defendant in the suit asked the Court to reverse the decision. (*NationsBank of North Carolina v. Variable Annuity Life Insurance Co.*; *Ludwig v. Variable Annuity Life Insurance Co.*)

Maritime law. The dredging company blamed for the April 1992 flood of Chicago's underground tunnels tried to limit its liability for the episode by using federal maritime law. Great Lakes Dredge & Dock Co. apparently caused the flooding by breaching a freight tunnel as it was repairing bridges along the Chicago River. The city of Chicago and thousands of individuals and businesses whose property was damaged by the flooding filed damage suits under state tort law. The company claimed that federal maritime law, which limits liability to the value of the vessel involved in an accident, applied because the incident occurred on navigable waters and was substantially related to traditional maritime activity. The federal appeals court in Chicago agreed, but the city and one of the private businesses that filed suit urged the Court to reverse the ruling. (*Jerome B. Grubart, Inc. v. Great Lakes Dredge & Dock Co.*; *City of Chicago v. Great Lakes Dredge & Dock Co.*)

Plant Variety Protection Act. The Court agreed to decide a high-stakes fight between seed companies and farmers. At issue was a 1970 law that created patent-like protections for the development of new varieties of seeds. The Plant Variety Protection Act gives companies exclusive rights to market new kinds of seeds for eighteen years, but it allows farmers to save seed produced from their own crops for use on their own farms or for sale. Asgrow Seed Co. sued an Iowa farm family, Denny and Becky Winterboer, claiming they were violating the law by selling large quantities of saved seed to other farmers. The U.S. Court of Appeals for the Federal Circuit rejected the suit, ruling that farmers can sell up to half their crop as saved seed. The seed industry, backed by the Clinton administration, said the ruling could imperil future research and development. But the Winterboers said the decision recognized "the centuries-old right of farmers to sell seed grown on their farms to other farmers." (*Asgrow Seed Co. v. Winterboer*)

Courts and Procedure

Vacating judgments. The Court seized on a second chance to rule on the validity of a little-known procedure that critics said allowed businesses to buy their way out of unfavorable legal precedents. The procedure calls for courts to vacate—wipe out—a ruling in a case if the parties agree to settle the dispute before time for an appeal has ended. Consumer groups charged that insurance companies and other businesses often used the procedure—called "vacatur"—to nullify potentially costly legal precedents by agreeing to a less expensive settlement in the individual case. Judges usually agreed to the procedure in order to encourage settlements. And businesses defended the practice, saying rulings should not stay on the books unless they are final.

In its 1993-1994 term the Court agreed to review a case posing the issue but dismissed it on procedural grounds (see p. 60). In March 1994, however, the justices found a new chance to look at the question when a bankruptcy dispute pending before the Court was settled and one of the parties asked the justices to vacate the federal appeals court ruling in the case.

Bonner Mall Partnership, a real estate venture that had won the appeals court ruling, asked the Court simply to dismiss the case and leave the appellate decision standing. But U.S. Bancorp Mortgage Co. said the Court should vacate the ruling because it was "infected with a clear and substantial error." The justices then asked both sides for briefs on the vacatur procedure and decided to set the case for argument in the new term.

The Clinton administration filed a brief supporting the practice. It argued the procedure "furthers the judicial system's important interest in voluntary settlement of disputes." In an opposing brief a plaintiffs group, Trial Lawyers for Public Justice, said the procedure "distorts the development of the law by allowing a party with a deep pocket to eliminate an unreviewable precedent it dislikes simply by agreeing to a sufficiently lucrative settlement." *(U.S. Bancorp Mortgage Co. v. Bonner Mall Partnership)*

Arbitration. A botched termite inspection provoked a legal fight over a 1925 federal law aimed at promoting arbitration. An Alabama family, Wanda and Michael Dobson, found termites in their new house and sued the Terminix company, which had inspected the house before the sale. Terminix said that the contract called for arbitration and the Federal Arbitration Act required states to enforce arbitration clauses. But the Alabama Supreme Court ruled that the law applied only to transactions involving interstate commerce. Terminix, supported by a number of industry groups, urged the Court to reverse what it called a "hostile reading" of the federal law. *(Allied-Bruce Terminix Companies, Inc. v. Dobson)*

Criminal Law

Gun-Free Schools Zone Act. More than 100,000 youngsters in the United States—perhaps as many as 250,000—come to school each day carrying guns. To try to stem the problem, Congress in 1990 put into an omnibus anticrime bill a provision making it a federal crime to possess a firearm within 1,000 feet of a school.

Some lawmakers raised concerns at the time that the provision, called the Gun-Free Schools Zone Act, infringed on local law enforcement responsibilities. In signing the crime bill President George Bush criticized the gun-free schools provision, saying it "inappropriately overrides legitimate State firearms laws."

In November 1993 a federal appeals court in Texas went one step further. It ruled that the government could not prosecute anyone under the law unless it proved that the defendant's offense had an effect on interstate commerce. While the ruling stopped short of completely invalidating the law, the three-judge panel questioned whether the law could ever be constitutionally applied.

The court's decision overturned the conviction and six-month sentence of a San Antonio youth, Alfonso Lopez, who had been arrested in March 1992 at a public high school while carrying an unloaded .38-caliber handgun and five bullets. Lopez, a twelfth-grade student at the time, said he had been paid $40 to deliver the gun to another student for use in a "gang war."

The government asked the Supreme Court to review the appeals court decision, calling the measure a "permissible exercise of Congress's power" under the Constitution's Commerce Clause. ". . . [V]iolent crime *in general* imposes sufficient burdens on interstate commerce to permit Congress very broad latitude to enact measures rationally designed to reduce its incidence," the solicitor general's office argued. Supporting briefs were filed by a group of fifty members of Congress, several states, and an array of gun control, law enforcement, and education groups.

But John Carter, the assistant federal public defender representing Lopez, urged the Court to uphold the ruling. "The Commerce Clause, while supreme where properly implicated, does not confer upon Congress a general police power," Carter said. He also noted that Texas and the other states in the federal appeals court's jurisdiction had their own laws prohibiting the carrying of most firearms in or around schools. (*United States v. Lopez*)

Capital punishment. The Court carried three capital punishment cases over to its calendar for the new term. Two raised issues about what death row inmates must prove to overturn their convictions or sentences through a federal habeas corpus proceeding. The third presented the question of what standards a judge must meet to impose a death sentence after a jury recommends life imprisonment instead.

In one of the habeas corpus cases, a Missouri prison inmate sentenced to death for the fatal stabbing of a fellow prisoner failed to win a new trial despite strong, newly discovered evidence that he might not have committed the murder. Lawyers for the inmate, Lloyd E. Schlup, Jr., located a prison surveillance videotape that they said showed he was somewhere else at the time of the slaying. But the federal appeals court for Missouri, in a 2-1 decision, said the inmate was not entitled to a new trial unless he could show that no reasonable jury would have convicted him if the new evidence had been presented at trial. (*Schlup v. Delo*)

In the second case a Louisiana death row inmate, Curtis Lee Kyles, sought to overturn his 1984 murder conviction by showing that prosecutors concealed information casting doubt on the credibility of one of its witnesses. A federal appeals court panel, in another 2-1 decision, said that Kyles had failed to show that any errors in the trial could have affected the outcome. (*Kyles v. Whitley*)

In the third case an Alabama woman, Louise Harris, was sentenced to death for plotting to kill her husband even though the jury voted 7-5 to sentence her to life imprisonment without parole. She argued on appeal that a capital sentencing system in which judges "are free to reject jury life-without-parole verdicts without regard to any articulated standard or norm" violates the Constitution. (*Harris v. Alabama*)

Harmless error. The Court agreed to decide who has the burden of showing in habeas corpus cases whether a constitutional error at trial did or did not have an effect on the outcome. An Ohio prison inmate sought to overturn his kidnapping conviction because of prosecutorial misconduct. But the federal appeals court for Ohio ruled the inmate had to show that the misconduct had a substantial effect on the trial. The inmate argued that the government had to show the error was harmless. Ohio authorities, supported by the Clinton administration and forty-eight states, asked the Court to uphold the appellate ruling. (*O'Neal v. McAninch*)

Child pornography. The Clinton administration asked the Court to salvage the federal child pornography law. A federal appeals court in California ruled the law unconstitutional because it did not require the government to prove that the defendant knew minors were depicted in the material. The solicitor general's office agreed prosecutors had to prove the defendant's knowledge of the material, but it asked the Court to interpret the law to include such a requirement. (*United States v. X-Citement Video, Inc.*)

Election Law

Anonymous campaign literature. Margaret McIntyre riled school officials in Westerville, Ohio, by leafleting against a local school tax levy in 1988 and 1989. After the measure passed on its third try, the assistant school superintendent charged McIntyre with violating a state law that bans the distribution of anonymous campaign literature.

The Ohio Elections Commission fined McIntyre $100. McIntyre contested the fine and called the law a violation of the First Amendment. But the Ohio Supreme Court upheld the measure, saying it helped voters evaluate campaign literature and identify anyone responsible for fraud, false advertising, or libel.

In asking the Court to invalidate the law, McIntyre's lawyers argued that anonymous leaflets "have played an important part in the nation's political history by facilitating the expression of unpopular views." But Ohio's attorney general, who joined in urging the justices to review the case, said the law served a "compelling state interest" by helping protect "the integrity of the electoral process." A supporting brief filed by the Tennessee attorney general's office warned that a ruling against the law could cast doubt on campaign disclosure statutes on the books in forty-four states and the District of Columbia.

McIntyre died in May 1994, but the case was continued by her husband, Joseph McIntyre. (*McIntyre v. Ohio Elections Commission*)

Federal Election Commission. The Federal Election Commission (FEC) faced the prospect of wholesale overturning of prior decisions because of a court ruling against the commission's makeup. For years the commission had included, in addition to its six voting members, two "special deputies" appointed by officers of the House and the Senate. These deputies attended meetings but did not vote. The federal appeals court in Washington ruled in October 1993 that the arrangement violated the constitutional doctrine of separation of powers. The commission eliminated the two nonvoting positions but asked the Court to declare that past FEC decisions were still valid. (*FEC v. NRA Political Victory Fund*)

Federal Government

Veterans hospitals. The government asked the Court to review a potentially costly ruling allowing veterans to receive compensation for any injuries resulting from treatment at a Veterans Administration (VA) hospital without proving the medical care was faulty.

The case involved a Korean War veteran, Fred Gardner, who said he suffered severe nerve damage to one leg as a result of back surgery at a VA hospital in Texas. He sought compensation under a law providing benefits for "an injury, or an aggravation of an injury" that results from "hospitalization, medical or surgical treatment" at a VA facility.

The VA denied benefits, relying on a long-standing regulation that a veteran could be compensated for a medical injury only if it was caused by "carelessness, negligence, lack of skill, error in judgment, or similar instances of fault." But the U.S. Court of Appeals for the Federal Circuit nullified the regulation, saying it conflicted with the "plain language" of the statute.

In urging the Court to review the case, the government said the Federal Circuit's "no-fault" construction of the law would cost the VA $1 billion over five years. Gardner said the ruling was in line with the "simple and straightforward language of the statute." (*Brown v. Gardner*)

First Amendment

Honoraria ban. For years many members of Congress engaged in an ethically suspect practice of taking fees, called honoraria, for giving speeches or writing articles for businesses, trade associations, or other lobbying organizations. With its image battered by an array of ethics issues in the late 1980s, Congress finally moved to settle the controversy over honoraria by adopting a complete ban on such fees for House members in 1989 and for senators two years later.

In passing the Ethics Reform Act of 1989, however, lawmakers decided to cast the new ethics net over the rest of the federal government, too. The law prohibited employees of the executive and judicial branches from accepting honoraria as well, even if the payments were for speeches or articles written on their own time and completely unrelated to their official positions.

Career civil servants promptly challenged the broad ban as a violation of their First Amendment rights. Two government employee unions—the National Treasury Employees Union and the American Federation of Government Employees—filed the suit. Individual plaintiffs included a Nuclear Regulatory Commission attorney working on articles about Russian history, a mailhandler who wrote and spoke about the Quaker religion, and an employee of the Department of Health and Human Services who free-lanced as a theater critic for local newspapers.

Two lower federal courts agreed that the honoraria ban violated the free speech rights of executive branch employees. In its ruling the federal appeals court in Washington in March 1993 said the prohibition applied to writing or speaking "with no nexus to government work that could give rise to the slightest concern."

The Clinton administration asked the Court to review the ruling. Solicitor General Drew S. Days III argued that the "modest" burden on federal employees was outweighed by the government's interest in promoting "the integrity and the appearance of integrity of the federal workforce." But the government unions said the ban went too far because Congress had no evidence of abuses resulting from paying federal workers for writing articles or giving speeches unrelated to their work. *(United States v. National Treasury Employees Union)*

Advertising in railway stations. New York artist Michael Lebron found the perfect spot to display a photomontage criticizing the Coors Brewing Co. for supporting conservative political causes: a giant illuminated billboard in the middle of Penn Station in New York City. But Amtrak, which owns the station, refused, citing a policy against political advertisements. Lebron sued in federal court, claiming the policy amounted to "state action" violating the First Amendment because Amtrak was "a government-controlled institution." But Amtrak, created in 1970 as a "mixed-ownership government corporation," insisted the policy was not influenced by any federal regulation or federal officers. "Amtrak is not a federal actor for purposes of constitutional analysis," it argued. (*Lebron v. National Railroad Passenger Corporation (Amtrak)*)

Commercial speech. The Coors Brewing Co. attacked a 1934 federal law that prohibits brewers from including alcohol content on beer labels unless the information is required by state law. Two lower federal courts agreed the act violated First Amendment protections for commercial speech. The government asked the Court to reinstate the law, saying it helped prevent "strength wars" between brewers competing to sell beer or malt liquor on the basis of higher alcohol content. But Coors argued the law was unnecessary. It said alcohol content labeling has not led to strength wars for wine and liquor in the United States or for beer in countries such as Canada where alcohol content labeling is permitted. (*Bentsen v. Adolph Coors Company*)

Ideological alignments among the justices may shift in the new term with the arrival of Justice Breyer, seen here with Chief Justice Rehnquist, left, on the steps of the Supreme Court building. Breyer, known as a pragmatist and consensus builder, takes over for Justice Blackmum, who had been the Court's most liberal voice.

Individual Rights

Job discrimination. When fired workers file job discrimination suits, companies often look into the employee's work history and discover evidence of misconduct that might have justified the firing had it been known at the time. Federal appeals courts have split on what to do about such "after-acquired evidence." This year the Court got a second chance to decide the issue. The justices had granted review in a case posing the same issue in 1993 but dropped it after the suit was settled.

The question reached the Court again in an age discrimination suit filed by Christine McKennon, who was fired in 1990 from her job in the accounting department of the *Nashville Banner* after working for the newspaper for nearly forty years. When the newspaper's attorneys took McKennon's deposition, she admitted that she had copied the company's payroll ledger and other confidential financial documents, taken them home, and showed them to her husband. A federal district court judge issued a judgment for the newspaper, and a federal appeals court upheld the decision.

In asking the Court to review the case, McKennon's attorneys said that newly discovered evidence "cannot absolve an employer of discriminatory action." In a supporting brief a number of civil rights groups, including the American Association of Retired Persons, the American Civil Liberties Union, and the Lawyers' Committee for Civil Rights Under Law, argued that the after-acquired evidence rule "defeats the deterrent and compensatory purposes of the fair employment laws." The newspaper argued that McKennon's misconduct was "serious and material" and justified her dismissal. In a separate brief, employers' groups contended that permitting back pay awards to a fired worker after discovery of wrongdoing "rewards the employee for managing to conceal his misconduct from the employer." (*McKennon v. Nashville Banner Publishing Co.*)

County liability. Two drug raids on a nightclub outside a small town in east-central Alabama form the backdrop of a case testing whether county governments can be held liable for misconduct by local sheriffs. The owners of the nightclub claimed that Chambers County Sheriff James Morgan and other law enforcement officers violated their civil rights by trying to drive the club out of business. The suit also named as a defendant the Chambers County Commission, the county's governing body. The county got out of the suit on a preliminary motion by arguing that the sheriff was not a policy-making official for the county. The plaintiffs asked the Court to review the ruling, which they said could apply to other states. But the county commission said the ruling was a correct interpetation of sheriffs' powers under Alabama law and would not necessarily apply to other states. (*Swint v. Chambers County Commission*)

States

State tax refunds. The Court agreed to decide when states must provide refunds for taxpayers who have paid levies that are later declared unlawful. The case was brought by Charles Reich, a federal retiree in Georgia, who was seeking refunds for state income taxes paid on his federal pension. The Court in 1989 ruled that states could not tax federal retirement benefits unless they also taxed state and local pensions. In a follow-up ruling a year later, the Court said states generally must provide some form of retroactive remedy, such as a refund, when tax laws are struck down.

Georgia refused, however, to pay refunds to Reich because he had not contested the liability before paying the tax. Reich told the Court that he had no "clear and certain remedy free of duress" because he could have been penalized or prosecuted for failing to pay the tax when due. But Georgia authorities argued that states "may require taxpayers to pay first and litigate their liabilities" later. The ruling could directly affect federal retirees in at least eight other states. (*Reich v. Collins*)

Appendix

How the Court Works   311

Brief Biographies   323

Glossary of Legal Terms   342

United States Constitution   348

How the Court Works

The Constitution makes the Supreme Court the final arbiter in "cases" and "controversies" arising under the Constitution or the laws of the United States. As the interpreter of the law, the Court often is viewed as the least mutable and most tradition-bound of the three branches of the federal government. But the Court has undergone innumerable changes in its history, some of which have been mandated by law. Some of these changes are embodied in Court rules; others are informal adaptations to needs and circumstances.

The Schedule of the Term

Annual Terms

By law the Supreme Court begins its regular annual term on the first Monday in October, and the term lasts approximately nine months. This session is known as the October term. The summer recess, which is not determined by statute or Court rules, generally begins in late June or early July of the following year. This system—staying in continuous session throughout the year, with periodic recesses—makes it unnecessary to convene a special term to deal with matters arising in the summer.

The justices actually begin work before the official opening of the term. They hold their initial conference during the last week in September. When the justices formally convene on the first Monday in October, oral arguments begin.

Arguments and Conferences

At least four justices must request that a case be argued before it can be accepted. Arguments are heard on Monday, Tuesday, and Wednesday for seven two-week sessions, beginning in the first week in October and ending in mid-April. Recesses of two weeks or longer occur between the sessions of oral arguments so that justices can consider the cases and deal with other Court business.

The schedule for oral arguments is 10:00 a.m. to noon and 1 p.m. to 3 p.m. Because most cases receive one hour apiece for argument, the Court can hear up to twelve cases a week.

The Court holds conferences on the Friday just before the two-week oral argument periods and on Wednesday and Friday during the weeks when oral arguments are scheduled. The conferences are designed for consideration of cases already heard in oral argument.

Before each of the Friday conferences, the chief justice circulates a "discuss" list—a list of cases deemed important enough for discussion and a vote. Appeals are placed on the discuss list almost automatically, but as many as three-quarters of the petitions for certiorari are dismissed. No case is denied review during conference, however, without an initial examination by the justices and their law clerks. Any justice can have a case placed on the Court's conference agenda for review. Most of the cases scheduled for the discuss list also are denied review in the end but only after discussion by the justices during the conference.

Although the last oral arguments have been heard by mid-April each year, the conferences of the justices continue until the end of the term to consider cases remaining on the Court's agenda. All conferences are held in secret, with no legal assistants or other staff present. The attendance of six justices constitutes a quorum. Conferences begin with handshakes all around. In discussing a case, the chief justice speaks first, followed by each justice in order of seniority.

Decision Days

Opinions are released on Tuesdays and Wednesdays during the weeks that the Court is hearing oral arguments; during other weeks, they are released on Mondays. In addition to opinions, the Court also releases an "orders" list—the summary of the Court's action granting or denying review. The orders list is posted at the beginning of the Monday session. It is not announced orally but can be obtained from the clerk and the public information officer. When urgent or important matters arise, the Court's summary orders may be made available on a day other than Monday.

Unlike its orders, decisions of the Court are announced orally in open Court. The justice who wrote the opinion announces the Court's decision, and justices writing concurring or dissenting opinions may state their views as well. When more than one decision is to be rendered, the justices who wrote the opinion make their announcements in reverse order of seniority. Occasionally, all or a large portion of the opinion is read aloud. More often the author summarizes the opinion or simply announces the result and states that a written opinion has been filed.

Reviewing Cases

In determining whether to accept a case for review, the Court has considerable discretion, subject only to the restraints imposed by the

Visiting the Supreme Court

The Supreme Court building has six levels, two of which—the ground and main floors—are accessible to the public. The basement contains a parking garage, a printing press, and offices for security guards and maintenance personnel. On the ground floor are the John Marshall statue, the exhibition area, the public information office, and a cafeteria. The main corridor, known as the Great Hall, the courtroom, and justices' offices are on the main floor. The second floor contains dining rooms, the justices' reading room, and other offices; the third floor, the Court library; and the fourth floor, the gym and storage areas.

From October to mid-April, the Court hears oral arguments Monday through Wednesday for about two weeks a month. These sessions begin at 10 a.m. and continue until 3 p.m., with a one-hour recess starting at noon. They are open to the public on a first-come, first-served basis.

Visitors may inspect the Supreme Court chamber any time the Court is not in session. Historical exhibits and a free motion picture on how the Court works also are available throughout the year. The Supreme Court building is open from 9 a.m. to 4:30 p.m. Monday through Friday, except for legal holidays. When the Court is not in session, lectures are given in the courtroom every hour on the half hour between 9:30 a.m. and 3:30 p.m.

Constitution and Congress. Article III, section 2, of the Constitution provides that "In all Cases affecting Ambassadors, other public Ministers and Consuls, and those in which a State shall be Party, the supreme Court shall have original Jurisdiction. In all the other Cases ... the supreme Court shall have appellate Jurisdiction, both as to Law and Fact, with such Exceptions, and under such Regulations as the Congress shall make."

Original jurisdiction refers to the right of the Supreme Court to hear a case before any other court does. Appellate jurisdiction is the right to review the decision of a lower court. The vast majority of cases reaching the Supreme Court are appeals from rulings of the lower courts; generally only a handful of original jurisdiction cases are filed each term.

After enactment of the Judiciary Act of 1925, the Supreme Court gained broad discretion to decide for itself what cases it would hear. In 1988 Congress virtually eliminated the Court's mandatory jurisdiction, which obliged it to hear most appeals. Since then that discretion has been nearly unlimited.

Methods of Appeal

Cases come to the Supreme Court in several ways: through petitions for writs of certiorari, appeals, and requests for certification.

In petitioning for a writ of certiorari, a litigant who has lost a case in a lower court sets out the reasons why the Supreme Court should review the case. If a writ is granted, the Court requests a certified record of the case from the lower court.

The main difference between the certiorari and appeal routes is that the Court has complete discretion to grant a request for a writ of certiorari but is under more obligation to accept and decide a case that comes to it on appeal.

Most cases reach the Supreme Court by means of the writ of certiorari. In the relatively few cases to reach the Court by means of appeal, the appellant must file a jurisdictional statement explaining why the case qualifies for review and why the Court should grant it a hearing. Often the justices dispose of these cases by deciding them summarily, without oral argument or formal opinion.

Those whose petitions for certiorari have been granted must pay the Court's standard $300 fee for docketing the case. The U.S. government does not have to pay these fees, nor do persons too poor to afford them. The latter may file in forma pauperis (in the character or manner of a pauper) petitions. Another, seldom used, method of appeal is certification, the request by a lower court—usually a court of appeals—for a final answer to questions of law in a particular case. The Court, after examining the certificate, may order the case argued before it.

Process of Review

In the 1993-1994 term the Court was asked to review about 7,700 cases. All petitions are examined by the staff of the clerk of the Court; those found to be in reasonably proper form are placed on the docket and given a number. All cases, except those falling within the Court's original jurisdiction, are placed on a single docket, known simply as "the docket." Only in the numbering of the cases is a distinction made between prepaid and in forma pauperis cases on the docket. The first case filed in the 1994-1995 term, for example, would be designated 94-1. In forma pauperis cases contain the year and begin with the number 5001. The second in forma pauperis case filed in the 1994-1995 term would thus be number 94-5002.

Each justice, aided by law clerks, is responsible for reviewing all cases on the docket. In recent years a number of justices have used a "cert pool" system in this review. Their clerks work together to examine cases, writing a pool memo on several petitions. The memo then is given to the justices who determine if more research is needed. Other justices may prefer to review each petition themselves or have their clerks do it.

Petitions on the docket vary from elegantly printed and bound documents, of which multiple copies are submitted to the Court, to single sheets of prison stationery scribbled in pencil. The decisions to grant or deny review of cases are made in conferences, which are held in the conference room adjacent to the chief justice's chambers. Justices are summoned to the conference room by a buzzer, usually between 9:30 and 10:00 a.m. They shake hands with each other and take their appointed seats, and the chief justice then begins the discussion.

Discuss and Orders Lists

A few days before the conference convenes, the chief justice compiles the discuss list of cases deemed important enough for discussion and a vote. As many as three-quarters of the petitions for certiorari are denied a place on the list and thus rejected without further consideration. Any justice can have a case placed on the discuss list simply by requesting that it be placed there.

Only the justices attend conferences; no legal assistants or staff are present. The junior associate justice acts as doorkeeper and messenger, sending for reference material and receiving messages and data. Unlike with other parts of the federal government, few leaks have occurred about what transpires during the conferences.

At the start of the conference, the chief justice makes a brief statement outlining the facts of each case. Then each justice, beginning with the senior associate justice, comments on the case, usually indicating in the course of the comments how he or she intends to vote. A traditional but unwritten rule is that four affirmative votes puts a case on the schedule for oral argument.

Petitions for certiorari, appeals, and in forma pauperis motions that are approved for review or denied review during conference are placed on a certified orders list to be released the next Monday in open court.

Arguments

Once the Court announces it will hear a case, the clerk of the Court arranges the schedule for oral argument. Cases are argued roughly in the order in which they were granted review, subject to modification if more

On the bench, the chief justice sits in the center, with the most senior associate justice on his right and the second most senior associate justice on his left. The remaining seats are occupied alternately by the other justices in order of seniority.

time is needed to acquire all the necessary documents. Cases generally are heard not sooner than three months after the Court has agreed to review them. Under special circumstances the date scheduled for oral argument can be advanced or postponed.

Well before oral argument takes place, the justices receive the briefs and records from counsel in the case. The measure of attention the brief receives—from a thorough and exhaustive study to a cursory glance—depends both on the nature of the case and the work habits of the justice.

As one of the two public functions of the Court, oral arguments are viewed by some as very important. Others dispute the significance of oral arguments, contending that by the time a case is heard most of the justices already have made up their minds.

Time Limits

The time allowed each side for oral argument is thirty minutes. Because the time allotted must accommodate any questions the justices may wish to ask, the actual time for presentation may be considerably shorter than thirty minutes. Under the current rules of the Court, one counsel only will be heard for each side, except by special permission.

An exception is made for an amicus curiae, a "friend of the court," a person who volunteers or is invited to take part in matters before a court but is not a party in the case. Counsel for an amicus curiae may participate in oral argument if the party supported by the amicus allows use of part of its argument time or the Court grants a motion permitting argument by this counsel. The motion must show, the rules state, that the amicus's argument "is thought to provide assistance to the Court not otherwise available." The Court is generally unreceptive to such motions.

Court rules provide advice to counsel presenting oral arguments before the Court: "Oral argument should emphasize and clarify the written arguments appearing in the briefs on the merits." That same rule warns—with italicized emphasis—that the Court "looks with disfavor on oral argument read from a prepared text." Most attorneys appearing before the Court use an outline or notes to make sure they cover the important points.

Circulating the Argument

The Supreme Court has tape-recorded oral arguments since 1955. In 1968 the Court, in addition to its own recording, began contracting with private firms to tape and transcribe all oral arguments. The contract stipulates that the transcript "shall include everything spoken in argument, by Court, counsel, or others, and nothing shall be omitted from the transcript unless the Chief Justice or Presiding Justice so directs." But "the names of Justices asking questions shall not be recorded or transcribed; questions shall be indicated by the letter 'Q.' "

The marshal of the Court keeps the tapes during the term, and their use usually is limited to the justices and their law clerks. At the end of the term, the tapes are sent to the National Archives. Persons wishing to listen to the tapes or buy a copy of a transcript can apply to the Archives for permission to do so.

Transcripts made by a private firm can be acquired more quickly. These transcripts usually are available a week after arguments are heard. Those who purchase the transcripts must agree that they will not be photographically reproduced. Transcripts usually run from forty to fifty pages for one hour of oral argument.

Proposals have been made to tape arguments for television and radio use or to permit live broadcast coverage of arguments. The Court has rejected these proposals.

Use of Briefs

The brief of the petitioner or appellant must be filed within forty-five days of the Court's announced decision to hear the case. Except for in forma pauperis cases, forty copies of the brief must be filed with the Court. For in forma pauperis proceedings, the Court requires only that documents be legible. The opposing brief from the respondent or appellee is to be filed within thirty days of receipt of the brief of the petitioner or appellant. Either party may appeal to the clerk for an extension of time in filing the brief.

Court Rule 24 sets forth the elements that a brief should contain. These are: the questions presented for review; a list of all parties to the proceeding; a table of contents and table of authorities; citations of the opinions and judgments delivered in the lower courts; "a concise statement of the grounds on which the jurisdiction of this Court is invoked"; constitutional provisions, treaties, statutes, ordinances, and regulations involved; "a concise statement of the case containing all that is material to the consideration of the questions presented"; a summary of argument; the argument, which exhibits "clearly the points of fact and of law being presented and citing the authorities and statutes relied upon"; and a conclusion "specifying with particularity the relief which the party seeks."

The form and organization of the brief are covered by rules 33 and 34. The rules limit the number of pages in various types of briefs. The rules also set out a color code for the covers of different kinds of briefs. Petitions are white; motions opposing them are orange. Petitioner's briefs on the merits are light blue, while those of respondents are red. Reply briefs are yellow; amicus curiae, green; and documents filed by the United States, gray.

Questioning

During oral argument the justices may interrupt with questions or remarks as often as they wish. Unless counsel has been granted special permission extending the thirty-minute limit, he or she can continue talking after the time has expired only to complete a sentence.

The frequency of questioning, as well as the manner in which questions are asked, depends on the style of the justices and their interest in a particular case. Of the current justices, all but Clarence Thomas participate, more or less actively, in questioning during oral arguments. Thomas was reported to have asked no questions whatsoever from the bench during the 1993-1994 term.

Questions from the justices may upset and unnerve counsel by interrupting a well-rehearsed argument and introducing an unexpected element. Nevertheless, questioning has several advantages. It serves to alert counsel about what aspects of the case need further elaboration or more information. For the Court, questions can bring out weak points in an argument—and sometimes strengthen it.

The justices meet in a private conference room to decide what cases to hear and to take preliminary votes on cases after oral argument. No legal assistants or staff are present during the conferences.

Conferences

Cases for which oral arguments have been heard are then dealt with in conference. During the Wednesday afternoon conference, the cases that were argued the previous Monday are discussed and decided. At the all-day Friday conference, the cases argued on the preceding Tuesday and Wednesday are discussed and decided. Justices also consider new motions, appeals, and petitions while in conference.

Conferences are conducted in complete secrecy. No secretaries, clerks, stenographers, or messengers are allowed into the room. This practice began many years ago when the justices became convinced that decisions were being disclosed prematurely.

The justices meet in an oak-paneled, book-lined conference room adjacent to the chief justice's suite. Nine chairs surround a large rectangular table, each chair bearing the nameplate of the justice who sits there. The chief justice sits at the east end of the table, and the senior associate justice at the west end. The other justices take their places in order of seniority. The junior justice is charged with sending for and receiving documents or other information the Court needs.

On entering the conference room the justices shake hands with each other, a symbol of harmony that began in the 1880s. The chief justice begins the conference by calling the first case to be decided and discussing it. When the chief justice is finished, the senior associate justice speaks, followed by the other justices in order of seniority.

The justices can speak for as long as they wish, but they practice restraint because of the amount of business to be completed. By custom each justice speaks without interruption. Other than these procedural arrangements, little is known about what transpires in conference. Although discussions generally are said to be polite and orderly, occasionally they can be acrimonious. Likewise, consideration of the issues in a particular case may be full and probing, or perfunctory, leaving the real debate on the question until later when the written drafts of opinions are circulated up and down the Court's corridors between chambers.

Generally the discussion of the case clearly indicates how a justice plans to vote on it. A majority vote is needed to decide a case—five votes if all nine justices are participating.

Opinions

After the justices have voted on a case, the writing of the opinion or opinions begins. An opinion is a reasoned argument explaining the legal issues in the case and the precedents on which the opinion is based. Soon after a case is decided in conference, the task of writing the majority opinion is assigned. When in the majority, the chief justice designates the writer. When the chief justice is in the minority, the senior associate justice voting with the majority assigns the job of writing the majority opinion.

Any justice may write a separate opinion. If in agreement with the Court's decision but not with some of the reasoning in the majority opinion, the justice writes a concurring opinion giving his or her reasoning. If in disagreement with the majority, the justice writes a dissenting opinion or simply goes on record as a dissenter without an opinion. More than one justice can sign a concurring opinion or a dissenting opinion.

The amount of time between the vote on a case and the announcement of the decision varies from case to case. In simple cases where few points of law are at issue, the opinion sometimes can be written and cleared by the other justices in a week or less. In more complex cases, especially those with several dissenting or concurring opinions, the process can take six months or more. Some cases may have to be reargued or the initial decision reversed after the drafts of opinions have been circulated.

The assigning justice may consider the points made by majority justices during the conference discussion, the workload of the other justices, the need to avoid the more extreme opinions within the majority, and expertise in the particular area of law involved in a case.

The style of writing a Court opinion—majority, concurring, or dissenting—depends primarily on the individual justice. In some cases, the justice may prefer to write a restricted and limited opinion; in others, he or she may take a broader approach to the subject. The decision likely is to be influenced by the need to satisfy the other justices in the majority.

When a justice is satisfied that the written opinion is conclusive or "unanswerable," it goes into print. Draft opinions are circulated, revised, and printed on a computerized typesetting system. The circulation of the drafts—whether computer-to-computer or on paper—provokes further discussion in many cases. Often the suggestions and criticisms require the writer to juggle opposing views. To retain a majority, the author of the draft opinion frequently feels obliged to make major emendations to satisfy justices who are unhappy with the initial draft. Some opinions have to be rewritten several times.

One reason for the secrecy surrounding the circulation of drafts is that some of the justices who voted with the majority may find the majority draft opinion so unpersuasive—or one or more of the dissenting drafts so convincing—that they change their vote. If enough justices alter their votes, the majority may shift, so that a former dissent becomes the majority opinion. When a new majority emerges from this process, the task of writing, printing, and circulating a new majority draft begins all over again.

When the drafts of an opinion—including dissents and concurring views—have been written, circulated, discussed, and revised, if necessary, the final versions then are printed. Before the opinion is produced the reporter of decisions adds a "headnote" or syllabus summarizing the decision and a "lineup" showing how the justices voted.

Two hundred copies of the "bench opinion" are made. As the decision is announced in Court, the bench opinion is distributed to journalists and others in the public information office. Another copy, with any necessary corrections noted on it, is sent to the U.S. Government Printing Office, which prints 3,397 "slip" opinions, which are distributed to federal and state courts and agencies. The Court receives 400 of these, and they are available to the public free through the Public Information Office as long as supplies last. The Government Printing Office also prints the opinion for inclusion in *United States Reports,* the official record of Supreme Court opinions.

The Court also makes opinions available electronically, through its so-called Hermes system, to a number of large legal publishers, the Government Printing Office, and other information services. These organizations allow redistribution of the opinions to their own subscribers and users. Opinions are available on the Internet through Case Western Reserve University. The Hermes system was established as a pilot project in 1991 and expanded and made permanent in 1993.

The public announcement of opinions in Court probably is the Court's most dramatic function. It may also be the most expendable. Depending on who delivers the opinion and how, announcements can take a considerable amount of the Court's time. Opinions are given simultaneously to the public information officer for distribution. Nevertheless, those who are in the courtroom to hear the announcement of a ruling are participating in a very old tradition. The actual delivery may be tedious or exciting, depending on the nature of the case, the eloquence of the opinion, and the style of its oral delivery.

Brief Biographies

William Hubbs Rehnquist

Born: October 1, 1924, Milwaukee, Wisconsin.

Education: Stanford University, B.A., Phi Beta Kappa, and M.A., 1948; Harvard University, M.A., 1949; Stanford University Law School, LL.B., 1952.

Family: Married Natalie Cornell, 1953; died, 1991; two daughters, one son.

Career: Law clerk to Justice Robert H. Jackson, U.S. Supreme Court, 1952-1953; practiced law, 1953-1969; assistant U.S. attorney general, Office of Legal Counsel, 1969-1971.

Supreme Court Service: Nominated as associate justice of the U.S. Supreme Court by President Richard Nixon, October 21, 1971; confirmed, 68-26, December 10, 1971; nominated as chief justice of the United States by President Ronald Reagan, June 17, 1986; confirmed, 65-33, September 17, 1986.

President Reagan's appointment of William H. Rehnquist as chief justice in 1986 was a clear indication that the president was hoping to shift the Court to the right. Since his early years as an associate justice in the 1970s, Rehnquist has been one of the Court's most conservative justices.

Rehnquist, the fourth associate justice to become chief, argues that the original intent of the Framers of the Constitution and the Bill of Rights is the proper standard for interpreting those documents today. He also takes a literal approach to individual rights. These beliefs have led him to dissent from the Court's rulings protecting a woman's privacy-based right to abortion, to argue that no constitutional barrier exists to school prayer, and to side with police and prosecutors on questions of criminal law. In 1991 he wrote the Court's decision upholding an  administration ban on abortion counseling at publicly financed clinics and in 1992 vigorously dissented from the Court's affirmation of *Roe v. Wade*, the 1973 opinion that made abortion legal nationwide.

Born in Milwaukee, Wisconsin, October 1, 1924, Rehnquist attended Stanford University, where he earned both a B.A. and M.A. He received a second M.A. from Harvard before returning to Stanford for law school. His classmates there recalled him as an intelligent student with already well-entrenched conservative views.

After graduating from law school in 1952, Rehnquist came to Washington, D.C., to serve as a law clerk to Supreme Court justice Robert H. Jackson. There he wrote a memorandum that later would come back to haunt him during his Senate confirmation hearings. In the memo Rehnquist favored separate but equal schools for blacks and whites. Asked about those views by the Senate Judiciary Committee in 1971, Rehnquist repudiated them, declaring that they were Justice Jackson's—not his own, although Jackson was a moderate.

Following his clerkship, Rehnquist decided to practice law in the Southwest. He moved to Phoenix and immediately became immersed in Arizona Republican politics. From his earliest days in the state, he was associated with the party's conservative wing. A 1957 speech denouncing the liberalism of the Warren Court typified his views at the time.

During the 1964 presidential race, Rehnquist campaigned ardently for Barry Goldwater. It was then that Rehnquist met and worked with Richard G. Kleindienst, who later, as President Richard Nixon's deputy attorney general, would appoint Rehnquist to head the Justice Department's Office of Legal Counsel as an assistant attorney general. In 1971 Nixon nominated him to the Supreme Court.

Rehnquist drew opposition from liberals and civil rights organizations before winning confirmation and again before being approved as chief justice in 1986. The Senate voted to approve his nomination in December 1971 by a vote of 68-26 at the same time that another Nixon nominee, Lewis F. Powell, Jr., was winning nearly unanimous confirmation. In 1986 Rehnquist faced new accusations of having harassed voters as a Republican poll watcher in Phoenix in the 1950s and 1960s. He was also found to have accepted anti-Semitic restrictions in a property deed to a Vermont home. Despite the charges, the Senate approved his appointment 65-33. Liberal Democratic senators cast most of the no votes in both confirmations.

Despite his strong views, Rehnquist is popular among his colleagues and staff. When he was nominated for chief justice, Justice William J. Brennan, Jr., the leader of the court's liberal bloc, said Rehnquist would be "a splendid chief justice." After becoming chief justice, Rehnquist was credited with speeding up the court's conferences, in which the justices decide what cases to hear, vote on cases, and assign opinions.

Rehnquist was married to Natalie Cornell, who died in 1991. They had two daughters and a son. In 1994 news reports said that Rehnquist was dating Cynthia Holcomb Hall, a judge on the Ninth U.S. Circuit Court of Appeals.

John Paul Stevens

Born: April 20, 1920, Chicago, Illinois.

Education: University of Chicago, B.A., Phi Beta Kappa, 1941; Northwestern University School of Law, J.D., 1947.

Family: Married Elizabeth Jane Sheeren, 1942; three daughters, one son; divorced 1979; married Maryan Mulholland Simon, 1980.

Career: Law clerk to Justice Wiley B. Rutledge, U.S. Supreme Court, 1947-1948; practiced law, Chicago, 1949-1970; judge, U.S. Court of Appeals for the Seventh Circuit, 1970-1975.

Supreme Court Service: Nominated as associate justice of the U.S. Supreme Court by President Gerald R. Ford, November 28, 1975; confirmed, 98-0, December 17, 1975.

When President Gerald R. Ford nominated federal appeals court judge John Paul Stevens to the Supreme Court seat vacated by veteran liberal William O. Douglas in 1975, Court observers struggled to pin an ideological label on the new nominee. The consensus that finally emerged was that Stevens was neither a doctrinaire liberal nor conservative, but a judicial centrist. His subsequent opinions bear out this description, although in recent years he has leaned more toward the liberal side.

Stevens is a soft-spoken, mild-mannered man who occasionally sports a bow tie under his judicial robes. A member of a prominent Chicago family, he had a long record of excellence in scholarship, graduating Phi Beta Kappa from the University of Chicago in 1941. After a wartime stint in the navy, during which he earned the Bronze Star, he returned to Chicago to enter Northwestern University Law School, from which he graduated magna cum laude in 1947. From there Stevens left for Washington, where he served as a law clerk to Supreme Court justice  Wiley B. Rutledge. He returned to Chicago to join the prominent law firm of Poppenhusen, Johnston, Thompson & Raymond, which specialized in antitrust law. Stevens developed a reputation as a preeminent antitrust lawyer, and after three years with Poppenhusen he left in 1952 to form his own firm, Rothschild, Stevens, Barry & Myers. He remained there, engaging in private practice and teaching part time at Northwestern and the University of Chicago law schools, until his appointment by President Richard Nixon in 1970 to the U.S. Court of Appeals for the Seventh Circuit.

Stevens developed a reputation as a political moderate during his undergraduate days at the University of Chicago, then an overwhelmingly liberal campus. Although he is a registered Republican, he has never been active in partisan politics. Nevertheless, Stevens served as Republican counsel in 1951 to the House Judiciary Subcommittee on the Study of Monopoly Power. He also served from 1953 to 1955, during the Eisenhower administration, as a member of the attorney general's committee to study antitrust laws.

Stevens has frequently dissented from the most conservative rulings of the Burger and Rehnquist courts. For example, he dissented from the Burger Court's 1986 decision upholding state antisodomy laws and the Rehnquist Court's 1989 decision permitting states to execute someone for committing a murder at the age of sixteen or seventeen. He has taken liberal positions on abortion rights, civil rights, and church-state issues. Among his most important opinions is a 1985 decision striking down an Alabama law that allowed a moment of silence for prayer or silent meditation at the beginning of each school day.

In 1942 Stevens married Elizabeth Jane Sheeren. They have four children. They were divorced in 1979. Stevens subsequently married Maryan Mulholland Simon, a longtime neighbor in Chicago.

Sandra Day O'Connor

Born: March 26, 1930, El Paso, Texas.

Education: Stanford University, B.A., 1950; Stanford University Law School, LL.B., 1952.

Family: Married John J. O'Connor III, 1952; three sons.

Career: Deputy county attorney, San Mateo, California, 1952-1953; assistant attorney general, Arizona, 1965-1969; Arizona state senator, 1969-1975; Arizona Senate majority leader, 1972-1975; judge, Maricopa County Superior Court, 1974-1979; judge, Arizona Court of Appeals, 1979-1981.

Supreme Court Service: Nominated as associate justice of the U.S. Supreme Court by President Ronald Reagan August 19, 1981; confirmed, 99-0, September 21, 1981.

Sandra Day O'Connor was the Court's first woman justice, and in 1992, after a decade on the Court, she emerged as a coalition builder in the Court's legal doctrine on abortion and other controversial issues.

Pioneering came naturally to O'Connor. Her grandfather left Kansas in 1880 to take up ranching in the desert land that eventually would become the state of Arizona. O'Connor, born in El Paso, Texas, where her mother's parents lived, was raised on the Lazy B Ranch, the 198,000-acre spread that her grandfather founded in southeastern Arizona near Duncan. She spent her school years in El Paso, living with her grandmother. She graduated from high school at age sixteen and then entered Stanford University.

Six years later, in 1952, Sandra Day had won degrees with great distinction, both from the university, in economics, and from Stanford Law School. At Stanford she met John J. O'Connor III, her future husband, and William H. Rehnquist, a future colleague on the Supreme Court. While in law school, Sandra Day was an editor of the *Stanford Law Review* and a member of Order of the Coif, both reflecting her academic leadership.

Despite her outstanding law school record, she found securing a job as an attorney difficult in 1952 when relatively few women were practicing law. She applied, among other places, to the firm in which William French Smith—first attorney general in the Reagan administration—was a partner, only to be offered a job as a secretary.

After she completed a short stint as deputy county attorney for San Mateo County (California) while her new husband completed law school at Stanford, the O'Connors moved with the U.S. Army to Frankfurt, Germany. There Sandra O'Connor worked as a civilian attorney for the army, while John O'Connor served his tour of duty. In 1957 they returned to Phoenix, where, during the next eight years, their three sons were born. O'Connor's life was a mix of parenthood, homemaking, volunteer work, and some "miscellaneous legal tasks" on the side.

In 1965 she resumed her legal career full time, taking a job as an assistant attorney general for Arizona. After four years in that post she was appointed to fill a vacancy in the state Senate, where she served on the judiciary committee. In 1970 she was elected to the same body and two years later was chosen its majority leader, the first woman in the nation to hold such a post. O'Connor was active in Republican Party politics, serving as co-chair of the Arizona Committee for the Re-election of the President in 1972.

In 1974 she was elected to the Superior Court for Maricopa County, where she served for five years. Then in 1979 Gov. Bruce Babbitt—acting, some said, to remove a potential rival for the governorship—appointed O'Connor to the Arizona Court of Appeals. It was from that seat that President Reagan chose her as his first nominee to the Supreme Court, succeeding Potter Stewart, who had retired. Reagan described her as "a person for all seasons."

By a vote of 99-0 the Senate confirmed O'Connor September 21, 1981, and she became the first woman associate justice of the U.S. Supreme Court.

O'Connor has helped push the Court in conservative directions in a number of areas, including criminal law and affirmative action. In 1989 she wrote the Court's opinion striking down a local minority contractor set-aside program. The same year she also wrote the Court's opinion permitting the death penalty for mentally retarded defendants. O'Connor has also been a strong voice for restricting state prisoners' ability to use federal habeas corpus to overturn criminal convictions or sentences.

Throughout the 1980s, O'Connor voted to uphold state laws regulating abortion procedures or restricting government funding of abortions. In 1992, however, she joined with two other Republican-appointed justices, Anthony M. Kennedy and David H. Souter, to form a majority for preserving a modified form of the Court's original abortion rights ruling, *Roe v. Wade*. In a jointly authored opinion the three justices said that *Roe*'s "essential holding"—guaranteeing a woman's right to an abortion during most of her pregnancy—should be reaffirmed. But the joint opinion also said that states could regulate abortion procedures as long as they did not impose "an undue burden" on a woman's choice—a test that O'Connor had advocated in previous opinions.

Antonin Scalia

Born: March 11, 1936, Trenton, New Jersey.

Education: Georgetown University, A.B., 1957; Harvard University Law School, LL.B., 1960.

Family: Married Maureen McCarthy, 1960; five sons, four daughters.

Career: Practiced law, Cleveland, 1960-1967; taught at the University of Virginia, 1967-1971; general counsel, White House Office of Telecommunications Policy, 1971-1972; chairman, Administrative Conference of the United States, 1972-1974; head, Justice Department Office of Legal Counsel, 1974-1977; taught at the University of Chicago Law School, 1977-1982; judge, U.S. Court of Appeals for the District of Columbia, 1982-1986.

Supreme Court Service: Nominated as associate justice of the U.S. Supreme Court by President Ronald Reagan June 17, 1986; confirmed, 98-0, September 17, 1986.

After Warren E. Burger retired from the Court and Ronald Reagan named William H. Rehnquist to succeed him as chief justice, the president's next move—appointing Antonin Scalia as associate justice—was not surprising. On issues dear to Reagan, Scalia clearly met the president's tests for conservatism. Scalia, whom Reagan had named to the U.S. Court of Appeals for the District of Columbia in 1982, became the first Supreme Court justice of Italian ancestry. A Roman Catholic, he opposes abortion. He also has expressed opposition to "affirmative action" preferences for minorities.

Deregulation, which Reagan pushed as president, was a subject of considerable interest to Scalia, a specialist in administrative law. From 1977 to 1982 he was editor of the magazine *Regulation,* published by the American Enterprise Institute for Public Policy Research.

In contrast to the hours of floor debate over Rehnquist's nomination as chief justice, only a few brief speeches were given in opposition to the equally conservative Scalia before he was confirmed, 98-0. He has since become the scourge of some members of Congress because of his suspicion of committee reports, floor speeches, and other artifacts of legislative history that courts traditionally rely on to interpret a statute.

Born in Trenton, New Jersey, March 11, 1936, Scalia grew up in Queens, New York. His father was a professor of Romance languages at Brooklyn College, and his mother was a schoolteacher. Scalia graduated from Georgetown University in 1957 and from Harvard Law School in 1960. He worked for six years for the firm of Jones, Day, Cockley & Reavis in Cleveland and then taught contract, commercial, and comparative law at the University of Virginia Law School.

Scalia served as general counsel of the White House Office of Telecommunications Policy from 1971 to 1972. He then headed the Administrative Conference of the United States, a group that advises the government on questions of administrative law and procedure. From 1974 through the Ford administration he headed the Justice Department's Office of Legal Counsel, a post Rehnquist had held three years earlier. Scalia then returned to academia, to teach at the University of Chicago Law School.

Scalia showed himself to be a hard worker, an aggressive interrogator, and an articulate advocate. On the appeals court he was impatient with what he saw as regulatory or judicial overreaching. In 1983 he dissented from a ruling requiring the Food and Drug Administration

(FDA) to consider whether drugs used for lethal injections met FDA standards as safe and effective. The Supreme Court agreed, reversing the appeals court in 1985.

Scalia was thought to be the principal author of an unsigned decision in 1986 that declared major portions of the Gramm-Rudman-Hollings budget-balancing act unconstitutional. The Supreme Court upheld the decision later in the year.

On the Supreme Court Scalia quickly became a forceful voice for conservative positions. He joined in conservative decisions limiting procedural rights in criminal cases and in a series of rulings in 1989 limiting remedies in employment discrimination cases. He also strongly dissented from rulings upholding affirmative action and reaffirming abortion rights.

In many of his constitutional law opinions, Scalia argued for an "original intent" approach that limited rights to those intended when the Constitution was adopted. He also sharply challenged the use of legislative history in interpreting statutes. He argued that judges should look only to the words of the statute itself.

Anthony McLeod Kennedy

Born: July 23, 1936, Sacramento, California.

Education: Stanford University, A.B., Phi Beta Kappa, 1958; Harvard University Law School, LL.B., 1961.

Family: Married Mary Davis, 1963; two sons, one daughter.

Career: Practiced law, San Francisco, 1961-1963, Sacramento, 1963-1975; professor of constitutional law, McGeorge School of Law, University of the Pacific, 1965-1988; judge, U.S. Court of Appeals for the Ninth Circuit, 1975-1988.

Supreme Court Service: Nominated as associate justice of the U.S. Supreme Court by President Ronald Reagan November 11, 1987; confirmed, 97-0, February 3, 1988.

Quiet, scholarly Anthony M. Kennedy, President Reagan's third choice for his third appointment to the Supreme Court, made all the difference when the Court's conservative majority began coalescing in 1989.

Kennedy proved to be a crucial fifth vote for the Court's conservative wing in civil rights cases, a firm supporter of state authority over defendants' rights in criminal cases, and a strict constructionist in the mode of Chief Justice William H. Rehnquist in most cases. Kennedy's presence effectively ushered in a new era on the Court. Reagan's earlier appointees, Sandra Day O'Connor and Antonin Scalia, had moved the Court somewhat to the right. But when Kennedy succeeded Lewis F.

Powell, Jr., a moderate conservative and a critical swing vote, the balance of power shifted. On a range of issues where Powell often joined the Court's four liberals, Kennedy has gone the other way. Kennedy, however, broke with the hardline conservatives in 1992. He voted to disallow prayer at public school graduations and to uphold a woman's right to abortion.

Before Kennedy's nomination in November 1987, the Senate and the country had agonized through Reagan's two unsuccessful attempts to replace Powell, first with Robert H. Bork and then with Douglas H. Ginsburg. The Senate rejected Bork's nomination after contentious hearings, and Ginsburg withdrew his name amid controversy about his qualifications and admitted past use of marijuana.

A quiet sense of relief prevailed when Reagan finally selected a nominee who could be confirmed without another wrenching confrontation. Later, Republicans would note the irony in Kennedy's tipping the balance of the Court because anti-Bork Democrats had so willingly embraced him as a moderate.

Kennedy spent twelve years as a judge on the U.S. Court of Appeals for the Ninth Circuit. But unlike Bork, who wrote and spoke extensively for twenty years, Kennedy's record was confined mostly to his approximately five hundred judicial opinions. His views thus were based in large part on issues that were distilled at the trial level and further refined by legal and oral arguments. Furthermore, Kennedy sought to decide issues narrowly instead of using his opinions as a testing ground for constitutional theories. He continued this approach in the decisions he has written on the high Court.

Kennedy has taken conservative positions on most criminal law and civil rights issues. He also voted in 1989 to overturn the Court's original abortion rights ruling, *Roe v. Wade*. In 1992, however, he disappointed conservatives by joining with Justices Sandra Day O'Connor and David H. Souter in the pivotal opinion reaffirming *Roe v. Wade*. Kennedy has also taken liberal positions on some First Amendment issues. In his first full term on the Court, he helped form the 5-4 majority that overturned state laws against burning or desecrating the U.S. flag.

A native Californian, Kennedy attended Stanford University from 1954 to 1957 and the London School of Economics from 1957 to 1958. He received an A.B. from Stanford in 1958 and an LL.B. from Harvard Law School in 1961. Admitted to the California bar in 1962, he was in private law practice until 1975, when President Gerald R. Ford appointed him to the appeals court. From 1965 to 1988 he taught constitutional law at McGeorge School of Law, University of the Pacific. Confirmed by the Senate, 97-0, February 3, 1988, Kennedy was sworn in as an associate justice of the Supreme Court February 18.

He and his wife, the former Mary Davis, have three children.

David Hackett Souter

Born: September 17, 1939, Melrose, Massachusetts.

Education: Harvard College, B.A., 1961; Rhodes scholar, Oxford University, 1961-1963; Harvard University Law School, LL.B., 1966.

Family: Unmarried.

Career: Private law practice, Concord, New Hampshire, 1966-1968; assistant attorney general, New Hampshire, 1968-1971; deputy attorney general, New Hampshire, 1971-1976; attorney general, New Hampshire, 1976-1978; associate justice, New Hampshire Superior Court, 1978-1983; associate justice, New Hampshire Supreme Court, 1983-1990; judge, U.S. Court of Appeals for the First Circuit, 1990.

Supreme Court Service: Nominated as associate justice of the U.S. Supreme Court by President George Bush July 23, 1990; confirmed, 90-9, October 2, 1990.

At first the Senate did not know what to make of David H. Souter, a cerebral, button-down nominee who was President Bush's first appointment to the Court. Souter was little known outside of his home state of

New Hampshire, where he had been attorney general, a trial judge, and a state supreme court justice.

Unlike Antonin Scalia and Anthony M. Kennedy, his immediate predecessors on the Court, Souter had virtually no scholarly writings to dissect and little federal court experience to scrutinize. Only three months earlier Bush had appointed him to the U.S. Court of Appeals for the First Circuit. Souter had yet to write a legal opinion on the appeals court.

During his confirmation hearings, the Harvard graduate and former Rhodes scholar demonstrated intellectual rigor and a masterly approach to constitutional law. His earlier work as state attorney general and New Hampshire Supreme Court justice had a conservative bent, but he came across as more moderate during the hearings.

Under persistent questioning from Democratic senators, Souter refused to say how he would vote on the issue of abortion rights. Abortion rights supporters feared he would provide a fifth vote for overturning the 1973 *Roe v. Wade* decision. Senators in both parties, however, said they were impressed with his legal knowledge. He was confirmed by the Senate 90-9; dissenting senators cited his refusal to take a stand on abortion.

On the bench Souter proved to be a tenacious questioner but reserved in his opinions. He generally voted with the Court's conservative majority in his first term. But in the 1991-1992 term he staked out a middle ground with Justices Sandra Day O'Connor and Kennedy in two crucial cases. In a closely watched abortion case Souter joined with the other two Republican-appointed justices in writing the main opinion reaffirming the "essential holding" of *Roe v. Wade*. The three also joined in forming a 5-4 majority to prohibit school-sponsored prayers at public high school graduation ceremonies.

In the Court's next two terms Souter moved markedly to the left, while Kennedy and O'Connor appeared to move back toward the right. Although Souter continued to vote most often with the Court's conservatives, he took liberal positions in a number of civil rights, church-state, and criminal law cases. On the final day of the Court's 1993-1994 term, Souter wrote the Court's opinions in two closely watched cases that reaffirmed racial line-drawing in legislative redistricting cases and struck down a New York law creating a special school district for an exclusively Jewish community.

Souter is known for his intensely private, ascetic life. He was born September 17, 1939, in Melrose, Massachusetts. An only child, he moved with his parents to Weare, New Hampshire, at age eleven. Except for college, he lived in Weare until 1990.

Graduating from Harvard College in 1961, Souter attended Oxford University on a Rhodes Scholarship from 1961 to 1963, then returned to Cambridge for Harvard Law School. Graduating in 1966, he worked for two years in a Concord law firm. In 1968 he became an assistant attorney general, rose to deputy attorney general in 1971, and in 1976 was appointed attorney general. Under conservative governor Meldrim Thomson, Jr., Attorney General Souter defended a number of controversial orders, including the lowering of state flags to half-staff on Good Friday to observe the death of Jesus. He prosecuted Jehovah's Witnesses who obscured the state motto "Live Free or Die" on their license plates.

Souter served as attorney general until 1978, when he was named to the state's trial court. Five years later Gov. John H. Sununu appointed Souter to the state Supreme Court. Sununu was Bush's chief of staff when Souter was named to the U.S. Supreme Court.

Souter, a bachelor, is a nature enthusiast and avid hiker.

Clarence Thomas

Born: June 23, 1948, Savannah, Georgia.

Education: Immaculate Conception Seminary, 1967-1968; Holy Cross College, B.A., 1971; Yale University Law School, J.D., 1974.

Family: Married Kathy Grace Ambush, 1971; one son; divorced 1984; married Virginia Lamp, 1987.

Career: Assistant attorney general, Missouri, 1974-1977; attorney, Monsanto Co., 1977-1979; legislative assistant to Sen. John C. Danforth, R-Mo., 1979-1981; assistant secretary of education for civil rights, 1981-1982; chairman, Equal Employment Opportunity Commission, 1982-1990; judge, U.S. Court of Appeals for the District of Columbia, 1990-1991.

Supreme Court Service: Nominated as associate justice of the U.S. Supreme Court by President George Bush July 1, 1991; confirmed, 52-48, October 15, 1991.

The Senate's 52-48 vote on Clarence Thomas was the closest Supreme Court confirmation vote in more than a century and followed a tumultuous nomination process that culminated in accusations against Thomas of sexual harassment. The charges, brought out in nationally televised hearings, were never proved and led the nominee to accuse the Senate of a "high-tech lynching."

Thomas, who took his judicial oath on October 23, 1991, succeeded Thurgood Marshall, the Court's last consistent liberal and a man whose six-decade legal career shaped the country's civil rights struggle. Marshall was the first black justice, and Thomas became the second.

Thomas also was the fifth conservative appointment by a Republican president in ten years, a historic record that raised the stakes for the Democratically controlled Senate and led in part to the politics surrounding the confirmation. Thomas was only forty-three when President Bush nominated him, and senators noted that Thomas likely would be affecting the outcome of major constitutional rulings well into the twenty-first century. His confirmation also solidified the conservative majority on the Court that began asserting itself in the late 1980s.

Most difficult for Thomas were the eleventh-hour allegations from a former employee that he had sexually harassed her when he was assistant secretary of education for civil rights and then chairman of the Equal Employment Opportunity Commission (EEOC). In an unprecedented move, senators abruptly postponed a scheduled confirmation vote and reconvened hearings to take testimony from accuser Anita F. Hill, a University of Oklahoma law professor; Thomas; and witnesses for both.

In the end most senators said Hill's charges and Thomas's defense— a categorical denial—were inconclusive. Senators fell back on their previous positions based on Thomas's judicial philosophy or his determined character and rise from poverty in rural Georgia.

In Thomas's first three years on the Court, he closely aligned himself with fellow conservative Antonin Scalia. He voted with Scalia nearly 90 percent of the time in the 1992-1993 term and 88 percent of the time in the 1993-1994 term. Often Scalia and Thomas dissented alone in opinions that sharply challenged existing legal doctrine. In the 1991-1992 term, for example, Thomas wrote a dissenting opinion arguing against the use of the Eighth Amendment's Cruel and Unusual Punishment Clause in prison brutality suits. And in a massive separate opinion in a voting rights case in the 1993-1994 term, Thomas called for scrapping precedents that allowed courts to order the creation of majority-black districts for legislative or congressional seats.

Thomas graduated from Yale Law School in 1974 and became an assistant attorney general of Missouri and, three years later, a staff attorney for Monsanto Company. He worked for Sen. John C. Danforth, R-Mo., as a legislative assistant and served in the Department of Education as assistant secretary for civil rights for one year before being named chairman of the EEOC.

Thomas's wife, the former Virginia Lamp, is a lawyer who served as a legislative official with the U.S. Department of Labor during the Bush administration and since 1993 as a senior policy analyst with the House Republican Conference. They were married in 1987. He has a son from his first marriage, which ended in divorce in 1984.

Ruth Bader Ginsburg

Born: March 15, 1933, Brooklyn, New York.

Education: Cornell University, B.A., 1954; attended Harvard University Law School, 1956-1958; graduated Columbia Law School, J.D., 1959.

Family: Married Martin D. Ginsburg, 1954; one daughter, one son.

Career: Law clerk to U.S. District Court Judge Edmund L. Palmieri, 1959-1961; Columbia Law School Project on International Procedure, 1961-1963; professor, Rutgers University School of Law, 1963-1972; director, Women's Rights Project, American Civil Liberties

Union, 1972-1980; professor, Columbia Law School, 1972-1980; judge, U.S. Court of Appeals for the District of Columbia, 1980-1993.

Supreme Court Service: Nominated as associate justice of the U.S. Supreme Court by President Bill Clinton, June 22, 1993; confirmed, 96-3, August 3, 1993.

Ruth Bader Ginsburg's path to the U.S. Supreme Court is a classic American story of overcoming obstacles and setbacks through intelligence, persistence, and quiet hard work. Her achievements as a student, law teacher, advocate, and judge came against a background of personal adversity and institutional discrimination against women. Ginsburg not only surmounted those hurdles for herself but also charted the legal strategy in the 1970s that helped broaden opportunities for women by establishing constitutional principles limiting sex discrimination in the law.

Born into a Jewish family of modest means in Brooklyn, Ruth Bader was greatly influenced by her mother Celia, who imparted a love of learning and a determination to be independent. Celia Bader died of cancer on the eve of her daughter's high school graduation in 1948.

Ruth Bader attended Cornell University, where she graduated first in her class and met her future husband, Martin Ginsburg, who became a tax lawyer and later a professor at Georgetown University Law Center in Washington.

At Harvard Law School Ruth Bader Ginsburg made law review, cared for an infant daughter, and then helped her husband complete his studies after he was diagnosed with cancer. He recovered, graduated, and got a job in New York, and she transferred to Columbia for her final year of law school.

Although she was tied for first place in her class when she graduated, Ginsburg was unable to land a Supreme Court clerkship or job with a top New York law firm. Instead, she won a two-year clerkship with a federal district court judge. She then accepted a research position at Columbia that took her to Sweden, where she studied civil procedure and began to be stirred by feminist thought. Ginsburg taught at Rutgers University Law School in New Jersey from 1963 to 1972. She also worked with the New Jersey affiliate of the American Civil Liberties Union (ACLU), where her caseload included several early sex discrimination complaints. In 1972 Ginsburg became the first woman to be named to a tenured position on the Columbia Law School faculty. As director of the national ACLU's newly established Women's Rights Project, she also handled the cases that over the course of several years led the Supreme Court to require heightened scrutiny of legal classifications based on sex. Ginsburg won five of the six cases she argued before the court.

President Jimmy Carter named Ginsburg to the U.S. Court of Appeals for the District of Columbia in 1980. There she earned a reputation as a judicial moderate on a sharply divided court. Although she is prochoice, she stirred controversy among abortion rights groups by criticizing some aspects of the way the Supreme Court's landmark abortion case, *Roe v. Wade,* was decided.

When Justice Byron R. White announced plans for his retirement in March 1993, Ginsburg was among the large field of candidates President Bill Clinton considered for the vacancy. Clinton considered and passed over two other leading candidates for the position before deciding to interview Ginsburg. White House aides told reporters later that Clinton had been especially impressed with Ginsburg's life story. Reaction to the nomination was overwhelmingly positive. On Capitol Hill Ginsburg won the support of some pivotal Republican senators, including Minority Leader Robert Dole of Kansas.

In three days of confirmation hearings before the Senate Judiciary Committee, Ginsburg depicted herself as an advocate of judicial restraint, but she also said courts sometimes had a role to play in bringing about social change. On specific issues she strongly endorsed abortion rights, equal rights for women, and the constitutional right to privacy. But she declined to give her views on many other issues, including capital punishment. Some senators said that she had been less than forthcoming, but the committee voted unanimously to recommend her for confirmation.

The full Senate confirmed her four days later by a vote of 96-3. Three conservative Republicans cast the only negative votes. Ginsburg was sworn in August 10, 1993, as the court's second female justice—joining Justice Sandra Day O'Connor—and the first Jewish justice since 1969.

In her first weeks on the bench, Ginsburg startled observers and drew some criticism with her unusually active questioning. She eased up a bit as the term progressed but continued to be one of the Court's most active interrogators during oral arguments. Although as a junior justice she wrote no major opinions, her voting appeared to bear out predictions made after her confirmation hearings. She took liberal positions on women's rights, civil rights, church-state, and First Amendment issues, but she had a more mixed record in other areas, including criminal law. She voted to back death penalty appeals in five out of seven capital punishment cases and sided with liberals in most of the closely divided criminal law rulings. Overall, however, she voted to uphold convictions or sentences in most of the Court's criminal law decisions of the term.

Stephen Gerald Breyer

Born: August 15, 1938, San Francisco, California.

Education: Stanford University, A.B., Phi Beta Kappa, 1959; Oxford University, B.A. (Marshall scholar), 1961; Harvard Law School, LL.B., 1964.

Family: Married Joanna Hare, 1967; two daughters, one son.

Career: Law clerk to Justice Arthur J. Goldberg, U.S. Supreme Court, 1964-1965; assistant to assistant attorney general, antitrust, U.S. Justice Department, 1965-1967; professor, Harvard Law School, 1967-1981; assistant special prosecutor, Watergate Special Prosecution Force, 1973; special counsel, Senate Judiciary Committee, 1974-1975; chief counsel, Senate Judiciary Committee, 1979-1980; judge, U.S. Court of Appeals for the First Circuit, 1980-1994.

Supreme Court Service: Nominated as associate justice of the U.S. Supreme Court by President Bill Clinton May 17, 1994; confirmed, 87-9, July 29, 1994.

When President Bill Clinton introduced Stephen G. Breyer, his second Supreme Court nominee, at a White House ceremony on May 16,

1994, he described the federal appeals court judge as a "consensus-builder." The reaction to the nomination proved his point. Senators from both parties quickly endorsed Breyer. The only vocal dissents came from a few liberals and consumer advocates, who said Breyer was too probusiness.

Breyer, chosen to replace the retiring liberal justice Harry A. Blackmun, won a reputation as a centrist in fourteen years on the federal appeals court in Boston and two earlier stints as a staff member for the Senate Judiciary Committee. Breyer's work crossed ideological lines. He played a critical role in enacting airline deregulation in the 1970s and writing federal sentencing guidelines in the 1980s.

Born in 1938 to a politically active family in San Francisco, Breyer earned degrees from Stanford University and Harvard Law School. He clerked for Supreme Court Justice Arthur J. Goldberg and helped draft Goldberg's influential opinion in the 1965 case establishing the right of married couples to use contraceptives. Afterward he served two years in the Justice Department's antitrust division and then took a teaching position at Harvard Law School in 1967.

Breyer took leaves from Harvard to serve as an assistant prosecutor in the Watergate investigation in 1973, special counsel to the Judiciary

Committee's Administrative Practices Subcommittee from 1974 to 1975, and the full committee's chief counsel from 1979 to 1980. He worked for Sen. Edward Kennedy, D-Mass., but also established good relationships with Republican committee members. His ties to senators paid off when President Jimmy Carter nominated him for the federal appeals court in November 1980. Even though Ronald Reagan had been elected president, Republican senators allowed a vote on Breyer's nomination.

As a judge, Breyer was regarded as scholarly, judicious, and open-minded, with generally conservative views on economic issues and more liberal views on social questions. He wrote two books on regulatory reform that criticized economic regulations as anticompetitive and questioned priorities in some environmental and health rulemaking. He also served as a member of the newly created United States Sentencing Commission from 1985 to 1989. Later he defended the commission's guidelines against criticism from judges and others who viewed them as overly restrictive.

President Clinton interviewed Breyer before his first Supreme Court appointment in 1993 but chose Ruth Bader Ginsburg instead. He picked Breyer in 1994 after Senate Majority Leader George Mitchell took himself out of consideration and problems developed with two other leading candidates.

In his confirmation hearings before the Senate Judiciary Committee, Breyer defused two potential controversies by saying that he accepted Supreme Court precedents upholding abortion rights and capital punishment. The only contentious issue came when Sen. Howard Metzenbaum, a liberal Ohio Democrat, questioned Breyer's investment in the British insurance syndicate Lloyd's of London. Metzenbaum said Breyer should have recused himself from several environmental pollution cases because of the investment. Breyer said the cases could not have affected his holdings but also promised to get out of Lloyd's as soon as possible. Despite the issue, Metzenbaum joined in the committee's unanimous vote recommending Breyer's confirmation.

Sen. Richard Lugar of Indiana, a moderate Republican, took up the Lloyd's issue when the nomination reached the Senate floor on July 29. But Breyer was strongly supported by senators from both parties, including Kennedy and the Judiciary Committee's ranking Republican, Orrin Hatch of Utah. The Senate voted to confirm Breyer 87-9. Lugar and eight Republican conservatives cast the only no votes.

Breyer took the judicial oath of office in a private ceremony on August 3 at the vacation home of Chief Justice William H. Rehnquist. A formal swearing-in ceremony was held at the White House on August 12. Breyer joined Ginsburg as the Court's second Jewish justice. The Court had two Jewish members only once before, in the 1930s when Louis Brandeis and Benjamin Cardozo served together for six years.

Harry Andrew Blackmun (Retired)

Born: November 12, 1908, Nashville, Illinois.

Education: Harvard College, B.A., Phi Beta Kappa, 1929; Harvard University Law School, LL.B., 1932.

Family: Married Dorothy E. Clark, 1941; three daughters.

Career: Law clerk to John Sanborn, U.S. Court of Appeals for the Eighth Circuit, St. Paul, 1932-1933; practiced law, Minneapolis, 1934-1950; resident counsel, Mayo Clinic, Rochester, Minnesota, 1950-1959; judge, U.S. Court of Appeals for the Eighth Circuit, 1959-1970.

Supreme Court Service: Nominated as associate justice of the U.S. Supreme Court by President Richard Nixon, April 14, 1970; confirmed, 94-0, May 12, 1970; retired August 3, 1994.

During his first years on the Court, Harry A. Blackmun frequently was described as one of the "Minnesota Twins" along with the Court's other Minnesota native, Chief Justice Warren E. Burger. Blackmun and Burger, who retired in 1986, were friends who initially voted together on important decisions.

However, Blackmun, who originally impressed observers as a modest, even meek, addition to the Court's conservative bloc, has written some of the Court's most controversial, liberally oriented decisions. He was best known for writing the Court's 1973 decision, *Roe v. Wade*, establishing a constitutional right for women to have an abortion and for defending abortion rights in later decisions that permitted states to restrict abortion procedures and upheld prohibitions against government-funded abortions. With the retirement of Justices William J. Brennan, Jr., in 1990 and Thurgood Marshall in 1991, Blackmun became the Court's most liberal member.

Blackmun was born in Nashville, Illinois, November 12, 1908, but spent most of his early years in St. Paul, Minnesota, where his father was in business. His lifelong friendship with Burger began in grade school.

Blackmun went east after high school to attend Harvard College on a scholarship. He majored in mathematics and toyed briefly with the idea of becoming a physician. But he chose the law instead. After graduating from Harvard in 1929, Phi Beta Kappa, Blackmun entered Harvard Law School and received his degree in 1932. During his law school years,

Blackmun supported himself with a variety of odd jobs, including tutoring in math and driving the launch for the college crew team.

Following law school Blackmun returned to St. Paul, where he served for a year and a half as a law clerk to United States Circuit Court judge John B. Sanborn, whom Blackmun succeeded twenty years later. He left the clerkship at the end of 1933 and joined a law firm in Minneapolis, where he specialized in taxation, trusts and estates, and civil litigation. At the same time he taught for a year at Burger's alma mater, the St. Paul College of Law (since renamed the William Mitchell College of Law). In addition to his practice, Blackmun taught for two years during the 1940s at the University of Minnesota Law School.

In 1950 he accepted a post as "house counsel" for the world-famous Mayo Clinic in Rochester, Minnesota. Among his colleagues there, Blackmun quickly developed a reputation as a serious man, totally engrossed in his profession. The reputation followed him to the bench of the U.S. Court of Appeals for the Eighth Circuit, to which Blackmun was appointed by President Dwight D. Eisenhower in 1959. As a judge, Blackmun was known for his scholarly and thorough opinions.

President Richard Nixon nominated Blackmun for the Supreme Court in 1970 after the Senate had rejected two previous nominees— Clement Haynsworth, Jr., and G. Harrold Carswell—in bitter, partisan fights. Blackmun won unanimous Senate confirmation, 94-0. Later he referred to his selection with self-deprecating wit by calling himself "old number three."

In his final term on the Court, Blackmun issued a highly personal, 7,000-word statement declaring that he would no longer vote to uphold death penalty cases. He said he had become convinced that capital punishment could not be administered fairly. He also wrote the Court's opinion in an important case prohibiting lawyers from excluding potential jurors on the basis of sex.

Blackmun's total devotion to the law left little time for outside activities. He is an avid reader, delving primarily into judicial tomes. Over the years he also has been active in Methodist church affairs. Before he developed knee problems, Blackmun was a proficient squash and tennis player.

It was on the tennis court that Blackmun met his wife, Dorothy E. Clark. They were married in 1941 and have three daughters.

Glossary of Legal Terms

Accessory. In criminal law, a person not present at the commission of an offense who commands, advises, instigates, or conceals the offense.

Acquittal. A person is acquitted when a jury returns a verdict of not guilty. A person also may be acquitted when a judge determines that insufficient evidence exists to convict him or that a violation of due process precludes a fair trial.

Adjudicate. To determine finally by the exercise of judicial authority, to decide a case.

Affidavit. A voluntary written statement of facts or charges affirmed under oath.

A fortiori. With stronger force, with more reason.

Amicus curiae. Friend of the court; a person, not a party to litigation, who volunteers or is invited by the court to give his or her views on a case.

Appeal. A legal proceeding to ask a higher court to review or modify a lower court decision. In a civil case, either the plaintiff or the defendant can appeal an adverse ruling. In criminal cases a defendant can appeal a conviction, but the Double Jeopardy Clause prevents the government from appealing an acquittal. In Supreme Court practice an appeal is a case that falls within the Court's mandatory jurisdiction as opposed to a case that the Court agrees to review under the discretionary writ of certiorari. With the virtual elimination of the Court's mandatory jurisdiction in 1988, the Court now hears very few true appeals, but petitions for certiorari are often referred to imprecisely as appeals.

Appellant. The party who appeals a lower court decision to a higher court.

Appellee. One who has an interest in upholding the decision of a lower court and is compelled to respond when the case is appealed to a higher court by an appellant.

Arraignment. The formal process of charging a person with a crime, reading that person the charge, asking whether he or she pleads guilty or not guilty, and entering the plea.

Attainder, Bill of. A legislative act pronouncing a particular individual guilty of a crime without trial or conviction and imposing a sentence.

Bail. The security, usually money, given as assurance of a prisoner's due appearance at a designated time and place (as in court) to procure in the interim the prisoner's release from jail.

Bailiff. A minor officer of a court, usually serving as an usher or a messenger.

Brief. A document prepared by counsel to serve as the basis for an argument in court, setting out the facts of and the legal arguments in support of the case.

Burden of proof. The need or duty of affirmatively providing a fact or facts that are disputed.

Case law. The law as defined by previously decided cases, distinct from statutes and other sources of law.

Cause. A case, suit, litigation, or action, civil or criminal.

Certiorari, Writ of. A writ issued from the Supreme Court, at its discretion, to order a lower court to prepare the record of a case and send it to the Supreme Court for review.

Civil law. Body of law dealing with the private rights of individuals, as distinguished from criminal law.

Class action. A lawsuit brought by one person or group on behalf of all persons similarly situated.

Code. A collection of laws, arranged systematically.

Comity. Courtesy, respect; usually used in the legal sense to refer to the proper relationship between state and federal courts.

Common law. Collection of principles and rules of action, particularly from unwritten English law, that derive their authority from longstanding usage and custom or from courts recognizing and enforcing these customs. Sometimes used synonymously with case law.

Consent decree. A court-sanctioned agreement settling a legal dispute and entered into by the consent of the parties.

Contempt (civil and criminal). Civil contempt arises from a failure to follow a court order for the benefit of another party. Criminal contempt occurs when a person willfully exhibits disrespect for the court or obstructs the administration of justice.

Conviction. Final judgment or sentence that the defendant is guilty as charged.

Criminal law. The branch of law that deals with the enforcement of laws and the punishment of persons who, by breaking laws, commit crimes.

Declaratory judgment. A court pronouncement declaring a legal right or interpretation but not ordering a specific action.

De facto. In fact, in reality.

Defendant. In a civil action, the party denying or defending itself against charges brought by a plaintiff. In a criminal action, the person indicted for commission of an offense.

De jure. As a result of law or official action.

De novo. Anew; afresh; a second time.

Deposition. Oral testimony from a witness taken out of court in response to written or oral questions, committed to writing, and intended to be used in the preparation of a case.

Dicta. *See* Obiter dictum.

Dismissal. Order disposing of a case without a trial.

Docket. A calendar prepared by the clerks of the court listing the cases set to be tried.

Due process. Fair and regular procedure. The Fifth and Fourteenth amendments guarantee persons that they will not be deprived of life, liberty, or property by the government until fair and usual procedures have been followed.

Error, Writ of. A writ issued from an appeals court to a lower court requiring it to send to the appeals court the record of a case in which it has entered a final judgment and which the appeals court will review for error.

Ex parte. Only from, or on, one side. Application to a court for some ruling or action on behalf of only one party.

Ex post facto. After the fact; an ex post facto law makes an action a crime after it already has been committed, or otherwise changes the legal consequences of some past action.

Ex rel. Upon information from; usually used to describe legal proceedings begun by an official in the name of the state but at the instigation of, and with information from, a private individual interested in the matter.

Grand jury. Group of twelve to twenty-three persons impanelled to hear, in private, evidence presented by the state against an individual or persons accused of a criminal act and to issue indictments when a majority of the jurors find probable cause to believe that the accused has committed a crime. Called a "grand" jury because it comprises a greater number of persons than a "petit" jury.

Grand jury report. A public report, often called "presentments," released by a grand jury after an investigation into activities of public officials that fall short of criminal actions.

Guilty. A word used by a defendant in entering a plea or by a jury in returning a verdict, indicating that the defendant is legally responsible as charged for a crime or other wrongdoing.

Habeas corpus. Literally, "you have the body"; a writ issued to inquire whether a person is lawfully imprisoned or detained. The writ demands that the persons holding the prisoner justify the detention or release the prisoner.

Immunity. A grant of exemption from prosecution in return for evidence or testimony.

In camera. In chambers. Refers to court hearings in private without spectators.

In forma pauperis. In the manner of a pauper, without liability for court costs.

In personam. Done or directed against a particular person.

In re. In the affair of, concerning. Frequent title of judicial proceedings in which there are no adversaries but instead where the matter itself—such as a bankrupt's estate—requires judicial action.

In rem. Done or directed against the thing, not the person.

Indictment. A formal written statement, based on evidence presented by the prosecutor, from a grand jury. Decided by a majority vote, an indictment charges one or more persons with specified offenses.

Information. A written set of accusations, similar to an indictment, but filed directly by a prosecutor.

Injunction. A court order prohibiting the person to whom it is directed from performing a particular act.

Interlocutory decree. A provisional decision of the court before completion of a legal action that temporarily settles an intervening matter.

Judgment. Official decision of a court based on the rights and claims of the parties to a case that was submitted for determination.

Jurisdiction. The power of a court to hear a case in question, which exists when the proper parties are present and when the point to be decided is within the issues authorized to be handled by the particular court.

Juries. *See* Grand jury; Petit jury.

Magistrate. A judicial officer having jurisdiction to try minor criminal cases and conduct preliminary examinations of persons charged with serious crimes.

Majority opinion. An opinion joined by a majority of the justices explaining the legal basis for the Court's decision and regarded as binding precedent for future cases.

Mandamus. "We command." An order issued from a superior court directing a lower court or other authority to perform a particular act.

Moot. Unsettled, undecided. A moot question also is one that no longer is material; a moot case is one that has become hypothetical.

Motion. Written or oral application to a court or a judge to obtain a rule or an order.

Nolo contendere. "I will not contest it." A plea entered by a defendant at the discretion of the judge with the same legal effect as a plea of guilty, but it may not be cited in other proceedings as an admission of guilt.

Obiter dictum. Statements by a judge or justice expressing an opinion and included with, but not essential to, an opinion resolving a case before the court. Dicta are not necessarily binding in future cases.

Parole. A conditional release from imprisonment under conditions that, if the prisoner abides by the law and other restrictions that may be imposed, the prisoner will not have to serve the remainder of the sentence.

Per curiam. "By the court." An unsigned opinion of the court, or an opinion written by the whole court.

Petit jury. A trial jury, originally a panel of twelve persons who tried to reach a unanimous verdict on questions of fact in criminal and civil proceedings. Since 1970 the Supreme Court has upheld the legality of state juries with fewer than twelve persons. Fewer persons serve on a "petit" jury than on a "grand" jury.

Petitioner. One who files a petition with a court seeking action or relief, including a plaintiff or an appellant. But a petitioner also is a person who files for other court action where charges are not necessarily made; for example, a party may petition the court for an order requiring another person or party to produce documents. The opposite party is called the respondent.

When a writ of certiorari is granted by the Supreme Court, the parties to the case are called petitioner and respondent in contrast to the appellant and appellee terms used in an appeal.

Plaintiff. A party who brings a civil action or sues to obtain a remedy for injury to his or her rights. The party against whom action is brought is termed the defendant.

Plea bargaining. Negotiations between a prosecutor and the defendant aimed at exchanging a plea of guilty from the defendant for concessions by the prosecutor, such as reduction of charges or a request for leniency.

Pleas. *See* Guilty; Nolo contendere.

Plurality opinion. An opinion supported by the largest number of justices but less than a majority. A plurality opinion typically is not regarded as establishing a binding precedent for future cases.

Precedent. A judicial decision that may be used as a basis for ruling on subsequent similar cases.

Presentment. *See* Grand jury report.

Prima facie. At first sight; referring to a fact or other evidence presumably sufficient to establish a defense or a claim unless otherwise contradicted.

Probation. Process under which a person convicted of an offense, usually a first offense, receives a suspended sentence and is given freedom, usually under the guardianship of a probation officer.

Quash. To overthrow, annul, or vacate; as to quash a subpoena.

Recognizance. An obligation entered into before a court or magistrate requiring the performance of a specified act—usually to appear in court at a later date. It is an alternative to bail for pretrial release.

Remand. To send back. When a decision is remanded, it is sent back by a higher court to the court from which it came for further action.

Respondent. One who is compelled to answer the claims or questions posed in court by a petitioner. A defendant and an appellee may be called respondents, but the term also includes those parties who answer in court during actions where charges are not necessarily brought or where the Supreme Court has granted a writ of certiorari.

Seriatim. Separately, individually, one by one.

Stare decisis. "Let the decision stand." The principle of adherence to settled cases, the doctrine that principles of law established in earlier judicial decisions should be accepted as authoritative in similar subsequent cases.

Statute. A written law enacted by a legislature. A collection of statutes for a particular governmental division is called a code.

Stay. To halt or suspend further judicial proceedings.

Subpoena. An order to present oneself before a grand jury, court, or legislative hearing.

Subpoena duces tecum. An order to produce specified documents or papers.

Tort. An injury or wrong to the person or property of another.

Transactional immunity. Protects a witness from prosecution for any offense mentioned in or related to his or her testimony, regardless of independent evidence against the witness.

Use immunity. Protects a witness from the use of his or her testimony against the witness in prosecution.

Vacate. To make void, annul, or rescind.

Writ. A written court order commanding the designated recipient to perform or not perform specified acts.

United States Constitution

We the People of the United States, in Order to form a more perfect Union, establish Justice, insure domestic Tranquility, provide for the common defence, promote the general Welfare, and secure the Blessings of Liberty to ourselves and our Posterity, do ordain and establish this Constitution for the United States of America.

Article I

Section 1. All legislative Powers herein granted shall be vested in a Congress of the United States, which shall consist of a Senate and House of Representatives.

Section 2. The House of Representatives shall be composed of Members chosen every second Year by the People of the several States, and the Electors in each State shall have the Qualifications requisite for Electors of the most numerous Branch of the State Legislature.

No Person shall be a Representative who shall not have attained to the age of twenty five Years, and been seven Years a Citizen of the United States, and who shall not, when elected, be an Inhabitant of that State in which he shall be chosen.

[Representatives and direct Taxes shall be apportioned among the several States which may be included within this Union, according to their respective Numbers, which shall be determined by adding to the whole Number of free Persons, including those bound to Service for a Term of Years, and excluding Indians not taxed, three fifths of all other Persons.][1] The actual Enumeration shall be made within three Years after the first Meeting of the Congress of the United States, and within every subsequent Term of ten Years, in such Manner as they shall by Law direct. The Number of Representatives shall not exceed one for every thirty Thousand, but each State shall have at Least one Representative; and until such enumeration shall be made, the State of New Hampshire shall be entitled to chuse three, Massachusetts eight, Rhode-Island and Providence Plantations one, Connecticut five, New-York six, New Jersey four, Pennsylvania eight, Delaware one, Maryland six, Virginia ten, North Carolina five, South Carolina five, and Georgia three.

When vacancies happen in the Representation from any State, the Executive Authority thereof shall issue Writs of Election to fill such Vacancies.

The House of Representatives shall chuse their Speaker and other Officers; and shall have the sole Power of Impeachment.

Section 3. The Senate of the United States shall be composed of two Senators from each State, [chosen by the Legislature thereof,][2] for six Years; and each Senator shall have one Vote.

Immediately after they shall be assembled in Consequence of the first Election, they shall be divided as equally as may be into three Classes. The Seats of the Senators of the first Class shall be vacated at the Expiration of the second Year, of the second Class at the Expiration of the fourth Year, and of the third Class at the Expiration of the sixth Year, so that one third may be chosen every second Year; [and if Vacancies happen by Resignation, or otherwise, during the Recess of the Legislature of any State, the Executive thereof may make temporary Appointments until the next Meeting of the Legislature, which shall then fill such Vacancies.][3]

No Person shall be a Senator who shall not have attained to the Age of thirty Years, and been nine Years a Citizen of the United States, and who shall not, when elected, be an Inhabitant of that State for which he shall be chosen.

The Vice President of the United States shall be President of the Senate, but shall have no Vote, unless they be equally divided.

The Senate shall chuse their other Officers, and also a President pro tempore, in the Absence of the Vice President, or when he shall exercise the Office of President of the United States.

The Senate shall have the sole Power to try all Impeachments. When sitting for that Purpose, they shall be on Oath or Affirmation. When the President of the United States is tried, the Chief Justice shall preside: And no Person shall be convicted without the Concurrence of two thirds of the Members present.

Judgment in Cases of Impeachment shall not extend further than to removal from Office, and disqualification to hold and enjoy any Office of honor, Trust or Profit under the United States: but the Party convicted shall nevertheless be liable and subject to Indictment, Trial, Judgment and Punishment, according to Law.

Section 4. The Times, Places and Manner of holding Elections for Senators and Representatives, shall be prescribed in each State by the Legislature thereof; but the Congress may at any time by Law make or alter such Regulations, except as to the Places of chusing Senators.

The Congress shall assemble at least once in every Year, and such Meeting shall [be on the first Monday in December],[4] unless they shall by Law appoint a different Day.

Section 5. Each House shall be the Judge of the Elections, Returns and Qualifications of its own Members, and a Majority of each shall constitute a Quorum to do Business; but a smaller Number may adjourn from day to day, and may be authorized to compel the Attendance of absent Members, in such Manner, and under such Penalties as each House may provide.

Each House may determine the Rules of its Proceedings, punish its Members for disorderly Behaviour, and, with the Concurrence of two thirds, expel a Member.

Each House shall keep a Journal of its Proceedings, and from time to time publish the same, excepting such Parts as may in their Judgment require Secrecy; and the Yeas and Nays of the Members of either House on any question shall, at the Desire of one fifth of those Present, be entered on the Journal.

Neither House, during the Session of Congress, shall, without the Consent of the other, adjourn for more than three days, nor to any other Place than that in which the two Houses shall be sitting.

Section 6. The Senators and Representatives shall receive a Compensation for their Services, to be ascertained by Law, and paid out of the Treasury of the United States. They shall in all Cases, except Treason, Felony and Breach of the Peace, be privileged from Arrest during their Attendance at the Session of their respective Houses, and in going to and returning from the same; and for any Speech or Debate in either House, they shall not be questioned in any other Place.

No Senator or Representative shall, during the Time for which he was elected, be appointed to any civil Office under the Authority of the United States, which shall have been created, or the Emoluments whereof shall have been encreased during such time; and no Person holding any Office under the United States, shall be a Member of either House during his Continuance in Office.

Section 7. All Bills for raising Revenue shall originate in the House of Representatives; but the Senate may propose or concur with Amendments as on other Bills.

Every Bill which shall have passed the House of Representatives and the Senate, shall, before it become a Law, be presented to the President of the United States; If he approve he shall sign it, but if not he shall return it, with his Objections to that House in which it shall have originated, who shall enter the Objections at large on their Journal, and proceed to reconsider it. If after such Reconsideration two thirds of that House shall agree to pass the Bill, it shall be sent, together with the Objections, to the other House, by which it shall likewise be reconsidered, and if approved by two thirds of that House, it shall become a Law. But in all such Cases the Votes of both Houses shall be determined by yeas and Nays, and the Names of the Persons voting for and against the Bill shall be entered on the Journal of each House respectively. If any Bill shall not be returned by the President within ten Days (Sundays excepted) after it shall have been presented to him, the Same shall be a Law, in like Manner as if he had signed it, unless the Congress by their Adjournment prevent its Return, in which Case it shall not be a Law.

Every Order, Resolution, or Vote to which the Concurrence of the Senate and House of Representatives may be necessary (except on a question of Adjournment) shall be presented to the President of the United States; and before the Same shall take Effect, shall be approved by him, or being disapproved by him, shall be repassed by two thirds of the Senate and House of Representatives, according to the Rules and Limitations prescribed in the Case of a Bill.

Section 8. The Congress shall have Power To lay and collect Taxes, Duties, Imposts and Excises, to pay the Debts and provide for the common Defence and general Welfare of the United States; but all Duties, Imposts and Excises shall be uniform throughout the United States;

To borrow Money on the credit of the United States;

To regulate Commerce with foreign Nations, and among the several States, and with the Indian Tribes;

To establish an uniform Rule of Naturalization, and uniform Laws on the subject of Bankruptcies throughout the United States;

To coin Money, regulate the Value thereof, and of foreign Coin, and fix the Standard of Weights and Measures;

To provide for the Punishment of counterfeiting the Securities and current Coin of the United States;

To establish Post Offices and post Roads;

To promote the Progress of Science and useful Arts, by securing for limited Times to Authors and Inventors the exclusive Right to their respective Writings and Discoveries;

To constitute Tribunals inferior to the supreme Court;

To define and punish Piracies and Felonies committed on the high Seas, and Offences against the Law of Nations;

To declare War, grant Letters of Marque and Reprisal, and make Rules concerning Captures on Land and Water;

To raise and support Armies, but no Appropriation of Money to that Use shall be for a longer Term than two Years;

To provide and maintain a Navy;

To make Rules for the Government and Regulation of the land and naval Forces;

To provide for calling forth the Militia to execute the Laws of the Union, suppress Insurrections and repel Invasions;

To provide for organizing, arming, and disciplining, the Militia, and for governing such Part of them as may be employed in the Service of the United States, reserving to the States respectively, the Appointment of the Officers, and the Authority of training the Militia according to the discipline prescribed by Congress;

To exercise exclusive Legislation in all Cases whatsoever, over such District (not exceeding ten Miles square) as may, by Cession of particular States, and the Acceptance of Congress, become the Seat of the Government of the United States, and to exercise like Authority over all Places purchased by the Consent of the Legislature of the State in which the Same shall be, for the Erection of Forts, Magazines, Arsenals, dock-Yards, and other needful Buildings;—And

To make all Laws which shall be necessary and proper for carrying into Execution the foregoing Powers, and all other Powers vested by this Constitution in the Government of the United States, or in any Department or Officer thereof.

Section 9. The Migration or Importation of such Persons as any of the States now existing shall think proper to admit, shall not be prohibited by the Congress prior to the Year one thousand eight hundred and eight, but a Tax or duty may be imposed on such Importation, not exceeding ten dollars for each Person.

The Privilege of the Writ of Habeas Corpus shall not be suspended, unless when in Cases of Rebellion or Invasion the public Safety may require it.

No Bill of Attainder or ex post facto Law shall be passed.

No Capitation, or other direct, Tax shall be laid, unless in Proportion to the Census or Enumeration herein before directed to be taken.[5]

No Tax or Duty shall be laid on Articles exported from any State.

No Preference shall be given by any Regulation of Commerce or Revenue to the Ports of one State over those of another; nor shall Vessels bound to, or from, one State, be obliged to enter, clear, or pay Duties in another.

No Money shall be drawn from the Treasury, but in Consequence of Appropriations made by Law; and a regular Statement and Account of the Receipts and Expenditures of all public Money shall be published from time to time.

No Title of Nobility shall be granted by the United States: And no Person holding any Office of Profit or Trust under them, shall, without the Consent of the Congress, accept of any present, Emolument, Office, or Title, of any kind whatever, from any King, Prince, or foreign State.

Section 10. No State shall enter into any Treaty, Alliance, or Confederation; grant Letters of Marque and Reprisal; coin Money; emit Bills of Credit; make any Thing but gold and silver Coin a Tender in Payment of Debts; pass any Bill of Attainder, ex post facto Law, or Law impairing the Obligation of Contracts, or grant any Title of Nobility.

No State shall, without the Consent of the Congress, lay any Imposts or Duties on Imports or Exports, except what may be absolutely necessary for executing it's inspection Laws: and the net Produce of all Duties and Imposts, laid by any State on Imports or Exports, shall be for the Use of the Treasury of the United States; and all such Laws shall be subject to the Revision and Controul of the Congress.

No State shall, without the Consent of Congress, lay any Duty of Tonnage, keep Troops, or Ships of War in time of Peace, enter into any Agreement or Compact with another State, or with a foreign Power, or engage in War, unless actually invaded, or in such imminent Danger as will not admit of delay.

Article II

Section 1. The executive Power shall be vested in a President of the United States of America. He shall hold his Office during the Term of four Years, and, together with the Vice President, chosen for the same Term, be elected, as follows

Each State shall appoint, in such Manner as the Legislature thereof may direct, a Number of Electors, equal to the whole Number of Senators and Representatives to which the State may be entitled in the Congress: but no Senator or Representative, or Person holding an Office of Trust or Profit under the United States, shall be appointed an Elector.

[The Electors shall meet in their respective States, and vote by Ballot for two Persons, of whom one at least shall not be an Inhabitant of the same State with themselves. And they shall make a List of all the Persons voted for, and of the Number of Votes for each; which List they shall sign and certify, and transmit sealed to the Seat of the Government of the United States, directed to the President of the Senate. The President of the Senate shall, in the Presence of the Senate and House of Representatives, open all the Certificates, and the Votes shall then be counted. The Person having the greatest Number of Votes shall be the President, if such Number be a Majority of the whole Number of Electors appointed; and if there be more than one who have such Majority, and have an equal Number of Votes, then the House of Representatives shall immediately chuse by Ballot one of them for President; and if no Person have a Majority, then from the five highest on the list the said House shall in like Manner chuse the President. But in chusing the President, the Votes shall be taken by States, the Representation from each State having one Vote; A quorum for this Purpose shall consist of a Member or Members from two thirds of the States, and a Majority of all the States shall be necessary to a Choice. In every Case, after the Choice of the President, the Person having the greatest Number of Votes of the Electors shall be the Vice President. But if there should remain two or more who have equal Votes, the Senate shall chuse from them by Ballot the Vice President.][6]

The Congress may determine the Time of chusing the Electors, and the Day on which they shall give their Votes; which Day shall be the same throughout the United States.

No Person except a natural born Citizen, or a Citizen of the United States, at the time of the Adoption of this Constitution, shall be eligible to the Office of President; neither shall any Person be eligible to that Office who shall not have attained to the Age of thirty five Years, and been fourteen Years a Resident within the United States.

In Case of the Removal of the President from Office, or of his Death, Resignation, or Inability to discharge the Powers and Duties of the said Office,[7] the Same shall devolve on the Vice President, and the Congress may by Law provide for the Case of Removal, Death, Resignation or Inability, both of the President and Vice President, declaring what Officer shall then act as President, and such Officer shall act accordingly, until the Disability be removed, or a President shall be elected.

The President shall, at stated Times, receive for his Services, a Compensation, which shall neither be encreased nor diminished during the Period for which he shall have been elected, and he shall not receive within that Period any other Emolument from the United States, or any of them.

Before he enter on the Execution of his Office, he shall take the following Oath or Affirmation:—"I do solemnly swear (or affirm) that I will faithfully execute the Office of President of the United States, and will to the best of my Ability, preserve, protect and defend the Constitution of the United States."

Section 2. The President shall be Commander in Chief of the Army and Navy of the United States, and of the Militia of the several States, when called into the actual Service of the United States; he may require the Opinion, in writing, of the principal Officer in each of the executive Departments, upon any Subject relating to the Duties of their respective Offices, and he shall have Power to grant Reprieves and Pardons for Offences against the United States, except in Cases of Impeachment.

He shall have Power, by and with the Advice and Consent of the Senate, to make Treaties, provided two thirds of the Senators present concur; and he shall nominate, and by and with the Advice and Consent of the Senate, shall appoint Ambassadors, other public Ministers and Consuls, Judges of the supreme Court, and all other Officers of the United States, whose Appointments are not herein otherwise provided for, and which shall be established by Law: but the Congress may by Law vest the Appointment of such inferior Officers, as they think proper, in the President alone, in the Courts of Law, or in the Heads of Departments.

The President shall have Power to fill up all Vacancies that may happen during the Recess of the Senate, by granting Commissions which shall expire at the End of their next Session.

Section 3. He shall from time to time give to the Congress Information of the State of the Union, and recommend to their Consideration such Measures as he shall judge necessary and expedient; he may, on extraordinary Occasions, convene both Houses, or either of them, and in Case of Disagreement between them, with Respect to the Time of Adjournment, he may adjourn them to such Time as he shall think proper; he shall receive Ambassadors and other public Ministers; he shall take Care that the Laws be faithfully executed, and shall Commission all the Officers of the United States.

Section 4. The President, Vice President and all civil Officers of the United States, shall be removed from Office on Impeachment for, and Conviction of, Treason, Bribery, or other high Crimes and Misdemeanors.

Article III

Section 1. The judicial Power of the United States, shall be vested in one supreme Court, and in such inferior Courts as the Congress may from time to time ordain and establish. The Judges, both of the supreme and inferior Courts, shall hold their Offices during good Behaviour, and shall, at stated Times, receive for their Services, a Compensation, which shall not be diminished during their Continuance in Office.

Section 2. The judicial Power shall extend to all Cases, in Law and Equity, arising under this Constitution, the Laws of the United States, and Treaties made, or which shall be made, under their Authority;—to all Cases affecting Ambassadors, other public Ministers and Consuls;—to all Cases of admiralty and maritime Jurisdiction;—to Controversies to which the United States shall be a Party;—to Controversies between two or more States;—between a State and Citizens of another State;[8]—between Citizens of different States;—between Citizens of the same State claiming Lands under Grants of different States, and between a State, or the Citizens thereof, and foreign States, Citizens or Subjects.[8]

In all Cases affecting Ambassadors, other public Ministers and Consuls, and those in which a State shall be Party, the supreme Court shall have original Jurisdiction. In all the other Cases before mentioned, the supreme Court shall have appellate Jurisdiction, both as to Law and Fact, with such Exceptions, and under such Regulations as the Congress shall make.

The Trial of all Crimes, except in Cases of Impeachment, shall be by Jury; and such Trial shall be held in the State where the said Crimes shall have been committed; but when not committed within any State, the Trial shall be at such Place or Places as the Congress may by Law have directed.

Section 3. Treason against the United States, shall consist only in levying War against them, or in adhering to their Enemies, giving them Aid and Comfort. No Person shall be convicted of Treason unless on the Testimony of two Witnesses to the same overt Act, or on Confession in open Court.

The Congress shall have Power to declare the Punishment of Treason, but no Attainder of Treason shall work Corruption of Blood, or Forfeiture except during the Life of the Person attainted.

Article IV

Section 1. Full Faith and Credit shall be given in each State to the public Acts, Records, and judicial Proceedings of every other State. And the Congress may by general Laws prescribe the Manner in which such Acts, Records and Proceedings shall be proved, and the Effect thereof.

Section 2. The Citizens of each State shall be entitled to all Privileges and Immunities of Citizens in the several States.

A Person charged in any State with Treason, Felony, or other Crime, who shall flee from Justice, and be found in another State, shall on Demand of the executive Authority of the State from which he fled, be delivered up, to be removed to the State having Jurisdiction of the Crime.

[No Person held to Service or Labour in one State, under the Laws thereof, escaping into another, shall, in Consequence of any Law or Regulation therein, be discharged from such Service or Labour, but shall be delivered up on Claim of the Party to whom such Service or Labour may be due.][9]

Section 3. New States may be admitted by the Congress into this Union; but no new State shall be formed or erected within the Jurisdiction of any other State; nor any State be formed by the Junction of two or more States, or Parts of States, without the Consent of the Legislatures of the States concerned as well as of the Congress.

The Congress shall have Power to dispose of and make all needful Rules and Regulations respecting the Territory or other Property belonging to the United States; and nothing in this Constitution shall be so construed as to Prejudice any Claims of the United States, or of any particular State.

Section 4. The United States shall guarantee to every State in this Union a Republican Form of Government, and shall protect each of them against Invasion; and on Application of the Legislature, or of the Executive (when the Legislature cannot be convened) against domestic Violence.

Article V

The Congress, whenever two thirds of both Houses shall deem it necessary, shall propose Amendments to this Constitution, or, on the Application of the Legislatures of two thirds of the several States, shall call a Convention for proposing Amendments, which, in either Case, shall be valid to all Intents and

Purposes, as Part of this Constitution, when ratified by the Legislatures of three fourths of the several States, or by Conventions in three fourths thereof, as the one or the other Mode of Ratification may be proposed by the Congress; Provided [that no Amendment which may be made prior to the Year One thousand eight hundred and eight shall in any Manner affect the first and fourth Clauses in the Ninth Section of the first Article; and][10] that no State, without its Consent, shall be deprived of its equal Suffrage in the Senate.

Article VI

All Debts contracted and Engagements entered into, before the Adoption of this Constitution, shall be as valid against the United States under this Constitution, as under the Confederation.

This Constitution, and the Laws of the United States which shall be made in Pursuance thereof; and all Treaties made, or which shall be made, under the Authority of the United States, shall be the supreme Law of the Land; and the Judges in every State shall be bound thereby, any Thing in the Constitution or Laws of any State to the Contrary notwithstanding.

The Senators and Representatives before mentioned, and the Members of the several State Legislatures, and all executive and judicial Officers, both of the United States and of the several States, shall be bound by Oath or Affirmation, to support this Constitution; but no religious Test shall ever be required as a Qualification to any Office or public Trust under the United States.

Article VII

The Ratification of the Conventions of nine States, shall be sufficient for the Establishment of this Constitution between the States so ratifying the Same.

Done in Convention by the Unanimous Consent of the States present the Seventeenth Day of September in the Year of our Lord one thousand seven hundred and Eighty seven and of the Independence of the United States of America the Twelfth. IN WITNESS whereof We have hereunto subscribed our Names,

George Washington,
President and
deputy from Virginia.

New Hampshire:	John Langdon, Nicholas Gilman.
Massachusetts:	Nathaniel Gorham, Rufus King.
Connecticut:	William Samuel Johnson, Roger Sherman.
New York:	Alexander Hamilton.

New Jersey:	William Livingston, David Brearley, William Paterson, Jonathan Dayton.
Pennsylvania:	Benjamin Franklin, Thomas Mifflin, Robert Morris, George Clymer, Thomas FitzSimons, Jared Ingersoll, James Wilson, Gouverneur Morris.
Delaware:	George Read, Gunning Bedford Jr., John Dickinson, Richard Bassett, Jacob Broom.
Maryland:	James McHenry, Daniel of St. Thomas Jenifer, Daniel Carroll.
Virginia:	John Blair, James Madison Jr.
North Carolina:	William Blount, Richard Dobbs Spaight, Hugh Williamson.
South Carolina:	John Rutledge, Charles Cotesworth Pinckney, Charles Pinckney, Pierce Butler.
Georgia:	William Few, Abraham Baldwin.

[The language of the original Constitution, not including the Amendments, was adopted by a convention of the states on September 17, 1787, and was subsequently ratified by the states on the following dates: Delaware, December 7, 1787; Pennsylvania, December 12, 1787; New Jersey, December 18, 1787; Georgia, January 2, 1788; Connecticut, January 9, 1788; Massachusetts, February 6, 1788; Maryland, April 28, 1788; South Carolina, May 23, 1788; New Hampshire, June 21, 1788.

Ratification was completed on June 21, 1788.

The Constitution subsequently was ratified by Virginia, June 25, 1788; New York, July 26, 1788; North Carolina, November 21, 1789; Rhode Island, May 29, 1790; and Vermont, January 10, 1791.]

Amendments

Amendment I

(First ten amendments ratified December 15, 1791.)

Congress shall make no law respecting an establishment of religion, or prohibiting the free exercise thereof; or abridging the freedom of speech, or of the press; or the right of the people peaceably to assemble, and to petition the Government for a redress of grievances.

Amendment II

A well regulated Militia, being necessary to the security of a free State, the right of the people to keep and bear Arms, shall not be infringed.

Amendment III

No Soldier shall, in time of peace be quartered in any house, without the consent of the Owner, nor in time of war, but in a manner to be prescribed by law.

Amendment IV

The right of the people to be secure in their persons, houses, papers, and effects, against unreasonable searches and seizures, shall not be violated, and no Warrants shall issue, but upon probable cause, supported by Oath or affirmation, and particularly describing the place to be searched, and the persons or things to be seized.

Amendment V

No person shall be held to answer for a capital, or otherwise infamous crime, unless on a presentment or indictment of a Grand Jury, except in cases arising in the land or naval forces, or in the Militia, when in actual service in time of War or public danger; nor shall any person be subject for the same offence to be twice put in jeopardy of life or limb; nor shall be compelled in any criminal case to be a witness against himself, nor be deprived of life, liberty, or property, without due process of law; nor shall private property be taken for public use, without just compensation.

Amendment VI

In all criminal prosecutions, the accused shall enjoy the right to a speedy and public trial, by an impartial jury of the State and district wherein the crime shall have been committed, which district shall have been previously ascertained by law, and to be informed of the nature and cause of the accusation; to be confronted with the witnesses against him; to have compulsory process for obtaining witnesses in his favor, and to have the Assistance of Counsel for his defence.

Amendment VII

In Suits at common law, where the value in controversy shall exceed twenty dollars, the right of trial by jury shall be preserved, and no fact tried by a jury, shall be otherwise re-examined in any Court of the United States, than according to the rules of the common law.

Amendment VIII

Excessive bail shall not be required, nor excessive fines imposed, nor cruel and unusual punishments inflicted.

Amendment IX

The enumeration in the Constitution, of certain rights, shall not be construed to deny or disparage others retained by the people.

Amendment X

The powers not delegated to the United States by the Constitution, nor prohibited by it to the States, are reserved to the States respectively, or to the people.

Amendment XI

(Ratified February 7, 1795)

The Judicial power of the United States shall not be construed to extend to any suit in law or equity, commenced or prosecuted against one of the United States by Citizens of another State, or by Citizens or Subjects of any Foreign State.

Amendment XII

(Ratified June 15, 1804)

The Electors shall meet in their respective states and vote by ballot for President and Vice-President, one of whom, at least, shall not be an inhabitant of the same state with themselves; they shall name in their ballots the person voted for as President, and in distinct ballots the person voted for as Vice-President, and they shall make distinct lists of all persons voted for as President, and of all persons voted for as Vice-President, and of the number of votes for each, which lists they shall sign and certify, and transmit sealed to the seat of the government of the United States, directed to the President of the Senate;—The President of the Senate shall, in the presence of the Senate and House of Representatives, open all the certificates and the votes shall then be counted;—The person having the greatest number of votes for President, shall be the President, if such number be a majority of the whole number of Electors appointed; and if no person have such majority, then from the persons having the highest numbers not exceeding three on the list of those voted for as President, the House of Representatives shall choose immediately, by ballot, the President. But in choosing the President, the votes shall be taken by states, the representation from each state having one vote; a quorum for this purpose shall consist of a member or members from two-thirds of the states, and a majority of all the states shall be necessary to a choice. [And if the House of Representatives shall not choose a President whenever the right of choice shall devolve upon them, before the fourth day of March next following, then the Vice-President shall act as President, as in the case of the death or other constitutional disability of the President.—][11] The person having the greatest number of votes as Vice-President, shall be the Vice-President, if such number be a majority of the whole number of Electors appointed, and if no person have a majority, then from the two highest numbers on the list, the Senate shall choose the Vice-President; a quorum for the purpose shall consist of two-thirds of the whole number of Senators, and a majority of the whole number shall be necessary to a choice. But no person constitutionally ineligible to the office of President shall be eligible to that of Vice-President of the United States.

Amendment XIII

(Ratified December 6, 1865)

Section 1. Neither slavery nor involuntary servitude, except as a punishment for crime whereof the party shall have been duly convicted, shall exist within the United States, or any place subject to their jurisdiction.

Section 2. Congress shall have power to enforce this article by appropriate legislation.

Amendment XIV

(Ratified July 9, 1868)

Section 1. All persons born or naturalized in the United States, and subject to the jurisdiction thereof, are citizens of the United States and of the State wherein they reside. No State shall make or enforce any law which shall abridge the privileges or immunities of citizens of the United States; nor shall any State deprive any person of life, liberty, or property, without due process of law; nor deny to any person within its jurisdiction the equal protection of the laws.

Section 2. Representatives shall be apportioned among the several States according to their respective numbers, counting the whole number of persons in each State, excluding Indians not taxed. But when the right to vote at any election for the choice of electors for President and Vice President of the United States,

Representatives in Congress, the Executive and Judicial officers of a State, or the members of the Legislature thereof, is denied to any of the male inhabitants of such State, being twenty-one years of age,[12] and citizens of the United States, or in any way abridged, except for participation in rebellion, or other crime, the basis of representation therein shall be reduced in the proportion which the number of such male citizens shall bear to the whole number of male citizens twenty-one years of age in such State.

Section 3. No person shall be a Senator or Representative in Congress, or elector of President and Vice President, or hold any office, civil or military, under the United States, or under any State, who, having previously taken an oath, as a member of Congress, or as an officer of the United States, or as a member of any State legislature, or as an executive or judicial officer of any State, to support the Constitution of the United States, shall have engaged in insurrection or rebellion against the same, or given aid or comfort to the enemies thereof. But Congress may by a vote of two-thirds of each House, remove such disability.

Section 4. The validity of the public debt of the United States, authorized by law, including debts incurred for payment of pensions and bounties for services in suppressing insurrection or rebellion, shall not be questioned. But neither the United States nor any State shall assume or pay any debt or obligation incurred in aid of insurrection or rebellion against the United States, or any claim for the loss or emancipation of any slave; but all such debts, obligations and claims shall be held illegal and void.

Section 5. The Congress shall have power to enforce, by appropriate legislation, the provisions of this article.

Amendment XV

(Ratified February 3, 1870)

Section 1. The right of citizens of the United States to vote shall not be denied or abridged by the United States or by any State on account of race, color, or previous condition of servitude.

Section 2. The Congress shall have power to enforce this article by appropriate legislation.

Amendment XVI

(Ratified February 3, 1913)

The Congress shall have power to lay and collect taxes on incomes, from whatever source derived, without apportionment among the several States, and without regard to any census or enumeration.

Amendment XVII

(Ratified April 8, 1913)

The Senate of the United States shall be composed of two Senators from each State, elected by the people thereof, for six years; and each Senator shall have one vote. The electors in each State shall have the qualifications requisite for electors of the most numerous branch of the State legislatures.

When vacancies happen in the representation of any State in the Senate, the executive authority of such State shall issue writs of election to fill such vacancies: *Provided,* That the legislature of any State may empower the executive thereof to make temporary appointments until the people fill the vacancies by election as the legislature may direct.

This amendment shall not be so construed as to affect the election or term of any Senator chosen before it becomes valid as part of the Constitution.

Amendment XVIII

(Ratified January 16, 1919)

Section 1. After one year from the ratification of this article the manufacture, sale, or transportation of intoxicating liquors within, the importation thereof into, or the exportation thereof from the United States and all territory subject to the jurisdiction thereof for beverage purposes is hereby prohibited.

Section 2. The Congress and the several States shall have concurrent power to enforce this article by appropriate legislation.

Section 3. This article shall be inoperative unless it shall have been ratified as an amendment to the Constitution by the legislatures of the several States, as provided in the Constitution, within seven years from the date of the submission hereof to the States by the Congress.][13]

Amendment XIX

(Ratified August 18, 1920)

The right of citizens of the United States to vote shall not be denied or abridged by the United States or by any State on account of sex.

Congress shall have power to enforce this article by appropriate legislation.

Amendment XX

(Ratified January 23, 1933)

Section 1. The terms of the President and Vice President shall end at noon on the 20th day of January, and the terms of Senators and Representatives at noon on the 3d day of January, of the years in which such terms would have ended if this article had not been ratified; and the terms of their successors shall then begin.

Section 2. The Congress shall assemble at least once in every year, and such meeting shall begin at noon on the 3d day of January, unless they shall by law appoint a different day.

Section 3.[14] If, at the time fixed for the beginning of the term of the President, the President elect shall have died, the Vice President elect shall become President. If a President shall not have been chosen before the time fixed for the beginning of his term, or if the President elect shall have failed to qualify, then the Vice President elect shall act as President until a President shall have qualified; and the Congress may by law provide for the case wherein neither a President elect nor a Vice President elect shall have qualified, declaring who shall then act as President, or the manner in which one who is to act shall be selected, and such person shall act accordingly until a President or Vice President shall have qualified.

Section 4. The Congress may by law provide for the case of the death of any of the persons from whom the House of Representatives may choose a President whenever the right of choice shall have devolved upon them, and for the case of the death of any of the persons from whom the Senate may choose a Vice President whenever the right of choice shall have devolved upon them.

Section 5. Sections 1 and 2 shall take effect on the 15th day of October following the ratification of this article.

Section 6. This article shall be inoperative unless it shall have been ratified as an amendment to the Constitution by the legislatures of three-fourths of the several States within seven years from the date of its submission.

Amendment XXI

(Ratified December 5, 1933)

Section 1. The eighteenth article of amendment to the Constitution of the United States is hereby repealed.

Section 2. The transportation or importation into any State, Territory, or possession of the United States for delivery or use therein of intoxicating liquors, in violation of the laws thereof, is hereby prohibited.

Section 3. This article shall be inoperative unless it shall have been ratified as an amendment to the Constitution by conventions in the several States, as provided in the Constitution, within seven years from the date of the submission hereof to the States by the Congress.

Amendment XXII

(Ratified February 27, 1951)

Section 1. No person shall be elected to the office of the President more than twice, and no person who has held the office of President, or acted as President, for more than two years of a term to which some other person was elected President shall be elected to the office of the President more than once. But this Article shall not apply to any person holding the office of President when this Article was proposed by the Congress, and shall not prevent any person who may be holding the office of President, or acting as President, during the term within which this Article become operative from holding the office of President or acting as President during the remainder of such term.

Section 2. This article shall be inoperative unless it shall have been ratified as an amendment to the Constitution by the legislatures of three-fourths of the several States within seven years from the date of its submission to the States by the Congress.

Amendment XXIII

(Ratified March 29, 1961)

Section 1. The District constituting the seat of Government of the United States shall appoint in such manner as the Congress may direct:
A number of electors of President and Vice President equal to the whole number of Senators and Representatives in Congress to which the District would be entitled if it were a State, but in no event more than the least populous State; they shall be in addition to those appointed by the States, but they shall be considered, for the purposes of the election of President and Vice President, to be electors appointed by a State; and they shall meet in the District and perform such duties as provided by the twelfth article of amendment.

Section 2. The Congress shall have power to enforce this article by appropriate legislation.

Amendment XXIV

(Ratified January 23, 1964)

Section 1. The right of citizens of the United States to vote in any primary or other election for President or Vice President, for electors for President or Vice President, or for Senator or Representative in Congress, shall not be denied or abridged by the United States or any State by reason of failure to pay any poll tax or other tax.

Section 2. The Congress shall have power to enforce this article by appropriate legislation.

Amendment XXV

(Ratified February 10, 1967)

Section 1. In case of the removal of the President from office or of his death or resignation, the Vice President shall become President.

Section 2. Whenever there is a vacancy in the office of the Vice President, the President shall nominate a Vice President who shall take office upon confirmation by a majority vote of both Houses of Congress.

Section 3. Whenever the President transmits to the President pro tempore of the Senate and the Speaker of the House of Representatives his written declaration that he is unable to discharge the powers and duties of his office, and until he transmits to them a written declaration to the contrary, such powers and duties shall be discharged by the Vice President as Acting President.

Section 4. Whenever the Vice President and a majority of either the principal officers of the executive departments or of such other body as Congress may by law provide, transmit to the President pro tempore of the Senate and the Speaker of the House of Representatives their written declaration that the President is unable to discharge the powers and duties of his office, the Vice President shall immediately assume the powers and duties of the office as Acting President.

Thereafter, when the President transmits to the President pro tempore of the Senate and the Speaker of the House of Representatives his written declaration that no inability exists, he shall resume the powers and duties of his office unless the Vice President and a majority of either the principal officers of the executive department or of such other body as Congress may by law provide, transmit within four days to the President pro tempore of the Senate and the Speaker of the House of Representatives their written declaration that the President is unable to discharge the powers and duties of his office. Thereupon Congress shall decide the issue, assembling within forty-eight hours for that purpose if not in session. If the Congress, within twenty-one days after receipt of the latter written declaration, or, if Congress is not in session, within twenty-one days after Congress is required to assemble, determines by two-thirds vote of both Houses that the President is unable to discharge the powers and duties of his office, the Vice President shall continue to discharge the same as Acting President; otherwise, the President shall resume the powers and duties of his office.

Amendment XXVI

(Ratified July 1, 1971)

Section 1. The right of citizens of the United States, who are eighteen years of age or older, to vote shall not be denied or abridged by the United States or by any State on account of age.

Section 2. The Congress shall have power to enforce this article by appropriate legislation.

Amendment XXVII

(Ratified May 7, 1992)

No law varying the compensation for the services of the Senators and Representatives shall take effect, until an election of Representatives shall have intervened.

Notes

1. The part in brackets was changed by section 2 of the Fourteenth Amendment.
2. The part in brackets was changed by the first paragraph of the Seventeenth Amendment.
3. The part in brackets was changed by the second paragraph of the Seventeenth Amendment.
4. The part in brackets was changed by section 2 of the Twentieth Amendment.
5. The Sixteenth Amendment gave Congress the power to tax incomes.
6. The material in brackets has been superseded by the Twelfth Amendment.
7. This provision has been affected by the Twenty-fifth Amendment.
8. These clauses were affected by the Eleventh Amendment.
9. This paragraph has been superseded by the Thirteenth Amendment.
10. Obsolete.
11. The part in brackets has been superseded by section 3 of the Twentieth Amendment.
12. See the Nineteenth and Twenty-sixth Amendments.
13. This Amendment was repealed by section 1 of the Twenty-first Amendment.
14. See the Twenty-fifth Amendment.

Source: House Committee on the Judiciary, *The Constitution of the United States of America, as Amended,* H. Doc. 100-94, 100th Cong., 1st sess., 1987.

Index

AT&T, 56, 91
ABF Freight System, Inc. v. National Labor Relations Board (1994), 106
Abortion, 10, 14-15, 26-31, 98-100. *See also Roe v. Wade* (1973)
Abortion clinics, 10, 19, 22-23, 25, 98-100, 266-291
 and Racketeer Influenced and Corrupt Organizations (RICO), 23-24, 113-118
ACLU. *See* American Civil Liberties Union (ACLU)
Adarand Constructors, Inc. v. Pena, 293
Administrative Procedure Act (APA), 94, 108
Affirmative action, 16, 293
Airline Deregulation Act, 297
Airline industry, 297
Air Transport Association, 297
Alabama
 jury selection, 37
 solid waste, 90
Albright v. Oliver (1994), 100
Allied-Bruce Terminix Companies, Inc. v. Dobson, 300
American Airlines v. Wolens, 297
American Association of Retired Persons (AARP), 306
American Bar Association, 48
American Civil Liberties Union (ACLU), 19, 48, 306
American Dredging Co. v. Miller (1994), 64-65
American Federation of Government Employees, 304
American Telephone & Telegraph Co. *See* AT&T
Amtrak, 304
AmWest Development, 119-131
Antarctica, 56

Anti-Drug Abuse Act (1988), 72, 85, 256
Anti-Head Tax Act (1973), 61
Anti-Injunction Act (1932), 260
Antitrust, 16
Arbitration, 300
Arkansas, 292, 295
Arkansas Writers' Project, Inc. v. Ragland (1987), 206, 207
Armed Career Criminal Act (1984), 84
Arnold, Richard, 1-2
Arrest, 71-72
Asgrow Seed Co., 299
Asgrow Seed Co. v. Winterboer, 299
Associated Industries of Missouri v. Lohman, Director of Revenue of Missouri (1994), 110
Attorney General of New York v. Grumet (1994), 168-193
Aviation law, 61
Aware Woman Center for Choice, 27-31, 267, 280. *See also* Abortion; Abortion clinics

Babbitt, Bruce, 1-2, 327
Bader, Celia, 336
Bais Rochel (school), 169
Balasar v. Illinois (1980), 84
Ballard v. United States (1946), 133
Banking law, 298
Bankruptcy law, 23-24, 60, 62
Barclays Bank PLC v. Franchise Tax Board of California (1994), 110-111
Beecham v. United States (1994), 83
Bentsen v. Adolph Coors Co., 304
Berger, Michael, 24
BFP v. Resolution Trust Corporation, as receiver of Imperial Federal Savings and Loan Association (1994), 62
Bible, Teresia, 37
Biden, Joseph, 16-17

Black Lung Benefits Act (1972), 108
Blackmun, Harry Andrew
  on abortion clinics, 30
  on bankruptcy law, 62
  biography, 340-341
  on cable television, 54, 96,
    210-211
  on church and state, 50, 51, 96, 177-
    178
  on Commerce Clause, 109-110
  on contempt, 12
  contempt of court decisions,
    68-69
  on criminal offenses, 76-77
  criminal offenses decisions,
    75-76
  on damage suits, 100, 101-102
  on the death penalty, 11-12, 15, 19,
    59-60, 73, 75, 341
  death penalty decisions, 46-49, 72-
    74, 256-261
  dissents, 11
  on evidence, 78
  on federal regulation, 91
  on freedom of speech, 97-98
  on hazardous waste, 89
  on insanity (criminal law), 80
  on interrogation, 80-81
  on interstate commerce, 11
  on job discrimination, 11,
    102-104
  on judicial disqualification, 70
  on juries, 82
  on jury selection, 12
  jury selection decisions, 36-39, 70-
    71, 131-136
  on labor relations, 105
  as a liberal, 11, 340
  on military law, 94
  mine safety decisions, 105-106
  on Native Americans, 95
  on property law, 39, 41,
    108-109, 162-163
  on reapportionment and
    redistricting, 33
  on remedies, 106-107
  remedies decisions, 107
  retirement of, 1, 6, 12, 338

  on securities law, 44, 46, 66-67,
    128-131
  on sentencing, 83-85
  on solid waste, 89-90
  on speedy trials, 85
  on taxation, 110
  taxation law decisions, 67-68
  on voting rights, 34, 35, 236, 238,
    244, 250-254
  on Voting Rights Act (1965),
    87-88
  on workers' compensation, 108
  on writ of certiorari, 60
Blakey, G. Robert, 27
Bleckley County (GA), 34,
  232-256. *See also* Voting rights
*Board of Education of Kiryas Joel
  Village School District v. Grumet*
  (1994), 49-52, 96, 168-193
*Board of Education of Monroe-
  Woodburg Central School District v.
  Grumet* (1994), 168-193
*Boca Grande Club, Inc. v. Florida
  Power & Light Co., Inc.* (1994), 65
Bokat, Stephen, 12, 19, 24, 57
Bolick, Clint, 19, 33, 36, 41
Bonner Mall Partnership, 299
Bork, Robert H., 331
Bowman, James, 37
Brafield, Lois, 39
Brandeis, Louis, 339
Breaking the Vicious Circle (Breyer), 5
Brennan, William J., 324, 340
Breyer, Joanna Hare, 13, 339
Breyer, Stephen Gerald, 55
  on abortion, 15
  on affirmative action, 16
  on antitrust, 16
  appointment of, 1-3
  as a moderate, 12
  biography, 3-6, 338-339
  Breaking the Vicious Circle (1993),
    5
  confirmation proceedings, 12-18
  and the Environmental Protection
    Agency (EPA), 13, 16
  on the Fourteenth Amendment, 16
  judicial decision making, 15

Lloyds of London investment, 13-14, 16, 17, 339
  on property law, 15
  and social security taxes, 16-17
  and the U.S. Sentencing Commission, 4-5
  on women's rights, 16
Brown v. Gardner, 303
Bryant v. Hill, 292
Buffer zones. *See* Abortion clinics
Burden of proof, 21, 76-77
Burger, Warren E., 254, 329, 340
Burns, Conrad, 17
Bush, George, 14, 32, 53, 102, 103, 111, 300, 332
Business law, 57, 61-68, 297-299
  aviation law, 61
  banking law, 23-24, 60, 298
  bankruptcy law, 62
  copyright, 62-63
  frequent flyer miles, 297
  insurance law, 64, 298
  interstate commerce, 22
  maritime law, 64-66, 298
  Plant Variety Protection Act (1970), 298-299
  protectionism, 22
  securities law, 66-67, 297-298
  taxation law, 67-68

Cable News Network (CNN), 55, 216
Cable television, 6, 21-22, 52-55, 95-96, 193-219. *See also* Television
Cable Television Consumer Protection and Competition Act (1992), 95, 193, 195, 196, 211, 213, 214
California, 238
  bankruptcy law, 62
  damage suits, 101
  death penalty, 11, 75
  federal courts, 69
  juries, 82
  labor law, 107-108
  settlements, 71
  taxation, 111
California Supreme Court, 81

Callins v. Collins, Director, Texas Department of Criminal Justice, Institutional Division (1994), 11
Campaign literature, anonymous, 302
Campbell, a/k/a/ Skyywalker v. Acuff-Rose Music, Inc. (1994), 62-63
Capital punishment. *See* Death penalty
Cardozo, Benjamin, 176, 339
Carswell, G. Harrold, 341
Carter, Jimmy, 4, 111, 337, 339
Carter, John, 301
Casey v. Planned Parenthood (1992), 15
Caspari, Superintendent, Missouri Eastern Correctional Center v. Bohlen (1994), 79-80
C & A Carbone, Inc. v. Town of Clarktown (1994), 89-90
Central Bank of Denver, 44-46, 66-67, 119-131
Central Bank of Denver, N.A. v. First Interstate Bank of Denver, N.A., and Jack K. Naber (1994), 44-46, 66-67, 119-131
Chemerinsky, Erwin, 20
Child pornography, 302
Church and state, 8, 22, 49-52, 96, 168-193
City of Chicago v. Environmental Defense Fund (1994), 88-89
City of Ladue v. Gilleo (1994), 97
Civil lawsuits, 60
Civil liberties, 57. *See also* First Amendment
Civil rights, 293. *See also* Equal Protection Clause; Individual rights; Job discrimination; Racial redistricting; Voting rights
Civil Rights Act (1964), 104, 191
Civil servants. *See* Federal employees
Class action lawsuits, 60
Clayton, Fay, 27
Clean Water Act (1972), 91

Clinton, Bill
  appointment of Ruth Bader
    Ginsburg, 337, 339
  appointment of Stephen Breyer, 1-3,
    12-18, 338
Clinton administration
  on abortion, 29
  on airline industry, 297
  on child pornography, 302
  and Equal Employment Opportu-
    nity Commission, 57
  on federal employees, 304
  on harmless error, 302
  on honoraria, 304
  on jury selection, 38
  on Plant Variety Protection Act
    (1970), 299
  on property law, 41
  on securities law, 45
  on taxation, 111
  and term limitations, 296
  on vacating judgments, 299
CNN. *See* Cable News Network
Coats, Dan, 17
Coffee, John, 46
Colgate-Palmolive Co., 111
Colorado National Bank, 44-46
Colorado Springs-Stetson Hills Public
  Building Authority, 119
Commerce Clause, 89-90, 109-110
Commercial speech, 97, 304
Committee for Public Education &
  Religious Liberty v. Nyquist (1973),
  171
Communications Act (1934), 207
Community Development Code
  (CDC) (Oregon), 154-168
Comprehensive Environmental
  Response, Compensation and
  Liability Act (1980, 1986), 89
Comptroller of the Currency, 298
Congress, term limitations, 292,
  294-297
Connor, Martin, 43
Conrail, 107
Consolidated Rail Corporation v.
  Gottshall (1994), 106-107

Constitution
  Eighth Amendment, 21
  Cruel and Unusual Punishment
    Clause, 79, 335
  Fifteenth Amendment, 34, 233
  Fifth Amendment, 39, 158
  Takings Clause, 24, 41, 157, 160,
    165, 166
  First Amendment. *See* separate en-
    try
  Fourteenth Amendment. *See*
    separate entry
  Fourth Amendment, 100, 180
  Nineteenth Amendment, 133
  Sixth Amendment, 133
  text of, 348-366
Constitutional law, 21. *See also* Due
  Process Clause; Equal Protection
  Clause; First Amendment
Contempt, 12
Contempt of court, 68-69
Coors Brewing Co., 304
Copyright Act, 63
Copyright law, 21, 62-63
Corporation for Public Broadcasting
  (CPB), 203
County liability, 306-307
Courts and procedure, 68-71,
  299-300
  arbitration, 300
  contempt of court, 68-69
  federal courts, 69
  judicial disqualification, 70
  jury selection, 70-71
  settlements, 71
  vacating judgments, 299-300
Coverdell, Paul, 17
Cox, Archibald, 4
Creedence Clearwater Revival
  (musical group), 63
Criminal law, 7, 20, 24, 71-86,
  300-302
  arrest, 71-72
  child pornography, 302
  criminal offenses, 75-77
  death penalty. *See* separate entry
  double jeopardy, 77
  evidence, 78

forfeiture, 78-79
Gun-Free School Zone Act (1990), 300-301
habeas corpus, 79-80
harmless error, 301-302
insanity, 80
interrogation, 80-82
juries, 82
prisons and jails, 82-83
sentencing, 83-85
speedy trial, 85-86
Criminal offenses, 75-77
Cruel and Unusual Punishment Clause, 79, 335
C-SPAN (television network), 55, 216
Cuomo, Mario, 52, 170
Curtis v. United States (1994), 83-84
Cutler, Lloyd, 2, 13

Dalton, Secretary of the Navy v. Specter (1994), 93-94
Damage suits, 100-102
Danforth, John C., 335
Davis v. United States (1994), 80-81
Days, Drew S., 53, 296, 304
de Grandy, Miguel, 32, 33, 219-231
Death penalty, 12, 14-15, 19, 46-49, 72-75, 256-266, 301
  in California, 11
  habeas corpus, 47, 48, 256-266, 301
Defense Base Closure and Realignment Act (1990), 93-94
Delaware Women's Health Organization, Inc. (DWHO), 26, 113-118. *See also* Abortion; Abortion clinics
Department of Revenue of Oregon v. ACF Industries, Inc. (1994), 111-112
Department of Taxation and Finance of New York v. Milhelm Attea & Bros., Inc. (1994), 112
Desktop Direct (corporation), 71
Digital Equipment Corporation, 71
Digital Equipment Corp. v. Desktop Direct, Inc. (1994), 71

Director, Office of Workers' Compensation Programs, Department of Labor v. Greenwich Collieries (1994), 108
Disability rights, 102
Discovery Channel, 55, 216
Dobson, Wanda and Michael, 300
Dolan, Dan, 39, 41
Dolan, Florence, 39, 154-168
Dolan, John, 39-40
Dolan v. City of Tigard (1994), 39-41, 108-109, 154-168
Dole, Robert, 337
Double jeopardy, 10, 11, 77
Double Jeopardy Clause, 10, 11, 21, 74, 77, 79-80
Douglas, William O., 325
Drug paraphernalia, 75-76
Drugs, 77
Due Process Clause, 42-43, 68, 113, 143-144, 147, 149, 150, 153, 165

Eighth Amendment, 21
  Cruel and Unusual Punishment Clause, 79, 335
Eisenhower, Dwight D., 341
Elder v. Holloway (1994), 100-101
Election law, 86-88, 302-303
  anonymous campaign literature, 302
  Federal Election Commission (FEC), 302-303
  reapportionment and redistricting, 86-87. *See also* Reapportionment and redistricting; Voting Rights Act (1965)
Ellis, Deborah, 38
Employment Retirement Income Security Act (ERISA), 64
Environmental law, 23, 88-91
  hazardous waste, 88-89
  solid waste, 89-90
  water, 90-91
Environmental Protection Agency (EPA), 13, 16, 88
Equal Opportunity Employment Commission (EEOC), 57
Equal Protection Clause, 33, 70, 131-132, 136-138, 139, 141, 160, 180, 183, 231

Erie Railroad Co. v. Tompkins (1938), 69

ERISA. See Employee Retirement Income Security Act (ERISA)

Establishment Clause, 169, 171-172, 174-176, 178, 181-185, 187-188, 191

Ethics Reform Act (1989), 303-304

Evidence, 78

Exchange Act (1975), 129, 130

Farmer v. Brennan, Warden (1994), 82-83

Farr, H. Barstow, 53

FCC. *See* Federal Communication Commission (FCC)

FDA. *See* Food and Drug Administration (FDA)

FEC v. NRA Political Victory Fund, 303

Federal Arbitration Act, 300

Federal Communications Commission (FCC), 53, 91, 193-219

Federal courts, 69

Federal Deposit Insurance Corporation (FDIC), 69, 101

Federal Deposit Insurance Corporation v. Meyer (1994), 101

Federal Election Commission (FEC), 302-303

Federal employees, 293, 303-304. *See also* Public employees

Federal Employers' Liability Act (FELA) (1988), 107

Federal government, 22, 91-95, 303
  commercial speech, 304
  employees, 293, 303-304
  employment discrimination, 22
  federal regulation, 91-92
  freedom of information, 93
  military, 93-95
  Native Americans, 95, 112
  railway stations, 304
  veterans hospitals, 303

Federal Labor Relations Authority, 93

Federal regulation, 90-91

Federal Rules of Civil Procedure, 60, 114

Federal Rules of Evidence, 78

Feminist Majority Foundation, 280

Fifteenth Amendment, 34
  and voting rights, 233

Fifth Amendment, 158
  property law, 39
  Takings Clause, 24, 41, 157, 160, 165, 166

Firearms. *See* Guns

First Amendment, 6, 21, 25, 95-98, 166, 303-304
  and abortion, 29, 30
  and abortion clinics, 19, 22, 27, 266-291
  anonymous campaign literature, 302
  and cable television, 52-54, 95-96, 194, 197-200, 205-208, 210-215, 218
  church and state, 96
  commercial speech, 97
  Establishment Clause, 169, 171-172, 174, 175-176, 178, 180-185, 187-188, 191
  freedom of speech, 97-98, 266-291
  Free Exercise Clause, 171
  Free Speech Clause, 180
  honoraria, 303-304
  and Racketeer Influenced and Corrupt Organizations (RICO), 117-118
  religion clauses, 180, 175, 187

First Interstate Bank of Denver, 44-46, 66-67, 120

Florence County School District Four v. Cater (1993), 102

Florida
  abortion clinics, 99, 266-291
  commercial speech, 97
  election districts, 219-231
  election law, 86-87
  evidence, 78
  voting districts, 31-33

Florida Supreme Court, 28-39, 268, 269, 272, 274, 277

Fogerty, John, 63

Fogerty v. Fantasy, Inc. (1994), 63

Foley, Thomas, 295-296

FOIA. *See* Freedom of Information Act (FOIA)

Food and Drug Administration
(FDA), 329-330
Ford, Gerald R., 325, 331-332
Foreclosure, 62
Forfeiture, 10, 21, 78-79
Fourteenth Amendment, 16, 34, 145,
157, 165
due process, 100
Due Process Clause, 143-144,
147-150, 153, 165
Equal Protection Clause, 131, 132,
136-139, 141, 160
and voting rights, 233
Fourth Amendment, 180
unreasonable search and seizure,
100
Free Exercise Clause, 171
Free Speech Clause, 180, 181
Freedom of expression, public
employees, 21
Freedom of Information Act (FOIA)
(1976), 93
Freedom of speech, 97-98
and abortion clinics, 19, 26-31,
98-99, 113-118, 266-291
Frequent flyer miles, 297
Frey, Andrew, 42-43
Friedman, Barry, 24
Frisby v. Schultz (1988), 275, 276

Gardner, Fred, 303
Georgia, 34
judicial disqualification, 70
voting rights, 232-256
Voting Rights Act (1965), 87-88
Georgia v. McCollum (1992), 37, 131,
138
Ginsburg, Douglas H., 331
Ginsburg, Martin, 336
Ginsburg, Ruth Bader, 1
on abortion, 337
on abortion clinics, 30
arrest decisions, 71-72
aviation law decisions, 61
on bankruptcy law, 62
biography, 335-337
on cable television, 6, 52, 55, 95-96,
213-218, 218-219

on church and state, 50, 96, 178-179
commercial speech decisions, 97
confirmation of, 17-18
on contempt of court, 69
on criminal law, 7
on criminal offenses, 77
criminal offenses decisions, 76
damage suit decisions, 100-101
on damage suits, 101-102
on the death penalty, 7, 48, 73, 75
on evidence, 78
on federal regulation, 91-92, 92
on the First Amendment, 6
on freedom of information, 93
on freedom of speech, 98
insurance law decisions, 64
on jury selection, 38
on labor relations, 105
on military law, 94, 95
on property law, 39, 41, 108-109,
162-167
on punitive damages, 42-43,
112-113, 149-153
questioning style, 7-8, 337
on reapportionment and
redistricting, 33
on remedies, 106-107
on securities law, 44, 46, 66-67,
128-131
on sentencing, 84-85
sentencing decisions, 85
on sexual harassment, 105
speedy trial decisions, 85-86
taxation decisions, 110-111
on voting rights, 6, 34, 35, 250-254,
254
on Voting Rights Act (1965), 87-88
on women's rights, 6
Goldberg, Arthur J., 4, 338
Goldwater, Barry, 324
Good, James Daniel, 78-79
Gramm-Rudman-Hollings Budget
Balancing Act (1985), 330
Great Lakes Dredge & Dock Co., 298
Grumet, Louis, 52
Gun-Free School Zone Act (1990),
300-301

Guns, 76-77, 293
Gustafson v. Alloyd Co., Inc., 298

Habeas corpus, 72, 74, 79-80, 86
and the death penalty, 47, 48,
256-266, 301
harmless error, 301-302
Hagen v. Utah (1994), 95
Hall, Cynthia Holcomb, 325
Hardy, Charles, 104-105
Harmless error, 301-302
Harris, Louise, 301
Harris, Reginald, 78
Harris, Teresa, 104-105
Harris v. Alabama, 301
Harris v. Forklift Systems, Inc. (1993),
104-105
Hatch, Orrin, 2-3, 17, 339
Hawaii, 78-79
Hawaiian Airlines, 107
Hawaiian Airlines, Inc. v. Norris
(1994), 107
Haynsworth, Clement, 341
Hazardous waste, 88-89
Health and Human Services Dept.
(HHS), 92
Heck v. Humphrey (1994), 101-102
Helms, Jesse, 17
Herman & McLean v. Huddleston
(1983), 119
HHS. *See* Health and Human
Services Dept. (HHS)
Hill, Anita F., 335
Hill, Bobbie, 295
Hobbs Anti-Racketeering Act (1934),
114
Holder, Jackie, 34, 36, 232-256
Holder v. Hall (1994), 33, 34-36,
87-88, 232-256
Holmes, Oliver W., 166
Honda Motor Co., 42-43, 112-113,
143-153
Honda Motor Co. v. Oberg (1994), 42-
43, 112-113, 143-153
Honoraria, 303-304
Howlett v. Birkdale Shipping Co., S.A.
(1994), 65
Hutchinson, Dennis, 24, 296

Ibanez, Silva Safille, 97
*Ibanez v. Florida Department of Busi-
ness and Professional Regulation,
Board of Accountancy* (1994), 97
ICC. *See* Interstate Commerce Com-
mission (ICC)
Indiana
damage suits, 101-102
speedy trials, 86
Indian reservations, 112
Indian Trader Statutes, 112
Individual rights, 20, 98-105, 306-307
abortion, 26-27, 98-100, 266-291.
See also separate entry
county liability, 306-307
damage suits, 100-102
disability rights, 102
job discrimination, 102-104, 306
sexual harassment, 104-105
Individuals with Disabilities
Education Act (1991), 102
Insanity (criminal law), 80
Insanity Defense Reform Act (1984),
80
Insurance law, 64, 298
Internal Revenue Code, 68. *See also*
Taxation
Internal Revenue Service (IRS), 68,
76. *See also* Taxation
Interrogation, 80-82
Interstate Agreement on Detainers
(IAD), 86
Interstate commerce, 11, 22, 61
Interstate Commerce Commission
(ICC), 92
IRS. *See* Internal Revenue Service

J. E. B. v. Alabama ex rel T. B.
(1994), 36-39, 70-71, 131-142
Jackson, Robert H., 30, 290, 324
Jackson v. Vasquez (1993), 263-264
Japanese-Americans, 30-31, 290-291
Job discrimination, 11, 102-104, 306
*John Hancock Mutual Life Insurance
Co. v. Harris Trust & Savings Bank,
as Trustee of Sperry Master Retire-
ment Trust No. 2* (1993), 64
Johnson, Robert, 232-256

Johnson, Speaker of the Florida House of Representatives v. de Grandy (1994), 31-33, 86-87, 219-231
Judges, military, 94-95
Judicial disqualification, 70
Juries, 21, 82
Jury instruction, 20
Jury selection, 12, 70-71
  and gender, 25, 36-39, 131-142
  and race, 132, 134, 140
Justice Dept., 220, 231

Kennedy, Anthony McLeod, 7
  on abortion, 98-99, 100, 117-118, 331
  on abortion clinics, 26, 29, 279-291
  biography, 330-332
  cable television decisions, 52-55, 95-96, 193-210
  on church and state, 10, 50, 182-185
  as a conservative, 8, 10, 330
  on criminal offenses, 76
  on damage suits, 100
  on the death penalty, 48, 74-75, 259
  death penalty decisions, 75
  on double jeopardy, 10
  on evidence, 78
  federal regulation decisions, 92
  on forfeiture, 10
  forfeiture decisions, 78-79
  on freedom of speech, 27, 98
  ideology of, 6
  on insurance law, 64
  on judicial disqualification, 70
  on jury selection, 38, 138-139
  labor relations decisions, 105
  as a liberal, 10
  on maritime law, 64-65
  maritime law decisions, 65
  on military law, 94
  as a moderate, 8
  on property law, 41
  on reapportionment and redistricting, 33, 230-231
  on school prayer, 331

securities law decisions, 44-46, 66-67, 119-128
  on sentencing, 85
  solid waste decisions, 89-90
  on speedy trials, 85-86
  taxation decisions, 111-112
  on voting rights, 35, 236, 237, 238
  Voting Rights Act decisions, 87-88
  voting rights decisions, 34-36, 232-236
  on writ of certiorari, 60
Kennedy, Edward, 2, 4, 17, 339
Kent County International Airport (Grand Rapids, MI), 61
Key Tronic Corp. v. United States (1994), 89
King, Martin Luther, 27
Kiryas Joel (NY), 49-52, 96, 168-193
Kleindienst, Richard G., 324
Kmiec, Douglas, 20, 31, 52
Kokkonen v. Guardian Life Insurance Co. of America (1994), 71
Korematsu v. United States (1944), 30-31, 290-291
Kyles, Curtis Lee, 301
Kyles v. Whitley, 301

Labor law, 25, 105-108
  mine safety, 105-106
  remedies, 106-108
  workers' compensation, 108
Labor relations, 105
Lampf, Pleva, Lipkind, Prupis & Petigrow v. Gilbertson (1991), 67
Landgraf v. USI Film Products (1994), 102-103, 104
Land-use policy, 8. *See also* Property law
Larkin v. Grendel's Den, Inc. (1982), 171, 172, 174, 176, 178, 181, 186
Lawyers' Committee for Civil Rights Under Law (organization), 306
Leahy, Norm, 296
Leathers v. Medlock (1991), 198, 206
Lebron v. National Railroad Passenger Corporation (Amtrak), 304

Lee v. Weisman (1992), 180, 181
Lemon v. Kurtzman (1971), 50, 51, 171, 178, 180, 182
Levitt, Arthur, 46
Liteky v. United States (1994), 70
Livadas v. Bradshaw, California Labor Commissioner (1994), 107-108
Lloyds of London (investment), 13-14, 16, 17, 339
Local laws, unconstitutional, 23 (table)
Lochner v. New York (1905), 165, 166
Lockhart v. United States (1983), 251
Longshore and Harbor Workers' Compensation Act (1972), 65, 108
Lopez, Alfonso, 300
Lott, Trent, 17
Louisiana, maritime law, 64-65
Ludwig v. Variable Annuity Life Insurance Co., 298
Lugar, Richard, 17, 339

Madsen v. Women's Health Center, Inc. (1994), 26-27, 98-99, 266-291. *See also* Abortion; Abortion clinics
Maislin Industries, U.S., Inc., v. Primary Steel (1990), 92
Maritime law, 64-66, 298
Marshall, Thurgood, 334, 340
Maryland, sentencing in, 84
McDermott, Inc. v. AmClyde (1994), 65-66
McDonald, Laughlin, 36
McFarland, Frank Basil, 46-49, 256-266
McFarland v. Scott, Director, Texas Department of Criminal Justice, Institutional Division (1994), 46-49, 72-73, 256-266
McGregor, Robert, 28, 280, 287
McIntyre, Margaret and Joseph, 302
McIntyre v. Ohio Elections Commission, 302
MCI Telecommunications Corp. v. American Telephone & Telegraph Co. (1994), 90-91
McKennon, Christine, 306
McKennon v. Nashville Banner Publishing Co., 306

Medicare, 92
Merrett 418 (Lloyds of London investment), 13
Metzenbaum, Howard, 3, 13, 16, 17, 339
Military justice system, 22
Military law, 93-95
Mine safety, 105-106
Mine Safety and Health Administration, 106
Miranda rule, 8, 20, 80, 81
Mississippi
    freedom of information, 93
    insanity (criminal law), 80
    maritime law, 64-65
Missouri
    habeas corpus, 79-80
    taxation, 110
Missouri Supreme Court, 110
Mitchell, Cleta, 296-297
Mitchell, George, 1, 1-2, 339
Money Laundering Act (1986), 76
Monroe-Woodbury Central School District (N.Y.), 168-193
Montana, illegal drugs in, 11, 21, 77
Montana Department of Revenue v. Kurth Ranch (1994), 77
Morales, Dan, 49
Morales v. Trans World Airline, Inc. (1992), 297
Morgan, James, 306-307
Morgan Stanley & Co., Inc. v. Pacific Mutual Life Insurance Co. (1994), 67, 298
Moshofsky, Bill, 41
Multinational corporations, taxation, 22
Murkowski, Frank H., 17

Naber, Jack, 120
Nader, Ralph, 3, 17
National Association of Broadcasters, 55
National Association for the Advancement of Colored People (NAACP), 220
    Cochran/Bleckley County Chapter, 232-256

National Cable Television Association, 55

National Firearms Act (1968), 76

National Labor Relations Board (NLRB), 25, 105, 106

National Labor Relations Board v. Health Care & Retirement Corporation of America (1994), 105

National Organization for Women, Inc. v. Scheidler (1994), 26-27, 99-100, 113-118

National Organization for Women (NOW), 26, 113-118

National Railroad Passenger Corporation. *See* Amtrak

National Treasury Employees Union, 304

NationsBank of North Carolina v. Variable Annuity Life Insurance, 298

Native Americans, 95, 112

Natural gas industry, 56

Nebraska, juries in, 82

Nevada, criminal law in, 71-72

Nevada Supreme Court, 72

New Hampshire, 238

New Inspirational Network (television network), 216

New Jersey, 238
  maritime law, 65

New Mexico, 176
  labor law, 106

Nichols v. United States (1994), 84-85

Nickles, Don, 17

Nineteenth Amendment, 133

Nixon, Richard, 324, 326, 341

North Briton (publication), 145

Northwest Airlines, Inc., v. Kent County (1994), 61

NOW. *See* National Organization for Women (NOW)

Oberg, Karl, 42-43, 143-153

O'Connor, John J., 327

O'Connor, Sandra Day, 7
  on abortion, 328, 331
  on abortion clinics, 30, 279-280
  biography, 326-328
  on cable television, 52, 54-55, 95-96, 213-218
  on church and state, 50, 52, 178-182
  on commercial speech, 97
  as a conservative, 8
  on contracts for minorities, 328
  on criminal offenses, 76, 77
  on death penalty, 46, 48-49, 72-73, 259, 261-262, 328
  death penalty decisions, 73-75
  disability rights decisions, 102
  on double jeopardy, 11, 77
  evidence decisions, 78
  on federal regulation, 92
  on forfeiture, 78-79
  freedom of speech decisions, 97-98
  on habeas corpus, 328
  habeas corpus decisions, 79-80
  on hazardous waste, 88-89
  ideology of, 6, 8
  on insurance law, 64
  interrogation decisions, 80-81
  jury decisions, 82
  on jury selection, 37, 38, 137-138, 140
  on land-use policy, 8
  on military law, 94
  Native American decisions, 95
  on property law, 41, 59
  on punitive damages, 8, 59
  on reapportionment and redistricting, 33, 229-230
  on remedies, 106
  on securities law, 8, 45, 298
  sentencing decisions, 83
  sexual harassment decisions, 104-105
  on solid waste, 90
  on taxation law, 68, 110-111
  on voting rights, 35, 232-236, 236-238, 244, 251
  on Voting Rights Act (1965), 88
  water law decisions, 90-91
  workers' compensation decisions, 108
  on writ of certiorari, 60

Oklahoma, death penalty in, 73
Olympic National Forest (WA), 90-91
O'Melveny & Myers v. Federal Deposit Insurance Corporation, as receiver for American Diversified Savings Bank (1994), 69
Operation Rescue, 26-28. *See also* Abortion; Abortion clinics
Orbison, Roy, 62
Oregon
  criminal offenses, 76
  property law, 39-41, 108-109, 154-168
  punitive damages, 112-113
  solid waste, 90
  taxation, 111-112
Oregon Constitution, 143, 149
Oregonians in Action (organization), 39, 41
Oregon Waste Systems, Inc. v. Department of Environmental Quality (1994), 90
Organized Crime Control Act of 1970, 113
Owens, Wilber C., 34

PBS. *See* Public Broadcasting System (PBS)
Pennsylvania, maritime law in, 65
Peterson, Edwin J., 161
Philadelphia Naval Shipyard, 94
Pitt, Harvey, 46
Plant Variety Protection Act (1970), 298-299
Plaut v. Spendthrift Farm, Inc., 67, 298
Pornography, child, 302
Porter, John, 37-39
Posters 'n' Things, Ltd. v. United States (1994), 75-76
Powell, Adam Clayton, 294
Powell, C. J., on voting rights, 254
Powell, Kitrick, 71-72
Powell, Lewis F., 324, 330-331
Powell v. McCormack (1969), 294

Powell v. Nevada (1994), 71-72
"Pretty Woman" (song), 62-63
Prisons and jails, 82-83
Privacy Act (1974), 93
Pro-Life Action Network (PLAN), 26, 99, 113-118. *See also* Abortion; Abortion clinics
Property law, 39-41, 108-109, 154-168
Property rights, 10, 15, 21, 24, 39-41
Protectionism, 22
Public Broadcasting System (PBS), 55, 216
Public employees, 98
  freedom of expression, 21. *See also* Federal employees
PUD No. 1 of Jefferson County v. Washington Department of Ecology (1994), 90-91
Punitive damages, 24, 42-43, 112-113, 143-153

Racial harassment, 103
Racial redistricting, 8, 31-33, 86-87, 219-231
Racketeer Influenced and Corrupt Organizations (RICO), 10, 26-27, 99-100, 113-118
  and abortion, 23-24, 113-118
Railroad industry, 106-107, 111-112, 304
Railway Labor Act (RLA), 107
Railway stations, 304
Ratzlaf v. United States (1994), 76
Reagan, Ronald, 111, 323, 328, 329, 330, 339
Reapportionment and redistricting, 19, 31-33, 219-231. *See also* Election law; Voting Rights Act (1965)
Redistricting. *See* Reapportionment and redistricting
Reed v. Farley, Superintendent, Indiana State Prison (1994), 85-86
Regulatory law, 20
Rehnquist, William Hubbs, 327
  on abortion, 10, 323
  on abortion clinics, 279-280
  abortion decisions, 26-27, 29-30, 98-99, 113-118, 266-277

on arrest, 71-72
biography, 323-325
on cable television, 54, 96
on church and state, 49, 50, 51, 96, 185-193
on Commerce Clause, 109-110
on commercial speech, 97
as a conservative, 8, 10, 12
on contempt of court, 69
copyright law decisions, 63
on criminal offenses, 76
damage suit decisions, 100
on the death penalty, 46, 48, 72-73, 74-75, 262-266
death penalty decisions, 73
on double jeopardy, 11, 77
on evidence, 78
on forfeiture, 78-79
on freedom of speech, 98
freedom of speech decisions, 26-27, 29-30
ideology of, 6
on individual rights, 323
on jury selection, 36, 38, 70-71, 139-140
military decisions, 93-94
on property law, 10, 24
property law decisions, 39-41, 108-109, 154-162
on punitive damages, 42-43, 59, 112-113, 149-153
on reapportionment and redistricting, 32, 33
on securities law, 45
on sentencing, 85
sentencing decisions, 83-84
on solid waste, 89-90
on voting rights, 35, 231-236, 254
on Voting Rights Act (1965), 88
on writ of certiorari, 60
Reich, Charles, 307
Reich v. Collins, 307
Remedies (labor law), 106-108
Resource Conservation and Recovery Act (1976), 88
Rhode Island, voting rights in, 237-238
RICO. *See* Racketeer Influenced and Corrupt Organization (RICO)

Rivers v. Roadway Express, Inc. (1994), 102-104
Roe v. Wade (1973), 10, 15, 29, 272, 323, 331, 333, 337, 340. *See also* Abortion
Romano v. Oklahoma (1994), 73
"Run Through the Jungle" (song), 63
Rutledge, Wiley B., 325

Sanborn, John B., 341
Sandoval v. California, 82
Satmar Hasidim (religious group), 49-52, 96, 168-193
Scalia, Antonin, 7
on abortion, 98-99, 329-330
on abortion clinics, 19, 26, 29, 30-31, 271, 273, 279-291
on affirmative action, 329
bankruptcy law decisions, 62
biography, 328-330
on cable television, 55, 95-96, 213-218
on church and state, 49, 50, 51, 96, 176, 177, 185-193
on civil rights, 59
on Commerce Clause, 109-110
as a conservative, 8, 10-11, 329, 335
on criminal law, 11
on criminal offenses, 76
damage suit decisions, 101-102
on the death penalty, 12, 46, 48, 74, 262-266
on deregulation, 329
dissensions, 11
on double jeopardy, 11, 77
on environmental law, 23
federal courts decisions, 69
federal regulation decisions, 91
on forfeiture, 78-79
on freedom of speech, 19
on hazardous waste, 89
hazardous waste decisions, 88-89
ideology of, 6
judicial disqualification decisions, 70
on jury selection, 36, 38, 57, 70-71, 140, 140-142
and legislative histories, 15
maritime law decisions, 64-65

on military law, 94
on property law, 41, 59
on punitive damages, 42-43, 144, 149
questioning style, 11
on reapportionment and redistricting, 31, 33, 86-87, 231
on remedies, 106
on securities law, 45
on sentencing, 85
settlements decisions, 71
on sexual harassment, 104-105
on statutory law, 22
on taxation law, 68
on voting rights, 238-249
on Voting Rights Act (1965), 88
on water law, 90-91
Scheidler, Joseph, 26, 113, 114
Schiro, Thomas, 73-74
Schiro v. Farley, Superintendent, Indiana State Prison (1994), 73-74
Schlup, Lloyd E., 301
Schlup v. Delo, 301
School desegregation, 293
Schools
guns in, 293
prayer in, 331
Securities Exchange Act (1934), 44
Securities Act (1933), 121, 123, 297-298
Securities Act (1934), 121, 122, 123, 124, 127
Securities Exchange Act (1934), 22, 66, 119, 128, 129
Securities and Exchange Commission (SEC), 46, 121, 124, 125, 126, 127, 130
Securities law, 22, 44-46, 66-67, 119-131, 297-298
Security Services, Inc. v. Kmart Corp. (1994), 91-92
Sekulow, Jay Alan, 30
Sentencing, 83-85
Settlements, 71
Sexual harassment, 25, 103, 104-105
Shannon v. United States (1994), 80
Shapiro, Stephen, 11, 57
Shaw, Theodore, 33

Shaw v. Reno (1993), 31, 33, 231, 239, 248
Sherman Antitrust Act (1976), 26, 113, 114, 255
Simmons v. South Carolina (1994), 74-75
Sixth Amendment, 133
Small Business Act (1993), 293
Smeal, Eleanor, 30-31
Smith, David, 40
Smith, Robert C., 17
Smith, William French, 327
Solid waste, 89-90
Souter, David Hackett, 7
on abortion, 100, 117-118, 331, 333
on abortion clinics, 30, 277
on bankruptcy law, 62
biography, 332-333
on cable television, 96
on church and state, 8, 186-187
church and state decisions, 49-52, 96, 168-185
confirmation proceedings, 14
copyright law decisions, 62-63
on damage suits, 100, 101-102
on the death penalty, 48, 73
on evidence, 78
on federal regulation, 91
federal regulation decisions, 91-92
on freedom of information, 93
on freedom of speech, 27, 98
ideology of, 6, 8
on interrogation, 80-81
on judicial disqualification, 70
on juries, 82
on jury selection, 38
on labor relations, 105
on military law, 94
on Native Americans, 95
prisons and jails decisions, 82-83
on property law, 39, 41, 108-109, 167-168
on racial redistricting, 8
on reapportionment and redistricting, 33
reapportionment and redistricting decisions, 31-33, 86-87, 219-229
remedies decisions, 107-108

on school prayer, 333
on securities law, 44, 46, 66-67
on sentencing, 83-84, 85
settlements decisions, 71
on solid waste, 89-90
on speedy trials, 85-86
taxation law decisions, 68
on voting rights, 34, 35, 250-254, 254-256
on Voting Rights Act (1965), 87-88
on workers' compensation, 108
South Carolina, 238
death penalty, 74-75
disability rights, 102
and parole, 59
Spector, Arlen, 94
Stansbury v. California (1994), 81
Staples v. United States (1994), 76-77
Starr, Kenneth, 56
State laws, unconstitutional, 23 (table)
States law, 109-112, 307
commerce clause, 109-110
taxation, 110-112, 307
Statutory law, 20
Stetson Hills, 119
Stevens, John Paul, 7
on abortion, 99, 326
on abortion clinics, 30, 271, 277-279
on antisodomy laws, 326
on bankruptcy law, 62
biography, 325-328
on cable television, 54, 96, 211-212
on church and state, 50, 96, 177-179
Commerce Clause decisions, 109-110
on criminal offenses, 76-77
on damage suits, 100, 101-102
on the death penalty, 48, 73, 75, 326
double jeopardy decisions, 77
on evidence, 78
on federal regulation, 90, 92
on freedom of speech, 97-98
freedom of speech decisions, 97
on habeas corpus, 79-80
on hazardous waste, 88-89
hazardous waste decisions, 89
ideology of, 6
on insanity (criminal law), 80

on interrogation, 80-81
job discrimination decisions, 102-103, 103-104
on judicial disqualification, 70
on jury selection, 38
on labor relations, 105
as a liberal, 11, 12
maritime law decisions, 65, 66
on military law, 94
on property law, 39, 41, 108-109, 160, 162-163
on punitive damages, 24
punitive damages decisions, 42-43, 112-113, 143-149
on reapportionment and redistricting, 33
remedies decisions, 106
on securities law, 44, 46, 66-67, 128-131
on sentencing, 83-84, 84-85
on speedy trials, 85-86
on taxation, 111-112
taxation decisions, 112
on voting rights, 34, 35, 236, 250-254, 254
on Voting Rights Act (1965), 87-88
on workers' compensation, 108
on writ of certiorari, 60
Stewart, Potter, 328
Storer v. Brown (1974), 295
Summit Women's Health Organization, Inc. (SWHO), 26, 113-118
Sununu, John H., 333
Superfund law, 89
Supreme Court
amicus curiae, 317
annual terms, 311
arguments, 315-316
briefs, 317-318
caseload, 6, 56-57, 58
case selection, 56, 59
conferences, 311-312, 319-320
Court Rule 24, 318
decision days, 312
dissenting opinions, 7 (table)
discuss lists, 315
methods of appeal, 314
opinions, 320-322

oral arguments, 311-312, 315-316
orders lists, 315
process of review, 314-315
questioning, 318
reversals of earlier rulings, 20,
  21 (table)
reviewing cases, 312-314
time limitations, 316-317
transcripts, 317
voting alignments, 7-8, 9 (table)
visiting hours, 313
and writ of certiorari, 59-60, 314
*Swint v. Chambers County
Commission,* 307

Takings Clause (Fifth Amendment),
  24, 41, 157, 160, 165, 166
Taxation, 110-112
  and illegal drugs, 21
  in Montana, 21
  multinational corporations, 22
  states, 307
Teitelbaum, Aaron, 169
Teitelbaum, Joel, 169, 185
Television, 52-55, 193-219. *See also*
  Cable television
Tennessee, 238
  paternity suits, 36-39, 70-71,
    131-142
  taxation, 110
  voting rights, 237
Tennessee Supreme Court, 59-60
Terminix (company), 300
Term limitations (congressional), 292,
  294-297
Terry, Randall, 26, 27
Texas
  death penalty, 19, 46-49, 72-73,
    256-266
  freedom of information, 93
  sexual harassment, 103
  voting rights, 237-238
Texas Resource Center, 47, 48,
  256-266
Thomas, Clarence
  on abortion, 98-99
  on abortion clinics, 26, 279-291
  on arrest, 71-72

on aviation law, 61
biography, 334-335
on cable television, 52, 55, 95-96,
  213-218
on church and state, 49, 51, 96,
  185-193
on civil rights, 59
on Commerce Clause, 109-110
confirmation proceedings, 14
as a conservative, 8, 10-11
on criminal offenses, 76
criminal offenses decisions, 76-77
damage suit decisions, 101
on damage suits, 100
on the death penalty, 46, 48, 72-73,
  74, 262-266
dissents, 11
on double jeopardy, 11, 77
on evidence, 78
on federal regulation, 91-92, 92
on forfeiture, 78-79
freedom of information decisions, 93
on freedom of speech, 98
on hazardous waste, 89
ideology of, 6
insanity (criminal law) decisions, 80
on insurance law, 64
interrogation decisions, 81-82
on jury selection, 36, 38, 57, 70-71,
  140-142
on maritime law, 64-65
on military law, 94
on property law, 41
on punitive damages, 144
questioning style, 11
on reapportionment and redistricting, 19, 31, 33, 86-87, 231
on redistricting, 19
remedies decisions, 106-107
on securities law, 45
on sentencing, 85
sexual harassment allegations,
  334-335
solid waste decisions, 90
on taxation, 110-111
taxation decisions, 110
on taxation law, 68

on voting rights, 34, 35, 236,
238-249, 254-256
on Voting Rights Act (1965), 88
on water law, 90-91
*Thomas Jefferson University dba
Thomas Jefferson Hospital v. Shalala,
Secretary of Health and Human
Services* (1994), 92
Thompson, Meldrim, 333
Thunder Basin Coal Co. v. Reich
(1994), 105-106
Thurmond, Strom, 15
Tort reform, 21
Torts, 112-113
punitive damages, 112-113
Trademark infringement, 71
Trademark law, 56
Transportation Dept., 61, 297
Trial Lawyers for Public Justice
(organization), 299-300
Tribe, Laurence, 8, 20, 31, 42-43
Tuilaepa v. California (1994), 75
Turner, Ted, 53
Turner Broadcasting System, 193-219
*Turner Broadcasting System, Inc. v.
Federal Communications Commission*
(1994), 52-55, 95-96, 193-219
2 Live Crew (rap group), 62-63

U.S. Bancorp Mortgage Co., 299-300
*U.S. Bancorp Mortgage Co. v. Bonner
Mall Partnership,* 299-300
U.S. Sentencing Commission, 4-5
U.S. Term Limits, Inc. v. Thornton,
292
U.S. Term Limits (organization), 295
Unisys Corp., 64
Unitah Indian Reservation, 95
United Airlines, 297
United Mine Workers, 25, 68-69
United Mine Workers v. Bagwell
(1994), 68-69
United States
v. Alvarez-Sanchez (1994), 81-82
v. Granderson (1994), 85
v. Irvine (1994), 68
v. Ivic, 114

v. James Daniel Good Real Property
(1993), 78-79
v. Lopez, 301
*v. National Treasury Employees
Union, 304*
v. X-citement Video, Inc., 302
United States Department of Defense v.
Federal Labor Relations Authority
(1994), 93
United Talmudic Academy, 169
Utah, 176

Vacating judgment, 299-300
Veterans Administration (VA), 303
Veterans hospitals, 303
Victor v. Nebraska (1994), 82
Virginia, contempt of court in, 68-69
Virginia Supreme Court, 69
Voting rights, 6, 11, 34-36, 231-256
Voting Rights Act (1965), 11, 23,
31-36, 86-88, 219, 226, 230, 232-256.
See also Election law; Reapportion-
ment and redistricting

Wallace, Peter, 33
Ward v. Rock Against Racism (1989),
207, 270
Washington (state), 292
water law, 90-91
Water (environmental law), 90-91
Waters v. Churchill (1994), 97-98
Weider, Abraham, 52
Weiss v. United States (1994), 94-95
Welch, Mandy, 48, 49
West Lynn Creamery, Inc. v. Healy
(1994), 109-110
White, Byron R., 337
on criminal law, 7
Williams, Spencer, 198, 202, 218
Williamson, Fredel, 78
Williamson v. United States (1994), 78
Wilson v. Seiter (1991), 82
Windle, Ed, 281
Winterboer, Denny and Becky, 299
Wisconsin, 237, 238
Women's rights, 6, 16, 25
Workers' compensation, 108
Writ of certiorari, 59-60